DEMONOLOGY

A COLLECTION

Tarl Warwick
2020

DEMONOLOGY

COPYRIGHT AND DISCLAIMER

All rights reserved. No part of this publication may be reproduced, distributed, or transmitted in any form or by any means, including photocopying, recording, or other electronic or mechanical methods, without the prior written permission of the publisher, except in the case of brief quotations embodied in critical reviews and certain other noncommercial uses permitted by copyright law.

In no way may this text be construed as condoning or encouraging any violent or illegal act. In no way does the author encourage or condone any violent or illegal act. All action is the responsibility of the reader.

DEMONOLOGY

PREFACE

This particular volume which I have compiled is a list of some of the most significant works related to (or explicitly about) demonology which I myself have encountered in my own literary forays; in a couple of cases I have added excerpts in the appendix from works which either contained valuable demonological materials but were by and large not quite reasonable to include, or very long works which would have filled up much of this volume, which after all is a compilation, those works being already made available for sale over the last few years after I edited them personally. In compiling this work I have removed a few errors in my own initial volumes.

Of note here are three important subtopics for the serious aficionado of deviltry:

1. The nature of the devil, that old serpent in the Christian tradition, and inclusions from other traditions of a non-Abrahamic nature.

2. The nature of demons, those minions of Tartarus, which have been said to plague the world since time immemorial.

3. The nature of human response and the historical impact of the aforementioned beliefs, for example, witch trials and pogroms, ritualistic behavior related to relieving witchcraft, etc.

In this volume which I have compiled we will observe nine entirely different takes on these questions: Some are rational, some superstitious. Some are more modern than others, a couple being explicitly academic. We will here behold that Satan is not just the tormentor of spirits chained in Hell, but is a Pentecostal minister, a vaguely cryptozoological entity

DEMONOLOGY

controlling astral bodies, and a superstition all rolled into one! While his demoniacal horde of twisted creatures-or-immaterial-spirits is at once a legion of devils bent on destroying the "true" Christian faith, and a conglomerate of unfortunate and fallen beings which do harm through character more than malice. As previously mentioned these eight works will be followed by an appendix with snippets from a few more works which I thought could not be reasonably included verbatim for the demonological aficionado.

The first work here compiled, **Demoniality**, is originally from the 17th century and was written by one Sinistrari of Ameno who I judge was familiar with the Turba Philosophorum and appears to both derive from and simultaneously deviate in part from the Daemonologie of King James I (which is also included in this compiled text.) The claims here are sure to raise some eyebrows in a modern audience and are arguably more audacious than most prior texts, even those from before the Renaissance began; namely:

1. Demons are real, and are the result of the creation of a being from less than the four natural elements. They come in various flavors according to their elemental composition (taken literally from the *Turba*.)

2. Demons may bring supernatural powers to individuals working with them.

3. Demons may *literally* copulate with humans by possessing corpses. This even King James himself described and denounced as false.

4. Sinistrari accepts the premise of the *Book of Tobit* from the apocryphal gospels and believes that demons may be warded off using aromas etc, not simply via faith or prayer, and partly secularizes them in a manner prior works from even a few decades before would never have dared.

DEMONOLOGY

Avowedly Catholic in background, Sinistrari repeats, *ad nauseam*, the claims of the church at the time in general however, regarding the system behind devilish magic- including the premise that congregants explicitly partake in physical contact with a literal Satan; indeed, even some animals are not immune to fornication with these spiritual entities and are said to have their manes braided by them during nocturnal rites.

The second work we come to is the infamous **Demonology** (or Daemonologie) of King James I- this particular tract caused the deaths of tens of thousands of people by exciting panic in his realms, which is interesting since he was also the author of "Counterblaste to Tobacco" which is the first truly comprehensive anti-smoking text in human existence.

As previously mentioned King James in his work decries the concept of spirits physically copulating with humans using corpses, a claim already apparently in vogue at the time, and one I have to presume had something to do with the rampant use of alcohol and occasionally ergot-tainted wheat and rye supply of the era. To King James, the Devil is no less devilish and spirits no less wicked than Sinistrari later reports, but James was a Protestant, not a Catholic, and so some of the claims differ a bit.

Here we see at large, the treatment of witchcraft which of course in the era was explicitly twain with demonic power. James endorses the concept of witches becoming insensible to all forms of pain, bearing branding marks of the presence of familiar spirits ("nipples" in irregular locations usually) as well as the practice of dunking the accused into a lake or river to see if they would float (which they normally did, given humans usually hold their breath and become semi-buoyant prior to such immersions!) James condemns Catholicism throughout the work, and claims that Catholic realms suffered less from perceived outbreaks of witchery because the Devil desired to cause people to convert to Catholicism, in a misguided belief

DEMONOLOGY

that the efficacy of the religion was the result of its veracity. In one slightly funny aside that I mentioned briefly in the foreword to my initial edition of this particular work, James refers to the Fourth Book of Agrippa (a spurious work Agrippa did not actually create) while ignoring a very real work by the same figure called *Female Preeminence* that denounces the "misogyny" of the era and applauds women as heroic and religiously inclined.

While the Catholics of the era made some use of discretion in persecuting the accused by labeling some forms of magic "not evil" (if not necessarily holy and sanctified!) such as herbal healing and midwifery, the protestant James condemns them all equally, and proposes the death penalty for any form of magic used outside the explicit context of the Christian religion.

We then come to a completely different third work, **Demonomania and Witchcraft**, which is a totally secular work delivered in 1871 as a historical piece to a medical audience in association with the "American Journal of the Insane." The mid 1800s were a time of rising rationalism and a three way battle between the forces of atheistic (or at least expressly irreligious) science, occult spiritual forces including the spiritist movement, and the orthodox religious forces of Catholic and mainline Protestant theology. This work relegates spirits to the realm of spooky nonsense in much the same way that yesteryears dragons in that era were becoming nothing more than piles of interesting bones mounted in a museum of creatures which were very much flesh and blood and held no supernatural character of any kind. The world was being spanned by railroads and medicine especially began to regard witch trials as examples of mass hysteria and mere superstition.

Here the author, Joseph Workman, speaks at length about (and refutes) King James, and other contemporary reports and sources; however he (in my humble opinion, wisely) points out that as of the 1870s people were just as gullible and just as easily moved to superstition as they had been centuries prior during the burning times. Indeed, not only was he correct, we would be correct today in claiming the same.

Fourth is **Demons and Tongues** which essentially claims that Satan is using the Pentecostal movement with its "speaking in tongues" and ecstatic rites as a vessel to pervert the world.

Fifth in this text is **Modern Vampirism**, from 1904 by Osbourne Eaves. This spiritualist extrapolation of demonology converts it from the realm of orthodox theology to that of occultism writ large, and turns the demon into a sort of malevolent astral body which can be warded off partly through the power of positive thinking and through being, simply, "good." Despite admitting that "Dracula" is fictional, Eaves mentions the novel anyways and derives from it directly!

Regardless of the obvious occult backdrop of the author (about which damnably little is known, sadly, considering how interesting this manuscript is), Eaves suggests avoiding hypnosis and seances, claiming them to be dangerous conduits for astral vampires; demons, as we may obviously class them. The latter sections speak at some length about the human aura (how is this markedly different from claims that humans have a sort of *animus* or spirit?) which is directly linked to the influence of astral entities, whether positive or negative, and which can be contagious.

The sixth book is **On the Operation of Demons** by Psellus (or Psellos) and comes from the late 17th century. It is delivered in the form of a dialogue between Timothy and Thracian, who are having a detailed conversation on subjects related to spirits and to people labeled "demoniac." In a stunning move, the author acknowledges (and this was uncommon prior to the enlightenment) that at least "some" cases of possession etc were the result of the use of narcotic

DEMONOLOGY

substances. This is today even admitted by orthodox theological minds, since the use of various psychotropics is absolutely and unarguably able to produce odd visions and sensations in a human using them.

Thracian here claims (in the Socratic dialogue given) that demons do not necessarily act out of pure malevolence, but out of a desire for the warmth and apparent comfort of a corporeal form, without which they are physically intangible. An example is given from the Bible itself: Jesus drives demons out of a man who then inhabit the bodies of a herd of pigs, but the pigs go insane and drown themselves in the ocean (one of the more bizarre stories of demons through human history!)

However, any rationalism exhibited by the author dissipates entirely when one considers the claims of this Thracian in regard to the behavior of certain demoniac cults! The eating of excrement is, in his opinion, while horrendous, merely a prelude to their frenetic rites of carnage, in which demons are exhorted to continue inhabiting their bodies by impregnating women, then cutting the infant out of their belly, torturing it, and finally burning it to ashes along with human excrement, using these as a sort of sacrament, and even utilizing it to cause others to become possessed, thus increasing their numbers.

Seventh in line in this compilation is **The Devil: His Origin, Greatness, and Decadence**, by Reville. This (liberally) Protestant work chronicles the slow development of the idea of the Devil (and his minions, and of Hell) through the ages, from a horrific dragon or fell beast, to an impious figure, from the wretched and malevolent to the merely tricky, all the way to the then-modern easily satirized little red man which more resembles a faun or satyr than a dragon or a demon-prince. I pointed out in my initial foreword to the work that this evolution has continued- Reville in the 1800s never got to witness the rebirth of fire and brimstone imagery in parts of the

DEMONOLOGY

West where Satan became both the face of religious fanaticism in the middle east, as well as a representative of imperialistic western business cabals (and occasionally a corporate mascot, often selling liquor or clothing!)

The initial development of Satan, as Reville correctly notes, was the result of Judaistic interposition with Persians (and other, even older civilizations, it ought to be noted!)

Reville never condemns the concept of a Satan existing (after all he was a religious man, if a forward-thinking one) but repeatedly remarks on the folly of different interpretations of the being, and of his hellish host, as throughout time, the ever-changing accepted views of both had already by that era become woefully self contradicting- a trend which shows no signs of letting up.

Eighth in line is **The Piasa: The Devil Among the Indians**, an excellent late 19th century academic work which catalogs some names and forms of the demonic among Native people in the Americas. This is exemplified especially by rock paintings and carvings along certain water routes- in fact I first heard of this book while reading a very good anthropological work by Claude Gagnon and Michel Muerger entitled "Lake Monster traditions" which listed this text in the bibliography and alluded to it while discussing the same carvings and the concept of the *Manitou*.

The Piasa, under various names, and various demonic cohorts, was present in carvings spanning pretty much the entire North American continent- stories appear to have transited from tribe to tribe and were related to European explorers frequently. I recall (although it is not retold in this work) that in some cases it was customary for passing Natives to fire arrows at some of the carvings of demonic beings, and that they were later erased when bows were replaced by firearms, slowly whittling away at them and rendering them extinct.

DEMONOLOGY

The author of this work remains rigorously academic throughout the work and its anthropological content is superb, however he makes the claim at the end of the work that resemblances of depictions of the Piasa to extinct dinosaur species is *best explained by the Natives coming to the continent while dinosaurs still existed*. This makes the work arguably even more valuable since it becomes, in itself, a historical piece from an era when science was gaining much more rigor but when the timeline of evolution was not particularly refined!

The ninth and final full work related here is **A Tryal of Witches**, which I have preserved in its initial old English (something I generally do not do)- specifically because it is a literal report from the Assizes dating to the actual period of the trial itself. It is a highly valuable primary source document and relates some of the most bizarre tales of supernatural powers or effects via the demonic ever recorded; including the mysterious appearance of pins or coins from the mouths of those suffering from demonic possession, that witches (by the agency of Satan and use of familiar spirits) could cause all manners of sicknesses (and did) and so forth. Sadly this is a document of hysteria and suffering which relates that based on what we would now deem not to be evidence at all, many were condemned and put to death in these cases.

It is worth noting that the actual reports here- though they consider witchcraft and demonic possession to be very literal and real- actually provide fairly good evidence for not just mass panic but the misuse of the "legal system" as it existed then for property purposes, literally a neighbor killing off someone they didn't like by pretending sickness. In a few cases it looks like individuals subjected to mass panic may have developed a case of what we now call *Pica* (which often involves eating inedible materials which the body may of course vomit up later.)

Here the Devil and his legions are very real and the only

DEMONOLOGY

solution given is death by hanging or burning, but the text accidentally memorializes the exact opposite and gives evidence to the contrary of its own religiously zealous claims!

In conclusion to those main sections I would note that it was *explicitly* my intent to vary the backgrounds of the works to be included in the text; I have read other works on demonology and while some are quite good, many of them only present the subject from one of three basic premises, at least, those made for a Western and largely Judeochristian or secular audience:

1. Satan exists. Demons exist. They have agency. You should avoid them as malevolent or might burn forever in Hell.

2. Spiritual forces exist, but not Satan or Hell. An occultist can consort with them with some caution.

3. Satan, demons, and all the rest, are mere superstitious nonsense and prattle.

I wanted to drag all of these basic opinions together along with works (especially Osbourne's work on Vampires) which are tangential or pseudo-related to the topics at hand and flesh it out with a bit more potential to cause the reader to consider the idea of the demonic from perspectives they may not hold in and of themselves.

At the end of the work you will find a full bibliography including many works not mentioned, for all of your reading needs. Some I have personally edited, others are available elsewhere.

~Tarl Warwick
October, 2020

CONTENTS

Demoniality (p. 14-82)

Demonology (Of King James I) (p. 83-138)

Demonomania and Witchcraft (p. 139-156)

Demons and Tongues (p. 157-213)

Modern Vampirism (p. 214-256)

On the Operation of Demons (p. 257-280)

The Devil: His Origin, Greatness, and Decadence (p. 281-331)

The Piasa: The Devil Among the Indians (p. 332-378)

A Tryal of Witches (p. 379-408)

Appendix (p. 409-420)

Bibliography (p. 421-424)

DEMONOLOGY

A COLLECTION

DEMONIALITY

Sinistrari of Ameno, 17th Century

PREFACE TO THE
FIRST EDITION

I was in London in the year 1872, and I hunted after old books.

They caused me to live in past ages, happy to escape from the present, and to exchange the petty passions of the day for the peaceable intimacy of Aldus, Dolet or Estienne. One of my favorite booksellers was Mr Allen, a venerable old gentleman, whose place of business was in the Euston road, close to the gate of Regent's park. Not that his shop was particularly rich in dusty old books; quite the reverse: it was small, and yet never filled.

Scarcely four or five hundred volumes at a time, carefully dusted, bright, arrayed with symmetry on shelves within reach of one's hand; the upper shelves remained unoccupied. On the right, Theology; on the left, the Greek and Latin Classics in a majority, with some French and Italian books; for such were Mr Allen's specialties; it seemed as if he absolutely ignored Shakespeare and Byron, and as if, in his mind, the literature of his country did not go beyond the sermons of Blair or Macculloch.

What, at first sight, struck one most in those books, was the moderateness of their price, compared with their excellent state of preservation. They had evidently not been bought in a lot, at so much a cubic yard, like the rubbish of an auction, and yet the handsomest, the most ancient, the most venerable from

DEMONOLOGY

their size, folios or quartos, were not marked higher than 2 or 3 shillings; an octavo was sold for 1 shilling, the duodecimo six pence; each according to its size. Thus ruled Mr Allen, a methodical man, if ever there was one; and he was all the better for it, since, faithfully patronized by clergymen, scholars and collectors, he renewed his stock at a rate which more assuming speculators might have envied.

But how did he get those well bound and well preserved volumes, for which, everywhere else, five or six times more would have been charged? Here also Mr Allen had his method, sure and regular. No one attended more assiduously the auctions which take place every day in London: his stand was marked at the foot of the auctioneer's desk. The rarest, choicest books passed before his eyes, contended for at often fabulous prices by Quaritch, Sotheran, Pickering, Toovey, and other bibliopolists of the British metropolis; Mr Allen smiled at such extravagance; when once a bid had been made by another, he would not add a penny, had an unknown Gutenberg or Valdarfer's Boccaccio been at stake. But if occasionally, through inattention or weariness, competition slackened, Mr Allen came forward: six pence!, he whispered, and sometimes the article was left him; sometimes even, two consecutive numbers, joined together for want of having separately met with a buyer, were knocked down to him, still for the minimum of six pence which was his maximum.

Many of those slighted ones doubtless deserved their fate; but among them might slip some that were not unworthy of the honors of the catalog, and which, at any other time, buyers more attentive, or less whimsical might perhaps have covered with gold. This, however, did not at all enter into Mr Allen's calculation: the size was the only rule of his estimate.

Now, one day when, after a considerable auction, he had exhibited in his shop purchases more numerous than usual, I especially noticed some manuscripts in the Latin language, the paper, the writing and the binding of which denoted an Italian origin, and which might well be two hundred years old. The title of one was, I believe: *De Veneris*; of another, *De Viperis*; of a third (the present work): *De Daemonialitate, et Incubis, et Suecubis*.

All three, moreover, by different authors, and independent of each other. Poisons, adders, demons, what a collection of horrors! Yet, were it but for civility's sake, I was bound to buy something; after some hesitation, I chose the last one: Demons, true, but Incubi, Succubi, the subject is not vulgar, and still less so the way in which it seemed to me to have been handled. In short, I had the volume for sixpence, a boon price for a quarto: Mr Allen doubtless deemed such a scrawl beneath the rate of type.

That manuscript, on strong paper of the 17th century, bound in Italian parchment, and beautifully preserved, has 86 pages of text. The title and first page are in the author's hand, that of an old man; the remainder is very distinctly written by another, but under his direction, as is testified by autographic side notes and rectifications distributed all through the work. It is therefore the genuine original manuscript, to all appearances unique and unedited.

Our dealer in old books had purchased it a few days before at Sotheby's House, where had taken place (from the 6th to the 16th of December 1871) the sale of the books of baron Seymour Kirkup, an English collector, deceased in Florence. The manuscript was inscribed as follows on the sale catalog:

Ameno (R. P. Ludovicus, *Maria Cotta de De Daemonialitate, et Incubis, et Succubis*, Manuscript. Scec. XVII-XVIII.)

Who is that writer? Has he left printed works? That is a question I leave to bibliographers; for, notwithstanding

DEMONOLOGY

numerous investigations in special dictionaries, I have been unable to ascertain any thing on that score.

Brunet (Manuel du libraire art. Cotta d'Ameno) vaguely surmises his existence, but confuses him with his namesake, most likely also his fellow-townsman, Lazaro Agostino Cotta of Ameno, a barrister and literary man of Novara. "The author," says he, "whose real Christian names would seem to be Ludovico-Mariaj has written many serious works..."

The mistake is obvious. One thing is sure; our author was living in the last years of the 17th century, as appears from his own testimony, and had been a professor of Theology in Pavia.

Be that as it may, his book has seemed to me most interesting in divers respects, and I confidently submit it to that select public for whom the invisible world is not a chimera. I should be much surprised if, after opening it at random, the reader was not tempted to retrace his steps and go on to the end. The philosopher, the confessor, the medical man will find therein, in conjunction with the robust faith of the middle ages, novel and ingenious views; the literary man, the curioso, will appreciate the solidity of reasoning, the clearness of style, the liveliness of recitals (for there are stories, and delicately told). All theologians have devoted more or less pages to the question of material intercourse between man and the demon; thick volumes have been written about witchcraft, and the merits of this work were but slender if it merely developed the ordinary thesis; but such is not its characteristic. The ground-matter, from which it derives a truly original and philosophical stamp, is an entirely novel demonstration of the existence of Incubi and Succubi, as rational animals, both corporeal and spiritual like ourselves, living in our midst, being born and dying like us, and lastly redeemed, as we are, through the merits of Jesus Christ, and capable of receiving salvation or damnation.

DEMONOLOGY

In the Father of Ameno's opinion, those beings endowed with senses and reason, thoroughly distinct from Angels and Demons, pure spirits, are none other but the Fauns, Sylvans and Satyrs of paganism, continued by our Sylphs, Elfs and Goblins; and thus is connected anew the link of belief. On this score alone, not to mention the interest of details, this book has a claim to the attention of earnest readers: I feel convinced that attention will not be found wanting.

Isidore Liseux

May, 1875.

DEMONIALITY

The first author who, to my knowledge, invented the word "Demoniality" is John Caramuel, in his *Fundamental Theology*, and before him I find no one who distinguished that crime from *Bestiality*. Indeed, all Theological Moralists, following in the train of S. Thomas (2, 2, question 154), include under the specific title of Bestiality, "every kind of carnal intercourse with anything whatever of a different species." Such are the very words used by S. Thomas. Cajetanus, for instance, in his commentary on that question, classes intercourse with the Demon under the description of Bestiality; so does Sylvester, *de Luxuria*, Bonacina, *de Matrimonio*, question 4, and others.

However it is clear that in the above passage S. Thomas did not at all allude to intercourse with the Demon. As shall be demonstrated further on, that intercourse cannot be included in the very particular species of Bestiality; and, in order to make that sentence of the holy Doctor tally with truth, it must be admitted that when saying of the unnatural sin, "that committed through intercourse with a thing of different species, it takes the name of Bestiality", S. Thomas, by a thing of different species, means a living animal, of another species than man: For he could not here use the word thing in its most general sense to mean indiscriminately an animate or inanimate being. In fact, if a man should fornicate *cum cadavere humano*, he would have to do with a thing of a species quite different from his own (especially according to the Thomists, who deny the form of human corporeity in a corpse); similarly *si cadaveri bestiali copularetur*: and yet, *talis coitus* would not be bestiality, but pollution. What therefore S. Thomas intended here to specify with preciseness, is carnal intercourse with a living thing of a species different from man, that is to say, with a beast, and he never in the least thought of intercourse with the Demon.

Therefore, intercourse with the Demon, whether Incubus or Succubus (which is, properly speaking, Demoniality) differs in kind from Bestiality, and does not in connection with it form one very particular species, as Cajetanus wrongly gives it; for, whatever may have said to the contrary some Ancients, and later Caramuel in his *Fundamental Theology*, unnatural sins differ from each other most distinctly. Such at least is the general doctrine, and the contrary opinion has been condemned by Alexander VII: first, because each of those sins carries with itself its peculiar and distinct disgrace, repugnant to chastity and to human generation; secondly, because the commission thereof entails each time the sacrifice of some good by its nature attached to the institution of the venereal act, the normal end of which is human generation; lastly, because they each have a different motive which in itself is sufficient to bring about, in divers ways, the deprivation of the same good, as has been clearly shown by Fillucius, Grespinus and Caramuel.

It follows that Demoniality differs in kind from Bestiality, for each has its peculiar and distinct disgrace, repugnant to chastity and human generation. Bestiality is connection with a living beast, endowed with its own peculiar senses and impulses; Demoniality, on the contrary, is copulation with a corpse (according at least to the general doctrine which shall be considered hereafter), a senseless and motionless corpse which is but accidentally moved through the power of the Demon. Now, if fornication with the corpse of a man, a woman, or a beast differs in kind from Sodomy and Bestiality, there is the same difference with regard to Demoniality, which, according to general opinion, is the intercourse of man with a corpse accidentally set in motion.

Another proof: in sins against nature, the unnatural insemination (which cannot be regularly followed by generation) is a genus; but the object of such insemination is the difference which marks the species under the genus. Thus, whether insemination takes place on the ground, or on an inanimate body, it is pollution; if *cum homine in vase praepostero* it is Sodomy; with a beast, bestiality, crimes which unquestionably all differ from each other in species, just as the ground, the corpse, the man and the beast, passive objects *talis seminationis*, differ in species from each other. But the difference between the Demon and the beast is not only specific, it is more than specific; the nature of the one is corporeal, of the other incorporeal, which makes a generic difference.

Whence it follows that insemination practiced on different objects differ in species from each other; and that is substantiated.

It is also a trite doctrine with Moralists, established by the Council of Trent, session 14, and admitted by Theologians that in confession it suffices to state the circumstances which alter the species of sins. If therefore Demoniality and Bestiality belonged to the same very particular species, it would be enough that each time he has fornicated with the Demon, the penitent should say to his confessor; "I have been guilty of the sin of Bestiality" But that is not so: Therefore those two sins do not both belong to the same very particular species.

It may be urged that if the circumstances of a sensual intercourse with the Demon should be revealed to the

DEMONOLOGY

Confessor, it is on account of its offense against Religion, an offense which comes either from the worship rendered to the Demon, or from the homage or prayers offered up to him, or from the compact of fellowship entered into with him (S. Thomas, quest. 90). But, as will be seen hereafter, there are Incubi and Succubi to whom none of the foregoing applies, and yet *copula sequitur*.

There is consequently, in that special case, no element of irreligion, no other character *quam puri et simplicis coitus*; and, if of the same species as Bestiality, it would be adequately stated by saying: "I have been guilty of the sin of Bestiality;" which is not so.

Besides, it is acknowledged by all Theological Moralists that *copula cum daemone* is much more grievous than the same act committed with any beast soever. Now, in the same very particular species of sins, one sin is not more grievous than another; all are equally so; it comes to the same whether connection is had with a bitch, an ass, or a mare; whence it follows that if Demoniality is more grievous than Bestiality, those two acts are not of the same species. And let it not be argued, with Cajetahus, that Demoniality is more grievous on account of the offense to religion from the worship rendered to the Demon or the compact of fellowship entered into with him, as has been shown above, that is not always met with in the connection of man with Incubi and Succubi; moreover, if in the genus of unnatural sin Demoniality is more grievous than Bestiality, the offense to Religion is quite foreign to that aggravation, since it is foreign to that genus itself.

Now, having laid down the specific difference between Demoniality and Bestiality, so that the gravity thereof may be duly appreciated in view of the penalty to be inflicted (and that is our most essential object), We must inquire in how many different ways the sin of Demoniality may be committed. There is no lack of people who, infatuated with their small baggage of

DEMONOLOGY

knowledge , venture to deny what has been written by the gravest authors and is testified by every day experience; namely, that the Demon, whether Incubus or Succubus, unites carnally not only with men and women, but also with beasts.

They allege that it all comes from the human imagination troubled by the craft of the Demon, and that there is nothing in it but phantasmagoria and diabolical spells. The like happens, they say, to Witches or Sagas, who, under the influence of an illusion brought on by the Demon, fancy that they attend the nightly sports, dances, revels and vigils, and have carnal intercourse with the Demon, though in reality they are not bodily transferred to those places nor taking part in those deeds, as has been defined verbatim by a Capitule and two Councils.

Of course, it is not contested that sometimes young women, deceived by the Demon, fancy taking part, in their flesh and blood, in the nightly vigils of Witches, without its being any thing but an imaginary vision. Thus, in a dream, one sometimes fancies *cum foemina aliqua concumbere, et semen vere excernitur, non tamen concubitus ille realis est*, but merely fantastic, and often brought about by a diabolical illusion; and here the above mentioned Capitule and councils are perfectly right. But this is not always the case; on the contrary, it more often happens that Witches are bodily present at nightly vigils and have with the Demon a genuine carnal and corporeal connection, and that likewise Wizards copulate with the Succubus or female Demon. Such is the opinion of Theologians as well as of jurists, whose names will be found at length in the *Compendium Maleficarum*, or Chronicle of Witches, by Brother Francis Marie Guaccius. This doctrine is therein confirmed by eighteen instances adduced from the recitals of learned and truthful men whose testimony is beyond suspicion, and which prove that Wizards and Witches are indeed bodily present at vigils and most shamefully copulate with Demons, Incubi or Succubi. And, after all, to settle the question, we have the

DEMONOLOGY

authority of S. Austin, who, speaking of carnal intercourse between men and the Demons, expresses himself as follows, book 15, chapt, 23 of the City of God: "It is widely credited, and such belief is confirmed by the direct or indirect testimony of thoroughly trustworthy people, that Sylvans and Fauns, commonly called Incubi, have frequently molested women, sought and obtained from them coition. There are even Demons, whom the Gauls call Duses or Elves, who very regularly indulge in those unclean practices: The fact is testified by so many and such weighty authorities, that it were impudent to doubt it." Such are the very words of S. Austin.

Now, several authors profess, and it is confirmed by numerous experiments, that the Demon has two ways of copulating carnally with men or women: the one which it uses with Witches or Wizards, the other with men or women entirely foreign to witchcraft.

In the first case, the Demon does not copulate with Witches or Wizards until after a solemn profession, in virtue of which such wretched human beings yield themselves up to him. According to several authors who have related the judicial admissions of Witches when on the rack, and whose recitals have been collected by Francis-Marie Guaccius, *Compend. Malef.* book I, ch. 7, that profession consists of eleven ceremonials:

Firstly, the Novices have to conclude with the Demon, or some other Wizard or Magician acting in the Demon's place, an express compact by which, in the presence of witnesses, they enlist in the Demon's service, he giving them in exchange his pledge for honors, riches and carnal pleasures.

Secondly, they abjure the catholic faith, withdraw from the obedience to God, renounce Christ and the protection of the most blessed Virgin Mary, and all the Sacraments of the Church.

DEMONOLOGY

Thirdly, they cast away the Crown, or Rosary of the most blessed Virgin Mary, the girdle of S. Francis, or the strap of S. Austin, or the scapular of the Carmelites, should they belong to one of those Orders, the Cross, the Medals, the *Agnus Dei*, whatever other holy or consecrated object may have been about their person, and trample them all under foot.

Fourthly, in the hands of the Devil they vow obedience and subjection; they pay him homage and vassalage, laying their fingers on some very black book. They bind themselves never to return to the faith of Christ, to observe none of the divine precepts, to do no good work, but to obey the Demon alone and, to attend diligently the nightly conventicles.

Fifthly, they promise to strive with all their power, and to give their utmost zeal and care for the enlistment of other males and females in the service of the Demon.

Sixth, the Devil administers to them a kind of sacrilegious baptism, and after abjuring their Godfathers and Godmothers of the Baptism of Christ and Confirmation, they have assigned to them a new Godfather and a new Godmother, who are to instruct them in the arts of witchcraft; they drop their former name and exchange it for another, more frequently a scurrilous nickname.

Seventh, they cut off a part of their own garments, and tender it as a token of homage to the Devil, who takes it away and keeps it.

Eighth, the Devil draws on the ground a circle wherein stand the Novices, Witches and Wizards, and there they confirm by oath all their aforesaid promises.

Ninth, they request the Devil to strike them out of the book of Christ, and to inscribe them in his own. Then comes forth that very black book on which, as has been said before, they laid hands when doing homage, and they are inscribed therein with the Devil's claw.

Tenth, they promise the Devil sacrifices and offerings at stated times: Once a fortnight or at least each month, the murder of some child, or an homicidal act of sorcery, and other weekly misdeeds to the prejudice of mankind, such as hailstorms, tempests, fires, cattle plagues, etc.

Eleventh, the Demon imprints on them some mark, especially on those whose constancy he suspects. That mark, moreover, is not always of the same shape or figure: sometimes it is the image of a hare, sometimes a toad's or, sometimes a spider, a puppy, a doormouse. It is imprinted on the most hidden parts of the body: with men, under the eye-lids, or the armpits, or the lips, on the shoulder, the penis, or somewhere else; with women, it is usually on the breasts or the privy parts. Now, the stamp which imprints those marks is none other but the Devil's claw. This having been all performed in accordance with the instructions of the Teachers who have initiated the Novices, these promise lastly never to worship the Eucharist; to insult all Saints and especially the most blessed Virgin Mary; to trample under foot and vilify the holy images, the Cross and the relics of Saints; never to use the sacraments or sacramental ceremonials; never to make a full confession to the priest, but to keep always hidden from him their intercourse with the Demon. The Demon, in exchange, engages to give them always prompt assistance; to fulfill their desires in this world and to make them happy after their death. The solemn profession being thus performed, each has assigned to himself a Devil, called Magistellus or Assistant Master, with whom he retires in private for carnal satisfaction; the said Devil being, of course, in the shape of a woman if the initiated person is a man, in the shape of a man, sometimes of a satyr, sometimes of a buck-goat, if it is a woman who has been received a witch.

DEMONOLOGY

If the authors be asked how it comes to pass that the Demon, who has no body, yet has carnal intercourse with man or woman, they unanimously answer that the Demon assumes the corpse of another human being, male or female as the case may be, or that, from the mixture of other materials, he shapes for himself a body endowed with motion, and by means of which he is united with the human being; and they add that when women are desirous of becoming pregnant by the Demon (which only occurs by the consent and express wish of the said women), the Demon is transformed into a Succubus, *et juncta homini semen ab eo recipit*; or else he procures pollution from a man during his sleep, *et semen prolectum in suo nativo calore, et cum vitali spiritu conservat, et incubando foemince infert in ipsius matricem*, whence follows impregnation. Such is the teaching of Guaccius, book I, ch. 12, who supports it on a number of quotations and instances taken from various Doctors.

At other times also the Demon, whether Incubus or Succubus, copulates with men or women from whom he receives none of the sacrifices, homage or offerings which he is wont to exact from Wizards or Witches, as aforesaid. He is then but a passionate lover, having only one desire; the carnal possession of the loved ones. Of this there are numerous instances to be found in the authors, among which the case of Menippus Lycius, who, after frequent coitius with a woman, was by her entreated to marry her; but a certain philosopher, who partook of the wedding entertainment, having guessed what that woman was, told Menippus that he had to deal with a *Compusa,* that is, a Succubus Demon; whereupon the bride vanished bewailing: Such is the narrative given by Coelius Rhodiginus, Antiq., book 29, ch. 5. Hector Boethius (History of Scotland) also relates the case of a young Scot, who, during many months, with closed doors and windows, was visited in his bed-room by a Succubus Demon of the most bewitching beauty; caresses, kisses, embraces, entreaties, she resorted to every blandishment *ut secum coiret*: but she could not prevail on

DEMONOLOGY

the chaste young man.

We read likewise of numerous women incited to coition by the Incubus Demon, and who, though reluctant at first of yielding to him, are soon moved by his entreaties, tears and endearments; he is a desperate lover and must not be denied. And although this comes sometimes of the craft of some Wizard who avails himself of the agency of the Demon, yet the Demon not infrequently acts on his own account; and it happens not merely with women, but also with mares; if they readily comply with his desire, he pets them, and plaits their mane in elaborate and inextricable tresses; but if they resist, he ill-treats and strikes them, smites them with the glanders, and finally puts them to death, as is shown by daily experience.

A most marvelous and well high incomprehensible fact: the Incubus whom the Italians call Folletti, the Spaniards Duendes, the French Follets, do not obey the Exorcists, have no dread of exorcisms, no reverence for holy things, at the approach of which they are not in the least overawed; very different in that respect from the Demons who vex those whom they possess; for, however obstinate those evil Spirits may be, however restive to the injunctions of the Exorcist who bids them leave the body they possess, yet, at the mere utterance of the most holy name of Jesus or Mary, or of some verses of Holy Writ, at the mere imposition of relics, especially of a piece of the wood of the Holy Cross, or the sight of the holy images, they roar at the mouth of the possessed person, they gnash, shake, quiver, and display fright and awe. But the Folletti show none of those signs, and leave off their vexations but after a long space of time. Of this I was an eye-witness, and shall relate a story which verily passes human belief; but I take God to witness that I tell the precise truth, corroborated by the testimony of numerous persons.

About twenty five years ago, when I was a lecturer on Sacred Theology in the convent of the Holy Cross, in Pavia,

DEMONOLOGY

there was living in that city a married woman of unimpeachable morality, and who was most highly spoken of by all such as knew her, especially by the Friars; her name was Hieronyma, and she lived in the parish of S. Michael. One day, this woman had kneaded bread at home and given it out to bake. The ovenman brought her back her loaves when baked, and with them a large cake of a peculiar shape, and made of butter and Venetian paste, as is usual in that city. She declined to take it in, saying she had not made any thing of the kind. "But," said the ovenman, "I had no other bread but yours to bake today, therefore this cake also must have come from your house; your memory is at fault." The good lady allowed herself to be persuaded, and partook of the cake with her husband, her little girl three years old, and the house servant. The next night, whilst in bed with her husband, and both asleep, she suddenly woke up at the sound of a very slender voice, something like a shrill hissing, whispering in her ears, yet with great distinctness, and inquiring whether the cake had been to her taste. The good lady, frightened, set about guarding herself with a sign of the cross and repeatedly calling the names of Jesus and Mary. "Be not afraid," said the voice, "I mean you no harm; quite the reverse: I am prepared to do anything to please you; I am captivated by your beauty, and desire nothing more than to enjoy your embraces." And she felt somebody kissing her cheeks, so lightly, so softly, that she might have fancied being grazed by the finest down. She resisted without giving any answer, merely repeating over and over again the names of Jesus and Mary, and crossing herself; the tempter kept on thus for nearly half an hour, when he withdrew.

The next morning the dame called on her Confessor, a discreet and learned man, who confirmed her in her faith, exhorted her to maintain her energetic resistance and to provide herself with some holy relics. On the ensuing nights, like temptation with the same language and kisses, like constancy also on the part of the woman. Weary however of such painful and persistent molestation, taking the advice of her Confessor

DEMONOLOGY

and other grave men, she had herself exorcised by experienced Exorcists, in order to ascertain whether perchance she was not possessed. Having found in her no trace of the evil Spirit, they blessed the house, the bedroom, the bed, and enjoined on the Incubus to discontinue his molestation. All to no purpose: he kept on worse than ever, pretending to be lovesick, weeping and moaning in order to melt the heart of the lady, who however, by the grace of God, remained unconquered. The Incubus then went another way to work; he appeared in the shape of a lad or little man of great beauty, with golden locks, a flaxen beard that shone like gold, sea-green eyes calling to mind the flax-flower, and arrayed in a fancy Spanish dress. Besides he appeared to her even when in company, whimpering, after the fashion of lovers, kissing his hand to her, and endeavoring by every means to obtain her embraces. She alone saw and heard him: For everybody else, he was not to be seen.

The good lady kept persevering in her admirable constancy till, at last, after some months of courting, the Incubus, incensed at her disdain, had recourse to a new kind of persecution. First, he took away from her a silver cross filled with holy relics, and a holy wax or papal lamb of the blessed Pontiff Pius V, which she always carried on her person; then, leaving the locks untouched, he purloined her rings and other gold and silver jewelry from the casket wherein they were put away. Next, he began to strike her cruelly, and after each beating bruises and marks were to be seen on her face, her arms or other parts of her body, which lasted a day or two, then suddenly disappeared, the reverse of natural bruises which decrease slowly and by degrees. Sometimes, while she was nursing her little girl, he would snatch the child away from on her breast and lay it upon the roof, on the edge of the gutter, or hide it, but without ever harming it. Sometimes he would upset all the furniture, or smash to pieces saucepans, plates and other earthenware which, in the twinkling of an eye, he restored to their former state.

DEMONOLOGY

One night that she was lying with her husband, the Incubus, appearing in his customary shape, vehemently urged his demand which she resisted as usual. The Incubus withdrew in a rage, and shortly came back with a large load of those flag stones which the Genoese, and the inhabitants of Liguriain general, use for roofing their houses. With those stones he built around the bed a wall so high that it reached the tester, and that the couple could not leave their bed without using a ladder. This wall however was built up without lime; when pulled down, the flags were laid by in a corner where, during two days, they were seen by many who came to look at them; they then disappeared.

On S. Stephen's day, the husband had asked some military friends to dinner, and, to do honor to his guests, had provided a substantial repast. Whilst they were, as customary, washing their hands before taking their seats, suddenly vanished the table dressed in the dining-room; all the dishes, saucepans, kettles, plates and crockery in the kitchen vanished likewise, as well as the jugs, bottles and glasses. You may imagine the surprise,the stupor of the guests, eight in number; among them was a Spanish Captain of infantry, who, addressing the company, said to them: "Do not be frightened, it is but a trick; the table is certainly still where it stood, and I shall soon find it by feeling for it." Having thus spoken, he paced round the room with outstretched arms, endeavoring to lay hold of the table; but when, after many circuitous perambulations, it was apparent that he labored in vain and grasped at naught but thin air, he was laughed at by his friends; and it being already high time for having dinner, each guest took up his cloak and set about to return home. They had already reached the street door with the husband, who, out of politeness, was attending them, when they heard a great noise in the dining-room; they stood to ascertain the cause thereof, and presently the servant came up to announce that the kitchen was stocked with new vessels filled with food, and that the table was standing again in its former place.

DEMONOLOGY

Having gone back to the dining-room, they were stupefied to see the table was laid, with cloths, napkins, salt-cellars, and trays that did not belong to the house, and with food which had not been cooked there. On a large sideboard all were arrayed in perfect order crystal, silver and gold chalices, with all kinds of vases, decanters and cups filled with foreign wines, from the Isle of Crete, Campania, the Canaries, the Rhine, etc. In the kitchen there was also an abundant variety of meats in saucepans and dishes that had never been seen there before. At first, some of the guests hesitated whether they should taste of that food; however, encouraged by others, they sat down, and soon partook of the meal, which was found exquisite. Immediately afterwards, as they were sitting before a seasonable fire, everything vanished at once, the dishes and the leavings, and in their stead reappeared the cloth of the house and the victual which had been previously cooked; but, for a wonder, all the guests were satisfied, so that no one thought of supper after such a magnificent dinner. A clear proof that the substituted viands were real and nowise fictitious.

This kind of persecution had been going on some months, when the lady betook herself to the blessed Bernardine of Feltri, whose body is worshiped in the church of St James, a short distance from the walls of the city. She made a vow to him that she would wear, during a whole twelve months, a gray frock, tied round her waist with a piece of cord, and such as is worn by the Minor Brethren, the order to which had belonged the blessed Bernardine; this she vowed, in the hope of being, through his intercession, at last rid of the persecution of the Incubus. And accordingly, on the 28th of September, the vigil of the Dedication of the Archangel S. Michael, and the festival of the blessed Bernardine, she assumed the votive robe.

The next morning, which was S. Michael's festival, the afflicted woman proceeded to the church of St Michael, her own parish, already mentioned; it was about ten o'clock, a time when a crowd of people were going to mass. She had no sooner set foot on the threshold of the church, than her clothes and ornaments fell off to the ground, and disappeared in a gust of wind, leaving her stark naked. There happened fortunately to be among the crowd two cavaliers of mature age, who, seeing what had taken place, hastened to divest themselves of their cloaks with which they concealed, as well as they could, the woman's nudity, and having put her into a vehicle, accompanied her home.

The clothes and trinkets taken by the Incubus were not restored by him before six months had elapsed. I might relate many other most surprising tricks which that Incubus played on her, were it not wearisome. Suffice it to say that, for a number of years he persevered in his temptation of her, but that finding at last that he was losing his pains, he desisted from his vexatious importunity.

In the above case, as well as in others that may be heard or read of occasionally, the Incubus attempts no act against Religion; he merely assails chastity. In consequence, consent is not a sin through ungodliness, but through incontinence.

Now, it is undoubted by Theologians and philosophers that carnal intercourse between mankind and the Demon sometimes gives birth to human beings; that is how is to be born the Antichrist, according to some Doctors, such as Bellarmin, Suarez, Maluenda, etc. They further observe that, from a natural cause, the children thus begotten by Incubi are tall, very hardy and bold, very proud and wicked. Thus writes Maluenda; as for the cause, he gives it from Vallesius, Archphysician in Reggio: "What Incubi introduce *in utero*, is not *qualecumque neque quantum cumque semen*, but abundant, very thick, very warm, rich in spirits and free from serosity. This moreover is an easy thing for them, since they have but to choose ardent, robust men, *et abundantes multo semine, quibus succumbant*, and then women of a like constitution, *quibus incumbant*, taking care that both shall enjoy *voluptatem solito majorem, tanto enim*

DEMONOLOGY

abundanthis emittitur semen quanta cum majori voluptate excernitur."

Those are the words of Vallesius, confirmed by Maluenda who shows, from the testimony of various Authors, mostly classical, that such associations gave birth to Romulus and Remus, according to Livy and Plutarch; Servius Tullius, the sixth king of Rome, according to Dyonisius of Haltcarnassus and Pliny the Elder; Plato the Philosopher, according to Diogenes Laertius and Saint Hieronymus; Alexander the Great, according to Plutarch and Quintus-Curtius; Seleucus, king of Syria, according to Justinus and Appianus; Scipio Africanus the Elder, according to Livy; the emperor Caesar Augustus, according to Suetonius; Aristomenes the Messenian, an illustrious Greek commander, according to Strabo and Pausanias, as also Merlin or Melchin the Englishman, born from an Incubus and a nun, the daughter of Charlemagne; and, lastly, as shown by the writings of Cochlceus quoted by Maluenda, that damned Heresiarch Martin Luther.

However, with due deference to so many and such learned Doctors, I hardly see how their opinion can bear examination. For, as Pererius truly observes in his Commentary on the Genesis, ch. 6, the whole strength and efficiency of the human sperm resides in the spirits which evaporate and vanish as soon as issued from the genital vessels wherein they were warmly stored: All medical men agree on that point. It is consequently not possible that the Demon should preserve in a fit state for generation the sperm he has received; for it were necessary that whatever vessel he endeavored to keep it in should be equally warm with the human genital organs, the warmth of which is nowhere to be met with but in those organs themselves.

Now, in a vessel where that warmth is not intrinsic but extraneous, the spirits get altered, and no generation can take place. There is this other objection, that generation is a vital act

DEMONOLOGY

by which man, begetting from his own substance, carries the sperm through natural organs to the spot which is appropriate to generation. On the contrary, in this particular case, the introduction of sperm cannot be a vital act of the man who begets, since it is not carried into the womb by his agency; and, for the same cause, it cannot be said that the man, whose sperm it was, has begotten the fetus which proceeds from it. Nor can the Incubus be deemed its father, since the sperm does not issue from his own substance. Consequentially, a child would be born without a father, which is absurd. Third objection: when the father begets in the course of nature, there is a concurrence of two casualties; the one, material, for he provides the sperm which is the matter of generation; the other, efficient, for he is the principal agent of generation, as Philosophers agree in declaring. But, in this case, the man who only provided the sperm would contribute but a mere material, without any action tending to generation; he could therefore not be regarded as the father of the child begotten under those circumstances; and this is opposed to the notion that the child begotten by an Incubus is not his son, but the son of the man whose sperm the Incubus has taken.

Besides, there is not a shadow of probability in what was written by Vallesius and quoted from him by us (*Vide supra* 30); and I wonder that any thing so extravagant should have fallen from the pen of such a learned man.

Medical men are well aware that the size of the fetus depends, not indeed on the quantity of matter, but on the quantity of virtue, that is to say of spirits held by the sperm; there lies the whole secret of generation, as is well observed by Michael Ettmuller, Institute of Medical Physiology: "Generation," says he, "entirely depends upon the genital spirit contained within an envelope of thicker matter; that spermatic matter does not remain in the uterus, and has no share in the formation of the fetus; it is but the genital spirit of the male, combined with the genital spirit of the female, that permeates the pores, or, less frequently, the tubes of the uterus, which it fecundates by that means." Of what moment can therefore the quantity of sperm be for the size of the fetus? Besides, it is not always a fact that men thus begotten by Incubi are remarkable for the huge proportions of their body: Alexander the Great, for instance, who is said to have been thus born, as we have mentioned, was very short; as the poet said of him: *"Magnus Alexander corpore parvus erat."*

Besides, although it is generally a fact that those who are thus begotten excel other men, yet such superiority is not always shown by their vices, but sometimes by their virtues and even their morals; Scipio Africanus, for instance, Caesar Augustus and Plato the Philosopher, as is recorded of each of them respectively by Livy, Suetonius and Diogenes Laertius, had excellent morals. Whence may be inferred that, if other individuals begotten in the same way have been downright villains, it was not owing to their being born of an Incubus, but to their having, of their own free will, chosen to be such.

We also read in the Testament, Genesis, ch. 6, verse 4, that giants were born when the sons of God came in unto the daughters of men; that is the very letter of the sacred text. Now, those giants were men of great stature, says Baruch, ch. 3, verse 26, and far superior to other men. Not only were they distinguished by their huge size, but also by their physical power, their plundering habits and their tyranny. Through their criminal excesses the Giants were the primary and principal cause of the Flood, according to Cornelius a Lapide, in his *Commentary on Genesis*. Some contend that by Sons of God are meant the sons of Seth, and by Daughters of men the daughters of Cain, because the former practiced piety, religion and every other virtue, whilst the descendants of Cain were quite the reverse; but, with all due deference to Chrysostom, Cyrillus, Hilarius and others who are of that opinion, it must be conceded that it clashes with the obvious meaning of the text. Scripture says, in fact, that of the conjunction of the above mentioned were born men of huge bodily size: Consequently, those giants were not previously in existence, and if their birth was the result of that conjunction, it cannot be ascribed to the intercourse of the sons of Seth with the daughters of Cain, who being themselves of ordinary stature, could but procreate children of ordinary stature. Therefore, if the intercourse in question gave birth to beings of huge stature, the reason is that it was not the common connection between man and woman, but the performance of Incubi Demons who, from their nature, may very well be styled sons of God. Such is the opinion of the Platonist Philosophers and of Francis Georges the Venetian; nor is it discrepant from that of Josephus the Historian, Philo the Jew, S. Justinus the Martyr, Clement of Alexandria, and Tertullian, who look upon Incubi as corporeal angels who have allowed themselves to fall into the sin of lewdness with women. Indeed, as shall be shown hereafter, though seemingly distinct, those two opinions are but one and the same.

If therefore these Incubi, in conformity with general belief, have begotten Giants by means of sperm taken from man, it is impossible, as aforesaid, that of that sperm should have been born any but men of approximately the same size as he from whom it came; for it would be in vain for the Demon, when acting the part of a Succubus, to draw from man an unwonted quantity of prolific liquor in order to procreate therefrom children of higher stature; quantity has nothing to do here, since all depends, as we have said, upon the vitality of that liquor, not its quantity. We are therefore bound to infer that Giants are born of another sperm than man's, and that, consequently, the Incubus Demon, for the purpose of generation, uses a sperm which is not man's. But then, what is to be said?

Subject to correction by our Holy Mother Church, and as a mere expression of opinion, I say that the Incubus Demon, when having intercourse with women, begets the human fetus from his own sperm.

DEMONOLOGY

To many that proposition will seem heterodox and hardly sensible; but I beg of my reader not to condemn it precipitately; for if, as Celsus says, it is improper to deliver judgment without having thoroughly inquired into the law, no less unfair is the rejection of an opinion, before the arguments upon which it rests have been weighed and confuted. I have therefore to prove the above conclusion, and must necessarily premise with some statements.

Firstly, I premise, as an article of belief, that there are purely spiritual creatures, not in any way partaking of corporeal matter, as was ruled by the Council of Lateran, under the pontificate of Innocent III. Such are the blessed Angels, and the Demons condemned to ever-lasting fire. Some Doctors, it is true, have professed, subsequently even to this Council, that the spirituality of Angels and Demons is not an article of belief; others even have asserted that they are corporeal, whence Bonaventure Baron has drawn the conclusion that it is neither heretical nor erroneous to ascribe to Angels and Demons a twofold substance, corporeal and spiritual. Yet, the Council having formally declared it to be an article of belief that God is the maker of all things visible and invisible, spiritual and corporeal, who has raised from nothing every creature spiritual or corporeal, Angelic or terrestrial, I contend it is an article of belief that there are certain merely spiritual creatures, and that such are Angels; not all of them, but a certain number.

It may seem strange, yet it must be admitted not to be unlikely. If, in fact. Theologians concur in establishing among Angels a specific, and therefore essential, diversity so considerable that, according to St. Thomas, there are not two Angels of the same species, but that each of them is a species by himself, why should not certain Angels be most pure spirits, of a consequently very superior nature, and others corporeal, therefore of a less perfect nature, differing thus from each other in their corporeal or incorporeal substance? This doctrine has the advantage of solving the otherwise insoluble contradiction

DEMONOLOGY

between two (Ecumenical Councils, namely the Seventh General Synod and the above-mentioned Council of Lateran. For, during the fifth sitting of that Synod, the second of Nicea, a book was introduced written by John of Thessalonica against a pagan Philosopher, wherein occur the following propositions: "Respecting Angels, Archangels and their Powers, to which I adjoin our own Souls, the Catholic Church is really of opinion that they are intelligences, but not entirely bodiless and senseless, as you Gentiles aver; she on the contrary ascribes to them a subtle body, aerial or igneous, according to what is written: He makes the spirits His Angels, and the burning fire His Minister." And further on: "Although not corporeal in the same way as ourselves, made of the four elements, yet it is impossible to say that Angels, Demons and Souls are incorporeal; for they have been seen many a time, invested with their own body, by those whose eyes the Lord had opened." And after that book had been read through before all the Fathers in Council assembled, Tharasius, the Patriarch of Constantinople, submitted it to the approval of the Council, with these words: "The Father shows that Angels should be pictured, since their form can be defined, and they have been seen in the shape of men." Without a dissent, the Synod answered: "Yes, my Lord."

That this approbation by a Council of the doctrine set forth at length in the book of John establishes an article of belief with regard to the corporeality of Angels, there is not a shadow of doubt: So Theologians toil and moil in order to remove the contradiction apparent between that decision and the definition, above quoted, by the Council of Lateran. One of them, Suarez, says that if the Fathers did not disprove such an assertion of the corporeality of Angels, it is because that was not the question. Another contends that the Synod did approve the conclusion, namely that Angels might be pictured, but not the motive given, their corporeality. A third, Molina, observes that the definitions issued in Council by the Synod were thus issued only at the seventh sitting, whence he argues that those of the previous sittings are not definitions of belief. Others, lastly, write that neither the Council of Nicea nor that of Lateran intended defining a question of belief, the Council of Nicea having spoken according to the opinion of the Platonists, which describes Angels as corporeal beings and was then prevailing, whilst that of Lateran went with Aristotle, who, in his 12th book of Metaphysics, lays down the existence of incorporeal intelligences, a doctrine which has since carried the day with most Doctors over the Platonists.

But any one can discern the invalidity of those answers, and Bonaventure Baro (Scot. *Defense*, tome 9) proves to evidence that they do not bear. In consequence, in order to agree the two Councils, we must say that the Council of Nicea meant one species of Angels, and that of Lateran another; the former, corporeal, the latter on the contrary absolutely incorporeal; and thus are reconciled two otherwise irreconcilable Councils.

Secondly, I premise that the word Angel applies, not indeed to the kind, but to the office; the Holy Fathers are agreed thereupon (St. Ambrose, on the Epistle to the Hebrews; St. Austin, City of God; St. Gregory, Homily 84 on Scripture; St. Isidorus. Supreme Goodness). An Angel, very truly says St. Ambrose, is thus styled, not because he is a spirit, but on account of his office: *Nuntius* in Latin, that is to say Messenger; it follows that whoever is entrusted by God with a mission, be he spirit or man, may be called an Angel, and is thus called in the Holy Scriptures, where the following words are applied to Priests, Preachers and Doctors, who, as Messengers of God, explain to men the divine will (Malachi, ch. 2, V. 7). "The priest's lips should keep knowledge, and they should seek the law at his mouth, for he is the Angel of the Lord of Hosts." The same prophet, ch. 3, V. I, bestows the name of Angel on St. John the Baptist, when saying: "Behold, I will send my Angel and he shall prepare the way before me." That this prophecy literally applies to St. John the Baptist is testified by our Lord Jesus Christ, in the Gospel, according to St. Matthew, ch. 1 1, V. 10. Still more: God himself is called an Angel, because he has "been sent by His Father to herald the law of mercy. To witness, the prophecy of Isaiah." Ch. 9, V. 6, according to Septuagint: "He shall be called an Angel of Wonderful Counsel." And more plainly still in Malachi, ch. 3, V. I; "The Lord whom you seek shall suddenly come to his temple., even the Angel of the covenant whom you delight in," a prophecy which literally applies to our Lord Jesus Christ. There is consequently nothing absurd in the contention that some Angels are corporeal, since men, who assuredly have a body, are called Angels.

Thirdly, I premise that neither the existence nor the nature of the natural things in this world has been sufficiently investigated to allow of denying a fact, merely because it has never been previously spoken of or written about. In the course of time have not new lands been discovered which the Ancients knew not of? New animals, herbs, plants, fruits and seeds, never seen elsewhere? And if that mysterious Austral land came at last to be explored, as has been to this day vainly tried by so many travelers, what unforeseen disclosures would be the result! Through the invention of the microscope and other instruments used by modern experimental Philosophy, combined with the more exact methods of investigation of Anatomists, have there not been, and are there not, every day, brought to light the existence, qualities and characteristics of a number of natural things unknown to ancient Philosophers, such as fulminating gold, phosphorus, and a hundred other chemical compounds, the circulation of the blood, the lacteal vessels, the lymph ducts and other recent anatomical discoveries? To deride a doctrine because it does not happen to be mentioned in any ancient author would therefore be absurd, especially bearing in mind this axiom of Logic; *locus ab auctoritate negativa non tenet.*

Fourthly, I premise that Holy Scripture and ecclesiastical tradition do not teach us any thing beyond what is requisite for the salvation of the soul, namely Faith, Hope and Charity. Consequently, from a thing not being stated either by Scripture or tradition it must not be inferred that that thing is not in existence. For instance, Faith teaches us that God, by His Word, made things visible, and invisible, and also that, through the merits of our Lord Jesus-Christ, grace and glory are conferred on every rational creature. Now, that there be another World than the one we live in, and that it be peopled by men not born of Adam but made by God, in some other way, as is implied by those who believe the lunar globe to be inhabited; or further, that in the very World we dwell in, there be other rational creatures besides man and the Angelic Spirits, creatures generally invisible to us and whose being is disclosed but accidentally, through the instrumentality of their own power; all that has nothing to do with Faith, and the knowledge or ignorance thereof is no more necessary to the salvation of man than knowing the number or nature of all physical things.

Fifthly, I premise that neither Philosophy nor Theology is repugnant to the possible existence of rational creatures having spirit and body and distinct from man. Such repugnance could be supported only on God, and that is inadmissible, since he is almighty, or on the thing to be made, and that likewise cannot be supported; for, as there are purely spiritual creatures, such as Angels, or merely material, such as the World, or lastly semi-spiritual and semi-corporeal, of an earthly and gross corporeality, such as man, so there may well be in existence a creature endowed with a rational spirit and a corporeality less gross, more subtle than man's. No doubt, moreover, but that after Resurrection, the souls of the blessed will be united with a glorious and subtle body; from which may be inferred that God may well have made a rational and corporeal creature whose body naturally enjoys the subtlety which will be conferred by the grace on the glorious body.

But, the possible existence of such creatures will be still better set forth by solving the arguments which can be adduced against our conclusion, and replying to the questions it may raise.

DEMONOLOGY

First question: Should such creatures be styled rational animals? And if so, in what do they differ from man, with whom they would have that definition in common?

I reply: Yes, they would be rational animals, provided with senses and organs even as man; they would, however, differ from man not only in the more subtle nature, but also in the matter of their body. In fact, as is shown by Scripture, man has been made from the grossest of all elements, namely clay, a gross mixture of water and earth; but those creatures would be made from the most subtle part of all elements, or of one or other of them; thus, some would proceed from earth, others from water, or air, or fire; and, in order that they should not be defined in the same terms as man, to the definition of the latter should be added the mention of the gross materiality of his body, wherein he would differ from said animals.

Second question: At what period would those animals have been originated, and where from? From earth, like the beasts, or from water, like quadrupeds, birds, etc.? Or, on the contrary, would they have been made, like man, by our Lord God?

I reply: It is an article of belief, expressly laid down by the Council of Lateran, that whatever is in fact and at present, was made in the origin of the world. By His almighty virtue, God, from the beginning of time, raised together from nothing both orders of creatures, spiritual and corporeal. Now, those animals also would be included in the generality of creatures. As to their formation, it might be said that God Himself, through the medium of Angels, made their body as he did man's, to which an immortal spirit was to be united. That body being of a nobler nature than that of other animals, it was meet that it should be united to an incorporeal and highly noble spirit.

Third question: Would those animals descend from one individual, as all men descend from Adam, or, on the contrary, would many have been made at the same time, as was the case for the other living things issued from earth and water, wherein were males and females for the preservation of the kind by generation? Would there be among them a distinction between the sexes? Would they be subject to birth and death, to senses, passions, want of food, power of growth? If so, what their nutrition? Would they lead a social life, as men do ? By what laws ruled? Would they build up cities for their dwellings, cultivate the arts and sciences, hold property, and wage war between themselves, as men are wont to?

I reply: It may be that all descend from one individual, as men descend from Adam; it may be also that a number of males and females were made initially, who preserved their kind by generation. We will further admit that they are born and die; that they are divided into males and females, and are moved by senses and passions, as men are; that they feed and grow according to the size of their body; their food, however, instead of being gross like that required by the human body, must be delicate and vapory, emanating through spirituous effluvia from whatever in the physical world abounds with highly volatile corpuscles, such as the flavor of meats, especially of roasts , the fume of wine, the fragrance of fruit, flowers, aromatics, which evolve an abundance of those effluvia until all their subtle and volatile parts have completely evaporated. To their being able to lead a social life, with distinctions of rank and precedence; to their cultivating the arts and sciences, exercising functions, maintaining armies, building up cities, doing in short whatever is requisite for their preservation, I have in the main no objection.

Fourth question: What would their figure be, human or otherwise? Would the ordering of the divers parts of their body be essential, as with other animals, or merely accidental, as with fluid substances, such as oil, water, clouds, smoke, etc.? Would those organic parts consist of various substances, as is the case with the organs of the human body, wherein are to be found very gross parts, such as the bones, others less gross, such as the cartilages, and others slender, such as the membranes?

I reply: As regards their figure, we neither can nor should be affirmative, since it escapes our senses, being too delicate for our sight or our touch. That we must leave to themselves, and to such as have the privilege of intuitive acquaintance with immaterial substances. But, so far as probability goes, I say that their figure tallies with the human body, save some distinctive peculiarity, should the very tenuity of their body not be deemed sufficient. I am led to that by the consideration that of all the works of God the human frame is the most perfect, and that whilst all other animals stoop to the ground, because their soul is mortal, God, as Ovid, the poet, says, in his Metamorphoses:

"Gave man an erect figure, bidding him behold the heavens. And raise his face towards the stars."

Man's soul having been made immortal for the heavenly abode. Considering that the animals we are speaking of Would be gifted with a spirit immaterial, rational and immortal, capable therefore of beatitude and damnation, it is proper to admit that the body to which that spirit is united may be like unto the most noble animal frame, that is to say to the human frame. Whence it follows that in the divers parts of that body there must be an essential order; that the foot, for instance, cannot be an appendage to the head, nor the hand to the belly, but that each organ is in its right place, according to the functions it has to perform. As to the constitutive parts of those organs, it is, in my opinion, necessary that there should be some more or less strong, others more or less slender, in order to meet the requirements of the organic working. Nor can this be fairly objected to on the ground of the slenderness of the bodies themselves; for the strength or thickness of the organic parts alluded to would not be absolute, but merely in comparison with the more slender ones. That, moreover, may be observed in all natural fluids, such as wine, oil, milk, etc; however homogeneous and similar to each other their component parts may look, yet they are not so; for some are like clay, others aqueous; there are fixed salts, volatile salts, brimstone, all of which are made obvious by a chemical analysis. So it would be in our case: For, supposing the bodies of those animals to be as subtle and slender as the natural fluids, air, water, etc., there would nevertheless be discrepancies in the quality of their constitutive parts, some of which would be strong when compared with others more slender, although the whole body which they compose might be called slender.

It may be objected that this is repugnant to what was said above concerning the essential ordering of the parts among themselves; that it is seen that, in fluid and subtle bodies, one part is not essentially but only accidentally connected with another; that a part of wine, for instance, just now contiguous with some other, soon comes in contact with a third, if the vessel be turned upside down or the wine shaken, and that all the parts together exchange positions at the same time, though it be still the same wine. Whence it should be inferred that, the bodies of those animals would have no permanent figure, and would consequently not be organic.

I reply that I deny the assumption. In fact, if in fluid bodies the essential ordering of the parts is not apparent, it subsists none the less, and causes a compound to preserve its own state. Wine, for instance, when expressed from the grapes, seems a thoroughly homogeneous liquor, and yet is not so; for there are gross parts which, in the long run, subside in the casks; there are also slender parts which evaporate, fixed parts, such as tartar; volatile parts, such as brimstone and alcohol; others again, half volatile and half fixed, such as phlegm. Those divers parts do not respectively maintain an essential order; for no sooner has the must been expressed from the grapes, and been styled brimstone or volatile spirits, than it continues so closely involved with the particles of tartar, which is fixed, as not to be in any way able to escape.

That is the reason why must recently expressed from the grapes is of no use for the distillation of the sulfurous spirits, commonly called brandy; but, after forty days fermentation, the particles of the wine change places; the spirits, no longer bound with the tartaric particles which they kept in suspension through their own volatility, whilst they were, in return, kept down by them and prevented from escaping, sever from those particles, and continue confused with the phlegmatic parts from which they become easily released by the operation of fire, and evaporate: Thus, by means of distillation, brandy is made, which is nothing but the brimstone of wine volatilized by heat with the most slender part of phlegm. At the end of forty days another fermentation begins, which extends more or less, according as the maturity of the wine is more or less perfect, and the termination of which is dependent on the greater or lesser abundance of sulfurous spirits. If abounding with brimstone, the wine sours and turns to vinegar; if, on the contrary, it holds but little brimstone, it ropes, and becomes what the Italians call *vino molle* or *vino guasto*. If the wine is at once ripe, as happens in other cases, it sours or ropes in less time, as is shown by everyday experience. Now, in said fermentation the essential order of the parts of wine is altered, but not so its quantity nor its matter, which neither changes nor decreases: A bottle that had been filled with wine is, after a certain time, found to be filled with vinegar, without any alteration in its quantity of matter; the essential order of its parts has alone been modified; the brimstone, which, as we have said, was united to the phlegm and separated from the tartar, becomes again involved and fixed with the tartar; so that, on distilling the vinegar, there issues from it first an insipid phlegm, and then spirits of vinegar, which are the brimstone of wine intermixed with particles of tartar that is less fixed. Now, the essential shifting of the aforesaid parts alters the substance of the juice of the grapes, as is clearly shown by the varied and contrary effects of must, wine, vinegar, and ropy or spoiled wine; for which cause the two first are fit, but the two last unfit materials for consecration. We have borrowed the above exposition of the economy of wine from the able work of Nicholas Lemery, perfumer to the King of France, *Course of Chemistry*, p. 2. C.Q.

If now we apply that natural doctrine to our subject, I say that, being given the corporeality of the animals in question, subtle and slender like the substance of liquids; being given also their organization and figure, which demand an essential order of the various parts, an adverse supposition could raise no argument contrary to their existence; for, just as the jumbling together of the parts of wine and the diversity of their accidental dispositions do not alter their essential order, even so it would be with the slender frame of our animals.

Fifth question: Would those animals be subject to diseases and other infirmities under which mankind lies, such as ignorance, fear, idleness, sensual paralysis, etc? Would they be wearied through labor, and require, for recruiting their strength, sleep, food, drink? And what food, what drink? Would they be fated to die, and might they be killed casually, or by the instrumentality of other animals?

I reply: Their bodies, though subtle, being material, they would of course be liable to decay; they might therefore suffer from adverse agencies, and consequently be diseased; that is, their organs might not perform, or painfully and imperfectly perform the office assigned to them, for therein consist all diseases whatever with certain animals, as has been distinctly explained by the most illustrious Michael Ettmuller, *Physiology* C.V thesis I. In sooth, their body being less gross than the human frame, comprising less elements mixed together, and being therefore less composite, they would not so easily suffer from adverse influences, and would therefore be less liable to disease than man; their life would also exceed his; for, the more perfect an animal, as a species, the longer its days; thus mankind, whose existence extends beyond that of other animals.

DEMONOLOGY

For I do not believe in the centenary existence of crows, stags, ravens and the like, of which Pliny tells his customary stories; and although his dreams have been reechoed by others without previous inquiry, it is no less clear that before writing thus, not one has faithfully noted the birth nor the death of those animals: They have been content with taking up the strange fable, as has been the case with the Phoenix, whose longevity is discarded as a story by Tacitus, *Annals* b. 6. It were therefore to be inferred that the animals we are speaking of would live longer still than man; for, as shall be said below, they would be more noble than he; consequently also, they would be subject to the other bodily affections, and require rest and food, as mentioned prior. Now, as rational beings amenable to discipline, they might also continue ignorant, if their minds did not receive the culture of study and instruction, and some among them would be more or less versed in science, more or less clever, according as their intelligence had been more or less trained.. However, generally speaking, and considering the whole of the species, they would be more learned than men, not from the subtlety of their body, but perhaps because of the greater activity of their mind or the longer space of their life, which would enable them to learn more things than men: Such are indeed the motives assigned by S. Austin (*Divine Demon*, ch. 3. and *Spirit and Soul* ch. 3;), to the prescience of the future in Demons. They might indeed suffer from natural agencies; but they could hardly be killed, on account of the speed with which they could escape from danger; it is therefore most unlikely that they could, without the greatest difficulty, be put to death or mutilated by beast or by man, with natural or artificial weapons, so quick would they be at avoiding the impending blow. Yet, they might be killed or mutilated in their sleep, or in a moment of inadvertence, by means of a solid body, such as a sword brandished by a man, or the fall of a heavy stone; for, although subtle, their body would be divisible, just like air which, though vaporous, is yet divided by a sword, a club, or any other solid body. Their spirit, however, would be indivisible, and like the human soul, entire in the whole and in each and every part of the body. Consequently, the division of their body by another body, as aforesaid, might occasion mutilation and even death , for the spirit, itself indivisible, could not animate both parts of a divided body.

True, just as the parts of air, separated by the agency of a body, unite again as soon as that body is withdrawn, and constitute the same air as before, even so the parts of the body divided, as above-mentioned, might unite and be revived by the same spirit. But then, it must be inferred that those animals could not be slain by natural or artificial agencies: And it were more rational to keep to our first position; for, if sharing matter with other creatures, it is natural that they should be liable to suffer through those creatures, according to the common rule, and even unto death.

Sixth question: Could their bodies penetrate other bodies, such as walls, wood, metals, glass, etc? Could many of them abide together on the same material spot, and to what space would their body extend or be restrained?

I reply: In all bodies, however compact, there are pores, as is apparent in metals where, more than in other bodies, it would seem there should be none; through a perfect microscope the pores of metals are discerned, with their different shapes. Now, those animals might, through the pores, creep into, and thus penetrate any other bodies, although such pores were impervious to other liquors or material spirits, of wine, ammonia salt, or the like, because their bodies would be much more subtle than those liquors.

However, notwithstanding many Angels may abide together on the same material spot, and even confine themselves in a lesser and lesser space, though not infinitely, as is shown by Scott, yet it were rash to ascribe the same power to those animals; for, their bodies are determined in substance and impervious to each other; and if two glorious bodies cannot abide together on the same spot, though a glorious and a non glorious one may do so, according to some Doctors, much less would it be possible for the bodies of those animals, which are indeed subtle, yet do not attain to the subtlety of the glorious body. As regards their power of extension or compression, we may instance the case of air, which, rarefied and condensed, occupies more or less room, and may even, by artificial means, be compressed into a narrower space than would be naturally due to its volume; as is seen with those large balls which, for amusement, one inflates by means of a blow-pipe or tube: Air, being forced into them and compressed, is held in larger quantity than is warranted by the capacity of the ball. Similarly the bodies of the animals we are speaking of might, by their natural virtue, extend to a larger space, not exceeding however their own substance; they might also contract, but not beyond the determined space due to that same substance. And, considering that of their number, as with men, some would be tall and some short, it were proper that the tall should be able to extend more than the short, and the short to contract more than the tall.

Seventh question: Would those animals be born in original sin, and have been redeemed by the Lord Christ? Would the grace have been conferred upon them and through what sacraments? Under what law would they live, and would they be capable of beatitude and damnation?

I reply: It is an article of belief that Christ has merited grace and glory for all rational creatures without exception. It is also an article of belief that glory is not conferred on a rational creature until such creature has been previously endowed with grace, which is the disposition to glory. According to a like article, glory is conferred but by merits. Now, those merits are grounded on the perfect observance of the commands of God, which is accomplished through grace. The above questions are thus solved. Whether those creatures did or did not sin originally is uncertain. It is clear, however, that if their first Parent had sinned as Adam sinned, his descent would be born in original sin, as men are born. And, as God never leaves a rational creature without a remedy, so long as it treads the way, if those creatures were infected with original or with actual sin, God would have provided them with a remedy; but whether it is the case, and of what kind is the remedy, is a secret between God and them. Surely, if they had sacraments identical with or different from those in use in the human Church militant, for the institution and efficacy thereof they would be indebted to the merits of Jesus Christ, the Redeemer and universal Atoner of all rational creatures. It would likewise be highly proper, nay necessary, that they should live under some law given them by God, and through the observance of which they might merit beatitude; but what would be that law, whether merely natural or written, Mosaic or Evangelical, or different from all these and specially instituted by God, that we are ignorant of. Whatever it might be though, there would follow no objection exclusive of the possible existence of such creatures.

The only argument, and that a rather lame one, which long meditations has suggested to me against the possibility of such creatures, is that, if they really existed in the World, we should find them mentioned somewhere by Philosophers, Holy Scripture, Ecclesiastical Tradition, or the Holy Fathers: Such not being the case, their utter impossibility should be inferred.

But that argument which, in fact, calls in question their existence rather than their possibility, is easily disposed of by our premises; for no argument can stand in virtue of a negative authority. Besides, it is not correct to assert that neither the Philosophers, nor the Scriptures, nor the Fathers have handed down any notion of them. Plato, as is reported by Apuleius (The Demon of Socrates) and Plutarch (his and Osiris) declared that Demons were beings of the animal kind, passive souls, rational intelligences, aerial bodies, everlasting; and he gave them the name of Demons which of itself is nowise offensive, since it means replete with wisdom; so that, when authors allude to the Devil (or Evil Angel), they do not merely call him Demon, but

DEMONOLOGY

Cacodemon, and say likewise Eudemon, when speaking of a good Angel. Those creatures are also mentioned in Scripture and by the Fathers, as shall be said hereafter.

Now that we have proved that those creatures are possible, let us go a step further, and show that they exist. Taking for granted the truth of the recitals concerning the intercourse of Incubi and Succubi with men and beasts, recitals so numerous that it would look like impudence to deny the fact, as is said by St Austin, whose testimony is given above, I argue: Where the peculiar passion of the sense is found, there also, of necessity, is the sense itself; for, according to the principles of philosophy, the peculiar passion flows from nature, that is to say, that, where the acts and operations of the sense are found, there also is the sense, the operations and acts being but its external form.

Now, those Incubi and Succubi present acts, operations, peculiar passions, which spring from the senses; they are therefore endowed with, senses. But senses cannot exist without concomitant composite organs, without a combination of soul and body. Incubi and Succubi have therefore body and soul, and, consequentially, are animals; but their acts and operations are also those of a rational soul; their soul is therefore rational; and thus, from first to last, they are rational animals.

Our minor is easy of demonstration in each of its parts. And indeed, the appetitive passion of coition is a sensual passion; the grief, sadness, wrath, rage, occasioned by the denial of coition, are sensual passions, as is seen with all animals; generation through coition is evidently a sensual operation. Now, all that happens with Incubi, as has been shown above: They incite women, sometimes even men; if denied, they sadden and storm, like lovers: *amantes, amentes*; they perfectly practice coition, and sometimes beget. It must therefore be inferred that they have senses, and consequently a body; consequently also, that they are perfect animals. More than that,

DEMONOLOGY

with closed doors and windows they enter wherever they please; their body is therefore slender; they foreknow and foretell the future, compose and divide, all which operations are proper to a rational soul; they therefore possess a rational soul and are, in sooth, rational animals. Doctors generally retort that it is the Evil Spirit that perpetrates those impure acts, simulates passions, love, grief at the denial of coition, in order to entice souls to sin and to undo them; and that, if he copulates and begets, it is with assumed sperm and body, as aforesaid.

But then, there are Incubi that have to do with horses, mares and other beasts, and, as shown by every day experience, ill treat them if rebel to coition; yet, in those cases, it can no longer be adduced that the Demon simulates the appetite for coition in order to bring about the ruin of souls, since those of beasts are not capable of everlasting damnation. Besides, love and wrath with them are productive of quite opposite effects. For, if the loved woman or beast humors them, those Incubi behave very well; on the contrary, they use them most savagely when irritated and enraged by a denial of coition: this is amply proved by daily experience: Those Incubi therefore have truly sexual passions. Besides, the Evil Spirits, the incorporeal Demons which have to do with Sorceresses and Witches, constrain them to Demon Worship, to the abjuration of the Orthodox Faith, to the commission of enchantments and foul crimes, as preliminary conditions to the infamous intercourse, as has been above-stated. Now, Incubi pretend to nothing of the kind; they are therefore no Evil Spirits. Lastly, as written by Guaccius, at the mere utterance of the name of Jesus or Mary, at the sign of the Cross, the approach of Holy Relics or consecrated objects, at exorcisms, adjurations or priestly injunctions, the Evil Demon either shudders and takes to flight, or is agitated and howls, as is daily seen with energumens and is shown by numerous narratives of Guaccius concerning the nightly revels of Witches, where, at a sign of the Cross or the name of Jesus said by one of the assistants. Devils and Witches all vanish together. Incubi, on the contrary, stand all those ordeals without taking to flight or showing the least fear; sometimes even they laugh at exorcisms, strike the Exorcists themselves, and rend the sacred vestments. Now, if the evil Demons, subdued by our Lord Jesus Christ, are stricken with fear by his name, the Cross and the holy things; if, on the other hand, the good Angels rejoice at those same things, without however inciting men to sin nor to give offense to God, whilst the Incubi, without having any dread of the holy things, provoke to sin, it is clear that they are neither evil Demons nor good Angels; but it is clear also that they are not men, though endowed with reason. What then should they be? Supposing them to have reached the goal, and to be pure spirits, they would be damned or blessed, for correct Theology does not admit of pure spirits on the way to salvation. If damned, they would revere the name and the Cross of Christ; if blessed, they would not incite men to sin; they would therefore be different from pure spirits, and thus, have a body and be on the way to salvation.

Besides, a material agent cannot act but on an equally material passive. It is indeed a trite philosophical axiom, that agent and patient must have a common subject; pure matter cannot act on any purely spiritual thing. Now, there are natural agents which act on those Incubi Demons: These are therefore material or corporeal. Our minor is proved by the testimony of Dioscorides, Pliny, Aristotle, and Apuleius, quoted by Guaccius, *Comp. Maleficarum*, b. 3, ch. 13, folio 316; it is confirmed by our knowledge of numerous herbs, stones and animal substances which have the virtue of driving away Demons, such as rue, St-John's wort, verbena, germander, palma Christi, centaury, diamonds, coral, jet, jasper, the skin of the head of a wolf or an ass, women's catamenia, and a hundred others: Wherefore it is written: "For such as are assaulted by the Demon it is lawful to have stones or herbs, but without recourse to incantations. It follows that, by their own native virtue, stones or herbs can bridle the Demon" else the above mentioned Canon would not permit their use, but would on the contrary forbid it

DEMONOLOGY

as superstitious. We have a striking instance thereof in Holy Scripture, where the Angel Raphael says to Tobit, ch. 6, v. 8, speaking of the fish which he had drawn from the Tigris: "If thou puttest on coals a particle of its liver, the smoke thereof will drive away all kinds of Demons."

Experience demonstrated the truth of those words; for, no sooner was the liver of the fish set on fire, than the Incubus who was in love with Sarah was put to flight.

To this Theologians usually retort that such natural agents merely initiate the ejection of the Demon, and that the completed effect is due to the supernatural force of God or of the Angel; so that the supernatural force is the primary, direct and principal cause, the natural force being but secondary, indirect and subordinate. Thus, in order to explain how the liver of the fish burnt by Tobit drove away the Demon, Vallesius asserts that the smoke thereof had been endowed by God with the supernatural power of expelling the Incubus, in the same manner as the material fire of Hell has the virtue of tormenting Demons and the souls of the Damned. Others, such as Lyranus and Cornelius, profess that the smoke of the heart of the fish initiated the ejection of the Demon by native virtue, but completed it by angelical and heavenly virtue; by native virtue, insomuch that it opposed a contrary action to that of the Demon; for the Evil Spirit applies native causes and humors, the native qualities of which are combated by the contrary qualities of natural things known to be capable of driving away Demons; that opinion is shared by all those who treat of the art of exorcisms.

But that explanation, however plausible the facts upon which it rests, can at most be received as regards the Evil Spirits which possess bodies or, through malefic ways, infect them with diseases or other infirmities; it does not at all meet the case of Incubi. For, these neither possess bodies nor infect them with diseases; they, at most, molest them by blows and ill-treatment.

DEMONOLOGY

If they cause the mares to grow lean because of their not yielding to coition, it is merely by taking away their provender, in consequence of which they fall off and finally die. To that purpose the Incubus need not use a natural agent, as the Evil Spirit does when imparting a disease; it is enough that it should exert its own native organic force. Likewise, when the Evil Spirit possesses bodies and infects them with diseases, it is most frequently through signs agreed upon with himself, and arranged by a witch or a wizard, which signs are usually natural objects, imbued with their own noxious virtue, and of course opposed by other equally natural objects endowed with a contrary virtue. But not so the Incubus: It is of his own accord, and without the cooperation of either witch or wizard, that he inflicts his molestation. Besides, the natural things which put the Incubi to flight exert their virtue and bring about a result without the intervention of any exorcism or blessing; it cannot therefore be said that the ejection of the Incubus is initiated by natural, and completed by divine virtue, since there is in this case no particular invocation of the divine name, but the mere effect of a natural object, in which God cooperates only as the universal agent, the author of nature, the first of efficient causes.

To illustrate this subject, I give two stories, the first of which I have from a Confessor of Nuns, a man of weight, and most worthy of credit; the second I was eyewitness to.

In a certain monastery of holy Nuns there lived, as a boarder, a young maiden of noble birth, who was tempted by an Incubus that appeared to her by day and by night and with the most earnest entreaties, the manners of a most passionate lover, incessantly incited her to sin; but she, supported by the grace of God and the frequent use of the sacraments, stoutly resisted the temptation. But, all her devotions, fasts and vows notwithstanding, despite the exorcisms, the blessings, the injunctions showered by exorcists on the Incubus that he should desist from molesting her; in spite of the crowd of relics and other holy objects collected in the maiden's room, of the lighted candles kept burning there all night, the Incubus nonetheless persisted in appearing to her as usual, in the shape of a very handsome young man. At last, among other learned men, whose advice had been taken on the subject, was a very erudite Theologian who, observing that the maiden was of a thoroughly phlegmatic temperament, surmised that that Incubus was an aqueous Demon (there are in fact, as is testified by Guaccius, igneous, aerial, phlegmatic, earthly, subterranean demons who avoid the light of day), and prescribed an uninterrupted fumigation in the room. A new vessel, made of glass-like earth, was accordingly brought in, and filled with sweet cane, cubeb seed, roots of both aristolochies, great and small cardamon, ginger, long-pepper, caryophyllae, cinnamon, cloves, mace, nutmegs, calamus, storax, benzoin, aloe wood and roots, one ounce of triasandalis, and three pounds of half brandy and water; the vessel was then set on hot ashes in order to force up the fumigating vapor, and the cell was kept closed. As soon as the fumigation was done, the Incubus came, but never dared enter the cell; only, if the maiden left it for a walk in the garden or the cloister, he appeared to her, though invisible to others and throwing his arms round her neck, stole or rather snatched kisses from her, to her intense disgust. At last, after a new consultation, the Theologian prescribed that she should carry about her person pills made of the most exquisite perfumes, such as musk, amber, chive, Peruvian balsam, and others. Thus provided, she went for a walk in the garden, where the Incubus suddenly appeared to her with a threatening face, and in a rage. He did not approach her, however, but, after biting his finger as if meditating revenge, disappeared and was never more seen by her.

Here is the other story. In the great Carthusian Friary of Pavia there lived a Deacon, Austin by name, who was subjected by a certain Demon to excessive, unheard of and scarcely credible vexations; although many exorcists had made repeated endeavors to secure his riddance, all spiritual remedies had proved unavailing. I was consulted by the Vicar of the convent, who had the cure of the poor clerk. Seeing the inefficacy of all customary exorcisms, and remembering the above-related instance, I advised a fumigation like unto the one that has been detailed, and prescribed that the Deacon should carry about his person fragrant pills of the same kind; moreover, as he was in the habit of using tobacco, and was very fond of brandy, I advised tobacco and brandy perfumed with musk. The Demon appeared to him by day and by night, under various shapes, as a skeleton, a pig, an ass, an Angel, a bird; with the figure of one or other of the Friars, once even with that of his own Abbot or Prior, exhorting him to keep his conscience clean, to trust in God, to confess frequently; he persuaded him to let him hear his sacramental confession, recited with him the psalms *Exsurgat Deus* and *Qui habitat* and the Gospel according to St John: And when they came to the words *Verbum carofactum est*, he bent his knee, and taking hold of a stole which was in the cell, and of the Holy-water sprinkle, he blessed the cell and the bed, and, as if he had really been the Prior, enjoined on the Demon not to venture in future to molest his subordinate; he then disappeared, thus betraying what he was, for otherwise the young deacon had taken him for his Prior. Now, notwithstanding the fumigations and perfumes I had prescribed, the Demon did not desist from his wonted apparitions; more than that, assuming the features of his victim, he went to the Vicar's room, and asked for some tobacco and brandy perfumed with musk, of which, said he, he was extremely fond. Having received both, he disappeared in the twinkling of an eye, thus showing the Vicar that he had been played with by the Demon; and this was amply confirmed by the Deacon, who affirmed upon his oath that he had not gone that day to the Vicar's cell. All that having been related to me, I inferred that, far from being aqueous like the Incubus who was in love with the maiden above spoken of, this Demon was igneous, or, at the very least, aerial, since he delighted in hot substances such as vapors, perfumes, tobacco and brandy. Force was added to my surmises by the temperament of the young deacon, which was choleric and sanguine, choler predominating however; for, those Demons never approach but those whose temperament tallies with their own. Another confirmation of my sentiment regarding their corporeality. I therefore advised the Vicar to let his penitent take herbs that are cold by nature, such as water-lily, liver-wort, spurge, mandrake, house-leek, plantain, henbane, and others similar, make two little bundles of them and hang them up, one at his window, the other at the door of his cell, taking care to strew some also on the floor and on the bed. Marvelous to say! The Demon appeared again, but remained outside the room, which he would not enter; and, on the Deacon inquiring of him his motives for such unwonted resort, he burst out into invectives against me for giving such advice, disappeared, and never came again.

The two stories I have related make it clear that, by their native virtue alone, perfumes and herbs drove away Demons without the intervention of any supernatural force; Incubi are therefore subject to material conditions, and it must be inferred that they participate of the matter of the natural objects which have the power of putting them to flight, and consequently they have a body; that is what was to be shown.

But, the better to establish our conclusion, it behooves to impugn the mistake into which have fallen the Doctors above quoted, such as Vallesius and Cornelius a Lapide, when they say that Sarah was rid from the Incubus by the virtue of the Angel Raphael, and not by that of the simple fish caught by Tobit on the banks of the Tigris. Indeed, saving the reverence due to such great doctors, such a construction manifestly clashes with the clear meaning of the Text, from which it is never justifiable to deviate, so long as it does not lead to absurd consequences. Here are the words spoken by the Angel to Tobias: "If thou puttest on coals a particle of its heart, the smoke thereof will expel all kinds of Demons, whether from man or woman, so that they shall never return, and its gall is good for anointing eyes that have whiteness, and healing them." (Tobit, ch. 6, 8-9). Pray notice that the Angel's assertion respecting the virtue of the heart or liver and gall of that fish is absolute, universal; for, he does not say "If thou puttest on coals particles of its heart, thou wilt put to flight all kinds of Demons, and if thou anoint with its gall eyes that have a whiteness, they shall be healed." If he had thus spoken, I could agree with the construction that Raphael had brought about, by his own supernatural virtue, the effects which the mere application of the smoke and the gall might not have sufficed to produce; but he does not speak thus, and, on the contrary, says absolutely, that such is the virtue of the smoke and the gall.

It may be asked whether the Angel spoke the precise truth regarding the virtue of those things, or whether he might have lied; and likewise, whether the whiteness was withdrawn from the eyes of the elder Tobit by the native force of the gall of the fish, or by the supernatural virtue of the Angel Raphael? To say that the Angel could have lied would be an heretical blasphemy; he therefore spoke the precise truth; but it would no longer be so if all kinds of Demons were not expelled by the smoke of the liver of the fish, unless aided by the supernatural force of the Angel, and especially, if such aid was the principal cause of the effect produced, as the Doctors assert in the present case. It would doubtless be a lie if a physician should say: Such an herb radically cures pleurisy or epilepsy, and if it should only begin the cure, the completion of which required the addition of another herb to the one first used; in the same manner, Raphael would have lied when averring that the smoke of the liver expelled all kinds of demons, so that they should not return, if that result had been only begun by the smoke, audits completion had been principally due to the virtue of the Angel. Besides, that flight of the demon was either to take place universally and by any one whomsoever putting the liver of the fish on the coals, or else it was only to occur in that particular case, the younger Tobit putting the liver on. In the first hypothesis, any person making that smoke by burning the liver should be assisted by an Angel, who, through his supernatural virtue should expel the Demons miraculously and regularly at the same time; which is absurd; for, either words have no meaning, or a natural fact cannot be regularly followed by a miracle; and, if the Demon was not put to flight without the assistance of the Angel, Raphael would have lied when ascribing that virtue to the liver. If, on the contrary, that effect was only to be brought about in that particular case, Raphael would again have lied when assigning to that fish, universally and absolutely, the virtue of expelling the Demon: Now, to say that the Angel lied is not possible.

The whiteness was withdrawn from the eyes of the elder Tobit, and his blindness healed, through the native virtue of the gall of that same fish, as Doctors aver. In fact, that the gall of the simple fish, which the Italians call *bocca in capo* and of which Tobias made use, is a highly renowned remedy for removing the whiteness from the eyes, all are agreed, Dioscorides, Galen, Pliny, Aclanius, Vallesius, etc. The Greek Text of Tobit, ch. 1, 13, says: "He poured the gall on his father's eyes, saying; 'have confidence, father; but, there being erosion, the old man rubbed his eyes, and the scales of the whiteness came out at the corners.'" Now, since, according to the same text, the Angel had disclosed to Tobias the virtue of the liver and gall of the fish, and since, through its native virtue, the gall cured the elder Tobit 's blindness, it must be inferred that it was likewise through its native force that the smoke of the liver put the Incubus to flight; which inference is conclusively confirmed by the Greek text, which, Tobit, ch. 8, 2 instead of the reading in the Vulgate: "He laid a part of the liver on burning coals," says explicitly: "He took the ashes of the perfumes, and put the heart and the liver of the fish thereupon, and made a smoke therewith; the which smell when the evil spirit had smelled, he fled." The Hebrew text says: "Asmodeus smelled the smell, and fled."

From all those texts it appears that the Demon took to flight on smelling a smoke which was prejudicial and hurtful to himself, and nowise from the supernatural virtue of the Angel. If, in ridding Sarah from the assaults of the Incubus Asmodeus, the operation of the smoke of the liver was followed by the intervention of Raphael, it was in order to bind the Demon in the wilderness of High Egypt, as related, Tobit, ch. 8, 3; for, at such a distance, the smoke of the liver could neither operate on the Demon, nor bind him. And here we have the means of reconciling our opinion with that of the above mentioned Doctors, who ascribe to Raphael's power Sarah's complete riddance from the Demon; for, I say with them, that the cure of Sarah was completed by the binding of the Demon in the wilderness, the deed of the Angel; which I concede; but I maintain that the deliverance properly called, that is to say, the ejection from Sarah's bedroom, was the direct effect of the virtue of the liver of the fish.

A third principal proof of our conclusion regarding the existence of those animals, in other words, respecting the corporeality of Incubi, is adduced by the testimony of St Hieronymus, in his Life of St Paul, the first Hermit. St Anthony, says he, set on a journey to visit St Paul. After traveling several days, he met a Centaur, of whom he inquired the hermit's abode; whereupon the Centaur, growling some uncouth and scarcely intelligible answer, showed the way with his outstretched hand, and fled with the utmost speed into a wood. The Holy Abbot kept on his way, and, in a dale, met a little man, almost a dwarf, with crooked hands, horned brow, and his lower extremities ending with goat's feet. At the sight of him, St Anthony stood still, and fearing the arts of the Devil, comforted himself with a sign of the Cross. But, far from running away, or even seeming frightened at it, the little fellow respectfully approached the old man, and tendered him, as a peace offering, dates for his journey. The blessed St Anthony having then inquired who he was: "I am a mortal," replied he, "and one of the inhabitants of the Wilderness, whom Gentility under its varied delusions, worships under the names of Fauns, Satyrs, and Incubi; I am on a mission from my flock: We request thee to pray for us unto the common God, whom we know to have come for the salvation of the world, and whose praises are sounded all over the earth." Rejoicing at the glory of Christ, St Anthony, turning his face

DEMONOLOGY

towards Alexandria, and striking the ground with his staff, cried out: "Woe be unto thee thou harlot City, who worships animals as Gods!" Such is the narrative of St Hieronymus, who expatiates at length on the fact, explaining its import in a long discourse.

It were indeed rash to doubt the truth of the above recital, constantly referred to by the greatest of the Doctors of the Holy Church, St Hieronymus, whose authority no Catholic will ever deny. Let us therefore investigate the circumstances thereof which most clearly confirm our opinion.

Firstly, we must observe that if ever a Saint was assailed by the arts of the Demon, saw through his infernal devices, and carried off victories and trophies from the contest, that Saint was St Anthony, as is shown by his life written by St Athanasius. Now, since in that little man St Anthony did not recognize a devil but an animal, saying: "Woe be unto thee, thou harlot City, who worships animals as Gods!" It is clear that it was no devil or pure spirit ejected from heaven and damned, but some kind of animal. Still more: St Anthony, when instructing his friars and cautioning them against the assaults of the Demon, said to them, as related in the Roman Breviary (Festival of St Anthony, Abbot b. I); "Believe me, my brethren, Satan dreads the vigils of pious men, their prayers, fasts, voluntary poverty, compassion and humility; but, above all, he dreads their burning love of our Lord Christ, at the mere sign of whose most Holy Cross he flies disabled." As the little man, against whom St Anthony guarded himself with a sign of the Cross, neither took fright nor fled, but approached the Saint confidently and humbly, offering him some dates, it is a sure sign that he was no Devil.

Secondly, we must observe that the little man said: "also am a mortal," whence it follows that he was an animal subject to death, and consequently called into being through generation; for, an immaterial spirit is immortal, because simple, and consequently is not called into being through generation from pre-existent matter, but through creation, and, consequently also, cannot lose it through the corruption called death; its existence can only come to an end through annihilation. Therefore, when saying he was mortal, he professed himself an animal.

Thirdly, we must observe that he said he knew that the common God had suffered in human flesh. Those words show him to have been a rational animal, for brutes know nothing but what is sensible and present, and can therefore have no knowledge of God. If that little man said that he and his fellows were aware of God having suffered in human flesh, it shows that, by means of some revelation, he had acquired the notion of God, as we have ourselves the revealed faith. That God assumed human flesh and suffered in it, is the essence of the two principal articles of our Faith; the existence of God one and threefold, His Incarnation, Passion and Resurrection. All that shows, as I said, that it was a rational animal, capable of the knowledge of God through revelation, like ourselves, and endowed with a rational, and consequently, immortal soul.

Fourthly, we must observe that, in the name of his whole flock whose delegate he professed to be, he besought St Anthony to pray for them to the common God. Where from I infer that that little man was capable of beatitude and damnation, and that he was not *in termino* but *in via*; for, from his being, as has been shown above, rational and consequently endowed with an immortal soul, it flows that he was capable of beatitude and damnation, the proper share of every rational Creature, Angel or man. I likewise infer that he was on the way, *in via*, that is, capable of merit and demerit; for, if he had been at the goal, *in termino*, he would have been either blessed or damned. Now, he could be neither the one nor the other; for, St. Anthony's prayers, to which he commended himself, could have been of no assistance to him, if finally damned, and, if blessed, he stood in no need of them. Since he commended himself to

DEMONOLOGY

those prayers, it shows they could be of avail to him, and, consequently, that he was on the way to salvation, *in statu vice et meriti*.

Fifthly, we must observe that the little man professed to be delegated by others of his kind, when saying: "I am on a mission from my flock," words from which many inferences may be deduced. One is, that the little man was not alone of his kind, an exceptional and solitary monster, but that there were many of the same species, since congregating they made up a flock, and that he came in the name of all; which could not have been, had not the will of many centered in him. Another is, that those animals lead a social life, since one of them was sent in the name of many. Another again is, that, although living in the Wilderness, it is not assigned to them as a permanent abode; for St Anthony having never previously been in that desert, which was far distant from his hermitage, they could not have known who he was nor what his degree of sanctity; it was therefore necessary that they should have become acquainted with him elsewhere, and, consequently, that they should have traveled beyond that wilderness.

Lastly, we must observe that the little man said he was one of those whom the Gentiles, blinded by error, call Fauns, Satyrs, and Incubi: And by these words is shown the truth of our principal proposition: That Incubi are rational animals, capable of beatitude and damnation.

The apparition of such little men is of frequent occurrence in metallic mines, as is written by Gregorius Agricola in his book *De Animal, subterran*. They appear to the miners, clothed like themselves, play and caper together, laugh and titter, and throw little stones at them for the sake of amusement; a sign, says the above-named Author, of excellent success, and of the finding of some branch or body of a mineral tree.
Peter Thyraeus, of Neuss, in his book *De Terrijication*.

nocturn. denies the existence of such little men, and supports his denial upon the following truly puerile arguments: Given such little men, says he, where do they live, how and where do they dwell? How do they keep up their kind, through generation or otherwise? Are they born, do they die, with what food do they sustain themselves? Are they capable of beatitude and damnation, and by what means do they procure their salvation? Such are the arguments upon which Thyrseus relies for denying that existence.

But it really shows little judgment in a man, to deny that which has been written by grave and credible Authors, and confirmed by every day experience. Thyraeus's arguments are worthless and have been already refuted, prior and following. The only question which remains to be answered is this: Where do those little men, or Incubi, dwell? To that I reply: as has been shown above, according to Guaccius, some are earthly, some aqueous, some aerial, some igneous, that is to say, that their bodies are made of the most subtle part of one of the elements, or, if of the combination of many elements, that yet there is one which predominates, either water or air, according to their nature. Their dwellings will consequently be found in that element which is prevalent in their bodies: Igneous Incubi, for instance, will only stay forcibly, may be will not stay at all, in water or marshes, which are adverse to them; and aqueous Incubi will not be able to rise into the upper part of ether, the subtlety of which region is repugnant to them. We see the like happen to men who, accustomed to thicker air, cannot reach certain lofty ridges of the Alps where the air is too subtle for their lungs.

Many testimonies of Holy Fathers, gathered by Molina, in his *Commentary of St Thomas*, would go to prove the corporeality of Demons; but, taking into account the above-quoted decision of the Council of Lateran, concerning the non-corporeality of Angels, we must understand that the Holy Fathers had in view those Incubi Demons which are still on the

DEMONOLOGY

way to salvation, and not those that are damned. However, to make matters short, we merely give the authority of St Austin, that eminent Doctor of the Church, and it will be clearly seen how thoroughly his doctrine harmonizes with ours.

St Austin, then, in his *Commentary on Genesis*, book 2, ch. 17, writes as follows concerning Demons: "They have the knowledge of some truths, partly through the more subtle acumen of their senses, partly through the greater subtlety of their bodies," and, book 3, ch. 1: "Demons are aerial animals, because they partake of the nature of aerial bodies." In his Epistle 115 to Hebridius, he affirms that they are "aerial or ethereal animals, endowed with very sharp senses." In *The City of God*, book II, ch. 13, he says that "the worst Demon has an aerial body." Book 21, ch. 10, he writes: "The bodies of certain Demons, as has been believed by some learned men, are even made of the thick and damp air which we breathe." Book 15, ch. 23: "He dares not define whether Angels, with an aerial body, could feel the lust which would incite them to communicate with women." In his *commentary on Psalm 85*, he says that "the bodies of the blessed will, after resurrection, be like unto the bodies of Angels" Psalm 14, he observes that; "the body of Angels is inferior to the soul." And, in his book *De Divinit Daemonum*, he everywhere, and especially in ch. 23, teaches that "Demons have subtle bodies."

Our doctrine can also be confirmed by the testimony of the Holy Scriptures, which, however diversely construed by commentators, are yet capable of adaptation to our proposition. First, Psalm 77, 24 and 25, it is said: "The Lord had given them of the bread of heaven; man did eat angels' food." David here alludes to Manna, which fed the People of Israel during the whole time that they wandered in the wilderness. It will be asked in what sense it can be said of Manna that it is the Bread of Angels. I am aware that most Doctors construe this passage in a mystical sense, saying that Manna figures the Holy Eucharist, which is styled the bread of Angels because Angels enjoy the sight of God who, by concomitance, is found in the Eucharist.

A most proper construction assuredly, and which is adopted by the Church in the office of the Most Holy Body of Jesus Christ; but it is in a spiritual sense. Now, what I want, is the literal sense; for, in that Psalm, David does not speak, as a prophet, of things to be, as he does in other places where a literal sense is not easily to be gathered; he speaks here as a historian, of things gone by. That Psalm, as is evident to whoever reads it, is a pure anacephalaeosis, or summing up of all the benefits conferred by God on the Hebrew People from the exodus from Egypt to the days of David, and the Manna of the Wilderness is spoken of in it; how, and in what sense is it styled the Bread of Angels? That is the question.

I am aware that others look upon the Bread of Angels as bread prepared by Angels, or sent down from Heaven by the ministry of Angels. But Cardinal Hugo explains that qualification by saying that that food partly produced the same effect upon the Jews, which the food of Angels produces upon the latter. Angels, in fact, are not liable to any infirmity; on the other hand Hebrew commentators, and Josephus himself, assert that whilst in the Wilderness, living upon Manna, the Jews' neither grew old, nor sickened, nor tired; so that Manna was like unto the bread that Angels feed upon, who know neither old age, nor sickness, nor fatigue.

These interpretations should indeed be received with the respect due to the authority of such eminent Doctors. There is however one difficulty in this: That, by the ministry of Angels, the pillars of the cloud and fire, the quails, and the water from the rock were provided for the Hebrews, no less than the Manna; and yet they were not styled the pillar, the water or the beverage of Angels. Why therefore should Manna be called Bread of Angels, because provided by their ministry, when the qualification Beverage of Angels is not given to the water drawn from the rock likewise by their ministry? Besides, in Holy Scripture, when it is said of bread that it is the bread of somebody, it is always the bread of him who feeds on it, not of him who provides or makes it. Of this there are numberless instances: Thus. Exodus, ch. 23, 25: "That I may bless thy bread and thy water"; 2 Kings,ch. 12, 3: "Eating of his bread"; Tobit ch. 4, 17: "Give of thy bread to the hungry" and 18: "Pour out thy bread on the burial of the Just"; Ecc. ch. 11, 1: "Scatter thy bread over the flowing waters"; Isaiah, ch. 58, v. , 77: "Deal thy bread to the hungry"; Jeremiah ch. 1, 19: "Let us put wood into his bread"; Matthew, ch. 15, 26: "It is not meet to take the children's bread"; Luke, ch. 11, 3: "Our daily bread." All those passages clearly show that, in Scripture, the bread of somebody is the bread of him who feeds upon it, not of him who makes, brings or provides it. In the passage of the Psalm we have quoted, Bread of Angels may therefore easily be taken to mean the food of Angels, not incorporeal indeed, since these require no material food, but corporeal, that is to say of those rational animals we have discoursed of, who live in the air, and, from the subtlety of their bodies and their rationality, approximate so closely to immaterial Angels as to fall under the same denomination.

I deduce that, being animals, consequently reproducible through generation and liable to corruption, they require food for the restoration of their corporeal substance wasted by effluvia; for the life of every sensible being consists in nothing else but the motion of the corporeal elements which flow and ebb, are acquired, lost and recruited by means of substances spirituous, yet material, assimilated by the living thing, either through the inhalation of air, or by the fermentation of food which spiritualizes its substance, as shown by the most learned Ettmuller (*Institute of Medical Physiology* ch. 2).

But, their body being subtle, equally subtle and delicate must be its food. And, just as perfumes and other vaporous and volatile substances, when adverse to their nature, offend and put them to flight, as testified by what we related above, in the like manner, when agreeable, they delight in and feed upon them. Now, as is written by Cornelius, "Manna is nothing but an emanation of water and earth, refined and baked by the heat of the sun, and then coagulated and condensed by the cold of the following night"; of course, I am speaking of the Manna sent down from Heaven for the nourishment of the Hebrews, and which differs all in all from nostrate or medicinal manna: the latter, in fact, according to Ettmuller (*Dilucid Physiology* ch. 1), "is merely the juice or transudation of certain trees which, during the night, gets mixed up with dew, and, the next morning, coagulates and thickens in the heat of the sun." The manna of the Hebrews, on the contrary, derived from other principles, far from coagulating, liquefied in the heat of the sun, as is shown by Scripture, Exodus, ch. 16, v22. The manna of the Hebrews was therefore undoubtedly of a most subtle substance, consisting as it did of emanations of earth and water and being dissolved by the sun and made to disappear: Consequently, it may very well have been the food of the animals we are speaking of, and thus have been truly called by David Bread of Angels.

We have another authority in the Gospel according to St John, ch. 10, 16, where it is said: "And other sheep I have, which are not of this fold; them also I must bring, and they shall hear my voice, and there shall be one fold and one shepherd." If we inquire what are those sheep which are not of that fold, and what the fold of which the Lord Christ speaks, we are answered by all Commentators that the only fold of Christ is the Church to which the preaching of the Gospel was to bring the Gentiles, sheep of another fold than that of the Hebrews. They are, in fact, of opinion that the fold of Christ was the Synagogue, because David had said, Psalm 95, 7: "We are the people of his pasture, and the sheep of his hand", and also because Abraham and David had been promised that the Messiah should be born of their race, because he was expected by the Hebrew people, foretold by the Prophets who were Hebrews, and that his advent, his acts, his passion, death and resurrection were prefigured in the sacrifices, worship and ceremonials of the Hebrew law.

But, saving always the reverence due to the Holy Fathers and other Doctors, that explanation does not seem quite satisfactory. For it is an article of belief that the Church of the Faithful has been the only one in existence from the beginning of the world, and will thus endure to the end of time. The head of that Church is Jesus Christ, the mediator between God and men, by whose contemplation all things were made and created. Indeed, the faith in the divine Trinity, though less explicitly, and the Incarnation of the Word were revealed to the first man, and by him taught his children, who, in their turn, taught them their descendants. And thus, although most men had strayed into idolatry and deserted the true faith, many kept the faith they had received from their fathers, and observing the law of nature, stayed in the true Church of the Faithful, as is noticed by Cardinal Tolet in reference to Job, who was a saint among idolatrous Gentiles. And, although God had conferred especial favors upon the Hebrew people, prescribed for them peculiar laws and ceremonials, and separated them from the Gentiles, yet those laws were not obligatory on the Gentiles, and the faithful Hebrews did not constitute a Church different from that of the Gentiles who professed their faith in one God and the coming of the Messiah.

And thus it came to pass that even among the Gentiles there were some who prophesied the advent of Christ and the other dogmas of the Christian faith, to wit Balaam, Mercurius Trismegistus , Hydaspes, and the Sibyls mentioned by Lactantius, book I, ch. 6, as written by Baronius, *Apparat. Annal,* 18. That the Messiah was expected by the Gentiles is shown by many passages of Isaiah, and plainly testified by the prophecy of Jacob, the Patriarch, thus worded, Genesis, ch. 49, 10: "The scepter shall not depart from Judah, nor a law-giver from between his feet, until Shiloh (he who is to be sent) come, and unto him shall the gathering of the people be." Likewise in the prophecy of Haggai, ch. 2, 8: "I will shake all Nations, and the desire of all Nations shall come"; which passage is thus commented by Cornelius a Lapide: "The Gentiles before the advent of Christ, who believed in God and observed the law of nature, expected and desired Christ equally with the Jews." Christ himself disclosed and manifested himself to the Gentiles as well as to the Jews; for, at the same time as the Angel apprised the shepherds of his nativity, by means of the miraculous star he called the Magi to worship him, who, being Gentiles, were the first among the Nations, as the shepherds among the Jews, to acknowledge and worship Christ (*Vide St Fulgentius*, Sermon 6, upon Epiphany). In like manner, the advent of Christ was made known by preaching (I am not speaking of the Apostles) to the Gentiles before it was to the Jews. As is written by the Venerable Mother, Sister Maria of Agreda, in her *Life of Jesus Christ and the Blessed Virgin Mary*: "When the Blessed Virgin Mary, fleeing with St Joseph, from the persecution of Herod, carried the Infant Jesus into Egypt, she tarried there seven years; and, during that time, the Blessed Virgin herself preached to the Egyptians the faith of the true God and the advent of the Son of God in human flesh." Besides, the nativity of Christ was attended by numerous prodigies, not only in Judaea, but also in Egypt, where the idols tumbled and the oracles were hushed; in Rome, where a spring of oil gushed out, a gold colored globe was seen to descend from the skies on earth, three suns appeared, and an extraordinary ring, variegated like a rainbow, encircled the disc of the sun; in Greece, where the oracle of Delphi was struck dumb, and Apollo, asked the reason of his silence by Augustus, who was offering up a sacrifice in his own palace where he had raised an altar to him, answered: "A Hebrew child, who sways the Gods, and is himself a God, Bids me quit my seat and return to the infernal regions; Depart therefore from our altars henceforward mute."

There were many more prodigies warning the Gentiles of the advent of the Son of God; they have been collected from various Authors, by Baronius, and are to be found in his *Apparat Annul*. Ecclesiastes, and Cornelius, Commentary upon Haggai.

From all this it is clear that the Gentiles also belonged, like the Jews, to the fold of Christ, that is, to the same Church of the Faithful; it cannot therefore be correctly said that the words of Christ: "Other sheep I have, which are not of this fold", are applicable to the Gentiles, who had, in common with the Hebrews, the faith in God, the hope, prophecy, expectation, prodigies and preaching of the Messiah.

I therefore say that by the words other sheep may very well be understood those rational Creatures or animals of whom we have been treating hitherto. They being, as we have said, capable of beatitude and damnation, and Jesus Christ being the mediator between God and man, as also every rational Creature (for rational creatures attain to beatitude in consideration of the merits of Christ, through the grace he confers upon them, without which beatitude is impossible of attainment), every rational creature must have cherished, at the same time as the faith in one God, the hope of the advent of Christ, and have had the revelation of his nativity in the flesh and of the principles of the law of grace. Those were therefore the sheep which were not of that human fold, and which Christ had to bring; the sheep which were to hear His voice, that is, the announcement of His advent and of the evangelical doctrine, either directly through Himself, or through the Apostles; the sheep which, partaking with men of heavenly beatitude, were to realize one fold and one shepherd.

To this interpretation, which I hold to be in no way improper, force is added by what we related, according to St Hieronymus, of that little man who requested St. Anthony to pray, for him and his fellows, unto the common God, whom he knew to have suffered in human flesh. For, it implies that they were aware of the advent and of the death of Christ, whom, as

DEMONOLOGY

God, they were anxious to propitiate, since they sought, to that effect, the intercession of St Anthony.

Thereto tends also the fact mentioned by Cardinal Baronius (*Appar. Annal*. no. 129), after Eusebius and Plutarch, as being one of the prodigies which took place at the time of the death of Christ. He relates that in the reign of the Emperor Tiberius, when Christ suffered, whilst mariners bound from Greece to Italy, were by night, and during a calm, in the vicinity of the Echinade Isles, their ship was brought close to land. All the crew heard a loud voice calling Tramnus, the master of the ship. He having answered to his name, the voice replied: "When near such a marsh, announce that the great Pan is dead." Which Tramnus having done, there arose suddenly, as from a numberless multitude, groans and shrieks. Doubtless, they were Demons, or corporeal Angels, or rational animals living near the marsh on account of their aqueous nature, and who, hearing of the death of Christ, described by the name of Great Pan, burst into tears and bewailing, like some of the Jews who, after witnessing the death of Christ, went home smiting their breasts (Luke, ch. 23, 48). From all that has been deduced above, it is therefore clear that there are such Demons, succubi and incubi, endowed with senses and subject to the passions thereof, as has been shown; who are born through generation and die through corruption, are capable of beatitude and damnation, more noble than man, by reason of the greater subtlety of their bodies, and who, when having intercourse with man, male or female, fall into the same sin as man when copulating with a beast, which is inferior to him. Also, it not infrequently occurs that those Demons slay the men, women or mares with whom they have had protracted intercourse; and the reason is that, being liable to sin whilst on the way to salvation, *in via*, they must likewise be open to repentance; and, in the same manner as a man, who habitually sins with a beast, is enjoined by his confessor to destroy that beast, with a view to suppressing the occasion of relapsing, it may likewise happen that the penitent demon should slay the animal with which it sinned, whether man or beast; nor will death thus occasioned to a man be reckoned a sin to the Demon, any more than death inflicted on a beast is imputed as a sin to man; for, considering the essential difference between a Demon of that kind and man, the man will be the same thing to the Demon as the beast is to man.

I am aware that many, perhaps most of my readers, will say of me what the Epicureans and some Stoic Philosophers said of St Paul (Acts of the Apostles ch. 17, 18): "He seemeth to be a setter forth of strange gods," and will deride my doctrine. But they will none the less have to answer the foregoing arguments, to show what are those Incubi Demons, commonly called Goblins who dread neither exorcisms, nor the holy things, nor the Cross of Christ, and to explain the various effects and phenomena related when propounding that doctrine.

What we have hitherto deduced accordingly solves the question laid down prior, to wit: How a woman can be got with child by an Incubus Demon? In fact, it cannot be brought about by sperm assumed from a man, agreeably to the common opinion which we confuted, prior; it follows, therefore, that she is directly impregnated by the sperm of the Incubus, which, being an animal and capable of breeding, has sperm of its own. And thus is fully explained the begetting of Giants from the intercourse of the Sons of God with the Daughters of men; for that intercourse gave birth to Giants who, although like unto men, were of higher stature, and, though begotten by Demons, and consequently of great strength, yet equaled them neither in might nor in power. It is the same with mules, which are intermediate, as it were, between the kinds of animals from whose promiscuity they are sprung, and which excel indeed the most imperfect, but never equal the most perfect: Thus, the mule excels the ass, but does not attain the perfection of the mare, which have begotten it.

In confirmation of the above inference, we observe that animals sprung from the mixing of different kinds do not breed,

DEMONOLOGY

but are barren, as is seen with mules. Now we do not read of Giants having been begotten by other Giants, but of their having been born of the Sons of God, that is Incubi, and the Daughters of men: Being thus begotten of the Demoniac sperm mixed with the human sperm, and being, as it were, an intermediate species between the Demon and man, they had no generative power.

It may be objected that the sperm of Demons, which must, by nature, be most fluid, could not mix with the human sperm, which is thick, and that, consequently, no generation would ensue.

I reply that, as has been said above, the generative power lies in the spirit that comes from the generator at the same time as the spumy and viscous matter; it follows that, although most liquid, the sperm of the Demon, being nevertheless material, can very well mix with the material spirit of the human sperm, and bring about generation.

It will be retorted that, if the generation of Giants had really come from the combined sperms of Incubi and Women, Giants would still be born in our time, since there is no lack of women who have intercourse with Incubi, as is shown by the Acts of St Bernard and Peter of Alcantara, and other stories related by various authors.

I reply that, as has been said above, prior, from Guaccius, some of those Demons are earthly, some aqueous, some aerial, some igneous, and they all dwell in their respective element. Now, it is well known that animals are of larger size, according to the element they live in; thus with fishes, many of which are diminutive, it is true, as happens with animals that live on land; but, the element water being larger than the element earth, since the container is always larger than the contents, fishes as a species, surpass in size the animals that dwell on land, as shown by whales, tunnies, cachalots, and other cetaceous and viviparous fish which surpass by far all animals that live on land. Consequently, these Demons being animals, as has been shown, their size will be proportionate to the extent of the element they dwell in, according to their nature. And, air being more extensive than water, and fire than air, it follows that ethereal and Igneous Demons will by far surpass their earthly and aqueous fellows, both in stature and might. It would be to no purpose to instance, as an objection, birds which, although inhabitants of the air, a more extensive element than water, are smaller, as a species, than fishes and quadrupeds; for, if birds do indeed travel through the air by means of their wings, they no less belong to the element earth, where they rest; otherwise, some fishes that fly, such as the sea swallow, would have to be classed among aerial animals, which it is not.

Now, it must be observed that, after the flood, the air which surrounds our earthy and aqueous globe, became, from the damp of the waters, thicker than it had been before; and, damp being the principle of corruption, that may be the reason why men do not live as long as they did before the flood. It is also on account of that thickness of the air that ethereal and igneous Demons, more corpulent than the others, can no longer dwell in that thick atmosphere, and if they do descend into it occasionally, do so only by force, much as divers descend into the depths of the sea.

Before the flood, when the air was not yet so thick, Demons came upon earth and had intercourse with women, thus procreating Giants whose stature was nearly equal to that of the Demons, their fathers. But now it is not so: The Incubi Demons who approach women are aqueous and of small stature; that is why they appear in the shape of little men, and, being aqueous, they are most lecherous. Lust and damp go together. Poets have depicted Venus as born of the sea, in order to show, as explained by Mythologists, that lust takes its source in damp. When, therefore, Demons of short stature impregnate women nowadays, the children that are born are not giants, but men of ordinary size. It should, moreover, be known that when Demons have carnal intercourse with women in their own natural body, without having recourse to any disguise or artifice, the women do not see them, or if they do, see but an almost doubtful, barely sensible shadow, as was the case with the female we spoke of, prior, who, when embraced by an Incubus, scarcely felt his touch. But, when they want to be seen by their mistresses, *atque ipsis delectationem in congressu carnali afferre*, they assume a visible disguise and a palpable body. By what means this is effected, is their secret, which our short-sighted Philosophy is unable to discover. The only thing we know is that such disguise or body could not consist merely in concrete air, since this must take place through condensation, and therefore by the influence of cold; a body thus formed would feel like ice, *et ita in coitu mulieres non delectaret*, but would give them pain; and it is the reverse that takes place.

Being admitted the distinction between spiritual Demons, which have intercourse with witches, and Incubi, who have to do with women that are nowise witches, we have to weigh the grievousness of the crime in both cases.

The intercourse of witches with Demons, from its accompanying circumstances, apostasy from the Faith, worshiping of the Devil, and so many other ungodly things related above, is the greatest of all sins which can be committed by man; and, considering the enormity against Religion which is presupposed by coition with the Devil, Demoniality is assuredly the most heinous of all carnal crimes. But, taking the sin of the flesh as such, exclusive of the sins against Religion, Demoniality should be reduced to simple pollution. The reason is, and a most convincing one, that the Devil who has to do with witches is a pure spirit, has reached the goal and is damned, as has been said above; if, therefore, he copulates with witches, it is in a body assumed or made by himself, according to the common opinion of Theologians.

Though set in motion, that body is not a living one; and

DEMONOLOGY

it follows that the human being, male or female, *coiens cum tali corpore,* is guilty of the same offense as if copulating with an inanimate body or a corpse, which would be simple pollution, as we have shown elsewhere. It has, moreover, been truly observed by Cajetanus, that such intercourse can very well carry with it the disgraceful characteristics of other crimes, according to the body assumed by the Devil, and the part used: Thus, if he should assume the body of a kinswoman or of a nun, such a crime would be incest or sacrilege; if coition took place in the shape of a beast, or in *vase praepostero*, it would be Bestiality or Sodomy.

As for intercourse with an Incubus, wherein is to be found no element, not even the least, of an offense against Religion, it is hard to discover a reason why it should be more grievous than Bestiality and Sodomy. For, as we have said above, if Bestiality is more grievous than Sodomy, it is because man degrades the dignity of his kind by mixing with a beast, of a kind much inferior to his own. But, when copulating with an Incubus, it is quite the reverse; for the Incubus, by reason of his rational and immortal spirit, is equal to man; and, by reason of his body, more noble because more subtle, he is more perfect and more dignified than man. Consequently, when having intercourse with an Incubus, man does not degrade, but rather dignifies his nature; and, taking that into consideration, Demoniality cannot be more grievous than Bestiality.

It is, however, commonly held to be more grievous, and the reason I take to be this: That it is a sin against Religion to hold any communication with the Devil, either with or without compact, for instance by being habitually or familiarly connected with him, by asking his assistance, counsel or favor, or by seeking from him the revelation of things to be, the knowledge of things gone by, absent, or otherwise hidden. Thus, men and women, by mixing with Incubi, whom they do not know to be animals but believe to be devils, sin through intention, *ex conscientia erronea*, and their sin is intentionally

DEMONOLOGY

the same, when having intercourse with Incubi, as if such intercourse took place with devils; in consequence, the grievousness of their crime is exactly the same.

PENALTIES

As regards the penalties applicable to Demoniality, there is no law that I know of, either civil or canonical, which inflicts a punishment for a crime of that kind. Since, however, such a crime implies a compact and fellowship with the Demon, and apostasy of the faith, not to speak of the malefice and other almost numberless outrages perpetrated by Sorcerers, as a rule it is punished, out of Italy, by the gallows and the stake. But, in Italy, it is but very seldom that offenders of that kind are delivered up by the Inquisitors to the secular power.

BIOGRAPHICAL NOTICE

Father Ludovico Maria Sinistrari, of the Order of Reformed Minors of the strict Observance of St. Francis, was born in Ameno, a small town of the district of St. Julius, in the diocese of Novara, on the 26th of February 1622. He received a liberal education and went through a course of humanities in Pavia, where, in the year 1647, he entered the Order of Franciscans. Devoting himself henceforward to tuition, he was first a professor of Philosophy; he then, during fifteen successive years, taught Theology in the same town, amid a numerous concourse of students attracted from all parts of Europe by his high repute. His sermons preached in the principal cities of Italy, at the same time as they caused his eloquence to be admired, were productive of the most happy results for piety. Equally endeared to the World and to Religion, he had been favored by nature with the most brilliant gifts; square frame, high stature, open countenance, broad forehead, sparkling eyes, high-colored complexion, pleasant conversation replete with sallies of wit, more valuable still, he was in possession of the gifts of grace, through which he was enabled to sustain, with unconquerable resignation, the assaults of an arthritic disease he was subject to; he was, moreover, remarkable for his meekness, candor and absolute submission to the rules of his Order. A man of all sciences, he had learned foreign languages without any master, and often, in the general Meetings of his Order, held in Rome, he supported, in public, *theses de omni scibili*. He, however, addicted himself more particularly to the study of Civil and Canon laws. In Rome he filled the appointment of Consulter to the supreme Tribunal of the Holy Inquisition; was some time Vicar general of the Archbishop of Avignon, and then Theologian attached to the Archbishop of Milan. In the year 1688, charged by the general Meeting of Franciscans with the compilation of the statutes of the Order, he performed this task in his treatise entitled *Practica criminalis Minorum illustrata*. He died in the year of our Lord 1701, on the 6th of March, at the age of seventy-nine.

LETTER OF THE REV. FATHER PROVINCIAL OF CAPUCHINS FOR THE PROVINCE OF PAVIA

Friday, 8 October 1875

MONS. ISIDORE LISEUX
   Paris.

I have gone through the work you sent me yesterday, and have, indeed, been satisfied with the edition; the time has not yet arrived for me to give my opinion on the value of the work itself. Here you would have met with no other works of the Rev. Father Sinistrari of Ameno than his book: Practica criminal is Minorum; De Deiictis et Poenis is to be found, I believe, in another of our convents; but you would have been given a most welcome reception.

I believe that Des Grieux can hardly have resided in the present St-Sulpice, which dates but from the year 1816 So far as a superficial glance has enabled me to ascertain, there are some other mistakes; but, altogether, the work is a good one, and you may accept of the congratulations of Your very little servant.

    Fr. A...

THE END

DEMONOLOGY

King James I, 1597

PREFACE

The fearful abounding at this time in this country, of these detestable slaves of the Devil, the Witches or enchanters, has moved me (beloved reader) to dispatch in post, this following treatise of mine, not in any way (as I protest) to serve for a show of my learning and ingenuity, but only (moved of conscience) to press thereby, so far as I can, to resolve the doubting hearts of many; both that such assaults of Satan are most certainly practiced, and that the instruments thereof, merits most severely to be punished: Against the damnable opinions of two principally in our age, whereof the one called SCOT an Englishman, is not ashamed in public print to deny, that there can be such a thing as Witchcraft: and so maintains the old error of the Sadducees, in denying of spirits. The other called WIERUS, a German physician, sets out a public apology for all these crafts-folks, whereby, procuring for their impunity, he plainly shows himself to have been one of that profession. And for to make this treatise the more pleasant and facile, I have put it in form of dialogue, which I have divided into three books: The first speaking of Magic in general, and Necromancy in special. The second of Sorcery and Witchcraft: and the third, contains a discourse of all these kinds of spirits, and specters that appear and trouble people, together with a conclusion of the whole work. My intention in this labor, is only to prove two things, as I have already said: the one, that such devilish arts have been and are. The other, what exact trial and severe punishment they merit: and therefore reason , what kind of things are possible to be performed in these arts, and by what natural causes they may be, not that I touch every particular thing of the Devil's power, for that were infinite: but only, to speak scholastically, (since this can not be spoken in our language) I reason upon type, leaving appearance, and differences to be comprehended therein. As for example, speaking of the power of Magicians, in the first book and sixth chapter: I say, that they can suddenly be brought unto them, all kinds of dainty dishes, by their familiar spirit: Since as a thief he delights to steal and as a spirit, he can quickly and secretly transport the same. Now under this kind, may be comprehended all particulars, depending thereupon. Such as the bringing wine out of the wall, (as we have heard oft to have been practiced) and such others; which particulars, are sufficiently proved by the reasons of the general. And such like in the second book of Witchcraft in special, and fifth chapter, I say and prove by diverse arguments, that witches can, by the power of their master, cure or cause diseases: Now by these same reasons, that proves their power by the Devil of diseases in general, is as well proved their power in special: as of weakening the nature of some men, to make them unable for women: and making it to abound in others, more then the ordinary course of nature would permit. And such like in all other particular sicknesses; but one thing I will pray you to observe in all these places, where I reason upon the Devils' power, which is the different ends and scopes, that God as the first cause, and the Devil as his instrument and second cause shoots at in all these actions of the Devil, (as Gods hang-man:) For where the Devils' intention in them is ever to perish, either the soul or the body, or both of them, that he is so permitted to deal with: God by the contraries, draws ever out of the evil glory to himself, either by the wrack of the wicked in his justice, or by the trial of the patient and amendment of the faithful, being awakened up with that rod of correction. Having thus declared unto thee then, my full intention in this Treatise, you will easily excuse, I doubt not, as well my pretermitting, to declare the whole particular rites and secrets of these unlawful arts: as also their infinite and wonderful practices, as being neither of them pertinent to my purpose: the reason whereof, is given in the last of the first chapter of the third book: And who likes to be curious in these things, he may read, if he will here of their practices, Bodinus'

DEMONOLOGY

Daemonomanie, collected with greater diligence, then written with judgment, together with their confessions, that have been at this time apprehended. If he would know what has been the opinion of the ancients, concerning their power: he shall see it well described by Hyperius, and Hemminguie, two late German writers: Besides innumerable other new theologies, that write largely upon that subject: And if he would know what are the particular rites, and curiosities of these black arts (which is both unnecessary and perilous,) he will find it in the fourth book of Cornelius Agrippa, and in Wierus, of whom I spake prior. And so wishing my pains in this Treatise (beloved reader) to be effectual, in arming all them that read the same, against these above mentioned errors, and recommending my good will to your friendly acceptance, I bid you heartily farewell.

JAMES Rx.

FIRST BOOK

I

Philomathes and Epistemon reason the matter.

Phi. I am surely very glad to have met with you this day, for I am of opinion, that you can better resolve me of some things, whereof I stand in great doubt, nor any other whom with I could have met.

Epi. In what I can, that you like to ask at me I will willingly and freely tell my opinion, and if I prove it not sufficiently, I am heartily content that a better reason carry it away then.

Phi. What think you of these strange news, which now only furnishes purpose to all men at their meeting: I mean of these Witches.

Epi. Surely they are wonderful: and I think such clear and plain confessions in that purpose, have never fallen out in any age or country.

DEMONOLOGY

Phi. No question if they be true, but thereof the Doctors doubt.

Epi. What part of it doubt you of?

Phi. Even of all, for ought I can yet perceive: and namely, that there is such a thing as witchcraft or witches, and I would pray you to resolve me thereof if you may: For I have reasoned with sundry in that matter, and yet could never be satisfied therein.

Epi. I shall with good do the best I can: But I think it the more difficult, since you deny the thing itself in general: for as it is said in the logic schools; do not try to prove a negative (*Contra negantem principia non est disputandum*).

Always for that part, that witchcraft, and witches have been, and are, the former part is clearly proved by the Scriptures, and the last by daily experience and confessions.

Phi. I know you will allege me Saules Pythonisse: but that as appears will not make much for you.

Epi. Not only that place, but divers others: But I marvel why that should not make much for me.

Phi. The reasons are these, first you may consider, that Saul being troubled in spirit, and having fasted long before, as the text testifies, and being come to a woman that was wont to have such knowledge, and that to inquire at such important news, he having so guilty a conscience for his heinous offenses, and specially, for that same unlawful curiosity, and horrible defection: And then the woman crying out upon the sudden in great admiration, for the uncouth sight that she alleged to have seen discovering him to be the King, though disguised, and denied by him before: It was no wounder I say, that his sense being thus distracted, he could not perceive her voice, he being himself in another chalmer, and seeing nothing. Next what could be, or was raised? The spirit of Samuel? Profane and against all Theology: the Devil in his likeness? As unapparent, that either God those days had been sure, what spirit spake to them in their visions, or then that he could foretell what was to come there after; for prophecy proceeds only of God: and the Devil has no knowledge of things to come.

      Epi. Yet if you will mark the words of the text, you will find clearly, that Saul saw that apparition: for giving you that Saul was in another Chalmer, at the making of the circles and conjurations, needful for that purpose (as none of that craft will permit any others to behold at that time) yet it is evident by the text, that how some that once that unclean spirit was fully risen, she called in upon Saul. For it is said in the text, that Saul knew him to be Samuel, which could not have been, by the hearing tell only of an old man with an mantel, since there were many more old men dead in Israel other than Samuel: And the common wear of that whole country was mantels. As to the next, that it was not the spirit of Samuel, I grant: In the proving whereof you need not to insist, since all Christians of whatsoever sect agree upon that: And none but either the merely ignorant, or necromancers or witches doubts thereof. And that the Devil is permitted at some times to put himself in the likeness of the Saints, it is plain in the Scriptures, where it is said, that Satan can transform himself into an Angel of light. Neither could that bring any inconvenience with the visions of the prophets, since it is most certain, that God will not permit him so to deceive his own: but only such as willfully deceive themselves, by running unto him, whom God then suffers to fall in their own snares, and justly permits them to be deluded with great efficacy of deceit, because they would not believe the truth (as Paul says). And as to the Devil's foretelling of things to come, it is true that he knows not all things future, but yet that he knows part, the tragic event of this histories declare, (which the wit of woman could never have fore-spoken) not that he has any prescience, which is only proper to God: or yet knows anything by looking upon God, as in a mirror (as the good Angels do) he being for ever debarred from the favorable presence and countenance of his creator, but only by one of these two means, either as being worldly wise, and taught by a continual experience, ever since creation, judges by likelihood of things to come, according to the like that has passed before, and the natural causes, in respect of the vicissitude of all things worldly: Or else by Gods employing of him in turn, and so foreseen thereof: as appears to have been in this, whereof we find the very like in Micheas prophetic discourse to King Achab. But to prove this my first proposition, that there can be such a thing as witchcraft, and witches, there are many more places in the Scriptures then this (as I said before). As first in the law of god, it is plainly prohibited: But certain it is, that the law of God speaks nothing in vain, nether does it lay curses, or enjoin punishments upon shadows, condemning that to be ill, which is not in essence or being as we call it. Secondly it is plain, where wicked Pharaohs' wise-men imitated a number of Moses miracles, to harden the tyrants heart thereby. Thirdly, said not Samuel to Saul, that disobedience is as the sin of witchcraft? To compare to a thing that were not, it were too too absurd. Fourth, was not Simon Magus, a man of that craft. And fifth, what was she that had the spirit of Python? beside innumerable other places that were irksome to recite.

II.

What kind of sin the practitioners of these unlawful arts commit. The division of these arts. And what are the means that allures any to practice them.

Phi. But I think it very strange, that God should permit any man (since they bear his own image) to fall in so gross and filthy a defection.

Epi. Although man in his creation was made to the image of the creator, yet through his fall having once lost it, it is but restored again in part by grace only to the elect: So all the rest falling away from God, are given over in the hands of the Devil that enemy, to bear his image: and being once so given over, the greatest and the grossest impiety, is the pleasantest, and most delightful unto them.

Phi. But may it not suffice him to have indirectly the rule, and procure the perdition of so many souls by alluring

DEMONOLOGY

them to vices, and to the following of their own appetites, suppose he abuse not so many simple souls, in making them directly acknowledge him for their master.

Epi. No surely, for he uses every man, whom of he has the rule, according to their complexion and knowledge: And so whom he finds most simple, he most plainly discloses himself unto them. For he being the enemy of mans' salvation, uses all the means he can to entrap them so far in his snares, as it may be unable to them thereafter (suppose they would) to rid themselves out of the same.

Phi. Then this sin is a sin against the holy Ghost.

Epi. It is in some, but not in all.

Phi. How is that? Are not all these that run directly to the Devil in one category?

Epi. God forbid, for the sin against the holy Ghost has two branches: The one a falling back from the whole service of God, and a refusal of all his precepts. The other is the doing of the first with knowledge, knowing that they do wrong against their own conscience, and the testimony of the holy spirit, having once had a taste of the sweetness of Gods' mercies. Now in the first of these two, all sorts of necromancers, enchanters or witches, are comprehended: But in the last, none but such as errs with this knowledge that I have spoken of.

Phi. Then it appears that there are more sorts not just one, that are directly professors of his service: And if so be, I pray you tell me how many, and what are they?

Epi. There are principally two sorts, whereunto all the parties of that unhappier art are redacted; whereof the one is called magic or necromancy, the other sorcery or witchcraft.

Phi. What I pray you? And how many are the names, whereby the Devil allures persons in any of these snares?

Epi. Even by these three passions that are within ourselves: Curiosity in great imaginations: thrift of revenge, for some torture deeply apprehended: or greedy appetite, caused through great poverty. As to the first of these, curiosity, it is only the enticement of magicians, or necromancers: and the other two are the allures of the sorcerers, or witches, for that old and crafty serpent, being a spirit, he easily pays our affections, and so conforms himself thereto, to deceive us to our destruction.

III.

The significations and etymologies of the words of magic and necromancy: The difference betwixt it and witchcraft: What are the entrances and beginnings, that brings any to the knowledge thereof.

Phi. I would gladly first hear, what thing is it that you call magic or necromancy.

Epi. This word, "magic," in the Persian tongue, imports as much as to be any contemplator or interpreter of Divine and heavenly sciences; which being first used among the Chaldaeans, through their ignorance of the true divinity, was esteemed and reputed among them, as a principal virtue: And therefore, was named unjustly with an honorable stile, which name the Greeks imitated, generally importing all these kinds of unlawful arts. And this word, "necromancy," is a Greek word, compounded of (nekron) and (manteia), which is to say the prophecies by the dead. This last name is given, to this black and unlawful science by the figure Synecdoche, because it is a principal part of that art, to serve themselves with dead carcasses in their divination.

Phi. What difference is there betwixt this art, and witchcraft.

Epi. Surely, the difference vulgarly put betwixt them, is very specious, and in a manner true, for they say, that the witches are servants only, and slaves to the Devil; but the necromancers are his masters and commanders.

Phi. How can that be true? Any men being specially addicted to this service, can be his commanders?

Epi. Yea, they may be: but it is only secondary (*secundum quid*): For it is not by any power that they can have over him, but only as he grants it (*ex pacto*) willingly. Whereby he obliges himself in some trifles to them, that he may on the other part obtain the fruition of their body and soul, which is the only thing he hunts for.

Phi. A very inequitable contract forsooth: But I pray you discourse unto me, what is the effect and secrets of that art?

Epi. That is too vast a question you ask of me: Yet I shall do good-will, the most summaries that I can, to run through the principal points thereof. As there are two sorts of folks, that may be enticed to this art, to wit, learned or unlearned; so are there two means, which are the first stirrirs-up and feeders of their curiosity, thereby to make them to give themselves over to the same: Which two means, I call the Devil's School, and his rudiments. The learned have their curiosities weakened up; and fed by that which I call his school: this is the *Astrologie judiciar*. For divers men having attained to a great perfection learning, and yet remaining over-bare (alas) of the spirit of regeneration and fruits thereof: Finding all natural things common, as well to the stupid peasants as unto them, they assay to vindicate unto them a greater name, by not only knowing the course of things heavenly, but likewise to attain to the knowledge of things to come thereby. Which, at the first face appearing lawful unto them, in respect the ground thereof seems to proceed of natural causes only: They are so allured thereby, that finding their practice to prove true in sundry things, they study to know the cause thereof: and so mounting from degree to degree, upon the slippery and and uncertain scale of curiosity; they are at last enticed, that where lawful arts of sciences fails, to satisfy their restless minds, even to seek to that black and unlawful science of magic. Where, finding at the first, that such divers forms of circles and conjurations rightly joined thereunto, will raise such divers forms of spirits, to resolve them of their doubts: and attributing the doing thereof, to the power inseparably tied, or inherent in the circles, and many words of God, all confused together; they blindly glory of themselves, as if they and by their quickness of mind, made a conquest of Pluto's dominion, and had become Emperors over the Stygian habitat. Where, in the meantime (miserable wretches) they are become in very deed, bond-slaves

DEMONOLOGY

to their mortal enemy: And their knowledge, for all that they presume thereof, is nothing increased, except in knowing evil, and the horrors of Hell for punishment thereof, as Adams' was by the eating of the forbidden tree.

IV.

The Description of the Rudiments and School, which are the entrances to the art of magic: And in special the differences betwixt Astronomy and Astrology: Division of Astrology in divers parts.

Phi. But I pray you likewise forget not to tell what are the Devils' rudiments.

Epi. His rudiments, I call first in general, all that which is called vulgarly the virtue of words, herbs, and stones: These are used by unlawful charms, without natural causes. As likewise all kinds of practices, frights, or other like extraordinary actions, which cannot abide the true touch of natural reason.

Phi. I would have you to make that plainer, by some particular examples; for your proposition is very general.

Epi. I mean either by such kind of charms as commonly daft wives use, for healing of certain goods, for preserving them from evil eyes, by knitting round trees, or various kinds of herbs, to the hair or tails of the goods: By curing the worm, by stemming of blood, by healing of hoarseness, by turning of the riddle, or doing of such like innumerable things by words, without applying any thing, meet to the part offended, as Mediciners do. Or else by staying married folks, to have natural intercourse with others, (by knitting so many knots upon a point at the time of their marriage) and such like things, which man uses to practice in such arts. For the unlearned men (being naturally curious, and lacking the true knowledge of God) find these practices to prove true, as sundry of them will do, by the power of the Devil for deceiving men, and not by any inherent virtue in these vain words and practices; and being desirous to

DEMONOLOGY

win a reputation to themselves in suchlike turns, they either (if they be of the shameless sort) seek to be learned by some that are experimented in that art, (not knowing it to be evil at the first) or else being of the grosser sort, run directly to the Devil for ambition or desire of gain, and plainly contracts with him thereupon.

Phi. But methinks these means which you call the School and rudiments of the Devil, are things lawful, and have been approved for such in all times and ages: As in special, this science of astrology, which is one of the special members of the Mathematicians.

Epi. There are two things which the learned have observed from the beginning, in the science of the heavenly creatures, the planets, stars, and such like: The one is their course and ordinary motions, which for that cause is called astronomy: Which word is a compound of (nomos) and (asteron) that is to say, the law of the stars: And this art indeed is one of the members of the mathematics, and not only lawful, but most necessaries and commendable. The other is called astrology, being compounded of (asteron) and (logos) which is to say, the word, and preaching of the stars: Which is divided in two parts: The first by knowing thereby the powers of the simple, and sicknesses, the course of the seasons and the weather, being ruled by their influence, which part depending upon the former, although it be not of itself a part of mathematics: yet it is not unlawful, being moderately used, but not so necessary and commendable as the former. The second part is to trust so much to their influences, as thereby to foretell what common-weals shall flourish or decay, or what persons shall be fortunate or unfortunate, or what side shall win in any battle, or what man shall obtain victories at singular combat, or what way, and of what age shall men die, or what horse shall win at match-running; and diverse others have more curiously than profitably written at large. Of this root last spoken of, springs innumerable branches; such as the knowledge by the nativities; the chiromancy, geomancy, hydromancy, arithmancy, practiced, and held in great reverence by the gentiles of old.

DEMONOLOGY

And this last part of astrology whereof I have spoken, which is the root of their branches, was called by them luck (*pars fortunae*). This part now is utterly unlawful to be trusted in, or practiced among Christians, as leaning to no ground of natural reason: and it is this part which I called before the Devil's school.

    Phi. But yet many of the learned are of the contrary opinion.

    Epi. I grant, yet I could give my reasons to fortify and maintain my opinion, if to enter into this disputation it wold not draw me quite off the ground of our discourse; besides the wasting of the whole day thereupon: One word only I will answer to them, and that in the Scriptures (which must be an infallible true ground to all true Christians.) That in the Prophet Jeremiah it is plainly forbidden, to believe or hearken unto them that prophecies and predicts by the course of the planets and stars.

V.

How far the using of charms is lawful or unlawful: The description of the forms of circles and conjurations. And what causes the magicians themselves to weary thereof.

    Phi. Well, you have said far enough in that argument. But how prove you now that these charms or unnatural practices are unlawful: For so, many honest and merry men and women have publicly practiced some of them, that I think if you wold accuse them all of witchcraft, you would affirm more nor you will be believed in.

    Epi. I see if you had taken good tent (to the nature of that word, whereby I named it,) you would not have been in this doubt, nor mistaken me, so far as you have done: For although, as none can be scholars in a school, and not be subject to the master thereof: so none can study and put in practice (for study is not alone, and knowledge, is not more perilous and offensive; and it is the practice only that makes the greatness of the

DEMONOLOGY

offense.) The circles and art of magic, without committing a horrible defection from God: And yet as they that read and learn their rudiments, are not the more subject to any schoolmaster, if it please not their parents to put them to the school thereafter; so they who ignorantly prove these practices, which I call the Devil's Rudiments, unknowing them to be baits, cast out by him, for trapping such as God will permit to fall in his hands: This kind of folk I say, no doubt, are to be judged the best of, in respect they use no invocation nor help of him (by their knowledge at least) in these turns, and so have never entered themselves in Satan's service; yet to speak truly for my own part (I speak but for myself) I desire not to make so near a comparison: For in my opinion our enemy is craftier, and we very weak, (except the greater grace of God) to assay such hazards, wherein he pleases to trap us.

Phi. You have reason forsooth; for as the common Proverb says: They that eat with the Devil, have need of long spoons. But now I pray you go forward in the describing of this art of magic.

Epi. Thus they have come once unto this perfection in evil, in having any knowledge (whether learned or unlearned) of this black art: they then begin to be weary of the raising of their master, by conjured circles; being both so difficult and perilous, and so come plainly to a contract with him, wherein is special;y contained forms and effects.

Phi. But I pray you or ever you go further, discourse with me somewhat of their circles and conjurations; and what should be the cause of their wearying thereof: For it should seem that that form should be the cause of their wearying thereof: For it should seem that that form should be less fearful yet, than the direct haunting and society, with that foul and unclean spirit.

Epi. I think you take me to be a witch my self, or at the least would fain swear yourself apprentice to that craft: Always as I may, I shall shortly satisfy you, in that kind of conjurations, which are contained in such books, which I call the Devil's School: There are four principal parts; the persons of the conjurations, the action of the conjuration; the words and rites used to that effect; and the spirits that are conjured. You must first remember to lay the ground, that I told you before: Which is, that it is no power inherent in the circles, or in the holiness of the names of God blasphemously used: nor in whatsoever rites or ceremonies at that time used, that either can raise any infernal spirit, or yet limit him perforce within or without these circles. For it is he only, the father of all lies, who having first of all prescribed that form of doing, feigning himself to be commanded and restrained thereby, will be loath to pass the bounds of these injunctions; as well thereby to make them glory in the inspiring over him (as I said before:) As likewise he may make himself so to be trusted in these little things, that he may have the better commodity thereafter, to deceive them in the end with a trick once for all; I mean the everlasting perdition of their soul and body. Then laying this ground, as I have said, these conjurations must have few or more in number of the persons, the conjurers, (always passing the singular number) according to the qualities of the circle, and forms of apparitions. Two principal things cannot well in that errand be wanted: holy water (whereby the Devil mocks the Papists) and some present of a living thing unto him. There are likewise certain seasons, days and hours, that they observe in this purpose: These things being all ready, and prepared, circles are made triangular, quadrangular, round, double or single, according to the form of apparition that they crave. But to speak of the diverse forms of the circles, of the innumerable characters and crosses that are within and without, and out-through the same, of the diverse forms of apparitions, that that crafty spirit deludes them with, and of all such particulars in that action, I remit it to others that have busied their heads in describing of the same; as being but curious, and altogether unprofitable. And this far only I touch, that when the conjured Spirit appears, which will not be while after manic circumstances, long prayers, and much muttering and murmuring of the conjurers; like a Papist priest, dispatching a hunting Mass: how soon I say, he appears, if they have missed one iota of all their rites; or if any of their feet once slid over the circle through terror of his fearful apparition, he pays himself at that time in his own hand, of that due debt which they owe him; and otherwise would have delayed longer to have paid him: I mean he carries them with him body and soul. If this be not now a just cause to make them weary of these forms of conjuration, I leave it to you to judge upon; considering the length of the labor, the precise keeping of days and hours (as I have said) The terribleness of apparition, and the present peril that they stand in, in missing the least circumstance or rite, that they ought to observe: And on the other part, the Devil is glad to move them to a plain and square dealing with him as I said before.

VI.

The Devil's contract with the Magicians: The division thereof in two parts: What is the difference betwixt Gods miracles and the Devils'.

Phi. Indeed, there is cause enough, but rather than leave him at all, then to run more plainly to him, if they were wise he dealt with. But go forward now I pray you to these turns, how they become once deacons in this craft.

Epi. From time that they once plainly begin to contract with him: The effect of their contract consists in two things; in forms and effects, as I began to tell already, were it not you interrupted me (for although the contract be mutual; I speak first of that part, wherein the Devil obliges himself to them) by forms, I mean, in what shape or fashion he shall come unto them, when they call upon him. And by effects, I understand, in what special sorts of services he binds himself to be subject unto them. The quality of these forms and effects, is less or greater, according to the skill and art of the magician. For as to the forms, to some of the baser sort of them he obliges himself to appear at their calling upon him, by such a proper name which he shows unto them, either in likeness of a dog, a cat, an ape, or such-like other beast; or else to answer by a voice only. The effects are to answer to such demands, as concerns curing

DEMONOLOGY

of diseases, their own particular menagerie: or such other base things as they require of him. But to the most curious sort, in the forms he will oblige himself, to enter in a dead body, and there out of to give such answers, of the event of battles, of matters concerning the estate of commonwealths, and such like other great questions: yea to some he will be a continual attender, in form of a page: He will permit himself to be conjured, for the space of so many years, either in a tablet or a ring, or such like thing, which they may easily carry about with them: He gives them power to sell such wares to others, whereof some will be dearer, and some more cheap; according to the lying or true speaking of the spirit that is conjured therein. Not but that in very deed, all Devils must be liars; but so they abuse the simplicity of these wretches, that becomes their scholars, that they make them believe, that at the fall of Lucifer, some spirits fell in the air, some in the fire, some in the water, some in the land: In which Elements they still remain. Whereupon they build, that such as fell in the fire, or in the air, are truer then they, who fell in the water or in the land, which is all but mere stupidity, and forged by the author of all deceit. For the fell may not be weighed, as a solid substance, to stick in any one part: But the principal part of their fall, consisting in quality, by the falling from the grace of God wherein they were created, they continued still thereafter, and shall do while the latter day, in wandering through the world, as Gods hang-men, to execute such turns as he employs them in. And when any of them are not occupied in that, return they must to their prison in Hell (as it is plain in the miracle that Christ wrought at Gennezareth.) Therein at the latter day to be all enclosed for ever: and as they deceive their scholars in this, so do they in imprinting in them the opinion that there are so many Princes, Dukes, and Kings among them, every one commanding fewer or more Legions, and excelling in diverse arts, and quarters of the earth. For though that I will not deny that there be a form of order among the Angels in Heaven, and consequently, was among them before their fall; yet, either this idea; or that God will permit us to know by damned Devils, such heavenly mysteries of his,

DEMONOLOGY

which he would not reveal to us neither by Scripture nor Prophets, I think no Christian will once think it. But by the contrary of all such mysteries contented with an humble ignorance, they being things not necessary for our salvation. But to return to the purpose, as these forms, wherein Satan obliges himself to the greatest of the magicians, are wonderfully curious; so are the effects correspondent unto the same: For he will oblige himself to teach them arts and sciences, which he may easily do, being so learned a knave as he is: To carry them news from any part of the world, which the agility of a spirit may easily perform: to reveal to them the secrets of any persons, so being they be once spoken, for the thought none knows but God; except so far as you may guess by their countenance, as one who is doubtlessly learned enough in the Physiognomy: Yea, he will make his scholars to creep in credit with Princes, by foretelling them many great things; part true, part false: for if all were false, he would lose credit at all hands; but always doubtsome, as his Oracles were. And he will also make them to please Princes, by fair banquets and dainty dishes, carried in short space from the farthest part of the world. For no man doubts but he is a thief, and his agility (as I spake before) makes him to come such speed. Such-like, he will guard his scholars with fair armies of horse-men and foot-men in appearance, castles and forts: Which all are but impressions in the air, easily gathered by a spirit, drawing so near to that substance himself: As in like manner he will learn them many low tricks at cards, dice, and such like, to deceive mens' senses thereby: and such innumerable false practices; which are proven by many examples in this age: As they who are acquainted with that Italian called Scoto, yet living, can report. And yet are all these things but deluding of the senses, and no ways true in substance, as were the false miracles wrought by King Pharaoh's magicians, for counterfeiting Moses: For that is the difference betwixt Gods miracles and the Devils, God is a creator, what he makes appear in miracle, it is so in effect. As Moses' rod being cast down, was no doubt turned in a natural serpent: where as the Devil (as Gods' ape) counterfeiting that by common proof,

DEMONOLOGY

that simple illusionists will make an hundred things seem both to our eyes and ears other ways than they are. Now as to the magicians' part of the contract, it is in a word that thing, which I said before, the Devil hunts for in all men.

Phi. Surely ye have said much to me in this art, if all that you have said be as true as wonderful.

Epi. For the truth in these actions, it will be easily confirmed, to any that pleases to take pain upon the reading of diverse authentic histories, and the inquiring of daily experiences. And as for the truth of the possibilities, that they may be, and in what manner, I trust I have alleged nothing whereunto I have not joined such probable reasons, as I leave to your discretion: To weigh and consider: One word only I omitted; concerning the form of making of this contract, which is either written with the magicians' own blood: or else being agreed upon (in terms his school-master) touches him in some part, though peradventure no mark remain: as it happens with all witches.

VII.

The reason why the art of magic is unlawful. What punishments they merit: And who may be accounted guilty of that crime.

Phi. Surely you have made this art to appear very monstrous and detestable. But what I pray you shall be said to such as maintains this art to be lawful, for as evil as you have made it?

Epi. I say, they favor of the pan themselves, or at least little better, And yet I wold be glad to hear their reasons.

Phi. There are two principally, that ever I heard used; beside that which is founded upon the common Proverb (that the necromancers command the Devil, which you have already refuted.) The one is grounded upon a received custom, we see that diverse Christian Princes and Magistrates severe punishers of witches, will not only over-see magicians to live within their dominions; but even sometimes delight to see them prove some of their practices. The other reason is, that Moses being brought up (as it is expressly said in the Scriptures) in all the sciences of the Egyptians; whereof no doubt, this was one of the principals. And he notwithstanding of this art, pleasing God, as he did, consequently that art professed by so godly a man, could not be unlawful.

Epi. As to the first of your reasons, grounded upon custom: I say; an evil custom can never be accepted for a good law, for the tremendous ignorance of the word in some Princes and Magistrates, and the contempt thereof in others, moves them to sin heavily against their office in that point. As to the other reason, which seems to be of greater weight, if it were formed in a syllogism; it behooved to be in many terms, and full of fallacies (to speak in terms of logic) for first, that that general proposition; affirming Moses to be taught in magic, I see no necessity. For we must understand that the spirit of God there, speaking of sciences, understands them that are lawful; for except they be lawful, they are but abusively called sciences, and are but ignorance indeed: The picture is not the thing. (*Nam homo pictus, non est homo*.) Secondly, giving that he had been taught in it, there is great difference, betwixt knowledge and practicing of a thing (as I said before) For God knows all things, being always good, and of our sin and our infirmity proceeds our ignorance. Third, giving that he had both studied and practiced the same (which is more monstrous than to be believed by any Christian) yet we know well enough, that before that ever the spirit of God began to call Moses, he was fled out of Egypt, being forty years of age, for the slaughter of an Egyptian, and in his good father Iethroes' land, first called at the flaming bush, having remained there another forty years in exile; so that suppose he had been the wickedest man in the world before, he then became a changed and regenerated man, and very little of old Moses remained in him. Abraham was an idolater in Ur of Chaldaea, before he was called: And Paul being called Saul, was a most sharp persecutor of the Saints of God, while that name was changed.

DEMONOLOGY

Phi. What punishment then think you merits these magicians and necromancers?

Epi. The like no doubt, that sorcerers and witches merit; and rather so much greater, as their error proceeds of the greater knowledge, and so draws nearer to the sin against the holy oversees them, which is seen by the miserable ends of many that ask counsel of them: for the Devil has never better tidings to tell to any, then he told to Saul: Neither is it lawful to use so unlawful instruments, were it never for so good a purpose: for that axiom in Theology is most certain and infallible: Evil is never to be done; thus good may happen.

SECOND BOOK

I.

Proved by the Scripture, that such a thing can be: And the reasons refuted of all such as would call it but an imagination and melancholic humor.

Phi. Now Since you have satisfied me now so fully, concerning magic or necromancy I will pray you to do the like in sorcery or witchcraft.

Epi. That field is likewise very large: and although in the mouths and pens of many, yet few know the truth thereof, so well as they believe themselves, as I shall so shortly as I can, make you (God willing) as easily to perceive.

Phi. But I pray you before you go further, let me interrupt you here with a short digression: which is, that many can scarcely believe that there is such a thing as witchcraft. Whose reasons I will shortly allege unto you, that you may satisfy me as well in that, as you have done in the rest. For first, whereas the Scripture seems to prove witchcraft to be, by diverse examples, and especially by sundry of the same, which you have alleged; it is thought by some, that these places speak of magicians and necromancers only, and not of witches. As in special, these wise men of Pharaohs, that counterfeited Moses' miracles, were magicians say they, and not witches: As likewise that Pythonisse that Saul consulted with: And so was Simon Magus in the new testament, as that very style imports. Secondly, where you would opine the daily practice, and confession of so many, that is thought likewise to be but melancholic imaginations of simple raving creatures. Thirdly, if witches had such power of witching of folks to death, (as they say they have) there had been none left alive long since in the world, but they: at the least, no good or godly person of whatsoever estate, could have escaped their devilry.

Epi. Your three reasons as I take, are grounded the first of them negative upon the Scripture: The second affirmative upon physic: and the third upon the certain proof of experience. As to your first, it is most true indeed, that all these wise men of Pharaoh were magicians of art: As likewise it appears well that the Pythonisse, with whom Saul consulted, was of that same profession: and so was Simon Magus. But you omitted to speak of the Law of God, wherein are all magicians, diviners, enchanters, sorcerers, witches, and whatsoever of that kind that consults with the Devil, plainly prohibited, and alike threatened against. And besides that, she who had the Spirit of Python, in the Acts, whose spirit was put to silence by the Apostle, could be no other thing but a sorcerer or witch, if you admit the vulgar distinction, to be in a manner true, whereof I spake in the beginning of our conference. For that spirit whereby she conquered such gain to her master, was not at her raising or commanding, as she pleased to appoint, but spake by her tongue, as well, publicly, as privately: Whereby she seemed to draw nearer to the fort of demoniacs or the possessed, if that conjunction betwixt them, had not been of her own consent: as it appeared by her, not being tormented therewith: And by her conquering of such gain to her masters (as I have already said.) As to your second reason grounded upon physic, in attributing their confessions or apprehensions, to a natural melancholic humor: Any that pleases physically to consider upon the natural humor of melancholy, according to all the physicians, that ever write thereupon, they all find that this will be over short a cloak to cover their knavery with: For as the humor of melancholy in the self is black, heavy and terrestrial, so are the symptoms thereof, in any persons that are subject thereunto, unsteadiness, paleness, desire of solitude: and if they come to the highest degree thereof, mere folly and mania: where as by the contrary, a great number of them that have ever been convicted or confessors of witchcraft, as may be presently seen by many that have at this time confessed: they are by the contrary, I say, some of them rich and worldly-wise, some of them fat or corpulent in their bodies, and most part of them altogether given over to the pleasures of the flesh, continual haunting of company, and all kind of merriness, both lawful and unlawful, which are things directly contrary to the symptoms of melancholy, whereof I spake, and further experience daily proves how loath they are to confess without torture, which witnesses their guiltiness, whereby the contrary, the melancholics never spare to betray themselves, by their continual discourses, feeding thereby their humor in that which they think no crime. As to your third reason, it scarcely merits an answer. For if the Devil their master were not bridled, as the scriptures teaches us, suppose there were no men nor women to be his instruments, he could find ways enough without any help of others to wrack all mankind: whereunto he employs his whole study, and goes about like a roaring lion (as Peter says) to that effect, but the limits of his power were set down before the foundations of the world were laid, which he has not power in the least but to transgress. But beside all this, there is over great a certainty to prove that they are, by the daily experience of the harms that they do, both to men, and whatsoever thing men possesses, whom God will permit them to be the instruments, so to trouble or visit, as in my discourse of that art, you shall hear clearly proved.

II.

The etymology and signification of that word of sorcery. The first entrance and apprenticeship of them that gives themselves to that craft.

       Phi. Come on then I pray you, and return where you left.

       Epi. This word of sorcery is a Latin word, which is taken from casting of the lot, and therefore he that uses it, is called *Sortiarius* a sort. As to the word of witchcraft, it is nothing but a proper name given in our language. The cause wherefore they were called *sortiary*, proceeded of their practices seeming to come of lot or chance: Such as the turning of the riddle: the knowing of the form of prayers, or such like tokens: If a person diseased would live or die. And in general, that name was given them for using of such charms, and rites, as that craft teaches them. Many points of their craft and practices are common betwixt the magicians and them: for they serve both one master, although in diverse fashions. And as I divided the necromancers, into two sorts, learned and unlearned; so must I divide them in other two, rich and of better accomplishment, poor and of baser degree. These two degrees now of persons, that practice this craft, answer to the passions in them, which (I told you before) the Devil used as means to entice them to his service, for such of them as are in great misery and poverty, he allures to follow him, by promising unto them great riches, and worldly commodity. Such as though are rich, yet burn in a desperate desire of revenge, he allures them by promises, to get their turn, satisfied to their hearts contentment. It is to be noted now, that the old and crafty enemy of ours, assails none, though touched with any of these two extremities, except he first find an entrance ready for him, either by the great ignorance of the person he deals with, joined with an evil life, or else by their carelessness and contempt of God: And finding them in an utter despair, for one of these two former causes that I have spoken of; he prepares the way by feeding them craftily in their humor, and filling them further and further with despair, while he finds the time proper to discover himself unto them. At which time, either upon their walking solitary in the fields, or else lying asleep in their bed; but always without the company of any other, he either by a voice, or in likeness of a man inquires of them, what troubles them: and promises them, a sudden and certain way of remedy, upon condition on the other part, that they follow his advice; and do such things as he will require of them: Their minds being prepared beforehand, as I have already spoken, they easily agreed unto that demand of his: And sun sets on another tryst, where they may meet again. At which time, before he proceed any further with them, he first persuades them to addict themselves to his service: which being easily obtained, he then discovers what he is unto them: makes them to renounce their God and Baptism directly, and gives them his mark upon some secret place of their body, which remains sorely unhealed, while his next meeting with them comes, and thereafter ever insensible, howsoever it be nipped or pricked by any, as is daily proved, to give them a proof thereby, that as in that doing, he could hurt and heal them; so all their ill and well doing thereafter, must depend upon him. And besides that, the intolerable dolor that they feel in that place, where he has marked them, serves to awaken them, and not to let them rest, while at their next meeting again: fearing least other ways they might either forget him, being as a new apprentice, and not well enough founded yet, in that fiendish folly: or else remembering of that horrible promise they made him, at their last meeting, they might be afraid at the same, and desire to call it back. At their third meeting, he makes a show to be careful to perform his promises, either by teaching them ways how to get themselves revenged, if they be of that sort: Or else by teaching them lessons, how by most vile and unlawful means, they may obtain gain, and worldly commodity, if they be of the other sort.

III.

The Witches actions divided in two parts. The actions proper to their own persons. Their actions toward others. The form of their conventions, and adoring of their master.

Phi. You have said now enough of their initiating in that

DEMONOLOGY

way. It rests then that you discourse upon their practices, how they be passed as apprentices: for I would fain hear what is possible to them to perform in very deed. Although they serve a common master with the necromancers, (as I have before said) yet serve they him in another form. For as the means are diverse, which allures them to the unlawful arts of serving of the Devil; so by diverse ways use they their practices, answering to these means, which first the Devil, used as instruments in them; though all tending to one end: To wit, the enlarging of Satans' tyranny, and crossing of the propagation of the Kingdom of Christ, so far as lies in the possibility, either of the one or other sort, or of the Devil their master. For where the magicians, as allured by curiosity, in the most part of their practices, seeks principally the satisfying of the same, and to win to themselves a popular honor and estimation: These witches on the other part, being enticed ether for the desire of revenge, or of worldly riches, their whole practices are either to hurt men and their guides, or what they possess, for satisfying of their cruel minds in the former, or else by the wrack in whatsoever sort, of any whom God will permit them to have power off, to satisfy their greedy desire in the last point.

 Epi. In two parts their actions may be divided; the actions of their own persons, and the actions proceeding from them towards any other. And this division being well understood, will easily resolve you, what is possible to them to do. For although all that they confess is no lie upon their part, yet doubtlessly in my opinion, a part of it is not indeed, according as they take it to be: And in this I mean by the actions of their own persons. For as I said before, speaking of magic, that the Devil deludes the senses of these scholars of his, in many things, so say I the like of these witches.

 Phi. Then I pray you, first to speak of that part of their own persons, and then you may come next to their actions towards others.

 Epi. To the effect that they may perform such services of their false master, as he employs them in, the Devil, as Gods' ape, counterfeits in his servants this service and form of

DEMONOLOGY

adoration, that God prescribed and made his servants to practice. For as the servants of God, publicly uses to convene for serving of him, so makes he them in great numbers to convene (though publicly they dare not) for his service. As none convenes to the adoration and worshiping of God, except they be marked with his seal, the Sacrament of Baptism: So none serves Satan, and convenes to the adoring of him, that are not marked with that mark, whereof I already spake. As the minister sent by God teaches plainly at the time of their public conventions, how to serve him in spirit and truth: so that unclean spirit, in his own person teaches his Disciples, at the time of their convening, how to work all kind of mischief: And craves contemplation of all their horrible and detestable proceedings passed, for advancement of his service. Yea, that he may the more vilely counterfeit and scorn God, he oft times make his slaves to convene in these very places, which are definite and ordained for the convening of the serving of God (I mean by Churches) But this far, which I have yet said, I not only take it to be true in their opinions, but even so to be indeed. For the form that he used in counterfeiting God among the gentiles makes me so to think: As God spake by his oracles, spake he not so by his? As God had as well bloody sacrifices, as others without blood, had not he the like? As God had churches sanctified to his service, with altars, priests, sacrifices, ceremonies and prayers; had he not the like polluted to his service? As God gave responses by Urim and Thummim, gave he not his responses by the entrails of beasts, by the singing of fowls, and by their actions in the air? As God by visions, dreams, and ecstasies revealed what was to come, and what was his will unto his servants; used he not the like means to forewarn his slaves of things to come? Yea, even as God loved cleanness, hated vice, and impurity, and appointed punishments therefore: used he not the like (though falsely I grant, but in eschewing the less inconvenient, to draw them upon a greater) yet dissimulated he not I say, so far as to appoint his priests to keep their bodies cleaned and undefiled, before their asking responses of him? And fained he not God to be a protector of every virtue, and a just avenger of the contrary? This reason then moves me, that as he is that same Devil; and as crafty now as he was then; so will he not spare at all in these actions that I have spoken of, concerning the witches persons: But further, witches ofttimes confesses not only his convening in the church with them, but his occupying of the pulpit: Yea, their form of adoration, to be the kissing of his hinder parts. Which though it seem ridiculous, yet may it likewise be true, seeing we read that in Calicute, he appearing in form of a Ram, has publicly that dishonest homage done unto him, by every one of the people: So ambitious is he, and greedy of honor (which procured his fall) that he will even imitate God in that part, where it is said, that Moses could see but the hinder parts of God for the brightness of his glory: And yet that speech is spoken.

IV.

What are the ways possible, whereby the witches may transport themselves to places far distant. And what are impossible and mere illusions of Satan. And the reasons thereof.

Phi. But what way say they or think you that it is possible that they can come to these unlawful conventions?

Epi. There is the thing which I esteem their senses to be deluded in, and though they lie not in confessing of it, because they think it to be true, yet not to be so in substance or effect: for they say, that by diverse means they may convened, either to the adoring of their master, or to the putting in practice any service of his, committed unto their charge: one way is natural, which is natural riding, walking or sailing, at what hour their master comes and advertises them. And this way may be easily believed: Another way is somewhat more strange: and yet it is possible to be true: which is being carried by the force of the spirit which is their conductor, either above the earth or above the sea swiftly, to the place where they are to meet; which I am persuaded is to be likewise possible, in respect that as Habakkuk was carried by the Angel in that form to the den

DEMONOLOGY

where Daniel laid; so think I, the Devil will be ready to imitate God, as well in that as in other things, which is much more possible to him to do, being a spirit, then to a mighty wind, being but a natural meteor, to transport from one place to another a solid body, as is commonly and daily seen in practice: But in this violent form they cannot be carried, but a short distance, agreeing with the space that they may retain their breath: for if it were longer, their breath could not remain unextinguished, their body being carried in such a violent and forceful manner, as be example: If one fall off a small height, his life is but in peril, according to the hard or soft landing: but if one fall from a high and mighty rock, his breath will be forcibly banished from the body, before he can even fall to the earth, as if often seen by experience. And in this transporting they say themselves, that they are invisible to any other, except among themselves; which may also be possible in my opinion. For if the Devil may form what kind of impressions he pleases in the air, as I have said before, speaking of magic, why may he not far more easily thicken and obscure it so the air, that is next about them by contracting it straight together, that the beams of any other mans' eyes, cannot pierce through the same, to see them? But the third way of their coming to their conventions, is, that where in I think them deluded: For some of them say, that being transformed in the likeness of a little beast or fowl, they will come and pierce through whatsoever house or church, though all ordinary passages be closed, by whatsoever open, the air may enter in at. And some say, that their bodies lying still as in an ecstasy, their spirits will be ravished out of their bodies, and carried to such places. And for verifying thereof, will give evident tokens, as well by witnesses that have seen their body lying senseless in the meantime, as by naming persons, whom with they met, and giving tokens of what purpose was among them, whom otherwise they could not have known, for this form of journeying, they affirm to use most, when they are transported from one country to another.

    Phi. Surely I long to hear your own opinion of this: For they are like old wives tattles about the fire. The reasons that

DEMONOLOGY

moves me to think that these are mere illusions, are these. First for them that are transformed in likeness of beasts or fowls, can enter through so narrow passages, although I may easily believe that the Devil could by his workmanship upon the air, make them appear to be in such forms, either to themselves or to others: Yet how he can contract a solid body within so little room, I think it is directly contrary to itself, for to be made so little, and yet not diminished: To be so straightly drawn together, and yet feel no pain; I think it is so contrary to the quality of a natural body, and so like to the little transubstantiation God in the Papists Mass, that I can never believe it. So to have this happen, is so proper to a solid body, that as all philosophers conclude, it cannot be any more without one, then a spirit can have one. For when Peter came out of the prison, and the doors all locked: It was not by any contracting his body in so little room, but the giving place of the door, though unseen by the jailers. And yet is there no comparison when this is done, betwixt the power of God, and of the Devil. As to their form of ecstasy and spiritual transporting, it is certain the souls going out of the body, is the only definition of natural death: and who are once dead, God forbid wee should think that it should lie in the power of all the Devils in Hell, to restore them to their life again: Although he can put his own spirit in a dead body, which the necromancers commonly practice, as you have heard. For that is the office properly belonging to God; and besides that, the soul once parting from the body, cannot wander any longer in the world, but to its own resting place must it go immediately, abiding the conjunction of the body again, at the latter day. And what Christ or the prophets did miraculously in this case, it cannot in no Christian mans opinion be made common with the Devil. As for any tokens that they give for proving this, it is very possible to the Devils' craft, to persuade them to these means. For he being a spirit, may he not so ravish their thoughts, and dull their senses, that their body lying as dead, he may object to their spirits as it were in a dream, and (as the Poets write of Morpheus) represent such forms of persons, of places, and other circumstances, as he pleases to delude them with? Yea, that he may deceive them with the greater efficacy, may he not at that same instant, by fellow angels of his, delude such other persons so in that same fashion, whom with he makes them to believe that they met; that all their reports and tokens, though thoroughly examined, may every one agree with an other. And that whatsoever actions, either in hurting men or beasts: or whatsoever other thing that they falsely imagine, at that time to have done, may by himself or his fellows, at that same time be done indeed; so as if they would give for a token of their being ravished at the death of such a person within so short space thereafter, whom they believe to have poisoned, or witched at that instant, might he not at that same hour, have smitten that same person by the permission of God, to the farther deceiving of them, and to move others to believe them? And this is surely the likeliest way, and most according to reason, which my judgment can find out in this, and whatsoever other unnatural points of their confession. And by these means shall we fail surely, betwixt Charybdis and Scylla, in eschewing the not believing of them altogether on the one part, lest that draw us to the error that there are no witches: and on the other part in believing of it, make us to eschew the falling into innumerable absurdities, both monstrously against all divine theology, and human philosophy.

V.

Witches' actions towards others. Why there are more women of that craft than men? What things are possible to them to effectuate by the power of their master. The reasons thereof. What is the surest remedy of the harms done by them.

Phi. Forsooth your opinion in this, seems to carry most reason with it, and since you have ended, then the actions belonging properly to their own persons: say forward now to their actions used towards others.

Epi. In their actions used towards others, three things ought to be considered. First the manner of their consulting thereupon: Next their part as instruments: And last their masters part, who puts the same in execution. As to their consultations thereupon, they use them often in the churches, where they convene for adoring: at what time their master inquiring at them what they would beat: every one of them proposes unto, what wicked turn they would have done, either for obtaining of riches, or for revenging them upon any whom they have malice at; who granting their demand, as no doubt willingly he will, since it is to do evil, he teaches them the means, whereby they may do the same. As for little trifling turns that women have ado with, he causes them to take dead corpses, and to make powders thereof, mixing such other things there among, as he gives unto them.

    Phi. But before you go further, permit me I pray you to interrupt you one word, which you have put me in memory of, by speaking of women. What can be the cause that there are twenty women given to that craft, where there is one man?

    Epi. The reason is easy, for as that sex is frailer then man is, so is it easier to be entrapped in these gross snares of the Devil, as was over well proved to be true, by the Serpents' deceiving of Eve at the beginning, which makes him the homelier with that sex ever since.

    Phi. Return now where you left off.

    Epi. To some others at these times he teaches, how to make pictures of wax or clay: That by the roasting thereof, the persons that they bear the name of, may be continually melted or dried away by continual sickness. To some he gives such stones or gems, as will help to cure or cast on diseases: And to some he teaches kinds of uncouth poisons, which Mediciners understand not (for he is far more cunning then man in the knowledge of all the occult proprieties of nature) not that any of these means which he teaches them (except the poisons which are composed of things natural) can of themselves help anything to these turns, that they are employed, but only being Gods' ape, as well in that, as in all other things. Even as God by his Sacraments which are earthly of themselves works a heavenly effect, though no ways by any cooperation in them: And as

DEMONOLOGY

Christ by clay and spittle wrought together, opened the eyes of the blind man, suppose there was no virtue in that which he outwardly applied, so the Devil will have his outward means to be shown as it were of his doing, which has no part of cooperation in his turns with him, how far that ever the ignorant be abused in the contrary. And as to the effects of these two former parts, to wit, the consultations and the outward means, they are so wonderful as I dare not allege any of them, without joining a sufficient reason of the possibilities thereof. For leaving all the small trifles among wives, and to speak of the principal points of their craft. For the common trifles thereof, they can do without conversing well enough by themselves: These principal points I say are these: They can make men or women to love or hate other, which may be very possible to the Devil to effectuate, seeing as he is a subtle spirit, knows well enough how to persuade the corrupted affection of them whom God will permit him so to deal with: They can lay the sickness of one upon an other, which likewise is very possible unto him: For since by Gods permission, he laid sickness upon Job, why may he not far more easily lay it upon any other: For as an old practitioner, he knows well enough what humor dominates most in any of us, and as a spirit he can subtly drum up the same, making it decrease, or to abound, as he thinks meet for troubling of us, when God will so permit him. And for the taking off of it, no doubt he will be glad to relieve such of present pain, as he may think by these means to persuade to be caught in his everlasting snares and fetters. They can bewitch and take the life of men or women, by roasting of the pictures, as I spake of before, which likewise is very possible to their master to perform, for although, (as I said before) that instrument of wax have not virtue in that turn doing, yet may he not very well even by that same measure that his conjured slaves melts that wax at the fire, may he not I say at these same times, subtle as a spirit so weaken and scatter the spirits of life of the the patient, as may make him on the one part, for faintness, to sweat out the humor of his body: And on the other part, for not the concurrence of these spirits, which causes his digestion, so debilitate his stomach, that his humor radically, continually, sweating out on the one part, and no new good luck being put in the place thereof, for lack of digestion on the other, he at last shall vanish away, even as his picture will do at the fire. And that knavish and cunning workman, by troubling him only at some times, makes a proportion so near betwixt the working of the one and the other, that both shall end as it were at one time. They can raise storms and tempests in the air, either upon sea or land, though not universally, but in such a particular place and prescribed bounds, as God will permit them so to trouble: Which likewise is very easy to be discerned from any other natural tempests that are meteors, in respect of the sudden and violent raising thereof, together with the short enduring of the same. And this is likewise very possible to their master to do, he having such affinity with the air as being a spirit, and having such power of the forming and moving thereof, as you have heard me already declare: For in the Scripture, that style of the Prince of the air is given unto him. They can make folks to become frenetic or insane, which likewise is very possible to their master to do, since they are but natural sicknesses: and so he may lay on these kinds, as well as any others. They can make spirits either to follow and trouble persons, or haunt certain houses, and frighten oftentimes the inhabitants: as has been known to be done by our witches at this time. And likewise they can make some to be possessed with spirits, and so to become demoniacs: and this last sort is very possible likewise to the Devil their master to do, since he may easily send his own angels to trouble in what form he pleases, any whom God will permit him so to use.

    Phi. But will God permit these wicked instruments by the power of the Devil their master, to trouble any of these means, any that believes in him?

    Epi. No doubt, for there are three kinds of folks whom God will permit so to be tempted or troubled; the wicked for their horrible sins, to punish them in the like measure; The godly that are sleeping in any great sins or infirmities and weakness in faith, to waken them up the faster by such an uncouth form: and even some of the best, that their patience may be tried before the world, as Jobs' was. For why may not God use any kind of extraordinary punishment, when it pleases him; as well as the ordinary rods of sickness or other adversities?

Phi. Who then may be free from these Devilish practices?

Epi. No man ought to presume so far as to promise any impunity to himself: for God has before all beginnings preordained as well the particular sorts of plagues as of benefits for every man, which in the own time he ordains them to be visited with, and yet ought we not to be the more afraid for that, of any thing that the Devil and his wicked instruments can do against us: For we daily fight against the Devil in a hundred other ways: And therefore as a valiant captain, afraid no more being at the combat, nor ever strays from his purpose for the smoking shot of a cannon, nor the small clack of a pistol: suppose he be not certain what may light upon him; Even so ought we boldly to go forward in fighting against the Devil without any greater terror, for these his rarest weapons, nor for the ordinary whereof we have daily the proof.

Phi. Is it not lawful then by the help of some other witch to cure the disease that is cast on by that craft?

Epi. No ways lawful: For I gave you the reason thereof in that axiom of theology, which was the last words I spake of magic.

Phi. How then may these diseases be lawfully cured?

Epi. Only by earnest prayer to God, by amendment of their lives, and by sharp persevering everyone, according to his calling of these instruments of Satan, whose punishment to the death will be a salutary sacrifice for the patient. And this is not only the lawful way, but likewise the most sure: For by the Devil's means, can never the Devil be cast out, as Christ said. And when such a cure is used, it may well serve for a short time, but at the last, it will doubtlessly tend to the utter perdition of the patient, both in body and soul.

VI.

What sort of folks are least or most subject to receive harm by witchcraft. What power they have to harm the magistrate, and upon what respects they have any power in prison: And to what end may or will the Devil appear to them therein. Upon what respects the Devil appears in sundry shapes to sundry of them at any time.

Phi. But who dare take upon him to punish them, if no man can be sure to be free from their unnatural invasions?

Epi. We ought not the more of that restrain from virtue, that the way whereby we climb thereunto be straight and perilous. But besides that, as there is no kind of persons to subject to receive harm of them, as these that are of infirm and weak faith (which is the best buckler against such invasions:) so have they so small power over none, as over such as zealously and earnestly pursues them, without sparing for any worldlier respect.

Phi. Then they are like the pest, which smites these sickest, that flies it farthest, and apprehends deepest the peril thereof.

Epi. It is even so with them: For neither is it able to them to use any false cure upon a patient, except the patient first believe in their power, and so hazard the tinsel of his own soul, nor yet can they have less power to hurt any, nor such as condemns most their doings, so being it come of faith, and not of any vain arrogance in themselves.

Phi. But what is their power against the magistrate?

Epi. Less or greater, according as he deals with them. For if he be slothful towards them, God is very able to make them instruments to waken and punish his sloth. But if he be the contrary, he according to the just law of God, and allowable law of all nations, will be diligent in examining and punishing of them: God will not permit their master to trouble or hinder so good a work.

DEMONOLOGY

Phi. But what if they be once in hands and captivity, have they any further power in their craft?

Epi. That is according to the form of their detention. If they be but apprehended and detained by any private person, upon other private respects, their power no doubt either in escaping or in doing hurt, is no less nor ever it was before. But if on the other part, their apprehending and detention be by the lawful magistrate, upon the just respects of their guiltiness in that craft, their power is then no greater than before that ever they meddled with their master. For where God begins justly to strike by his lawful Lieutenants, it is not in the Devil's power to defraud or bereave him of the office, or effect of his powerful and revenging scepter.

Phi. But will never their master come to visit them, if they be once apprehended and put in prison?

Epi. That is according to the state that these miserable wretches are in: For if they be obstinate in still denying, he will not spare, when he finds time to speak with them, either if he find them in any comfort, to fill them more and more with the vain hope of some manner of relief: or else if he find them in a deep despair, by all means to augment the same, and to persuade them by some extraordinary means to put themselves down, which very commonly they do. But if they be penitent and confess, God will not permit him to trouble them any more with his presence and allurements.

Phi. It is not good using his counsel I see then. But I would earnestly know when he appears to them in prison, what forms uses he then to take?

Epi. Divers forms, even as he uses to do at other times unto them. For as I told you, speaking of magic, he appears to that kind of craftsmen ordinarily in a form, according as they agree upon it among themselves: Or if they be but apprentices, according to the quality of their circles or conjurations: Yet to these capped creatures, he appears as he pleases, and as he finds meet for their humors. For even at their public conventions, he appears to divers of them in divers forms, as we have found by the difference of their confessions in that point: For he deluding them with vain impressions in the air, makes himself to seem more terrible to the grosser sort, that they may thereby be moved to fear and reverence him the more: And less monstrous and uncouth again to the craftier sort, least otherwise they might be startled and flee at his ugliness.

Phi. How can he then be felt, as they confess they have done him, if his body be but of air?

Epi. I hear little of that among their confessions, yet may he make himself palpable, either by assuming any dead body, and using the ministry thereof, or else by deluding as well their sense of feeling as seeing; which is not impossible to him to do, since all our senses, as we are so weak, and even by ordinary sicknesses will be often times deluded.

Phi. But I would hear one word further yet, concerning his appearing to them in prison, which is this: May any other that chances to be present at that time in the prison, see him as well as they.

Epi. Sometimes they will, and sometimes not, as it pleases God.

VII.

Two forms of the Devils' visible conversing in the earth, with the reasons wherefore the one of them was communed in the time of Papistry: And the other sense. Those that deny the power of the Devil, deny the power of God, and are guilty of the error of the Sadducees.

Phi. Has the Devil then power to appear to any other, except to such as are his sworn disciples: especially since all oracles, and such like kinds of illusions were taken away and abolished by the coming of Christ?

Epi. Although it be true indeed, that the brightness of the Gospel at his coming, scaled the clouds of all these gross errors among the gentiles: yet that these abusing spirits, ceases not attempting at some times to appear, daily experience teaches us. Indeed this difference is to be marked betwixt the forms of

DEMONOLOGY

Satan's conversing visibly in the world. For of two different forms thereof, the one of them by the spreading of the Evangel, and conquest of the white horse, in the sixth chapter of the Revelation, is much hindered and become rarer there through. This his appearing to any Christians, troubling of them outwardly, or possessing of them in a constrained way. The other of them is become more common and more used by Satan, I mean by their unlawful arts, whereupon our whole purpose has been This we find by experience in this Island to be true. For we know, more ghosts and spirits were seen, nor tongue can tell, in the time of blind Papistry in these countries, where now by the contrary, a man shall scarcely all his time here once of such things. And yet were these unlawful arts far rarer at that time: and never were so much heard of, nor so rife as they are now.

Phi. What should be the cause of that?

Epi. The diverse nature of our sins procures at the Justice of God, diverse sorts of punishments answering thereunto. And therefore as in the time of Papistry, our fathers erring grossly, and through ignorance, that mist of errors overshadowed the Devil to walk the more familiarly among them: And as it were by frightening terrors, to mock and accuse their frightened errors. By the contrary, we now being sound of religion, and in our life rebelling to our profession, God justly by that sin of rebellion, as Samuel called it, accuses our life of so willfully fighting against our profession.

Phi. Since you are entered now to speak of the appearing of spirits: I would be glad to hear your opinion in that matter. For many deny that any such spirits can appear in these days as I have said.

Epi. Doubtlessly who denies the power of the Devil, would likewise deny the power of God, if they could for shame. For since the Devil is the very contrary opposite to God, there can be no better way to know God, then by the contrary; as by the ones power (though a creature) to admire the power of the great Creator: by the falsehood of the one to consider the truth of the other, by the injustice of the one, to consider the justice of the other: And by the cruelty of the one, to consider the mercy

DEMONOLOGY

of the other: And so forth in all the rest of the essence of God, and qualities of the Devil. But I fear indeed, there be over many Sadducees in this world, that deny all kinds of spirits: For convicting of whose error, there is cause enough if there were no more, that God should permit at sometimes spirits visibly to harm us.

THIRD BOOK

I.

The division of spirits in four principal kinds. The description of the first kind of them, called Spectra and umbrae mortuorum. What is the best way to be free of their trouble.

Phi. Pray you now then go forward in telling what you think fabulous, or may be done in that case.

Epi. The kind of the Devils conversing in the earth, may be divided in four different kinds, whereby they frighten and trouble the bodies of men: For of the abusing of the soul, I have spoken already. The first is, where spirits trouble some houses or solitary places: The second, where spirits follow certain people, and at divers hours trouble them: The third, when they enter within them and possess them: The fourth is the kind of spirits that are called vulgarly the fairies. Of the three former kinds, you have heard already, how they may artificially be made by witchery to trouble folks: Now it rests to speak of their natural coming as it were, and not raised by witchcraft. But generally I must forewarn you of one thing before I enter in this purpose: that is, that although in my discoursing of them, I divide them in divers kinds, you must notwithstanding thereof note my phrase of speaking in that: For doubtlessly they are in effect, but all one kind of spirits, who for abusing the more of mankind, take on these sundry shapes, and uses diverse forms of outward action, as if some were of nature better then other. Now I return to my purpose: As to the first kind of these spirits, that were called by the ancients by divers names, according as their actions were. For if they were spirits that haunted houses, by appearing in divers and horrible forms, and making great noises: they were called Lemures or Spectra. If they appeared in likeness of any defunct to some friends of his, they were called umbra mortuorum: And so innumerable visages they have, according to their actions, as I have said already. As we see by experience, how many appearances they have given them in our language in the like manner: Of the appearing of these spirits, we are certified by the Scriptures, where the Prophet Esau in the 13th and 14th chapters threatening the destruction of Babel and Edom, declares, that it shall not only be wracked, but shall become so great a solitude, as it shall be the inhabitance of howling spirits, and of Ziim and Iim, which are the proper Hebrew names for these spirits. The cause while they haunt solitary places, it is by reason, that they may terrorize and drive off the more the faith of such as them alone haunts such places. For our nature is such, as in companies we are not so soon moved to any such kind of fear, as being solitary, which the Devil knowing well enough, he will not therefore assail us but when we are weak: And besides that, God will not permit him so to dishonor the societies and companies of Christians, as in public times and places to walk visibly among them. On the other part, when he troubles certain houses that are dwelt in, it is a sure token either of gross ignorance, or of some gross and slanderous sins among the inhabitants thereof: which God by that extraordinary rod punishes.

Phi. But by what way or passage can these spirits enter in these houses, seeing they allege that they will enter, even while the doors and windows are locked?

Epi. They will choose the passage for their entrance, according to the form that they are in at that time. For if they have assumed a dead body, in which they lodge themselves, they can easily enough open without noise any door or window, and enter in thereat. And if they enter as a spirit only, any place where the air may come in at, is large enough an entry for them: For as I said before, a spirit can occupy no quantity.

Phi. And will God then permit these wicked spirits to

trouble the rest of a dead body, before the resurrection thereof? Or if he sill so, I think it should be of the reprobate only.

Epi. What more is the rest troubled of a dead body, when the Devil carries it out of the Grave to serve his turn for a space, nor when the witches takes it up and powder it, or when as swine roots up the graves? The rest of them that the Scripture speaks of, is not meant by a local remaining continually in one place, but by their resting from their travels and miseries of this world, while their latter conjunction again with the soul at that time to receive full glory in both. And that the Devil may use as well the ministry of the bodies of the faithful in these cases, as of the unfaithful, there is no inconvenience; for his haunting with their bodies after they are dead, can in no way defile them in respect of the souls absence. And for any dishonor it can be unto them, by what reason can it be greater, then the hanging, heading, or many such shameful deaths, that good men will suffer for there is nothing in the bodies of the faithful, more worthy of honor, or freer from corruption by nature, nor in these of the unfaithful, until such time they be purged and glorified in the latter day, as is daily seen by the vile diseases and corruptions, that the bodies of the faithful are subject unto, as you will see clearly proved, when I speak of the possessed and the demoniacs.

Phi. Yet there are sundry that affirm to have haunted such places, where these spirits are alleged to be: And could never hear nor see anything.

Epi. I think well: For that is only reserved to the secret knowledge of God, whom he will permit to see such things, and whom not.

Phi. But where these spirits haunt and trouble any houses, what is the best way to banish them?

Epi. By two means may only the remedy of such things be procured: The one is ardent prayer to God, both of these persons that are troubled with them, and of that church whereof they are. The other is the purging of themselves by amendment of life from such sins, as have procured that extraordinary plague.

DEMONOLOGY

Phi. And what means then these kinds of spirits, when they appear in the shadow of a person newly dead, or to die, to his friends?

Epi. When they appear upon that occasion, they are called wraiths in our language. Among the gentiles the Devil used that much, to make them believe that it was some good spirit that appeared to them then, either to forewarn them of the death of their friend; or else to discover unto them, the will of the defunct, or what was the say of his slaughter, as is written in the book of the histories Prodigious. And this way he easily deceived the gentiles, because they knew not God: And to that same effect is it, that he now appears in that manner to some ignorant Christians. For he dare not so delude any that knows that, neither can the spirit of the defunct return to his friend, or yet an angel use such a form.

Phi. And are not our war-wolves one sort of these spirits also, that haunt and troubles some houses or dwelling places?

Epi. There have indeed been an old opinion of such like things; For by the Greeks they were called lycanthropes which signifies wolf-men. But to tell you simply my opinion in this, if any such thing has been, I take it to have proceeded but of a natural super-abundance of melancholy, which as we read, that it has made some think themselves pitchers, and some horses, and some one kind of beast or other: So suppose I that it has so vivid the imagination and memory of some, as per *lucida interualla*, it has so highly occupied them, that they have thought themselves to be wolves indeed at these times: and so have counterfeited their actions in going on their hands and feet, pressing to devour women and livestock, fighting and snatching with all the town dogs, and in using such like other brutish actions, and so to become beasts by a strong apprehension, as Nebuchadnezzar was seven years: But as to their having and hiding of their hard and beast-like sloughs, I take that to be but folly, by uncertain report, the author of all lies.

DEMONOLOGY

II.

The description of the next two kinds of spirits whereof the one follows outwardly, the other possesses inwardly the persons that they trouble. That since all Prophecies and visions are now ceased, all spirits that appear in these forms are evil.

Phi. Come forward now to the rest of the these kinds of spirits.

Epi. As to the next two kinds, that is, either these that outwardly troubles and follows some person, or else inwardly possesses them: I will conjoin them in one, because as well the causes are alike in the persons that they are permitted to trouble; as also the ways whereby they may be remedied and cured.

Phi. What kind of persons are they that may be troubled?

Epi. Two kinds in special: Either such as being guilty of grievous offenses, God punishes by that horrible kind of scourge, or else being persons of the best nature peradventure, that you shall find in all the country about them, God permits them to be troubled in that sort, for the trial of their patience, and wakening up of their zeal, for admonishing of the beholders, not to trust over much in themselves, since they are made of no better stuff, and peradventure blotted with no smaller sins (as Christ said, speaking of them upon whom the tower in Siloam fell:) And for giving likewise to the spectators, matter to praise God, that they meriting no better are yet spared from being corrected in that fearful form.

Phi. These are good seasons for the part of God, which apparently moves him so to permit the Devil to trouble such persons. But since the Devil has ever a contrary respect in all the actions that God employs him in: Which is I pray you the end and mark he shoots at in this turn?

Epi. It is to obtain one of two things thereby, if he may: The one is the tinsel of their life, by inducing them to such perilous places at such time as he either follows or possesses them, which may procure the same: And such like, so far as God will permit him, by tormenting them to weaken their body, and cast them in incurable diseases. The other thing that he presses to obtain by troubling of them, is the tinsel of their soul, by enticing them to mistrust and blaspheme God: Either for the intolerable nature of their torments, as he assayed to have done with Job; or else for his promising unto them to leave the troubling of them, in case they would so do, as is known by experience at this same time by the confession of a young one that was so troubled.

Phi. Since you have spoken now of both these kinds of spirits comprehending them in one: I must now go back again in asking some questions of every one of these kinds in special. And first for these that follows certain persons, you know that there are two sorts of them: One sort that troubles and torments the person that they haunt with: Another sort that are serviceable unto them in all kind of their necessaries, and omits never to forewarn them of any sudden peril that they are to be in. And so in this case, I would understand whither both these sorts be but wicked and damned spirits: Or if the last sort be rather Angels, (as should appear by their actions) sent by God to assist such as he specially favors. For it is written in the Scriptures, that God sends Legions of Angels to guard and watch over his elect.

Epi. I know well enough where from that error which you allege has proceeded: For it was the ignorant gentiles that were the fountain thereof. Who for that they knew not God, they forged in their own imaginations, every man to be still accompanied with two spirits, whereof they called the one genius bonus, the other *genius malies*: the Greeks called them similarly, whereof the former they said, persuaded him to all the good he did: the other enticed him to all the evil. But praise God we that are Christians, and walk not among the Cymmerian conjectures of man, we know well enough, that it is the good spirit of God only, who is the fountain of all goodness, that persuades us to the thinking or doing of any good: and that it is our corrupted flesh and Satan, that entices us to the contrary. And yet the Devil for confirming in the heads of ignorant

DEMONOLOGY

Christians, that error first maintained among the Gentiles, he whiles among the first kind of spirits that I speak of, appeared in the time of Papistry and blindness, and haunted divers houses, without doing any evil, but doing as it were necessary turned up and down the house: and this spirit they called Brownie in our language, who appeared like a rough-man: yea, some were so blinded, as to believe that their house was all the better, as they called it, that such spirits resorted there.

Phi. But since the Devils' intention in all his actions, is ever to do evil, what evil was there in that form of doing, since their actions outwardly were good.

Epi. Was it not evil enough to deceive simple ignorants, in making them to take him for an Angel of light, and so to account of Gods enemy, as of their particular friend? Whereby the contrary, all we that are Christians, ought assuredly to know that since the coming of Christ in the flesh, and establishing of his Church by the Apostles, all miracles, visions, prophecies, and appearances of Angels or good spirits are ceased. Which served only for the first sowing of faith, and planting of the Church. Where now the Church being established, and the white horse whereof I spake before, having made his conquest, the law and Prophets are thought sufficient to serve us, or make us inexcusable, as Christ saith in his parable of Lazarus and the rich man.

III.

The description of a particular sort of that kind of following spirits, called Incubi and Succubi: And what is the reason wherefore these kinds of spirits haunt most the Northern and barbarous parts of the world.

Phi. The next question that I would ask, is likewise concerning this first of these two kinds of spirits that you have conjoined: and it is this; you know how it is commonly written and reported, that among the rest of the sorts of spirits that follow certain persons, there is one more monstrous above all the rest: in respect as it is alleged, they converse naturally with them whom they trouble and haunt with: and therefore I would know in two things your opinion herein: First if such a thing can be, and next if it be, whether there be a difference of sexes among these spirits or not.

Epi. That abominable kind of the Devils abusing of men or women, was called of old, Incubi and Succubi, according to the difference of the sexes that they conversed with. By two means this great kind of abuse might possibly be performed: The one, when the Devil only as a spirit, and stealing out the sperm of a dead body, abuses them that way, they not readily seeing any shape or feeling anything, but that which he so conveys in that part: As we read of a Monastery of Nuns which were burnt for their being that way abused. The other mean is when he borrows a dead body and so visibly, and as it seems unto them natural as a man converses with them. But it is to be noted, that in whatsoever way he uses it, that sperm seems intolerably cold to the person abused. For if he steal out the nature of a quick person, it cannot be so quickly carried, but it will both tine the strength and heat by the way, which it could never have had for lack of agitation, which in the time of procreation is the procurer and awakener up of these two natural qualities. And if he occupying the dead body as his lodging expel the same out thereof in the due time, it must likewise be cold by the participation with the qualities of the dead body where it comes of. And whereas you inquire if these spirits be divided in sexes or not, I think the rules of Philosophy may easily resolve a man of the contrary: For it is a sure principle of that art, that nothing can be divided in sexes, except such living bodies as must have a natural seed to generate by. But we know spirits have no seed proper to themselves, nor yet can they gender one with another.

Phi. How is it then that they say sundry monsters have been gotten by that way.

Epi. These tales are nothing but folly. For that they have no nature of their own, I have shown you already. And that the cold nature of a dead body, can work nothing in generation, it is more plain, as being already dead of itself as well as the rest of the body is, wanting the natural heat, and such other natural operation, as is necessary for working that effect, and in case such a thing were possible (which were all utterly against all the rules of nature) it would breed no monster, but only such a natural offspring, as would have come betwixt that man or woman and that other abused person, in case they both being alive had done with one other. For the Devil's part therein, is but the naked carrying or expelling of that substance: and so it could not participate with the quality of the same. Indeed, it is possible to the craft of the Devil to make a womens' bellies to swell after he has that way abused her, which he may do, either by stirring up her own humor, or by herbs, as we see beggars daily do. And when the time of her delivery should come to make her feel great dolor, like unto that natural course, and then subtly to slip into the Midwives hands, sticks, stones, or some monstrous thing brought from some other place, but this is more reported and guessed at by others, not believed by me.

Phi. But what is the cause that this kind of abuse is thought to be most common in such wild parts of the world, as Lapland, and Finland, or in our North Isle of Orkney and Scotland?

Epi. Because where the Devil finds greatest ignorance and barbarity, there assails he most openly, as I gave you the reason wherefore there was more witches of womankind rather than men.

Phi. Can any be so unhappy as to give their willing consent to the Devil's vile abusing them in this form?

Epi. Yea, some of the witches have confessed, that he had persuaded them to give their willing consent thereunto, that he may thereby have them fettered the more easily in his snares; But as the other compelled sort is to be pitted and prayed for, so is this most highly to be punished and detested.

Phi. Is it not the thing which we call the Mare, which takes folks sleeping in their beds, a kind of these spirits, whereof you are speaking?

Epi. No, that is but a natural sickness, which the

DEMONOLOGY

Mediciners have given that name of Incubus unto *ab incubando*, because it being a thick flume, falling into our breast upon the heart, while we are sleeping, interludes so our vital spirits, and takes all power from us, as makes us think that there were some unnatural burden or spirit, lying upon us and holding us down.

IV.

The description of the demoniacs and possessed. By what reason the Papists may have power to cure them.

Phi. Well, I have told you now all my doubts, and you have satisfied me therein, concerning the first of these two kinds of spirits that you have conjoined. Now I am to inquire only two things at you concerning the last kind, I mean, the demoniacs. The first is, whereby shall these possessed folks be discerned from them that are troubled with a natural frenzy or mania. The next is, how can it be that they can be remedied by the Papists' Church, whom we counting as heretics, it should appear that one Devil should not cast out another, for then would his kingdom be divided in itself, as Christ said.

Epi. As to your first question; there are divers symptoms, whereby that heavy trouble may be discerned from a natural sickness, and especially three, omitting the divers vain signs that the Papists attribute to it: such as the raging at holy water, their fleeing a back from the cross, their not abiding the hearing of God named, and innumerable such like vain things that were alike numerous and feckless to recite. But to come to these three symptoms then, whereof I spake, I account the one of them to be the incredible strength of the possessed creature, which will far exceed the strength of six of the strongest and burliest of any other men that are not so troubled. The next is the firming up so far of the patients breast and belly, with such an unnatural stirring and vehement agitation within them: And such an iron-like hardness of his sinews so stiffly bent out, that it were not possible to prick out as it were the skin of any other person so far: so mightily works the Devil in all the members

DEMONOLOGY

and senses of his body, he being locally within the same, suppose of his soul and affections thereof, he has no more power than of any other mans'. The last is, the speaking of sundry languages, which the patient is known by them that were acquainted with him never to have learned, and that with an uncouth and hollow voice, and all the time of his speaking, a greater motion being in his breast then in his mouth. But from this last symptom is excepted such, as are altogether in the time of their possessing bereft of all their senses being possessed with a dumb and blind spirit, whereof Christ relieved one, in the 12th chapter of Matthew. And as to your next demand, it is first to be doubted if the Papists or any not professing the only true religion, can relieve any of that trouble. And next, in case they can, upon what respects it is possible unto them. As to the former upon two reasons, it is grounded: first that it is known of many of them to be counterfeit, which while the Clergy invents for confirming of their rotten religion. The next is, that by experience we find that few, who are possessed indeed, are fully cured by them, but rather the Devil is content to release the bodily hurting of them, for a short space, thereby to obtain the perpetual hurt of the souls of so many that by these false miracles may be induced or confirmed in the profession of that erroneous religion: even as I told you before that he does in the false cures, or casting out of diseases by witches. As to the other part of the argument, in case they can, which rather (with reverence of the learned thinking otherwise) I am induced to believe, by reason of the faithful report that men found of religion, have made according to their fight thereof, I think if so be, I say these may be the respects, whereupon the Papists may have that power. Christ gave a commission and power to his Apostles to cast out Devils, which they according thereunto put in execution: The rules he bade them observe in that action, was fasting and prayer, the action itself to be done in his name. This power of theirs proceeded not then of any virtue in them, but only in him who directed them. As was clearly proved by Judas by his having as great power in that commission, as any of the rest. It is easy then to be understand that the casting out of

Devils, is by the virtue of fasting and prayer, and in calling of the name of God, suppose many imperfections be in the person that is the instrument, as Christ himself teaches us of the power that false Prophets shall have to cast out Devils. It is no wonder then, these respects of this action being considered, that it may be possible to the Papists, though erring in sundry points of religion, to accomplish this, if they use the right form prescribed by Christ herein. For what the worse is that action that they err in other things, more then their Baptism is the worse that they err in the other Sacrament, and have created many vain attachments to the Baptism itself.

Phi. Surely it is no little wonder that God should permit the body of any of the faithful to be so dishonored, as to be a dwelling place to that unclean spirit.

Epi. There is it which I told right now, would prove and strengthen my argument of the devils entering in the dead bodies of the faithful. For if he is permitted to enter in their living bodies, even when they are joined with the soul, how much more will God permit him to enter in their dead carrion, which is no more man, but the filthy and corruptible case of man. For as Christ said: It is not any thing that enters within man that defiles him, but only that which proceeds and comes from him.

V.

The description of the fourth kind of spirits called the fairies: What is possible therein, and what is but illusions. How far this dialogue entreats of all these things, and to what end.

Phi. Now I pray you come on to that fourth kind of spirits.

Epi. That fourth kind of spirits, which by the gentiles was called Diana, and her wandering court, and among us was called the fairy (as I told you) or our good neighbors, was one of the sorts of illusions that was made in the time of Papistry: for although it was held odious to prophecy by the Devil, yet whom these kind of spirits carried away, and informed, they were thought to be wisest and of best life. To speak of the many vain tales founded upon that illusion: How there was a King and Queen of the fairies, of such a jolly court and train as they had, how they had a manner, and duty, as it were, they ate and drank, and did all other actions like natural men and women: I think it like Virgils *Campi Elysy*, or anything that ought to be believed by Christians, except in general, that as I spake sundry times before, the Devil deluded the senses of sundry simple creatures, in making them believe that they saw and heard such things as were nothing so indeed.

Phi. But how can it be then, that many witches have gone to death with that confession, that they have been transported with the fairyfolk to such a hill, which opening, they went in, and there saw a fairy Queen, who being now lighter, gave them a stone that had various virtues, which at some times has been produced in judgment?

Epi. I say that, even as I said before of that imaginary ravishing of the spirit into the body. For may not the Devil object to their fantasy, their senses being dulled, and as it were asleep, such hills and houses within them, such glittering courts and streets, and whatsoever such like wherewith he pleased to delude them. And in the meantime their bodies being senseless, to convey in their hand any stone or such like thing, which he makes them to imagine to have received in such a place.

Phi. But what say you to their foretelling the death of certain persons, whom they allege to have seen in these places? That is, a sooth-dream (as they say) since they see it walking.

Epi. I think that either they have not been sharply enough examined, that gave so blunt a reason for their prophesies, or otherwise, I think it likewise as possible that the Devil may prophesy to them when he deceives their imaginations in that sort, as well as when he plainly speaks unto them at other times for their prophesying, is but by a kind of vision, as it were, wherein he commonly counterfeits God among the ethnics, as I told you before.

Phi. I would know now whether these kinds of spirits

may only appear to witches, or if they may also appear to any other.

Epi. They may do to both, to the innocent sort, either to terrorize them, or to seem to be a better sort of folks than unclean spirits are, and to the witches, to be a kind of safety for them, that ignorant magistrates may not punish them for it, as I told even now. But as the one sort, for being perforce troubled with them ought to be pitied, so ought the other sort (who may be discerned by their taking upon them to prophecy by them,) That sort I say, ought as severely to be punished as any other witches, and rather the more, that they go in dissemblance to work.

Phi. And what makes the spirits have such different names from others.

Epi. Even the knavery of that same Devil; who as he deludes the necromancers with innumerable feigned names for him and his angels, as in special, making Satan, Beelzebub, and Lucifer, to be three sundry spirits, where we find the two former, but divers names given to the Prince of all the rebelling angels by the Scripture. As by Christ, the Prince of all the Devils is called, Beelzebub in that place, which I alleged against the power of any heretics to cast out Devils. By John in the Revelation, the old tempter is called, Satan the Prince of all the evil angels. And the last, to wit, Lucifer, is but by allegory taken from the day star (so named in divers places of the Scriptures) because of his excellence (I mean the Prince of them) in creation before his fall: Even so I say he deceives the witches, by attributing to himself divers names: as if every divers shape that he transforms himself in, were a different kind of spirit.

Phi. But I have hard many more strange tales of this fairy, than those you have told me so far.

Epi. As well I do in that, as I did in all the rest of my discourse. For because the ground of this conference of ours, proceeded of your asking me at our meeting, if there was such a thing as witches or spirits: And if they had any power: I therefore have framed my whole discourse, only to prove that such things are and may be, by such number of examples as I show to be possible by reason: and keeps me from dipping any further in playing the part of a dictionary, to tell whatever I have read or heard in that purpose, which both would exceed faith, and, and rather would seem to teach such unlawful arts, not to disallow and condemn them, as it is the duty of all Christians to do.

VI.

Of the trial and punishment of witches. What sort of accusation ought to be admitted against them. What is the cause of the increasing so far of their number in this age.

Phi. Then to make an end of our conference, since I see it draws late, what form of punishment think you merits these magicians and witches? For I see that you account them to be all alike guilty?

Epi. They ought to be put to death according to the Law of God, the civil and imperial law, and municipal law of all Christian nations.

Phi. But what kind of death I pray you?

Epi. It is commonly used by fire, but that is an indifferent thing to be used in every country, according to the Law or custom thereof.

Phi. But ought no sex, age nor rank to be exempted?

Epi. None at all (being so used by the lawful magistrate) for it is the highest point of idolatry, wherein no exception is admitted by the law of God.

Phi. Then children may not be spared?

Epi. Yea, not a hair the less of my conclusion. For they are not that capable of reason as to practice such things. And for any being in company and not revealing thereof, their less and ignorant age will no doubt excuse them.

Phi. I see ye condemn them all that are of the counsel of such crafts.

Epi. No doubt, for as I said, speaking of magic, the consulters, trusters-in, over-seers, entertainers or stirrers-up of these witches, are equally guilty with themselves that are the practitioners.

Phi. Whether may the Prince then, or supreme magistrate, spare or oversee any that are guilty of that craft? Upon some great respects known to him?

Epi. The Prince Magistrate for further trials' cause, may continue the punishing of them such a certain space as he thinks convenient: But in the end to spare the life, and not to strike when God bids strike, and so feverishly punish in so odious a fault and treason against God, it is not only unlawful, but doubtless no less a sin in that magistrate, nor it was in Saul sparing of Agag. And so comparable to the sin of witchcraft itself, as Samuel alleged at that time.

Phi. Surely then, I think since this crime ought to be so severely punished. Judges ought to beware to condemn any, but such as they are sure are guilty, neither should the clattering report of a noble serve in so weighty a case.

Epi. Judges ought indeed to beware whom they condemn: For it is as great a crime (as Solomon says,) to condemn the innocent, as to let the guilty escape free. Neither ought the report of any one infamous person, be admitted for a sufficient proof, which can stand of no law.

Phi. And what may a number of guilty persons confessions, work against one that is accused?

Epi. The result must serve for interpreter of our law in that respect. But in my opinion, since in a matter of treason against the Prince, children or wives, or defamed persons, may of our law serve for sufficient witnesses and proofs. I think surely that by a far greater reason, such witnesses may be sufficient in matters of high treason against God: For who but witches can be proved, and so witnesses of the doings of witches.

Phi. Indeed, I say they will be loath to put any honest man upon their counsel. But what if they accuse folk to have been present at their imaginary conventions in the spirit, when their bodies lie senseless, as you have said?

Epi. I think they are not a hair the less guilty: For the

DEMONOLOGY

Devil dare never have borrowed their shadow or similitude to that turn, if their consent had not been at it: And the consent in these turns is death of the law.

Phi. Then Samuel was a witch: For the Devil resembled his shape, and played his person in gluing response to Saul.

Epi. Samuel was dead as well before that; and so none could slander him with meddling in that unlawful art. For the cause why, as I take it, that God will not permit Satan to use the shapes or similitude of any innocent persons at such unlawful times, is that God will not permit that any innocent persons shall be slandered with that vile defection: for then the Devil would find ways anew, to calumniate the best. And this we have in proof by them that are carried with the fairy, who never see the shadows of any in that court, but of them that thereafter are tried to have been brethren and sisters of that craft. And this was likewise proved by the confession of a young Lass, troubled with spirits, laid on her by witchcraft. That although she saw the shapes of diverse men and women troubling her, and naming the persons whom these shadows represents, yet never one of them are found to be innocent, but all clearly tried to be most guilty, and the most part of them confessing the same. And besides that, I think it has been seldom hard to tell of, that any who is guilty of that crime accused, as having known them to be their marrows by eyesight, and not by hearsay, but such as were so accused of witchcraft, could not be clearly tried upon them, were at the least publicly known to be of a very evil life and reputation: So jealous is God I say, of the fame of them that are innocent in such causes. And besides that, there are two other good helps that may be used for their trial: the one is the finding of their mark, and the trying the insensible nature thereof. The other is their fleeting on the water: for as in a secret murder, if the dead carcass be at any time thereafter handled by the murderer, it will gush out of blood, as if the blood were crying to the heaven for revenge of the murderer, God having appointed that secret supernatural sign, for trial of that secret unnatural crime, so it appears that God has appointed (for a supernatural sign of the monstrous impiety of the witches) that the water shall refuse to receive them in her bosom, that have shaken off them the sacred water of Baptism, and willfully refused the benefit thereof: No not so much as their eye are able to shed tears (threaten and torture them as you please) while first they repent (God not permitting them to dissemble their obstinacy in so horrible a crime) albeit the women kind especially, be able otherwise to shed tears at every light occasion when they will, yea, although it were altogether like the crocodiles.

Phi. Well, we have made this conference to last as long as leisure would permit: And to conclude then, since I am to take my leave of you, I pray God to purge this country of these Devilish practices, for they were never so rife in these parts, as they are now.

Epi. I pray God that so be to. But the causes are over manifest, that makes them to so so rife. For the great wickedness of the people on the one part, procures this horrible defection, whereby God justly punishes sin, by a greater iniquity. And on the other part, the consummation of the world, and our deliverance drawing near, makes Satan to rage the more in his instruments, knowing his kingdom to be so near an end. And so farewell for this time.

THE END

DEMONOLOGY

DEMONOMANIA AND WITCHCRAFT

Joseph Workman M.D., 1871

I presume there is hardly a member of this Association who has had the good fortune to be unacquainted with that distressing form of insanity, which is known under the designation Demonomania; and I am sure none who have had to encounter it in some of its intense forms, will deny that it is one of the greatest difficulties presented to our specialty. I fear that in its treatment we seldom derive much valuable aid from the quarter to which we have some right to look for it; yet we should feel most thankful for even the most trifling assistance in our arduous work.

Belief in diabolic possession as an existing fact of the present day, may, I think, be said to be extinct, unless among the least educated portions of society. It is not to be expected, that a doctrine, which, less than two centuries ago, pervaded the whole of Christendom, and was preached from every pulpit, and proclaimed from every bench of justice, could utterly die out among the uncultured masses in Any very short lapse of time. I have myself met with persons, not insane, who have avowed their belief in its present existence. I well remember one instance in the institution under my charge, when I requested a clergyman to see, and, with a view to her mental relief, to converse with a poor woman who was suffering under that strange form of insanity known as Lycanthropia. She believed herself to be a wolf, or a dog, and she declared she was laboring under Hydrophobia. She used to spit, and grin, and snap her teeth, as if anxious to bite, and would tell us to stand off, or she would destroy us. My simple minded clerical friend went to her bedside, and spoke to her very soothingly. She responded to his address in a series of lupine, or canine demonstrations, which utterly horrified him. He fled from the room, and when he recovered his mental equilibrium, said to me, "Oh Doctor! that

DEMONOLOGY

woman is possessed!" I replied, she certainly was, but not of the devil; for I had opened too many bodies of deceased maniacs, to believe that there was any necessity for ascribing their delusional extravagances to any supernatural agency. The ascription of insanity, and other maladies which involve a pathological condition of the brain and nervous system, to demoniacal influences, was, with our ancestors, a very easy mode of solving the great question of causation, which even now so much perplexes the cultivators of psycho-pathology. Across the long and deeply indented peninsula which we are now endeavoring to explore and to fathom, inch by inch, they made a very convenient short cut, which certainly saved them a great deal of time and laborious investigation; but their conclusion did not tend to the alleviation of human misery.

Of all the departments of diabolic sovereignty, none was so prolific in the literature of divinity and jurisprudence of the 15th, 16th, and 17th centuries, as sorcery and witchcraft. Bodin, one of the most brilliant and profound jurisconsults and historians that France ever produced, left a work upon each subject, which the most able writers of later times, have characterized as masterpieces of erudition; for Bodin renounces all claims to originality. He gives us the "opinions of a multitude of the greatest writers of pagan antiquity, and of the most illustrious of the fathers." In short he rests his whole argument on anecdotes. The last resource, as all men in the present day know, of all writers who fail to convince their readers by force of reason, and an appeal to the ordeal of common sense.

Shortly after the publication of Bodin's work on Sorcery, Wier, a physician of Cloves, in the middle of the 16th century, wrote a book, entitled, "De Prestigiis Daemonum." He, as a doctor, (of medicine be it noted,) declared his conviction that many of the so-called victims of diabolic possession were simply lunatics; a verdict which, I am sure every member of this association, living and moving, as we do, among the same class of unfortunates in the present day, will most unreservedly endorse.

It was hardly to be expected that this writer would, at a bound, over-leap the boundaries of popular error, and set at defiance that reverence for authority, which was then regarded as the cardinal virtue of all literature and all philosophy. He believed, (or affected to believe,) that the world was peopled by crowds of demons, who were constantly doing mischief; but he endeavored to reconcile their ubiquitous manifestations with the simple phenomena of corporeal disease; exactly that which we now do. He did not believe that the possessed ones had entered, as was then the universal belief, into any unholy compact with Satan, but that they were merely his passive subjects; nor that they were guilty of those evil deeds, of which many of them accused themselves; but rather that Satan had villainously persuaded them that they had actually, of their own free will and motion, so done.

If we should inquire what has been, among a variety of the learned of the present day, the advance made by them on the theory of Wier, what might be the response to our question? Wier did not, as James VI. of Scotland did, believe that witches raised terrific sea storms, and wrecked noble argosies, nor ride through the air on broomsticks, to participate in the horrid orgies of their Witch-Sabbath nor become, as James and other not less erudite authorities have told us, the concubines of Satan; yet he did believe that these poor demented beings were still the vassals of the Arch-Fiend.

Three editions of Wier's book were published in a short time, and it was translated into French in 1569. Its appearance in this language aroused the indignation of Bodin, who declared he could not find words meet to express his astonishment, that a puny doctor of physic should have dared to oppose himself to the authority of all ages; and to question the existence of the most notorious of all facts. He declared Wier's impiety to be even greater than his audacity, for he "had armed himself against God." He declared Wier's attempt to save from fire, those whom Scripture and the voice of the church had branded as the worst of criminals, the very climax of treason against the Almighty.

Bodin's second work was provoked by Wier's heresy, and it must certainly be one of the richest depositories of demoniacal erudition, and of Satanic inspiration, to be found in the whole domain of bibliography. Take as an example, the following deliverance, with respect to the best means of extorting from the accused, confessions of their guilt. "Sharp pincers should be inserted between the nails and flesh, such as are in use in Turkey."

We shall see, by and by, that James VI., was not unskilled in this witch art. "Some magistrates are in the habit," Bodin tells us, "of employing counterspells," which he declares to be a perilous course. He would have torture in ordinary cases only after failure of other means. He would first try terror, by letting them see the implements of torture, and hearing frightful cries, as if from one under the infliction. He tells of one functionary who had a countenance so terrific as to frighten all courage out of the guilty. This sort of experiment, he naively lets us know, is more proper towards timid than towards impudent persons. Spies who should feign being themselves accused of similar crime, he says, were most valuable witnesses.

The law of evidence, as laid down by Bodin, is so grotesquely ludicrous, that it would be impossible to restrain our laughter, did we not know that this famous jurisconsult's deliverances, on this subject, became a text authority, even more abiding than the commentaries of Blackstone, Coke, or Littleton, and that thousands were under its dictation consigned to the flames.

First and strongest among the proofs of diabolic

possession, he places the notarial document between Satan and his witch disciple, which, as it appears, needed not the sign manual of the former, but only that of the latter. The great German poet Goethe, in the preliminary arrangement between Faust and Mephistopheles, shows us that the signature of the endowed must be written with blood, for, says his high-commissioners hip;

"Blut ist ein gauz besondres Saft."

Bodin does not seem to insist upon red ink. Indeed it is probable that in the days of Bodin not many of the witches were competent in the art of penmanship, and therefore their signatures, in full, could hardly be insisted upon. They could not, however, have signed by the mark of the cross, for so orthodox a catholic as Bodin was, would well know, that this form of subscription would have upset the whole arrangement. He tells us that a second indisputable proof is, if the accused speak to the devil, and he, though invisible, answers.

How many asylum physicians, were the jurisprudence of today the same as in the time of Bodin, would be found most valuable corroborative witnesses, in this direction! Could we not tell very marvelous tales of the interviews and colloquies which some of our patients assure us they have had with Satan, or his emissaries?

It is also, says Bodin, a valid proof, if the witch has been found absent from her bed, when all the doors were locked. In this case she must have gone out through the key-hole, which, unless she really was a witch, she certainly could not do.

Bodin describes fifteen detestable species of crime perpetrated by sorcerers, or witches, some of which must, in the age of credulity in which he wrote, have appeared atrocious beyond all measure of punitive retribution. One of these was doing homage and sacrifice to the devil; and of this an unobliteratable proof remained in the mark of the "osculum in tergo" which I may be excused from rendering into plain English. All readers of witch history are well aware of the abominable indecencies involved in this judicial tenet.

The last of Bodins fifteen diabolic crimes, and the most tremendous of all, was that of sexual intercourse with demons, and the procreation of juniors, who, if we may believe all that has been recorded of them, were by no means unworthy of their illustrious sires; some indeed of the writers on the subject of demonology, seem to think the stock was enriched by this crossing-out process.

In support of this theory of multiplication of the race of demons, Bodin, who never wrote unauthorizedly, quotes freely from the early fathers, especially from Justin Martyr, Tertullian, Lactantius, and St. Augustine. The publication of Bodin's treatise gave a new and tremendous stimulus to public zeal in the discovery and extirpation of witches, and as he strongly advocated the punishment by burning, the result was an incalculable amount of human agony from this terrible infliction.

The most illustrious demonologist in our mother country was the British Solomon, James VI., of Scotland, and I. of England. He published his brochure on witches at Edinburgh in 1597, and shortly after his accession to the throne of England, he deemed it expedient, by a second edition in London, to enlighten his new subjects on the recondite science of which he was so profound a master. In his introduction he tells his readers that "the fearful abounding at this time, in this country, of those detestable slaves of the devil, the witches, or enchanters, has moved him of conscience to resolve the doubting hearts of many, both that such assaults of Satan are most certainly practiced, and that the instruments deserve most severely to be punished." He was not slow in following up his philanthropic purpose, for in the very first year of his English reign, he secured from a parliament overpowered by the forcible logic of his treatise, the enactment of the celebrated Witch Act, a law more bloody and more lasting than was the code of Draco, for it remained unrepealed until the middle of the last century. James had received from the witches of his native country much provocation. His conjugal alliance with the house of Denmark came very near frustration, in consequence of a terrific storm raised by the witches, during the voyage of James and his bride, to Scotland.

One Dr. Fian, was accused as the ringleader of a witch circle comprising some 40 or 50, who were all duly disposed of, according to the jurisprudence of the time.

He confessed, under the torture, as did many a wretched witch, to his guilt, but he, immediately after, retracted his confession. "Every form of torture was then in vain employed to vanquish his obduracy. The bones of his legs were broken into small pieces in the iron boot. All the tortures that Scottish law knew of were successively, but wonderful to say, not successfully applied. At last the King, (that 'most dread sovereign') who presided in person over the tortures, arising like 'the sun in his strength' suggested, (having no doubt read Bodin's treatise,) a new and more horrible device."

"The prisoner who had been removed during the deliberation, was brought in, and, in the words of the record of the trial, 'his nails upon all his fingers were riven and pulled off with an instrument called in Scottish a turkas, which in England we call a pair of pincers, and under every nail there was thrust in two needles over, even up to the heads; but so deeply had the devil entered into his heart, that he utterly denied all that which he before avouched, and he was burnt unconfessed.'"

Scotland has done due honor to many of her gifted sons; but I am not aware that she has yet erected a monument in

DEMONOLOGY

commemoration of this noblest of her martyrs.

It is hardly to be supposed that a monarch who was so highly eulogized by the most eminent and learned divines of his time, would fail to impress all classes with a strong conviction of the necessity of a vigilant enforcement of his Witch Act. It assuredly did not remain a dead letter on the statute book. Witch drowning, hanging, and burning soon became familiar facts in the land ruled by his "Dread Majesty" and yet witches did not decrease in number. On the contrary they seemed to spring up, phoenix like, from the ashes of the destroyed ones. It is a fact well known to British sportsmen, that hares are always most numerous in those parts where they are hunted. I remember once spending a considerable time, constantly out of doors, in a district where there was no hunting. I never saw a single hare there; but when my field duty brought me nearer to the hound kennels, then I would see one in almost every field. Indeed I knew of two sagacious old ones who resided in a meadow close to a kennel. It was said by skilled persons that these creatures, knowing that the hounds were never cast off so near home, had concluded that they would have quieter lodging here than further away from their persecutors.

Whether a similar state of matters obtained in the days of witchdom, I am unable to state. It is however an unquestionable fact, that wherever and whenever witches were most actively hunted after, they were most abundant. In the short period of Cromwell's usurpation, (and in justice to the illustrious house of the Stewarts, the fact should not be withheld,) more witches were destroyed in England, than in all the rest of the period during which the witch mania prevailed.

It has been calculated that from 1603 to 1680, the total put to death by regular legal process alone, was about 70,000, and if in the ten years of exclusion of the Stewarts from the throne, over 35,000 witches were destroyed, the annual number must have been over 35,000, or nearly 10 per day, Sundays not

DEMONOLOGY

excluded. In those days the office of witch-finder was one of no small distinction. In the county of Suffolk, one of this class of public functionaries, seems to have done keen service. His name was Matthew Hopkins. Butler in that imperishable depiction of Puritanical hypocrisy, ignorance, and superstition, his *Hudibras*, alludes to the efficiency with which this gifted personage performed his task (See Canto III., of part 2, line 139 *et postea*.)

> "Hath not this present parliament
> A ledger to the devil sent
> Fully empowered to treat about
> Finding revolted witches out?
> And has not he within a year
> Hanged three score of them in one shire?
> Some only for not being drowned,
> And some for sitting above ground
> Whole days and nights upon their breeches,
> And feeling pain, were hanged for witches.
> And some for putting knavish tricks
> Upon green geese and turkey chicks."

But "transient is the smile of fate," for Butler a little farther on tells us, this adept witch-finder;

> "After proved himself to be a witch
> And made a rod for his own breech."

Even the most zealous opponent of capital punishment might hesitate to say it was here inadmissible. Among the sixty Suffolk victims of that fearful year, was an unfortunate Episcopalian clergyman of eighty years old. The pious Baxter calls him an "old reading parson" and informs us that he confessed to being possessed of two imps, a good and a bad one; a circumstance in which I imagine he pretty much resembled ourselves. The one was always prompting him to evil deeds; but the other faithfully restrained him from them, until one unlucky day as he was walking on the sea-shore, he saw a ship at a distance. The evil imp urged him to sink the ship, and he did so, too promptly for the good imp to interpose. Have you, gentlemen, not met with men quite as potent in sinking ships as was this old doting "reading parson?" Verily you have, many such. I have under my care a man who built our asylum at Boston, and transported it to Toronto by means of a huge balloon, and this feat was but ft trifle compared with hundreds of others done by him.

Poor old Parson Lewis saw the ship, and he believed he could sink her, though many miles from him. She at once disappeared, therefore he had sunk her. It is too probable that when some of us reach four score years, we may have similar visual experience, but it is to be hoped we may not be similarly deceived; and it surely is no trivial blessing that we live in an age when natural phenomena are more rationally interpreted than they were in that of Cromwell.

The poor "old reading parson," was, to the entire satisfaction of Baxter, subjected to the ordeal of water in which he was more expert than he believed the ship had been, which he said he had sunk; but to escape drowning was but the most certain step to hanging, and he was hanged accordingly. It booted not that he had been for fifty years, an exemplary minister of religion.

Poor man! he shared in the superstition of the times; he confessed to his own demoniac possession; and in those days this was enough. Who knows but that he may himself, ere while, have lent a hearty cooperation in the destruction of witches? It would be an almost wondrous fact that he had not. I have not given in full the details of this poor man's sufferings. It is almost impossible to restrain one's risible proclivities, in the perusal of the worse than lunatic records of the judicial proceedings of our sapient ancestors, in witch cases, yet the subject is certainly not one at all harmonizing with merriment.

DEMONOLOGY

Would that we could erase from our history the entire record! But we cannot; perhaps it is best so, for who can say how nearly now we approach the domain of mental darkness, and puerile credulity? Until we shall have outlived the marvels of table-jumping, spiritualistic telegraphs between living experts and departed disciples, the inscrutable untying of Davenport knots, and the hundred and one other supenaturalities which follow one another in a succession which threatens to be as interminable as human gullibility, we shall do well not to laugh at the follies and faults of our forefathers.

At the close of the 17th century the belief in witchcraft had, partially at least, died out. A few trials and executions took place in the first 20 years of the 18th century, but unless among the very ignorant and a small section of the clergy, the doctrine seemed to have become obsolete. Though Chief Justice, Sir Matthew Hale, sentenced witches to death without compunction, and took advantage of the occasions for delivering to his audiences very learned and lengthened expositions of it, the reality of witchcraft and diabolism generally; and though Blackstone was a believer, and has told us that Addison also was of the number; yet, the superstition had to die, and to leave the poor witches to live. A judge of assize at the trial of one Jane Wenham, about the time last mentioned, had the hardihood to charge the jury strongly in the poor woman's favor; but he was a little in advance of the men whom he addressed, for despite his charge they brought in a verdict of guilty. The judge, however, readily obtained from government a reversal of the sentence which he had been reluctantly obliged to pass. But, poor man! now came his terrible trial; one of the witnesses for the prosecution had been the parson of Jane Wenham's parish; and he swore "on his faith as a clergyman he believed the woman to be a witch." The judge laid the birch on his parsonship rather smartingly; and he felt it. His brethren took up the cudgels, and waged a tremendous pamphlet war.

They finally drew up a declaration of their unabated

DEMONOLOGY

faith in witchcraft, which they closed with the portentous words, "*liberavimus animas noatras*" Thus did they ease their consciences. Assuredly the doctrine did not die in silence. From 1691 to 1718, when its moribund condition had become manifest, immense efforts were made to resuscitate it. Twenty-five books of various bulk, were published in its support, in England alone. One of these was written by the celebrated Richard Baxter. He was prompted to this labor of love by reading Cotton Mather's narrative of the Massachusetts witch trials.

Baxter was much edified by the details, and did his best to stir up the English public to an imitation of the efforts of Mather and his twin assassin Parris, whom many of you, gentlemen, will recognize as the grand center of that sewing circle, by virtue of whose hysterical and maniacal evolutions and revolutions, the witches' hill at Salem was so fearfully enriched with victims. I may be allowed to pass over in silence this afterpiece to the great European tragedy.

You are, no doubt, better read in its history than I am; and yet I can not help saying, I wish I knew less of it for it exposes to view the weaknesses, and wickedness of a few men belonging to a valuable class whom no good Christian desires to lower in popular esteem; yet it is my honest conviction that parson Parris, of Salem, was one of the greatest scoundrels that ever gave notoriety to the witch mania. But the very enormity of this man's exploits, in all probability, brought the witchcraft mania to a much earlier close on this continent than otherwise it might have had. His victims were, as an able writer in the Edinburgh Review for July, 1868, has truly said, "the wisest, gentlest, and purest Christians his parish contained. Had they not been such, who can say how long the murderous superstition would have survived; for the colony of Massachusetts was founded in the time of James I., who had given his royal patronage and exalted scriptural support, in propagation of this article of Satanic faith. The Puritan fathers who fled from the Devil, in the shape of bishops, in England, still found his ubiquitous Highness in even more multiform manifestation in the New World.

Every red Indian, who lurked and skulked around their clearings through the day, and at night ruthlessly fired their dwellings, and spared neither age nor sex was surely to them no other than a missionary from Hell, and when they found suitable opportunity they dealt with him as such. It was short logic, to ascribe all their terrible trials and sufferings to Satan. Had they continued to recognize his agency only in this relation, they would have escaped the honors of Salem witch-hill; but in those days no department of human affairs was considered exempt from Satanic domination.

Mr. Parris unfortunately got into a little altercation with some of his flock, on the delicate questions of salary, firewood, and the homestead title. All who opposed him, or spoke of him irreverently, he speedily cataloged, and by the aid of his little girl circle, and his two servants, John, and Tituba his wife, he managed to rid his congregation of not a few of these children of iniquity.

It must have been a scene infinitely richer than any of our modern spiritualistic circles can extemporize, when Mr. Parris assembled all the divines he could collect at his parsonage, and made his troop of girls go through their performances; for when they had ended their farce, a general groan issued from the reverend spectators, "over the manifest presence of the Evil One, and a passionate intercession for the afflicted children" was made. These children were suffering under the evil practices of the witches; that is to say, of those naughty people who grudged Mr. Parris a good salary, abundance of firewood, and his personal ownership of the parsonage.

It was a fearful thing in those times to be called a bad

DEMONOLOGY

name by a parson. It is very unpleasant even in the present day, to be met with harsh epithets, where we might hope for calm discussion. We must not, however, be over angry with those who have recourse to such weapons; for they would not wield them had they any better at command; and the rational world now regards all recourse to this sort of battle, as but tantamount to an acknowledgment of utter defeat.

The repeal of the witch laws in England, in 1738, was an anomalous constitutional fact, which in the present day could not occur there, nor in this country; for it was a measure in utter antagonism with popular sentiment.

The mass of the people, and the almost entire body of the clergy of all denominations, were opposed to it; and, for long years after, strenuous efforts for the restoration of the former regime were put forth. In 1768 John Wesley lamented the shocking decadence that had befallen "the belief in witches and apparitions."

I shall not venture to quote his words, lest they might sound offensive; suffice it to say they were more earnest than discreet. Five years after Wesley's protest, "the divines of the associated Presbeter of Scotland passed resolutions, declaring their belief in witchcraft, and deploring the skepticism that was then general." (Macaulay; *Hist*. VIII., p. 706.)

We surely should not be surprised to find that, even now, only a century from the above declarations of men who have left on the world abiding and deep marks of their genius and influence, the belief in witchcraft and diabolic possession still lingers among the uncultured portions of society. In September, 1863, a man was beaten to death, by a mob of 70 mechanics and small tradesmen, in the county of Essex, England, because they believed he was a witch. Some six months ago, at New market, England, a man who had agreed to expel a witch or some such unearthly thing, from a haunted house, was obliged to take legal process to recover the amount of the contract- some £18 or £20.

The Bench directed that he should be paid ordinary laboring-man's wages. How shameful! The defendant did not deny that the witch, or ghost, had been expelled. He must, therefore, have been benefited to the extent of the rent; so that if value was not given, it certainly was received. Perhaps the Judge had some suspicion that the ghost was of the Bryan O'Linn stamp.

> "Bryan O'Linn had no watch to put on,
> So he scooped out a turnip, to make him a one;
> He slipped in a cricket, clane under the skin,
> 'They'll think it is tickin',' says Bryan O'Linn."

The world abounds in Bryan O'Linn crickets, and if the Newmarket ghost was not one, I am sure it very easily might have been. What, however, has become of the great family of the witches? One would reasonably suppose that after they ceased to be exterminated, they must have multiplied with fearful rapidity.

It is not on record that, like the Kilkenny cats, they ate each other up; yet they died off as soon as they ceased to be killed. Seventy thousand, we are informed by history, were destroyed in England in a little over seventy years. At the present day there are in England, Ireland and Scotland about this number of insane persons lodged in asylums. Is there one of you, gentlemen, who live among this afflicted class in this country, who doubts that in the time of witch hunting and burning and hanging, at least one-half of the 70,000 lunatics whose support costs so much to the already over-taxed people of the United Kingdom, would have been far more cheaply disposed of? We protect, and house, and feed, and clothe, and soothe the poor witches- yea, and by these simple means, do we not expel the Devil out of a great many? We do! And is it not marvelous that kindness is so potent, even over this wretch? Unkindness had utterly failed to exorcise him; but since, the true Gospel of Him who restored to a distracted father, an epileptic lunatic son, sane in mind and sound in body, has been, not merely preached in frothy words, but acted out in heavenly deeds, what a change has come over the dream of witchdom! Thousands and thousands of unreal, innocent sorcerers and enchanters were burned and hanged, in former times; but the greatest of all the modern tribe escaped- and that man was Pinel. He drove out Satan, by unchaining him. The brute could not look Pinel in the face, for heavenly charity beamed from his bewitching eyes.

Wonderful yet to say, Pinel's head was saved from the block, by one of the possessed whom he had loosed from the bonds of Satan!

I am sure, gentlemen, you every one know how irresistible is the charm by which Pinel subdued Satan; for I know it is the one almost sole, curative agency by which our statistics are enriched- and certainly the statistics of American institutions for the treatment of insanity, need not blush under comparison with those of any other country.

Should it be alleged by critics of the outside world, less familiar than we are with the delusions of insanity, and with the terrible mental sufferings attendant upon some of them, that a brief exposition, such as this paper, of an antiquated and exploded fallacy, is at this day, before an association of alienistic physicians, uninstructive and uncalled for, I would simply observe, that very few of the delusions of the insane spring up indigenously.

If we carefully and closely investigate the early training, and the past domestic and social formative influences, which have molded the moral and intellectual characters of our patients, and have implanted in their minds those persistent habits of thought which become the semi-instinctive leaders and directors of maturer life, I think we shall not rashly conclude that their ravings are all of spontaneous generation.

Certainly there is not one of us who would not be gratified with the knowledge that the seed of these tares had never been sown. To root them out, and avoid injuring the wheat, is our task, and it is truly an arduous and a delicate one. I can think of no more distressing position for a physician to be placed in, than that of the responsible charge of an afflicted fellow-being, laboring under the delusion of having committed the unpardonable sin, because of his having become possessed by Satan. You all know how commonly this mental condition is associated with persistent suicidal propensity.

I could, as you are well aware, exhibit a multitude of details in confirmation of this fact; but such expositions of the frailties and sufferings of our patients, though attractive to the sensational and empty-headed classes, are by no means pleasant exercises to the writers; and assuredly they must prove very painful to those among our hearers, or readers, who have stood in close relation with the unhappy ones alluded to.

That there may be, or are, fulminating pulpit orators, who will not be admonished by anything short of the *experimentum crucis* who will not believe, before they have, as Thomas, thrust their fingers into the pierced side, and into the nail prints of their victims, I question not; for they are not unknown to me.

Is there not, gentlemen, a great lesson to the sane world, to be learned among the insane? If men require to learn the omnipotence of kindness, do you know of a better school than the modem lunatic asylum? If they require to be taught that unkindness, and cruelty, and terror, effect no real change of conduct and character, but on the contrary always render the subjects of them more obdurate and vicious than before, then let them take up their abodes for a sufficient time, among the inmates of our institutions. There they would be the right men in right places, and both themselves and the community at large would be immense gainers by the probation.

I have abstained from details of the atrocities resulting from the witchcraft superstition in the continental nations of Europe; not because they were less horrid than those perpetrated in our mother country, or because protestantism was more guilty, in this relation, than the olden church; but simply because the limits of a paper, for such an occasion as the present, preclude a wider excursion; and to tell the whole truth, I do not think that the confession of our neighbor's sins, instead of our own, is either a commendable, or a useful virtue, though we all know it is a very prevalent one.

Whether any good may result from the remarks which the experience of the members of this association may enable them to offer on the general subject of Demonomania, I dare not anticipate; but I can see no possibility of injury to the victims of this terrible form of mental alienation likely to proceed from them; and whithersoever duty calls us, thither unfaltering we are bound fearlessly to advance.

THE END

DEMONS AND TONGUES

Alma White, 1910

CHAPTER I

DEMON POSSESSION - GREATEST CALAMITY - SPIRITUAL BEARINGS LOST – SATAN'S MIGHTIEST WEAPON – THE LATTER RAIN - SPURIOUS LOVE - MIRACLES CLAIMED - RELIGIOUS DEMONS - PERVERT THE TRUTH - A CORRUPT TREE – VIGOROUS WARFARE NECESSARY - THE LONE PROPHET

"There is a way which seemeth right unto a man, but the end thereof are the ways of death"

(Prov. 14:12)

This scripture came to mind as we thought of the condition of backsliders, and others, who have been caught in the Satanic "Tongues" delusion, which, during the past few years, has swept like a pestilence over the globe. A person who has fallen from grace is in a deplorable state and is to be pitied, even when he realizes his condition, but how much more dreadful it is to be possessed with demons and not know it. Of all calamities that could possibly befall a person this side of eternity, this appeals to us as being the worst. When the Holy Spirit is grieved away, the door is open and demons enter as angels of light and take possession of the heart. They do not say, "We are demons and have come to sink your soul into perdition," but they talk like angels. In other words, they claim to be the Holy Ghost, and thus deceive and destroy the soul. From a personal knowledge of and actual acquaintance with many who have been swept away by the "Tongues" delusion, we know, that through disobedience or refusal to consecrate themselves to God, they lost their spiritual bearings and have been backslidden, some of them, for years. Of course it was Satan's opportunity to pick them up and make them dupes of his religion. When the truth is fully known it will be found that the "Tongues" adherents, with few exceptions, are persons of this character. When people refuse to take the rugged way of the Cross, they are continually looking for something to ease their consciences; Satan sees that they find it.

He stands at their right hand and says, "This is the way, walk ye in it," and without controversy they obey. When they repeatedly go against light, and refuse God's counsel and reproof, He turns away and leaves them to their fate. God helps those who do His will. "Not every one that saith unto me, Lord, Lord, shall enter into the kingdom of heaven; but he that doeth the will of my Father which is in heaven." (Matt. 7:21).

Apostate Gentiles have turned their ears unto fables, ignoring the word of God and walking after the traditions of men, hence the soil of their hearts is ready for the devil's own planting. The good seed finds no lodging-place. But God is merciful enough not to leave them without warning. He has a few people in these days of awful peril who are exposing the works of the devil, and faithfully proclaiming His word and truth. The so-called Apostolic movement, known as the "Tongues," is an invention of Satan to shut people's eyes to the apostate condition of Christendom.

Its purpose is to make a great religious display and lull the multitudes to sleep in their cradles of carnal security, just at the close of the Gentile age. Satan knows that his days are few and he must lose no time; that the day is not far distant when the angel will descend from heaven with a chain to bind him and cast him into the bottomless pit, where the key will be turned on him for a thousand years. His mightiest weapon of warfare is a counterfeit religion. He must make people believe that the world is growing better, and he disguises himself and comes as an angel of light, bringing with him this so-called Pentecostal baptism with the sign of tongues. To his satisfaction the great multitudes of professors have cooled off and many are ready for just such a counterfeit or to accept anything under the name of Pentecost he may hand out to them. He tells them that Zechariah's prophecy (Zech. 14:7), which says, "At evening time it shall be light," is being fulfilled in the spread of the "Tongues" movement over the globe, that "The Latter Rain" is falling upon the Gentiles and there is now a world-wide revival and that hundreds and thousands are receiving their Pentecost.

The prophecy which says, "At evening time it shall be light," and those concerning "the latter rain," have reference to the Jews, and will be fulfilled after they are gathered back to Palestine. All this talk about the latter rain is a misappropriation of Scripture that belongs to the Jews, as is plain to be seen: "Be glad then, ye children of Zion, and rejoice in the Lord your God: for he hath given you the former rain moderately, and he will cause to come down for you the rain, the former rain, and the latter rain in the first month. And the floors shall be full of wheat, and the fats shall overflow with wine and oil. And I will restore to you the years that the locust hath eaten, the cankerworm, and the caterpillar, and the palmerworm, my great army which I sent among you." (Joel 2:23-25).

Gentiles have no claim whatever to the literal fulfillment of the prophecies concerning the latter rain. Instead of light coming to them they are being enshrouded in the greatest spiritual darkness that has ever been known in the history of the Gospel age. Many persons have signed pledges and quit the drink and other habits without ever having been converted, and there may be in the "Tongues" movement those who have reformed, but this they could do and not have a particle of spiritual light. Salvation begins in the heart and works outward. Those who have once had the Spirit of God are not so likely to fall back into the old paths of outward sin; they are more likely to be brought under the power of some delusion, never getting their eyes open until they wake up in perdition.

DEMONOLOGY

Satan does not care how high a person's outward standard of morals may be just so his imps can have a lodging place in his heart. He can better accomplish his purpose when one is not outwardly wicked.

There is a spurious love existing among the "Tongues" folk which is extremely revolting. When Satan is trying to deceive a person with false religion he is too shrewd to come as a roaring lion, but brings his counterfeit of Divine love which always appeals to the carnal mind and is readily accepted by those who are caught by his heresies. The "Tongues" people claim miracle-working power in the healing of diseases just as the Christian Scientists have claimed it for years. At the beginning of each new era in the history of both Jews and Gentiles, there have been great demonstrations of power. The true Church will never lose the gifts of the Spirit nor the power of working miracles. It is not necessary, however, at the close of the Gentile dispensation for miracles to be worked to prove the divinity of Christ. His divinity has already been established.

In fulfillment of prophecy, men have hardened their hearts; the Holy Spirit has been rejected and demons are strongly entrenched in human habitations, and, like a criminal, apostate Christendom is under the Divine sentence and must pay the penalty. God owes no favors to those who have refused His counsel and insulted His Spirit. The gallows for their execution, figuratively speaking, is already prepared. There are a few people, however, who have kept their garments unspotted from the world and are robed and ready to meet their coming Lord when He appears in the clouds of His glory.

When a religious demon enters the heart, he will sing, preach and pray through his victim, and in fact do almost anything that one does who has real salvation. He is usually equipped with plenty of religious paraphernalia. He has a lingo that sounds like the language of Canaan, and the unwary pilgrim will be taken in his net. He even talks about the blood of the atonement and the coming of Christ. If He did not there would be no danger of his deceiving the very elect. He comes with an open Bible and claims that his arguments are based upon the word of God; he can quote scripture and pervert it to perfection.

A smooth-tongued hypocrite thus demonized can do more real damage than a host of sinners who make no profession. The fountain of iniquity from within sends forth an unclean stream; the tongue speaks perverse things. It is a critical time when those who profess to be righteous, neither call for justice nor plead for the truth, and we personally know that many among the "Tongues" people who claim "the baptism" with the sign of tongues, are ever ready to pervert the truth.

They will take up and spread an evil report and they always find a hearing among those of their own kind. The love of the truth is not in them.

Isaiah says of such, "They hatch cockatrice' eggs, and weave the spider's web; he that eateth of their eggs dieth, and that which is crushed breaketh out into a viper." No stronger statements than these could be made. There is nothing more deadly than the sting of a viper, and those who listen to falsehoods and repeat them hatch cockatrice' eggs, and a nest of vipers are turned loose to bite and destroy. When one listens to and accepts a lie he is becoming inoculated with the poison of a viper. Those who have the spirit of Jesus will not do such things; they will not subsist on falsehoods and take up an evil report and carry it to others. The spider weaves a web and captures his prey in its meshes, and so does a tale-bearer weave his stories so as to catch the innocent and unwary. A tale-bearer is an encumberer of the ground and should be looked upon as such by all who love the truth. "Their webs shall not become garments, neither shall they cover themselves with their works; their works are works of iniquity, and the act of violence is in their hands." (Isa. 59:6).

DEMONOLOGY

Truth is fallen to the ground and a false standard is lifted up. God will arise, and according to the deeds of the wicked He will repay "fury to his adversaries, recompense to his enemies."

When John the Baptist told his hearers of Jesus who would baptize them with the Holy Ghost and fire, he said, "And now also the ax is laid unto the root of the trees: every tree therefore which bringeth not forth good fruit is hewn down, and cast into the fire." (Luke 3:9). The "Tongues" tree is not only corrupt (doctrinally wrong), but it is lodging all kinds of unclean birds in its branches.

The Gospel ax must hew it down, and there are not many who are able to wield the ax. This tree sprang up in a day and bears unmistakably the fruit of corruption. Any person, however profligate he may be, can get the tongues. All he needs to do is to associate with the "Tongues" folk and seek according to their directions. If he has any difficulty they will assist him by their magic devices, even taking hold and working his jaws until satisfactory results are obtained. A legion of devils were cast out of the Gadarene and seven were cast out of Mary Magdalene. If we could only know how many are hiding underneath a cloak of profession among the "Tongues" people it would be a great revelation to some who are deceived. Many an old spiritualist has attended their meetings and felt himself perfectly at home.

He recognizes the same spirits operating in a "Tongues" meeting that he does in the seance. Devil worshipers in India have had the gift of tongues, and Mormon polygamists in our own land claim to speak with the "tongues of angels." There never was a better time for witchcraft to become rooted in fruitful soil. The leaders of the apostate holiness movements are full of pride and unholy ambition, living to gratify their fleshly appetites. The rugged way of the Cross is shunned and something that appeals to the senses is sought after by leaders

DEMONOLOGY

and people.

In old times, those who were possessed with strange spirits were taken out and stoned to death that the land might be rid of witches, and it is necessary to wage as vigorous warfare against this evil today as it was in olden times. We fully realize our great responsibility, and see more and more the fight we will have to make in the midst of this wicked and perverse generation, where multitudes of professed Christians are so utterly ignorant of the power of the Holy Spirit to save, sanctify and keep free from sin. Elisha was the only prophet and evangelist in Israel that could bid Naaman's leprosy depart. "And many lepers were in Israel in the time of Eliseus the prophet; and none of them was cleansed, saving Naaman the Syrian." (Luke 4:27). For one to be healed of leprosy was an unheard of thing, but there was one man at least whom God honored, who had found such favor with Him that He could use him in the healing of a leper.

God has raised up the Pillar of Fire and placed it in the breach to enlighten the people and to bring them to the knowledge of the truth. It is no small work to expose the devil as he appears in the disguise of the Holy Ghost in this "Tongues" movement. But we are going to make the effort and leave the consequences with God.

The principalities and powers of darkness cannot stand before a prevailing Church; not because its members have any strength or might of their own, but from the fact that the God of the universe hears their cries and co-operates with them. He has all power in heaven and in earth and besides Him there is no God. When man reaches the limit of his strength, he may expect something marvelous to take place, especially when the enemies of righteousness have set themselves to destroy the work that God has called him to do. The "Tongues" adherents, whether they are aware of it or not, are being used of the devil to destroy, if possible, the last ray of spiritual light in the old holiness movement, but God is raising up a standard against them. The Church moves heaven and heaven moves earth and hell. The Lord delights to honor those who honor Him and tells them to remember that their weapons of warfare are not carnal.

"Vengeance is mine; I will repay, saith the Lord." Soon the long night of sin will be brought to a close and the day will break for those who have been faithful. The eye of faith even now beholds the rosy-tinted morning that will herald the coming of our Lord and King to reign in glory upon the earth.

CHAPTER II

SIGN-SEEKERS - A SIGN OF THE LAST DAYS - SIGNS FROM BENEATH - TONGUEISM IS SPIRITISM - MYSTERY OF INIQUITY - JUDGED BY ITS FRUIT - WANDERING STARS – THE LOVE OF MONEY - A RICH "TONGUES" EDITOR

In the 12th chapter of Matthew we find that Jesus rebuked the Pharisees who were seeking after a sign. These Pharisees were so dead spiritually that they did not know their Messiah when He came. They claimed that He was an impostor, and utterly rejected Him. They said He cast out devils by Beelzebub the prince of devils. When they desired a sign of Him, He replied, "An evil and adulterous generation seeketh after a sign; and there shall no sign be given unto it, but the sign of the prophet Jonas." (Matt. 12:39). Christ himself is this sign, His death and burial being prefigured by the three days and nights that Jonah was in the whale, and His resurrection by the ejection of the prophet onto the dry land. He further said, "The men of Nineveh shall rise up in judgment with this generation, and shall condemn it."

That is, the generation that sought after a sign. When people turn aside from the truth and go to seeking signs, they open their hearts to be deceived by men and demons. These

DEMONOLOGY

Pharisees had no conviction and no desire to repent of their sins.

They were already condemned. Heathen Nineveh received Jonah's message and repented in sackcloth and ashes, and mercy was extended unto them; but the hypocritical Pharisees who were seeking after signs refused to repent, and in their rags of self righteousness were turned over to become the habitations of demons.

"When the unclean spirit is gone out of a man, he walketh through dry places, seeking rest, and findeth none. Then he saith, I will return into my house from whence I came out; and when he is come, he findeth it empty, swept and garnished. Then he goeth, and taketh with him seven other spirits more wicked than himself, and they enter in and dwell there; and the last state of that man is worse than the first. Even so shall it be also unto this wicked generation." (Matt. 12:43-45).

There is no better illustration of this evil generation to which Jesus referred than the present "Tongues" movement, composed, as it is, of hypocritical sign-seekers. They have signs among them, but they are from beneath and not from above. It is the same old spirit of necromancy and witchcraft that has been manifested in all ages. Witchcraft belongs to the works of the flesh; wherever people are given to the over-indulgence of their fleshly appetites, it is an easy matter to become the victims of witchcraft. Josiah, king of Israel, had the land cleansed of the workers with familiar spirits. 2 Kings 23:24-25 says, "Moreover the workers with familiar spirits, and the wizards, and the images, and the idols, and all the abominations that were spied in the land of Judah and in Jerusalem, did Josiah put away, that he might perform the words of the law which were written in the book that Hilkiah the priest found in the house of the Lord. And like unto him was there no king before him, that turned to the Lord with all his heart, and with all his soul, and with all his might, according to all the law of Moses; neither after him arose there any like him."

We must wage warfare against this demon-working power if we expect to please God and have our prayers answered. The country is full of witches and wizards presenting themselves as the teachers of righteousness. "Tongueism" is spiritism, and so subtle is the enemy that it is deceiving the people in all lands. Multitudes are being brought under the influence and charm of those who claim to have obtained the Holy Ghost baptism with the sign of tongues. Ignorant of the true principles of salvation they are unable to understand the strange spirits that operate in a "Tongues" meeting and are caught by the devil's baits. It is for this class of people more especially that we write, hoping that by some means they may be recovered from the snare of the wicked one and their eyes opened to their peril before they are hopelessly engulfed in the slime pits of "Tongueism" where all kinds of heresies are bred and fostered.

"For the mystery of iniquity doth already work: only he who now letteth will let, until he be taken out of the way. Even him, whose coming is after the working of Satan with all power and signs and lying wonders, And with all deceivableness of unrighteousness in them that perish; because they received not the love of the truth, that they might be saved. And for this cause God shall send them strong delusion, that they should believe a lie: That they all might be damned who believed not the truth, but had pleasure in unrighteousness." (2 Thess. 2:7-12).

When people refuse to be reined up and go through the spiritual discipline that God seeks to give them, He sends them strong delusions which they are unable to get rid of. No amount of arguing or reasoning will cause them to see their lost condition, and they go on deceiving and being deceived. They have forsaken sound doctrines and become the advocates of heresy. Paul, in his second epistle to Timothy (4: 3-4) says, "For

DEMONOLOGY

the time will come when they will not endure sound doctrine; but after their own lusts shall they heap to themselves teachers, having itching ears; And they shall turn away their ears from the truth, and shall be turned unto fables."

We never saw so many with itching ears as are found in the "Tongues" movement. They are listening to hear of signs and wonders and they sit fascinated while remarkable stories are being told of how people who, it has been claimed, have been healed of their bodily diseases, etc. A short time ago in London, we heard of a person whom the "Tongues" people claimed was healed on receiving a handkerchief that one of their leaders in Los Angeles, California, had blessed and sent to her. We have known this man for years. When we first met him he was a practicing physician and had salvation, but we have every evidence that he has been a backslider for years. We are to judge a tree by its fruit and we know that his ministry is not bringing forth the fruit of righteousness. Like others he is looking for signs and wonders, while those under his ministry are perishing for the bread of life. There is no evidence given among his followers that they have been truly converted. To show the character of the work this man is doing, he told us on one occasion that after a few minutes' talk in one of his meetings, the power fell and about one hundred persons were converted in their seats.

There was no repentance, no restitution, no crying, "God be merciful to me a sinner," no confession of sin, no godly sorrow, yet he claimed they were converted. Who ever heard of a Holy Ghost revival under such conditions. This is worse than a card-signing affair. After the three years' ministry of our Lord on earth there were only 120 persons who waited for the descent of the Holy Ghost in the upper room. In these last days of awful peril and old church apostasy we find a person who is presumptuous enough to claim that one hundred persons were converted under the above conditions in a single meeting. Jude says of such preachers, "These are spots in your feasts of charity, when they feast with you, feeding themselves without fear; clouds they are without water, carried about of winds; trees whose fruit withereth, without fruit, twice dead, plucked up by the roots: Raging waves of the sea, foaming out their own shame; wandering stars, to whom is reserved the blackness of darkness for ever."

This man, we positively know, has helped to prepare the soil in Los Angeles for the "Tongues" heresy. The Scripture says, "For by thy words thou shalt be justified, and by thy words thou shalt be condemned." He told us about some gold mines in which he was interested, and frankly stated that some day he expected to be a very rich man. His own words were sufficient proof that he had fallen from grace. Matthew 19:24 says, "It is easier for a camel to go through the eye of a needle, than for a rich man to enter into the kingdom of God." He evidently was not expecting to take the track that Jesus took, who said, "The foxes have holes, and the birds of the air have nests; but the Son of man hath not where to lay his head."

James says, "Your gold and silver is cankered; and the rust of them shall be a witness against you, and shall eat your flesh as it were fire." It was clearly manifested that he had an exalted opinion of himself and had the love of money in his heart. The Scripture says, "For the love of money is the root of all evil: which while some coveted after, they have erred from the faith, and pierced themselves through with many sorrows. But thou, O man of God, flee these things; and follow after righteousness, godliness, faith, love, patience, meekness. Fight the good fight of faith, lay hold on eternal life." (1 Tim. 6:10-12).

There is an editor of a "Tongues" publication in California who, we are told (by the "Tongues" people), is very rich, but she is looked upon by them as being a saint. James says to the rich men, "Go weep and howl for your miseries that shall come upon you." The people of this so-called Apostolic movement are not telling the rich among them to weep and

DEMONOLOGY

howl, they tell him to seek the tongues. Jesus said, "Lay not up for yourselves treasures upon earth, where moth and rust doth corrupt, and where thieves break through and steal: For where your treasure is, there will your heart be also." Men's hearts are always with their treasures. It cannot be otherwise. The only way to get the affections on things above is to become poor in this world's goods. "Poor, yet making many rich; as having nothing, and yet possessing all things." It is God's plan to keep His children dependent upon Him for their temporal supplies, and only in this way can they live the life of faith. "Without faith it is impossible to please him."

Rich men who make a profession of religion, openly defy God's word and trample His laws under their feet; they have persecuted His prophets and martyred His saints in all ages. Jesus called them a generation of vipers and said, "How can ye escape the damnation of hell?" There are not two roads to heaven; there is only one way- the way of faith- "The just shall live by faith."

CHAPTER III

HERESIES - DENYING UNITY OF GODHEAD - THE THIRD BLESSING - STRANGE MEETINGS - THE DEVIL'S FIRE - RENOUNCE FORMER TEACHINGS – QUOTATIONS - SEEKING TONGUES TO EASE CONSCIENCE - GOD'S WARNINGS - EVIL ANGELS - MULTITUDES BEING DECEIVED

We notice in looking over the "Tongues" publications that their pages are all stamped with heresy. They teach that the baptism with the Holy Ghost and tongues is a distinct work from sanctification. They call sanctification the "baptism with blood," and claim that the Holy Spirit has nothing to do with this baptism, that the Holy Spirit did not die for humanity. What could be more abominable in the sight of God than this? While like the third blessing heresy so popular among many backsliders a few years ago, this doctrine is much worse. Ephesians 4:5 says clearly there is but "One Lord, one faith, one baptism." When carnality is destroyed by the sanctifying power of the Holy Spirit people become one in Christ, having been baptized by one Spirit into one body.

Advocates of the "Tongues" heresy do violence to the unity of the Godhead. They divide up the work of salvation among the three persons and run into tri-theism, when they deny that the Holy Spirit is our sanctifier. The Word declares that there are not three Gods, but one God in three persons. The Holy Spirit is the third person, the executive of the Godhead. He convicts the sinner, regenerates the penitent and sanctifies the Christian.

The Word teaches that we are sanctified by the Holy Spirit, that is, the Holy Spirit applies the blood, cleansing the heart from all spiritual defilement, taking possession of the temple and occupying the throne of the heart. The disciples, the "Tongues" folk say, were sanctified before Pentecost. It seems strange that any one who has had spiritual light could be swept away by such doctrines. We have every evidence that the disciples had the carnal mind until Pentecost, when the Holy Ghost fell upon them and utterly expurgated the last remains of it. The baptism of the Holy Ghost and sanctification is one and the same work, and any one who teaches differently has either never known Christ or is a backslider under the control of demons. Why should we go back on this standard teaching which God has blessed in all past ages? The great work of Pentecost was the destruction of the carnal nature, or the execution of the old man of sin. The plan of salvation has never been changed; it has been the same in all ages. Two works of grace are set forth- regeneration and sanctification. Regeneration is the imparting of life by the Holy Spirit to the dead soul. Sanctification is the removal of the carnal nature, or the body of sin that, like a dead corpse, clings to the soul after it has been regenerated. In the seventh of Romans (verse 24) we read, "O wretched man that I am! who shall deliver me from the body of this death?" The next verse gives hope; through Jesus Christ there is deliverance. The Holy Spirit utterly destroys this body of sin and fits the temple for His own indwelling, and takes possession.

A few years ago an advocate of the third blessing heresy told us that the fact that the disciples were all of one accord in one place when the Holy Spirit descended proves that they were sanctified before Pentecost. He had been in Canada and different parts of the United States gathering a few people together and erroneously teaching them that it is impossible for regenerated people to be of one accord, and used this as his strong argument that the sanctification of the disciples took place before Pentecost. He almost succeeded in making some of our own converts believe he was right and tried to convince us that we had been teaching them wrong. While he stood with his Bible in hand delivering his message to us in our own home we opened a revised version and showed him that the "one accord" was missing; that the scripture simply reads, "When the day of Pentecost was now come, they were all together in one place." (Acts 2:1, R. V.).

When he saw the complete absence of "With one accord," on which he was basing his argument, he was utterly confused and began to whirl around in the floor and shout out, "Glory to God, glory to God, glory to God!" This ended his work in the West. A short time afterwards we learned that he had died.

The "Tongues" people believe in laying aside doctrines like a person would lay off a garment, then they say, "Become passive- cease to strive- and tongues will come." This is hypnotism- the same spirits at work that are found in the spiritualistic meetings. Paul repeatedly warns Timothy about the doctrines. 1 Tim. 4:16 says, "Take heed unto thyself, and unto the doctrine; continue in them; for in doing this thou shalt both save thyself, and them that hear thee." The 13th verse says, "Till I come, give attention to reading, to exhortation, to doctrine."

The fact is, we cannot get along without doctrine, but God forbid that we should endorse the doctrines of devils. There is no way for the devil to proceed with his work in a "Tongues" meeting until he has induced people to give up sound doctrines, then he can operate upon their mental and spiritual organisms, and after they have accepted the false he has them completely under the control of his imps, and most any kind of outburst of demon power is likely to follow. It may be speaking in tongues which no one can understand or even in language that some are familiar with. Seekers of the tongues often become unconscious and remain in that state for hours.

In the "Tongues" meetings it is a fact that under strange spells people have been known to writhe like serpents, bark like dogs, mew like cats, and mimic perfectly other animals. Satan understands languages and in some instances may speak through those who yield themselves to be used as his instrumentalities. As the Gentile age draws to a close, there will be greater manifestations of demon power than have ever been known in the history of the world. One Bible commentator has said the devil's fire will fall and many will be deceived. "Man has fox fire, and the devil has hell-fire, and God has heavenly fire. The Holy Ghost is God. If you seek a baptism separate from sanctification you open the door for men and devils to deceive you with their strange fire, for which Nadab and Abihu fell dead when they offered it unto the Lord."

It hardly seems possible that so many people could be deceived by the false doctrines current in the present "Tongues" movement. Those who have refused spiritual discipline are unable to tell the difference between the Holy Spirit, and imps of perdition when they come as angels of light. Professing to know God they failed to keep the rugged track and gave way to the works of the flesh in some form.

DEMONOLOGY

The devil saw his opportunity to deceive them and took advantage of it. We find that many persons who have become the victims of the "Tongues" delusion have claimed the baptism of the Holy Ghost for years. Of course they were backslidden when they came in contact with this demon worship and they concluded that they had never had their Pentecost, and threw open the doors of their hearts and invited the "Tongues" demon to come in, which he did, only too glad to get the chance. If a legion of devils begged Jesus to let them go into the swine they would have no hesitation in entering the heart of a human being who persistently entreats them to come in. The fact is these demon seducers are taking possession of those whose hearts were once the temple of the Holy Spirit without being resisted.

In accepting the "Tongues" heresy people virtually say that all previous claims they have made to salvation are false, and that for the first time in their lives they are being enlightened. They make God out a liar. If they had any salvation they would hold fast the profession of their faith without wavering, but, according to instructions, they renounce their former teachings and spiritual light as not being of God. The testimonies of such people amount to this, "We have been hypocrites during all the years of our Christian profession, we have been deceived by the devil, and we are just now getting our eyes open to the truth." In order to worm their way out of their entanglements they go to tinkering with the doctrines. First, the candidate must be immersed in water, then follow the various works which they divide up between the different persons of the Godhead, the ultimate end of which must be muttering or jabbering in tongues.

We quote the following from a "Tongues" paper published in Chicago: "Let it be settled once and for all, that the Holy Spirit cannot save any one, and that it is no part of His work to do so." This is simply blasphemy. What could please the devil more than to have men blaspheme the Holy Ghost? "Verily I say unto you, All sins shall be forgiven unto the sons of men, and blasphemies wherewith soever they shall blaspheme: But he that shall blaspheme against the Holy Ghost hath never forgiveness, but is in danger of eternal damnation." (Mark 3:28-29). There is no greater blasphemy against the Holy Ghost than is found in this "Tongues" movement! It certainly climaxes the works of the devil in all ages.

The following is also a quotation from this publication: "What a mistake it is to give the Holy Spirit credit for all the work the blessed Christ does for us, thus robbing Him of His glory." What else can this be but blasphemy? The Word says, "For there are three that bear record in heaven, the Father, the Word (Jesus), and the Holy Ghost: and these three are one." (1 John 5:7).

When a person says that the Holy Spirit has not power of execution he virtually says that neither God nor His Son have this power, and if the truth were only known, these blasphemers are taking all the power from God and giving it to the devil, who, with his imps, is operating through them. It certainly is time for the lovers of truth and righteousness to rise up in arms against this "Tongues" movement and contend for the faith that was once delivered to the saints.

Again we quote, from the same paper: "Large numbers who know that it is Christ that is received in conversion, and who believe in sanctification as a subsequent work of grace, declare that while they did not receive the Spirit in conversion, they certainly did in sanctification. Again we say, 'No,' Jesus Christ is made unto us wisdom, righteousness, sanctification, and redemption. Then if the Spirit reveals unto us after we are saved that the Christ we received as our Savior in conversion is also made unto us sanctification and faith appropriates it, it is not the Holy Spirit we receive, it is sanctification in Jesus Christ. Further, the Holy Spirit will witness clearly to our sanctification and will bring great blessing and joy to the heart of the person who is separated unto God through the precious

DEMONOLOGY

blood of Christ. But all this is not receiving the Holy Ghost."

A few years ago, we met people who had gone into the third blessing heresy. They went from one extreme to another. After they had claimed to receive the Holy Ghost, as a third work, they sought a blessing of dynamite. After having received it, they sought the blessing of lyddite, which, they said, was even stronger than dynamite. At this juncture those who had at first advocated the third blessing made a protest declaring that they would not go any further. Then their meetings broke up in a row. This was God's way of answering our prayers in behalf of those who were being swept away by the false doctrines.

The persistence shown by some of the adherents of the present "Tongues" heresies in trying to get others under the same demon-working power is shocking, but thank God, there are a few persons yet who cannot be brought under the control of demons. There is a saying that we have often heard, "You can fool some of the people all of the time, and all of the people some of the time, but you cannot fool all of the people all of the time."

We can say with St. Paul, "For I know whom I have believed, and am persuaded that he is able to keep that which I have committed unto him against that day." (2 Tim. 1:12). The next verse says, "Hold fast the form of sound words, which thou hast heard of me, in faith and love which is in Christ Jesus." Paul had reference here to sound doctrine. He says also that all that were in Asia turned away from him and mentions Phygellus and Hermogenes. These persons who turned away may have kept up their profession, but they embraced false doctrines, or in other words, the doctrines of devils. He mentioned Onesiphorus who had often refreshed Him and was not ashamed of his chain. By this we know that those who left him were ashamed of his chain.

There was too much reproach in connection with it for

them. They wanted a popular religion, and of course the devil had it for them. Paul declared that he was not ashamed of the Gospel, that it is the power of God unto salvation unto every one that believeth. The "Tongues" people laid down the Cross before they embraced the doctrines of devils. There is no reproach of the Cross connected with getting the modern tongues, from the fact they originated in perdition. There are some persons among them who claim they are being persecuted. This may be true, but it is not for righteousness' sake. No doubt some of them in their deceived and deluded condition actually suffer. There are all kinds of divisions and dissensions among those who are given up to demon worship. There are carnal professors who have not yielded themselves to these spirits who will oppose those who have. It is the same old carnal warfare that has been manifested in churches and political parties all down the ages. All classes of people are found seeking the tongues without repenting of their sins or meeting the conditions of the Scriptures in any sense. Those who have been rebelling against God for years will go to a "Tongues" meeting and seek tongues to ease their consciences.

Isaiah describes their spiritual condition: "The whole head is sick, and the whole heart faint. From the sole of the foot even unto the head there is no soundness in it; but wounds, and bruises, and putrefying sores; they have not been closed, neither bound up, neither mollified with ointment." Such persons ought to read the tenth and eleventh verses (chapter 1), and profit by them: "Hear the word of the Lord, ye rulers of Sodom; give ear unto the law of our God, ye people of Gomorrah. To what purpose is the multitude of your sacrifices unto me?" The "Tongues" movement is of the flesh and of the devil, and as truly can God call the leaders, "Rulers of Sodom," as He did backslidden Israel in the days of old. He will unsheathe His sword and uncover this mess of carnality. The day is not far distant when all those who have been found taking part in their meetings would gladly go into the holes and caves of the earth if they could hide from the presence of the Lord. The ghastly

DEMONOLOGY

works of the devil in "Tongueism" must and will be exposed.

For years God has been warning people that His judgments were about to fall upon the earth, and those who have had spiritual understanding of the Word have stood in the pulpit and drawn vivid pictures of the power of demons that will be manifest in the latter days. Many books have been written against spiritualism and witchcraft, but alas for preachers, writers and others, demon power is manifesting itself in a different way from what they expected. While they have been at ease in Zion, Satan has marshaled his hosts and dressed up his imps like angels from heaven and sent them out to make one grand onslaught with his deceptive arts. His chief end is to blaspheme the Holy Ghost and sweep true religion off the face of the earth.

Stories that are being circulated in regard to the healing of diseases, are his strongest bait. Many go to the "Tongues" meetings and seek to be healed of their diseases, and have no thought of restraining their appetites or otherwise disciplining their bodies, or of glorifying God in their lives as cross bearers. They want to see signs and wonders, but God will have nothing to do with them, and of course it is the devil's opportunity to build up his own kingdom by promising them health.

When Israel murmured and gave way to their fleshly lusts the Psalmist says that God "cast upon them the fierceness of his anger, wrath, and indignation, and trouble, by sending evil angels among them." We see here that one of God's ways of punishing people is by sending evil angels among them. He is punishing the backslidden holiness organizations today by letting these vultures from the pit swoop down upon them and prey on their carnal members. He is the same yesterday, today and forever. His ways are past finding out. When people cling to the Cross and walk in His precepts: He will not allow them to be deceived, but if they give way to fleshly lusts, refuse and rebel, He will give them over to seducing spirits. Of all the

DEMONOLOGY

abominations that have been known in the past centuries on the earth, this abomination of "Tongues" we believe is the worst.

But God has been merciful enough not to leave those who are being deluded without sufficient warning. The multitudes are being deceived through hypocritical preachers and professors. Jesus said, "Beware of false prophets, which come to you in sheep's clothing, but inwardly they are ravening wolves. Ye shall know them by their fruits. Do men gather grapes of thorns, or figs of thistles?" (Matt. 7:15-16). We fail to see any good fruit from the world-wide revival that the "Tongues" people claim is in progress. They actually have the audacity to tell us that four hundred people in a certain locality have received the baptism of the Holy Ghost.

They say most of those who are receiving this baptism are young women, and that young women more readily receive the tongues than others. They should read Acts 16:16-18 and find out where their so-called baptism originated: "And it came to pass, as we went to prayer, a certain damsel possessed with a spirit of divination met us, which brought her masters much gain by soothsaying: The same followed Paul and us, and cried, saying, 'These men are the servants of the most high God, which shew unto us the way of salvation.' And this did she many days. But Paul, being grieved, turned and said to the spirit, I command thee in the name of Jesus Christ to come out of her. And he came out the same hour." Paul permitted this unclean spirit to cry out many days before he rebuked him, and no sooner was it done than the masters of the young woman, seeing that their gains were lost, drew Paul and Silas before the rulers and had them beaten and cast into prison.

The devil was certainly enraged when he had these two saints cast into prison and their feet put into stocks. Demons in that locality would not consent to vacate their strongholds without a protest, and no doubt a conference of arch-fiends was held in pandemonium to devise plans by which the work of Paul and Silas might be stopped, but we find them at midnight singing praises unto God. After the demons were routed, God had to work a miracle to deliver His servants. And so it is today, when a person dares in the name of Jesus Christ to rebuke the devil and tear the mask off those who are deceiving others, he will have the combined forces of perdition to meet, but the same God who sent an earthquake to shake the jail at Philippi is on hands to take a part in this kind of battle. He can send angels, pestilences, earthquakes, cyclones, or other forces to thwart the work of demons and establish His kingdom in the hearts of believers. Praise His name.

> "I'd rather be the least of them,
> Who are the Lord's alone,
> Thou wear a royal diadem,
> And sit upon a throne."

CHAPTER IV

PERILOUS TIMES - GREAT REVIVAL PREDICTED - SINS OF THE FLESH - SEDUCING SPIRITS - RAPID GROWTH - THE GREAT APOSTASY – DISSENSIONS - REVIVAL AT EPHESUS - SCEVA'S SEVEN SONS - THE CLASHING OF SWORDS - SUFFICIENT WARNING

The "Tongues" leaders claim that organized Christianity is on the eve of a profound and universal reformation; also that there has been a world-wide outpouring of the Holy Spirit as an earnest of what is to follow. It is claimed that the apostate church will gradually return to its first works. Nothing could be more unscriptural than this. No church once fallen has ever been reclaimed. When an organization fails to lift up the Gospel standard, and to honor the doctrines of the New Testament, God turns away from it and raises up another body to represent Him. It is useless to try to reform a fallen church, but it is possible to awaken a few to its condition, and get them to a place of safety.

DEMONOLOGY

"This know also, that in the last days perilous times shall come. For men shall be lovers of their own selves, covetous, boasters, proud, blasphemers, disobedient to parents, unthankful, unholy, Without natural affection, truce breakers, false accusers, incontinent, fierce, despisers of those that are good, Traitors, heady, high minded, lovers of pleasures more than lovers of God." (2 Tim. 3:1-4). The modern churches are full of people of this character; they have a form of godliness, but deny the power thereof, and the commandment is, "from such turn away." God will give people a chance to make their escape if they wish to do so. It is useless to stay with a fallen church expecting it to reform. For as it was in the days of Noah and Lot, so shall it be in the winding up of this dispensation.

The flood came and swept the ante-diluvians away, and fire and brimstone were rained upon Sodom after the angels had hurried Lot and some of the members of his family out. The apostate church is ripe for the tribulation judgments, and it cannot escape the wrath of God.

"For of this sort are they which creep into houses, and lead captive silly women laden with sins, led away with divers lusts." (2 Tim. 3:6). This is a true picture of the fallen church. Preachers and people are living self-indulgent lives, led away with divers lusts. Scarcely a daily newspaper can be picked up without an account of out-breaking sins among prominent church members in which ministers are involved. The sins of the flesh were the curse of the ante-diluvians, the sons of God intermarrying with the daughters of men and producing a race of giants, proud, haughty, self-indulgent and God-defying. The iniquity became so great that the flood was sent as the Almighty's protest. If you will take notice to the description given of the ante-diluvians, by the inspired writers you will find that the same sins which destroyed them are the curse of the nations today- they are eating and drinking, marrying and giving in marriage, thus showing that the flesh life predominates. The sins of the flesh, like the dreaded disease of leprosy, have eaten away the vitals of religious organizations which have fallen to the very depths and can never be recovered.

Of all the cunning craftiness that Satan has ever displayed as an angel of light, we believe the climax has been reached in this latter day sorcery of the "Tongues" movement, but we are not surprised, as it is in direct fulfillment of Scripture. 1 Tim. 4:1 says, "Now the Spirit speaketh expressly, that in the latter times some shall depart from the faith, giving head to seducing spirits, and doctrines of devils." Paul in this epistle to Timothy has no reference to people at large, but is showing the backslidden condition of the Gentile church in the last days. Multitudes who are giving heed to seducing spirits and doctrines of devils will never humble themselves enough to admit it. They are unwilling to believe that the enemy has been crafty enough to deceive them, but the fact is he has done so, and they might as well find it out first as last. In every land and clime the backslidden holiness movement has furnished fruitful soil for the "Tongues," just as the old church has for Christian Science.

This accounts for the rapidity with which the "Tongues" movement has spread over the globe. It has gone like wild-fire, sweeping almost everything in its course. We quote the following from a "Tongues" paper:

"It will soon be four years since the present outpouring of the Spirit became so general. Nothing we have ever seen spread so rapidly. Nothing on earth seemed to promise so much to the people of the earth. We saw from the first that if it was of God it would ultimately carry everything before it. We were soon convinced that it was from God, and just as fully convinced that it would practically revolutionize the theories and teachings of men so far as they relate to the baptism of the Holy Ghost. It was so manifestly from God that it seemed to us all who really knew the voice of God would gladly accept it. In all essentials it so closely resembles the samples given in the word of God that it seemed to us all the world would give it a glad welcome. The enemies denounced it fiercely as being of the devil. They seemed to think it a gigantic stroke of Satan to swallow up all the real spiritual life of the world. On the other hand many who had received the Holy Spirit failed to see the plan of God and thus the work suffered at their hands. It was sadly misrepresented both by its enemies and its friends."

No one with a knowledge of the Word and spiritual understanding can fail to see from the foregoing statements that the "Tongues" movement came from below and not from above. That the great apostasy of the latter days is upon us no one can doubt and the very fact that this movement could have such a rapid spread under these conditions is proof that it is not of God. After Pentecost the early church had to meet all kinds of opposition in the spread of the Gospel. The resistance on the part of the Jews, heathen and all classes was so great that none of the apostles died a natural death, with perhaps one exception. The world was not evangelized then in a few months or years. Down through the centuries it has taken the blood of hundreds and thousands of martyrs to establish New Testament doctrines and lift up the cross of Jesus Christ. In the history of every true religious organization the greatest heroism has been manifested.

Privations and sufferings and persecutions of every kind have always characterized the true Church. But what has this "Tongues" movement all amounted to? With one broad stroke Satan has swept the globe and left nothing behind but devastation and death. The means has been furnished for scores and hundreds to go to foreign lands to preach in what they supposed was the native tongue of the Hindus, Chinese and every other nationality. But to their surprise they find that their "tongues" are of no use to them, that they cannot be understood at all. Why did not the Holy Spirit reveal this to them before they started?

John 16:13 says, "Howbeit when he, the Spirit of truth

is come, he will guide you into all truth: for he shall not speak of himself; but whatsoever he shall hear, that shall he speak : and he will show you things to come." Those whom the "Tongues" people have sent to foreign lands, if they have not had the means to return, had to settle down and learn the language of the natives. Their great schemes of evangelizing the heathen proved to be air-castles or floating bubbles that burst when they reached their destination. The Holy Spirit is God, and we certainly credit Him with having intelligence superior to this. You will notice in the above quotation the writer says, "Many who had received the Holy Spirit failed to see the plan of God, and thus the work suffered at their hands."

Reader, imagine a person baptized with the Holy Ghost and yet unable to see God's plans and the work suffering at his hands. What kind of person is the Holy Ghost? Is He not the third person of the Trinity? "For there are three that bear record in heaven, the Father, the Word, and the Holy Ghost; and these three are one. And there are three that bear witness in earth, the Spirit, and the water, and the blood: and these three agree in one." (l John 5:7-8). What God knows the Holy Spirit knows, and the Holy Spirit will not direct any one contrary to the Father and the Son. Is it the third person of the Trinity that these people are receiving who claim to have the Holy Ghost with the sign of tongues? Verily, they have received an archfiend who has come in the disguise of an angel.

The same writer says, "It is more than sad to see some trying to establish their claims as originators and founders of the work." We might add, that so far as its origin is concerned there can be no doubt as to that, for the work unmistakably bears the marks of its father, the devil. The persons here referred to, who are trying to establish their claims as the originators of the "Tongues" movement of course claim they have received the baptism with the sign of tongues. If they have received the Holy Ghost why should they be making false claims or trying to organize something that God does not want organized? Why do they want to be called the "projectors" or "field directors," if this is contrary to the Holy Spirit whom they claim to have received? This writer also says, "Others have worked to get committees appointed or councils and have worked to get to be the chairman of such councils or committees." He also says, "Only a few of these men are ambitious schemers; most of them simply failed to see the plan of God." You see it is claimed here they have their Pentecost and are really friends to the work, but do not understand God's plan, yet they are accused of being ambitious for leadership and to be called the "projectors" and "directors" of the work. Are not these the manifestations of carnality? A person could not even be saved and have such unholy ambitions and desires.

Thank God, we are not ignorant of the devil's devices and are ready to expose his works anywhere they are found. With few exceptions, he has swallowed up nearly every religious publication in the land and stamped it with "Tongues," and on every page the trail of the serpent can be found. If St. Paul were present today to help us fight in this battle against principalities and powers, and against unclean spirits he would expose the black arts of these hypocrites and compel them to make a bonfire of their papers and books as he did in the days of old.

At Ephesus the mighty power of God was made manifest in the revival that followed Paul's preaching, who entered the synagogue and spoke boldly the things concerning the kingdom of God. In this revival "divers were hardened, and believed not, but spake evil of the way before the multitude." Then Paul departed from them and went to the school of Tyrannus where he continued to teach and preach for the space of two years. All that dwelt in Asia had the privilege of hearing the word of the Lord Jesus, both Jews and Greeks. God never turns people over to be ravaged by evil spirits until they have hardened their hearts against His truths. No man can go to perdition until the Holy Spirit has first given him up; neither can

DEMONOLOGY

a person become the victim of a strong delusion until He has turned away from him.

When He ceases to strive with him then evil spirits take possession. In Paul's revival, sinners were converted and believers sanctified; the sick were healed, and demons had to leave their human habitations. Among the Jews there were those who had hardened their hearts against the Gospel, but when they saw the sick healed and lunatics restored to their right minds they wanted to do some wonderful works also.

Sceva's seven sons were among the vagabond Jews who worked in curious arts. They took it upon themselves to call over those who had evil spirits the name of the Lord Jesus, saying, "We adjure you by Jesus whom Paul preacheth." An evil spirit in a man said, "Jesus I know, and Paul I know; but who are ye? And the man in whom the evil spirit was leaped on them, and overcame them, and prevailed against them, so that they fled out of that house naked and wounded."

These Jews did not want to meet the conditions that Paul laid down for their obtaining salvation, but they wanted to work miracles. This is exactly the condition among the "Tongues" people today- they will not repent of their sins and straighten up their lives, but they want to do great things. God has said that no flesh should glory in His presence. "The flesh lusteth against the Spirit, and the Spirit against the flesh." The "Tongues" movement is a movement of the flesh. It is corrupt to the very core. Among its adherents we have heard of the most out-breaking and flagrant sins. Free-loveism, like the coils of a serpent, has wrapped itself around some of the "Tongues" victims and sunk them into the lowest depths of immorality and degradation. These persons have invariably professed the Pentecostal baptism with tongues, some of them speaking, as they have claimed, in many different languages.

In the wake of a Holy Ghost revival the devil always

DEMONOLOGY

stirs up the forces of darkness and does his most ghastly work. When evil spirits are cast out they seek for other habitations and usually find an entrance to the hearts of those who have refused to walk in the light. When Jesus cast a legion of devils out of the Gadarene they entered into the swine and the whole herd plunged over the precipice into the sea. They much prefer to live in human beings and will take possession of them when the opportunity is given them to do so.

The swine is an unclean beast and is a type of carnality. Wherever the carnal nature is found in hearts evil spirits seek a lodging place. Jesus said, "The prince of this world cometh and findeth nothing in me." When carnality is destroyed Satan has no more claim on the human heart; there is nothing in it that belongs to him, hence it behooves every regenerated person to get sanctified as soon as possible after his conversion. May the Lord not only deliver people from eating swine flesh, but save them from the old corruptible nature of which it is a type.

Demons and swine are closely associated. We have known persons at the beginning of some of our revival meetings who could scarcely hold out against the pleadings of the Spirit, but after resisting for a time they grew hard and indifferent to the strongest appeals that were made to them; they became critical and could scarcely see any good in anything or anybody. Then they turned away altogether and sought the company of those who were of a reprobate mind. Such persons have found congenial affiliations among the "Tongues" people.

The seven sons of Sceva had heard the Gospel at Ephesus and were given the opportunity to repent and get right with God, but they failed to do so, and were found fleeing naked before their demoniacal pursuer. Any person who has been caught in the "Tongues" delusion, if he ever had the habiliments of righteousness, has lost them, and in his shame has no cloak with which to cover his spiritual nakedness. What a deplorable condition one is in who has turned away from God and has gone

DEMONOLOGY

to consulting witches and wizards! The lust of the flesh and the lust of the eyes and the pride of life will bring him to this. In the meantime he is utterly helpless and unable to see himself. No person can go through a Holy Ghost revival without being made better or worse. He must either yield to God and walk in the light that is falling upon his pathway or be brought under the control of evil spirits. When he refuses the counsel of the righteous he does so at the peril of his own soul.

Like the sons of Sceva and the man possessed with demons, there is often a clashing of swords among the "Tongues" people. Evil spirits are unwilling to be routed by their own kind without a protest. Some are stronger than others and refuse to vacate their tenements at the command of those who are presumptuous enough to attempt to rout them. In a Western city there were four different bands of "Tongues" all fighting one another and professing to have the Holy Spirit. They were so at loggerheads, some of them would tell those of other factions that they had devils in them. This continued until a prominent leader among them commanded the demons to come out of a young woman who was not of his band. It was a critical time for these modern sorcerers, for the young woman had been recognized by various "Tongues" leaders as having the real Pentecostal baptism, speaking fluently, they said, seven or more languages. When she fell to the floor in one of her spells she was approached by this honored advocate of "Tongues" who took it upon himself to command the evil spirits to come out of her.

One can imagine the consternation of many who were present. The news of this young woman's ability to speak in tongues had been heralded from city to city. She was just entering into womanhood and no one believed it was possible for demons to get possession of one so young and innocent. If it had been some one who was hardened in sin it would have appealed to them as being more reasonable, but for a young, beautiful girl brought up under the roof of parents who

DEMONOLOGY

professed to know God to be possessed with so many demons was more than they could comprehend. The father of the young woman, who was at first an enthusiastic "Tongueist," was completely at his wit's end; he took his daughter away from the meetings and had nothing more to do with them. The leader who commanded the evil spirits to come out is an advocate of the "Tongues" heresy and is widely known as a writer and publisher.

Another leader of one of these bands frankly admitted that some of his people had the devil's tongues and that their lives were crooked. We quote the following from a "Tongues" paper published by A. A. Boddy of England. This article written by the wife of the publisher, whether so intended or not, is a repudiation of the "Tongues" doctrine. We know of no editor that has been more widely quoted among the "Tongues" people than A. A. Boddy, and no doubt the appearance of this article has created consternation among those in the "Tongues" movement who have considered him authority in the past.

"The baptism is to be filled with God, and tongues will follow; but to speak in tongues only, is not, as I can see, a sufficient sign of the baptism. I am more and more convinced of this, that as soon as a person is truly born of God and has Christ in his life, then the Holy Ghost will fall and he will speak in tongues, if he expects to do so, but I do believe that merely speaking in tongues is not necessarily a convincing sign that a person has got God in him. Of course the deep spiritual work may be done after a person has spoken in tongues, if he goes on, but in the meantime, in many cases, much dishonor and damage is done to God's work. The trouble is so few know what the baptism really means. It means to be filled with God." -Mrs. Mary Boddy.

Undoubtedly this editor and wife have had experience with those who spoke in tongues that manifested demon power in some way, which they were not able to reconcile with the "baptism in the Holy Ghost," therefore they were forced to come to the conclusion that tongues was not always a sign of the "baptism." But most any one can get the tongues "f he expects to do so," whether he has God or not.

Are not these things sufficient warning to all who look with favor upon this movement of latter day sorcery and witchcraft? When once brought under the spell of witchcraft it is hard for one ever to be recovered. We have had persons who were caught in these Satanic traps, after they had gotten their eyes open to the whole thing as being the work of the devil, to come and tell us that they were physical wrecks and that it seemed impossible for them to ever recover from the awful effects of this demon- working power. They would sit in our services under the most powerful preaching, apparently unable to yield to the pleadings of the Spirit, yet realizing that they were in a lost condition. One young woman who had become the victim of "Tongues" told us that she had suffered such losses through it that her mother had died of a broken heart, and that she herself was unable to rally from the awful effects of it. In our work of evangelism from coast to coast, and across the sea, this is only one instance in many that we have encountered. While people are under the spell of demon power they find a strange pleasure in it which they imagine is the joy of the Holy Spirit. But think of their sorrowful condition when they awaken to the fact that their joy was not real, but only that which was imparted by demons. If there were not some kind of joy in connection with the "Tongues" experience the devil would not be able to deceive so many people.

CHAPTER V

STRANGE APPEARANCE OF A LEADER - PENTECOST
REPORTED AT LOS ANGELES - GOSPEL MEETINGS -
PEOPLE WARNED - DELIVERED THROUGH READING
PILLAR OF FIRE - IN GERMANY - REPULSIVE ALTAR
SCENES - A "TONGUES" MEETING - CALLED EACH

DEMONOLOGY

OTHER LIARS

In the spring of 1906, a colored man, introducing himself as Seymour, called at our Bible School at Denver. He was on his way to Los Angeles, California, and took the opportunity of visiting our School while passing through the city. We did not know he was in the building until he walked into the dining room. Some one had shown him through the building and brought him into the dining room.

He had a strange appearance which somewhat aroused our curiosity, and as he claimed to be a preacher of the Gospel we called on him to pray. He responded with a good deal of fervor, but oh the feeling that came over us! We thought of demons, snakes and other slimy creatures before he had finished praying. After he had left the room a number of the students told that they felt that he was possessed with evil spirits.

He was very untidy in his appearance; he wore no collar and had a greenish looking brass button exposed in the band of his shirt. In our evangelistic and missionary tours we have met all kinds of religious fakirs and tramps, but we felt that he excelled them all. There was a cause for our feeling this way; the Lord wanted us to see this man and learn something of him, knowing that Satan was going to use him in the out-breaking of the "Tongues" on the Pacific Coast.

It was only a short time after his arrival at Los Angeles that the news was being heralded around that there was a great revival breaking out in that city. It was said that God had raised up a colored man to bring Pentecost back to the earth again, and that people through his ministry were receiving the baptism of the Holy Ghost and speaking in tongues. A few weeks before, we had been at Los Angeles preaching and knew well the deplorable spiritual condition of the professed holiness people there. Most of them, while they made a profession, were backslidden in heart, and time and again under our ministry the Lord tried to get them to repent and confess their backslidings, but they absolutely refused to do so. A more self-righteous, self-sufficient people we never met.

Week after week we preached to them and urged them to repent and do their first works over. Two years previous to this we had a large Gospel tent erected in the very heart of the city, and preached for several weeks and truly the Lord gave us a harvest of souls. We preached in halls for weeks before and after the meetings in the tent, and the Lord did not fail to honor the messages in the salvation of souls. But the conditions were similar to those at Ephesus; divers were hardened and turned away from the truth. Night after night as the messages went forth under the unction of the Spirit the forces of darkness strongly resisted us, but God gave the victory. Hundreds and even thousands attended the services during our labors at Los Angeles. Preachers from high-steepled churches were frequently seen in the congregations, and one very prominent preacher who is now a bishop attended regularly, and, we understand, told his people that we were preaching the truth.

Before the gales of perdition began to blow, God let the holiness professors of Los Angeles see their tireless condition and gave them a chance to repent and get right with Him, but this, with few exceptions, they refused to do. The devil was even then preparing a net to catch their feet, and after they hardened their hearts and resisted the pleadings of the Spirit, they were taken into his net and carried away in the most hellish outburst of demoniacal power that has probably ever been known under the name of religion.

We had a presentiment of God's judgments coming on the city, simply from the fact that many, like the Sons of Sceva, had hardened their hearts against the truth and turned away. We frankly told them in the public services that something out of the ordinary was coming to Los Angeles, and there were at least

DEMONOLOGY

a score of persons present who had the same impression and testified to the fact. We did not know just how God was going to visit them, but knew a scourge of some kind was near at hand, and of all the calamities that could have fallen upon a people, we verily believe that this demoniacal out-breaking of tongues is the worst. It is bad enough to be possessed with demons, but when they get control of the vocal organs and talk about the blood of the atonement, the coming of Christ, etc., it is more than most people have ever thought they were capable of doing.

Many reliable persons, some of whom are with us today, have told us of things they saw in the so-called Azusa Street Mission. Some of our own missionaries, who were laboring in Los Angeles, went to see for themselves, and they declared that what they saw and heard from those who were under the spell of demons far exceeded anything they could have imagined or that ever had been told them. While dictating these lines Sister N , who is writing for us, stopped and told us the following story. "When I visited the Azusa Street Mission the first person that attracted my attention was a woman with a thin, white silk waist on who stood shaking from head to foot. She had a sad, far away look in her eyes. There were several rows of chairs in front of her that were filled with seekers. The colored man, Mr. Seymour, was preaching, but my attention was attracted to the woman who continued to shake until a man sitting in front of her slid down out of his chair and went under a spell. I then lost sight of the woman. The man who fell in the vision was pale and thin, and continued in his position on the floor until after a number of seekers had gathered around the altar. Then he arose and staggered to them and began to shake his hands in front of their faces and wave his arms over their heads and moan. He was apparently unconscious while he was doing this. Then he put his hands on the heads of the women and began to shake their hair. Some of them lost control of themselves and went under a spell. He rubbed a man's jaws until the victim tumbled over and remained apparently in an unconscious state for half an hour, when suddenly he began to stutter and jabber. Those who claimed to have the tongues cried out, 'He has the baptism, he has the baptism!' A young colored woman was doing her best to get the tongues; she went through all kinds of muscular contortions in her efforts to get her tongue to work. While work at the altar was going on a colored woman had her arms around a white man's neck praying for him. One man of mature years leaped out of his chair and began to stutter. He did not utter a distinct syllable, but as fast as he could make his tongue work he said tut- tut- tut- tut- tuttut-tut. This, of course, they claimed was evidence that he had the baptism. The woman with the silk waist on appeared again, this time singing a far-away tune that sounded very unnatural and repulsive. There were others who mingled their voices with hers in the production of these strange notes. While the altar call was being made a woman walked up to the front and kissed a man. It was evident that the man, who was one of the prominent workers in the mission,was not her husband or even a relative. Kissing between the sexes is a common occurrence in the 'Tongues' meetings."

The following in part is from the pen of one of our preachers, who in company with another brother attended a "Tongues" meeting:

"We arrived about eight o'clock. We took seats and sat quietly until 9 :30. The brother who was with me had met one of the leaders in L, and as the work around the altar had begun, we thought it would be all right for him to speak to this man and hand him some of our tracts. He then spoke to the preacher who was in charge, and asked him if we might have the privilege of giving out some of our literature. He gave his consent so all could hear him. He said, 'Take their tracts; they will do you no harm.' Of course we were glad to have the opportunity, and went through the audience and gave them out. Some of the people became very much excited and began to mutter in tongues. They asked God to strike us down with His judgments right there. This was said in plain English. One of the leaders, whom our brother had previously met, called him a liar, a

DEMONOLOGY

blasphemer, dishonest, etc. Then followed a controversy between this man and the preacher in charge; one telling the other he did not believe the half he had said. The people in the audience observing the discord saw that if one had the Lord the other did not. Of course these persons had the tongues. As a natural consequence the work at the altar was broken up, and the preacher in charge told the people to bring the papers and tracts we had handed to them to the platform. He wanted to make a bonfire out of them. A few responded to his request. He then called for a bucket and put the papers and tracts into it and burned them. During the meeting he acknowledged that some of their people had the devil's tongues. 'But of course,' he said, 'some have the genuine tongues.' There was one person at the altar who appeared to be an honest seeker, but the controversy between the leaders, and other things he heard evidently caused him to seriously consider the situation. He told of the good experience he once had, but for some time he had been dissatisfied and was struggling to get free. Scores like this man go to the "Tongues" meetings expecting to get something to satisfy their souls. They hear great reports in regard to the things that are going on under the name of Pentecost, and go, having no idea that it is the devil's counterfeit. 1 Cor. 10:20-21 says, 'But I say, that the things which the Gentiles sacrifice, they sacrifice to devils, and not to God; and I would not that ye should have fellowship with devils. Ye cannot drink the cup of the Lord, and the cup of devils; ye cannot be partakers of the Lord's table, and the table of devils.' One of the great arguments of the 'Tonguists' to prove that they have sought and obtained the Pentecostal baptism is the fact that the Lord will not give a person a stone when he asks bread, neither will He give him a serpent when he asks for a fish (Matt. 7:9-10). See how cunning the devil is! He knows the Lord will not give stones and serpents for bread and fish, and uses this argument to beguile those who are ignorant of his devices. It is true the Lord never deceives people, but when they sit down to the devil's table they have to take his bill of fare. He will turn the hearts of those who were once under the melting influence of the Holy Spirit into stone, and poison them with the venom of these 'Tongues' like the bite of a serpent. One who puts his hand into a nest of vipers is running a terrible risk even though he is reaching for bread."

We know of those who have become so hardened under the influence of this demon power they are entirely unlike what they were once. They will turn away with a cold indifference from those who are suffering on their account and manifest no sympathy whatever. In the meantime they will threaten them with the judgments of God because they refuse to sit down to the table of devils with them, and they imagine they are pleasing God when they make it hard for those who cannot be brought under the power of seducing spirits. John 16:2 says, "Yea, the time cometh that whosoever killeth you will think that he doeth God service."

We quote the following from a letter received from a man who, through reading the Pillar of Fire, was delivered from the devil's tongues in a city in Pennsylvania: "I attended the 'Tongues' meeting at H . Here I found men and women lying on the floor in all shapes, and the workers would put big blankets over them. These people on the floor would be jabbering all at once in what they called unknown tongues. While I was praying one of the workers got hold of me and said, Holy Ghost, we command Thee to go into this soul. The workers were jabbering and shaking their hands over me, and a hypnotic demon power (as I know now) took possession of me, and I fell among the people on the floor and knew nothing for ten hours. When I came to my senses I was weak and my jaws were so tired they ached. I believed then that this power was of God. They said I was wonderfully blessed, and Rev. W sent me from one place to another so that I could jabber in tongues. I was told that while I was speaking in tongues the people would fall on their faces and say, 'Yes, Lord,' 'We will, Lord,' thinking that it was God who was speaking through me. I am now jumping and praising God for delivering me from the devil's tongues. When we get the real power of God we can see that this "Tongues" movement is of

DEMONOLOGY

the devil. Your paper, the Pillar of Fire, is stirring up things here. The meetings in McK and H have been broken up. I am now going to towns where I spoke in tongues and telling them it is of the devil. I know if it had not been for the Pillar of Fire I would have gone to Hell. I am so glad that God has some of His own in the world yet. Keep praying for me."

In "*Der Evangelist*" we read the following about the "Tongues."

THE PENTECOSTAL MOVEMENT

N. Gropmann, Berlin-Rudorf, Germany, gives an account of one of his own experiences with the people of the above named movement in regard to speaking in "unknown tongues:"

He says, "At Brother H's home in Beek, Germany, I had the opportunity to get personally acquainted with a spirit of this kind. A sister belonging to the M. E. Church visited the annual conference at Muehlheim a. d. Ruhr, and on this occasion through laying on of hands by Mr. G of the same city received the gift of tongues. However, she soon found that instead of receiving her Pentecost she had let a demon take possession of her. She called for us to pray with her that she might be delivered from it and its influence. We responded and prayed with her for hours. Previous to this time the spirit had been talking about the things of God, such as Calvary, the blood, glory, revivals, etc. But now he begin to talk in a fearful, profane manner and call us all sorts of names. In the name of Jesus we commanded the unclean spirit to depart from her, but he, stoutly refusing, told us we better not waste our time, but go home, for he intended to stay. Therefore he began to torment the sister by accusing her of disloyalty to God and pronounced curse upon curse upon her, predicting her destruction and death in the near future. He began to tear and pull her around the room in a terrible way. The more we prayed the more furious he

DEMONOLOGY

became- cursing and swearing at us. I am not nervous, but I felt a cold shiver running down my back and felt as if the room was filled with demons. The climax was reached when we laid hands on her in the name of Jesus. We could not possibly be mistaken concerning the reality of things, for we heard him curse, swear and call us names. The language was so shocking that I could not very well mention any of it here. Often I was able to understand without the sister interpreting- a mixture of Latin, Italian and French. Now and then I was able to catch a word, for the spirit spoke very rapidly. I shiver to think that these cursing and swearing demons found and are finding entrance to the hearts of people. Where are people getting to when they give place to such devils? Is it not a sign of the times? Is this the beginning of 'strong delusions' which God will send upon the earth and into which people that refuse to walk in the light will be ensnared?" -From "*Der Evangelist*," Bremen, Germany, Vol. 60, Dec. 11, 1909.

Some professors of Christianity would not like to be found in dark rooms where spiritual seances are carried on, but they have no hesitation in congregating with those who give themselves over to strange workings of demon power under the name of religion. May God open their eyes to their deceived and lost condition before the doors of heaven are everlastingly closed against them.

Among the "Tongues" people there are those who claim to be prophets and prophetesses. From time to time the things that they prophesied have been published in their papers. Among those was a prophecy concerning Pike's Peak. This peak, they said, within four months would have a volcanic eruption, and the people of Cripple Creek and surrounding towns were warned to flee for their lives. Nearly four years have passed and there has been no burning crater with floods of lava to make its appearance. Prophecies were also made among them after the earthquake on the Pacific Coast of dreadful things that would soon come to pass which of course have never been fulfilled.

When the "Tongues" first broke out there were two divisions, one led by Seymour and the other led by Parham. Parham's crowd said Seymour's people had the devil in them, and vice versa. At the various "Tongues" meetings there was strife among the workers as to who should be the first to lay their hands on the seekers. When the jaws of the seeker began to work and he commenced to mutter in strange gibberish the worker who had his hands on him at the time would get the glory. Then they would slander one another behind their backs and say they were possessed with evil spirits, which of course was the truth. It was a case of the pot calling the kettle black.

Our workers have been stationed in Los Angeles during the whole history of the "Tongues" movement and have watched it closely from the very first outbreak of demon power in Seymour's meetings. The conditions have been such that it would be impossible to publish the things that have occurred there, things that they have actually seen and heard. The familiarity between the sexes in the public meetings has been shocking. Hell has certainly reaped an awful harvest and infidelity has become more strongly rooted than ever before on the Pacific Coast. The city of the angels, as it is called, is an infirmary for people of all manner of diseases and physical ailments. They have gone there from every land and clime in search of health, and all kinds of extravagances have been taught on the subject of divine healing by carnal, professors and leaders, some of whom were anxious to gain a following and thus become famous, and of course the soil was well prepared for the spreading of the "Tongues." The ministry of healing has been so perverted in Los Angeles that it is almost impossible to deal with the subject as it should be and place the gift of healing where it belongs. For years the devil has had the full length of rope there on this subject, and of course he has made good use of it. Many persons of wealth have wanted to be healed of their diseases, but they have had no use for salvation. The way of the

DEMONOLOGY

Cross is despised, and the flesh life has had the pre-eminence.

CHAPTER VI

GIFTS OF THE SPIRIT - DO ALL SPEAK IN TONGUES - THE AUTHOR'S CONVERSION - COMMAND OF LANGUAGE - THE JEWS AFTER THE RESTORATION - MIRACLE IN HEARING - MOSES' ROD - THE "GIFT" A FAILURE - GOOD MEMORIES

The 12th chapter of First Corinthians sets forth nine different gifts of the Spirit, one of these being the gift of tongues. "Now there are diversities of gifts, but the same Spirit. For to one is given by the Spirit the word of wisdom; to another the word of knowledge by the same Spirit; To another faith by the same Spirit; to another the gifts of healing by the same Spirit; To another the working of miracles; to another prophecy; to another discerning of spirits; to another divers kinds of tongues; to another the interpretation of tongues. But all these work that one and the selfsame Spirit, dividing to every man severally as he will."

We notice that "divers" is in italics and is not in the original. The right reading would be, "to another kinds of tongues." The gift of tongues and the interpreting are the last in the list. The question is asked in the 30th verse, "Do all speak in tongues?" This verse accords with the 11th showing that they do not. Neither is there any great stress put upon the gift of tongues, as will be seen in the first verse of the next chapter: "Though I speak with the tongues of men and of angels, and have not charity, I am become as sounding brass, or a tinkling cymbal."

Paul says in chapter 14, verse 19, "Yet in the church I had rather speak five words with my understanding, that by my voice I might teach others also, than ten thousand words in an unknown tongue." These scriptures are sufficient to show the

DEMONOLOGY

estimate that Paul put on the gift of tongues. The Corinthian church was born of the Holy Ghost under Paul's ministry and naturally we would expect the gifts of the Spirit to be made manifest and to be placed where they belong, but how about this latter-day movement which unmistakably bears every evidence of being born from beneath and not from above. The fruit of the Spirit is not in it. Neither are the gifts of the Spirit made manifest which the Corinthian church possessed. Their woeful lack of spiritual discernment is appalling. People who are converted often possess the gifts of the Spirit to a marvelous degree, but the "Tongues" people show that their lights have been totally eclipsed.

We know the fruit of the Spirit when we see it. We have been too long in the Christian warfare to be deceived by the witchcraft and sorcery in this movement.

At the age of 16 the writer experienced the new birth, and after years of faithful cross-bearing was sanctified wholly, or in other words baptized with the Holy Spirit. There was no manifestation of strange tongues in this baptism, but as truly as ever the disciples received the Holy Ghost on the day of Pentecost we were baptized by the same Spirit. The power of God rested upon us from day to day and marvelous results followed from our ministry in the conviction and conversion of sinners and the sanctification of believers. It would take volumes to give our readers even a partial account of the results which followed the outpouring of the Holy Spirit upon us.

Our natural timidity, which had hindered our service for the Master for so long, was swept away. Our tongue was touched with a live coal from the altar. There was no difficulty to command language in our own tongue. We were enabled to express our thoughts in words that we had never used before and scarcely knew the meaning of. They would come to our mind and fit into the right place when we were standing before an audience. At times the pressure of the Spirit was so great upon us it seemed the earthen vessel would almost break. Just before delivering a message where there were vital issues involved there were times when we were unable to stand on our feet for half or three-quarters of an hour, but when the moment came to deliver the message strength was given us.

We have never lost the power of the Holy Ghost. We still have the Spirit that discerns between the false and the true.

The question is often asked, will the Gentile church in the last days again possess the gift of tongues. Our answer is, all things are possible with God. If His name can be glorified through the gift in these last days we certainly should be on the lookout for it, but it will take some time for the people to recover from the effects of this counterfeit "Tongues" movement before God could get glory out of the real gift of tongues. When the Jews are gathered back to Palestine and the nations of the earth go up to Jerusalem to hear the Gospel preached, undoubtedly God will enable the sons of Abraham to speak in languages so they can be understood. The occasion will demand it. If nations are to be converted in a day, it will be necessary for them to understand the language of those who are ministering unto them. The gifts of the Spirit will be imparted, the dead will be raised and wonderful things be accomplished as it was in the days of old.

We have never seen a person who was actually raised from the dead, but we know the time is coming in the history of the Hebrews when the dead will be raised. We have seen a number of persons during the years of our ministry who we knew were dying, who in answer to the prayer of faith were brought back to life and health, but the breath had not entirely left their bodies.

We have had persons come to us who could understand but little English, and tell us that while we were preaching they understood every word we said. We remember a German

DEMONOLOGY

woman especially who was converted in one of our first revival meetings. She grasped our hand and gave us to understand, in German and broken English, that she had understood every word we had said. She was asked if she understood other preachers who had preached in the same meeting, and she affirmed that she did not. This is only one incident out of many of a similar character.

Acts 2:8 says, "And how hear we every man in his own tongue, wherein we were born?" We believe there is as much in hearing as in speaking. When the Holy Spirit speaks through a person it is possible for Him to make people to understand, even though they are not acquainted with the language in which the message is given. If we were called to foreign fields we would not expect to put in years learning the language of the people to whom we went to minister. We would have faith for divine illumination and help to acquire the language of the natives in a short time. If all the people who were present on the day of Pentecost heard Peter's message in their own language this was a greater miracle than the gift of tongues. Most any old clairvoyant can mutter and speak words that no one can understand, but there is a limit to the power of demons, there are things in the spiritual realm that they are unable to comprehend.

When Moses and Aaron cast their rod down before Pharaoh it became a serpent. Then Pharaoh called up the sorcerers and the magicians, and with their enchantments they did the same thing; they cast down their rods and they became serpents, but Aaron's rod swallowed up their rods. Pharaoh saw this, yet he continued to harden his heart and refused to let Israel go.

The Lord commanded Moses and Aaron to take their rod and stretch it out over the waters of Egypt that they might become blood. The fish in the rivers died, and the water became so unwholesome that no one could drink of it. The magicians continued to work with their enchantments and succeeded in turning some water to blood. The famine of water was upon them, and the Egyptians were everywhere digging around the river beds to find a pure stream, but for all this Pharaoh would not relent, he hardened his heart and went into his house.

When the plague of frogs was on the land and they came up into his bed-chamber and drought-troughs he had the magicians trying to bring up frogs with their enchantments, and they did so. But when the plague of lice came they could go no further. They repeatedly tried and failed. Then they acknowledged to Pharaoh that the finger of God was upon them, but still the king's heart was hardened. God continued His plagues until the magicians could not stand before Moses because of the boils, "for the boils were upon the magicians, and upon all the Egyptians" (Exodus 9:11). The claims that the "Tongues" people have made of being able to speak the languages of the heathen have been proved false time and again. They found that their so-called tongues were a complete failure in foreign lands. Oftentimes when they thought they were speaking in the tongues of angels they were using the vilest language that could possibly fall from the lips of a human being. We will give one instance with which we are familiar. A person who had received the tongues thought he was talking about the coming of Jesus, to a Chinaman, who listened for a while and then started after him with a knife, threatening his life. When the Chinaman was asked what caused him to become so angry, he said the person with the tongues was cursing him and his gods and using other language too shameful to repeat.

We have known persons who were reared in homes where several languages were spoken, and while they were unable to speak in more than one language, under the hypnotic spell of demons in the "Tongues" meetings they have been able to speak, in a measure, in these foreign tongues that they were familiar with when they were children. Of course they would come out of a spell claiming to have the "Tongues," when the fact is, under a prolonged nervous strain, through some kind of strange phenomena that we are unable to explain, they were enabled to recall things that had been forgotten for years. We note the fact that those who claim to have received the tongues are of extremely nervous temperament, many of whom, at some time in their lives, have suffered from nervous prostration.

The writer is personally acquainted with a number of persons of this kind who now are identified with the "Tongues" movement. It must be remembered that some people have good memories and as they go from place to place coming in contact with the "Tongues" people they learn a sort of lingo that makes it appear that they have received what they call their "Pentecost." All they need is to utter a few sentences in some foreign tongue and they are fellowshipped as having the baptism of the Holy Ghost. In this country there are multiplied thousands of people whose parents were foreigners, whose native tongue they never learned, but are more or less familiar with, and when seeking the tongues it is easy to recall the language they heard in their childhood days.

We remember certain phrases in the German language that we learned from a neighbor when we were a child. And this is no doubt true of many of the "Tongues" people. Most of them, we understand, can utter only a few sentences at best. We asked one of our missionaries if she could speak German. She said she could not, but we found that she could understand her parents when they were conversing in the German language. We suppose that in a "Tongues" meeting they would call such a person an interpreter. We have heard persons in the Western states mimic Chinamen perfectly, so that it was impossible to tell the difference.

And when "Tongueism" is sifted down it will be found that the cunning craftiness of depraved humanity figures in it more prominently than any one has any idea of.

DEMONOLOGY

CHAPTER VII

THE OLD RED DRAGON - SATAN'S AMBITION - WOMAN CLOTHED WITH THE SUN - WORKS OF THE FLESH - "AS IT WAS IN THE DAYS OF NOD" – SODOM - AN OBJECT LESSON - LOT'S PLEA - CUP OF INIQUITY FULL - FALLEN ANGELS - SATAN'S EFFORTS FOILED - NATURE OF DEMONS

When Satan lost his first estate as an archangel and fell from heaven, his tail drew the third part of the stars with him. These stars, or angels, were cast to the earth, where they have ever since been engaged in the service of the king of darkness. What an innumerable host there must be! Isaiah 14:12-14 says, "How art thou fallen from heaven, O Lucifer, son of the morning! How art thou cut down to the ground, which didst weaken the nations. For thou hast said in thine heart, I will ascend into heaven, I will exalt my throne above the stars of God: I will sit also upon the mount of the congregation in the sides of the north: I will ascend above the heights of the clouds: I will be like the most High." A further account of Lucifer says that he made the world as a wilderness and destroyed the cities thereof, and opened not the house of his prisoners; but notwithstanding all this, God said, "Thou shalt be brought down to hell, to the sides of the pit." It was Satan's ambition to become mightier than God, and while he knows now that this he can never accomplish, he is still trying to hold the world and its inhabitants, and with the hosts that co-operate with him he is waging vigorous warfare against the Son of God. This earth is the purchased possession of Jesus Christ, who, Revelation says, was the Lamb slain from the foundation of the world. The devil knows this, but will not relinquish his claims until he is forced to do so. But thank God, the time is short. A mighty angel will descend from heaven with a chain and cast him into the pit and lock him up, but until this has been accomplished his work of devastation and ruin will continue.

DEMONOLOGY

In the 12th chapter of Revelation we have an account of the war in heaven, and how Michael and his angels fought against Satan and prevailed over him. Here he is called a Great Red Dragon.

"There appeared a great wonder in heaven; a woman clothed with the sun, and the moon under her feet, and upon her head a crown of twelve stars, and she being with child cried, travailing in birth, and pained to be delivered. And there appeared another wonder in heaven; behold a great red dragon, having seven heads and ten horns, and seven crowns upon his head. And his tail drew the third part of the stars of heaven, and did cast them to the earth and the dragon stood before the woman which was ready to be delivered, for to devour her child as soon as it was born." This woman represents the Church at the beginning of the Gospel age, who brought forth a man child who was to rule the nations with a rod of iron. "And her child was caught up unto God, and to his throne." This child was none other than God's immaculate Son who was crucified on Calvary and caught up to heaven.

The Dragon succeeded in having Him put to death, but before He was caught up to heaven His Church was established on the earth, against which He said the gates of hell should not prevail. The woman (Church) had to flee to the wilderness where God had a place prepared for her. The Old Red Dragon, that symbolizes the flesh, has always pursued the Church, and stood ready to devour her offspring. Through the centuries past her place has been one of obscurity, she has had to hide away from the Dragon and those who are in league with Him.

Paul gives, in the fifth chapter of Galatians, a graphic account of the works of the flesh. "This I say then, walk in the Spirit, and ye shall not fulfill the lust of the flesh. For the flesh lusteth against the Spirit, and the Spirit against the flesh; and these are contrary the one to the other, so that ye cannot do the things that ye would. Now the works of the flesh are manifest,

DEMONOLOGY

which are these Adultery, fornication, uncleanness, lasciviousness, Idolatry, witchcraft, hatred, variance, emulations, wrath, strife, sedition, Heresies, Envyings, murders, drunkenness, revelings, and such like; of the which I tell you before, as I have also told you in times past, that they who do such things shall not inherit the kingdom of God." It was the Old Red Dragon working through fleshly lusts that caused the antediluvians to be destroyed by the flood.

Luke 17: 27 corroborates this, "They did eat, they drank, they married wives, they were given in marriage, until the day that Noe entered into the ark, and the flood came, and destroyed them all."

It is plain to be seen that these antediluvians were making provisions for the flesh until God in judgment sent the flood to sweep them away. The sins of the flesh have destroyed nations and drowned the multitudes of all ages in perdition. God rained fire and brimstone upon Sodom and Gomorrah because of their abominable fleshly lusts and practices. When Lot separated from Abraham he pitched his tent toward Sodom, symbolizing the life of the flesh which some people cleave to even after they have been born of the Spirit. The Red Dragon stands ever ready to devour the spiritual child, and without the strictest discipline no one who has been given up to the fleshly lusts and indulgences will be able to stand, even after he has been born of the Spirit. The tendency of people is to relapse into the old habits and to cling to the environments that will eventually result in their complete overthrow and destruction.

It is this old red flesh dragon back of the "Tongues" movement that has caused it to spread with such rapidity around the globe. The soil of fleshly lusts has been so well prepared among backsliders that there has been no difficulty for heresy and witchcraft, the works of the flesh, to become strongly rooted. The colored race are the descendants of Ham, and all, perhaps, are familiar with the conditions which caused God to

DEMONOLOGY

send a curse upon Ham, one of the sons of Noah. "Cursed be Canaan (Ham); a servant of servants shall he be unto his brethren. Blessed be the Lord God of Shem; and Canaan shall be his servant. God shall enlarge Japheth, and he shall dwell in the tents of Shem; and Canaan shall be his servant." (Gen. 9:25-27).

The reason that blessings were pronounced upon Shem and Japheth was because they took a garment and walked backwards and covered their father's nakedness. Ham, who had the first opportunity, failed to do so. There was no blush on his cheek when he saw the sorrowful plight that his father was in. He was a man who, no doubt, was given to fleshly lusts, and as the curse fell upon Adam and Eve in the Garden for disobedience, so God in like manner, sent a curse upon Ham for his lack of modesty and respect for his father. With due consideration for the colored people, and with a heart interest in their spiritual uplifting, we must say it was very fitting that the devil should choose a colored man to launch out the "Tongues" movement in which the works of the flesh are so plainly manifest in these last days when the Old Red Dragon has well-nigh swallowed up every religious movement on the globe.

There is no other race through which the Dragon could work more effectually than through the colored race.

The colored people today are not responsible for the sin of Ham, and can receive salvation through the atonement like all other nationalities that have come under the curse of the sin of our first parents. But that does not alter the fact that the curse of fleshly lusts did especially fall upon Ham and his descendants, and every colored person should be enlightened on this subject so that he may make vigorous warfare on this the besetting sin of his race. It is our duty to deal with every individual in such a manner as to be helpful to him in making the fight against the world, the flesh and the devil, and when we discover the weak places in people's characters we should deal with them honestly and with a spirit of divine love, warning them against the traps the enemy has set for them, and help to build them up rather than let them go on in ignorance and lose their souls.

The conditions were so dreadful in Sodom, where the people were cursed with the sins of the flesh that the men would have done violence to the angels who came to warn Lot if they had not been restrained. No wonder the wrath of God burned against them and rained fire down upon them. The contaminating influence of Sodom was so great that Lot, with the assistance of the angels, could not deliver all the members of his family. While his wife was being hastened from the city she looked back with longing eyes upon Sodom and the lightning of God struck her and turned her to a pillar of salt.

What an awful lesson for those who are fondly twining their affections around things that pertain to the flesh! Men and women pamper the flesh and indulge the appetites until they become so weak in mind, body and soul that they are almost beyond recovery. The Red Dragon, through the flesh, has cut human life down until people are old and feeble when they ought to be in their prime God had to smite the men in Sodom with blindness to keep them from seeking to carry out their evil designs with the angels. Think of these depraved human beings, the last night in Sodom, with the persistence of demons trying to force open the door of Lot's house bent on accomplishing their nefarious purposes.

The Almighty let these things go down on record for an object lesson to the world. He raised the curtain for a short time and exposed their shame and debauchery before he let it fall, never to rise again. The Old Red Dragon had swallowed the whole city and with wide open mouth was ready to devour the angels from heaven. Lot's plea to stop at Zoar was a plea for the indulgence of the flesh. He was not ready, like Elijah, to gird up his loins and run for his life. His muscles had become soft and his will power so weakened by the life in Sodom that it seemed a great undertaking to him to go any great distance from the city. The angel, seeing his weakness, granted his request to stop at Zoar until, perhaps, he could recuperate and make another effort, but before he was in a place of safety he had to reach the mountains.

There are some persons who are unused to the rugged way of the Cross whom the Lord will bear with for a time, but sooner or later they must reach the mountain top, where the flesh, with the affections and lusts, must be crucified.

When Joshua entered Canaan God commanded him to utterly exterminate the Canaanites. He was to make no covenants with them nor show any mercy. The Canaanites, descendants of Ham, like the inhabitants of Sodom and Gomorrah, had become so corrupt they were unfit to encumber the ground and God determined to destroy them. Their cup of iniquity was full, and while they were giants, Joshua was told to fear not their faces. At one time God sent hailstones upon the armies that fought against Joshua and killed more of them than were killed by the sword.

He caused the sun and the moon to stand still for a whole day when he was being avenged upon these workers of iniquity. God will fight for any one who will make war on the flesh. The unseen armies of heaven are at the command of those who wage vigorous warfare against all the sins of the flesh. He says of his spiritual priesthood, "But ye are a chosen generation, a royal priesthood, an holy nation, a peculiar people; that ye should show forth the praises of him who hath called you out of darkness into his marvelous light." (1 Peter 1:6).

When the Syrians warred against Israel the Lord opened the eyes of Elijah's servant that he might see the innumerable host of heaven that was ready to take part in the battle. The mountains were full of chariots and horses. Elisha said, "Fear not, for they that be with us are more than they that be with them." This shows how the angels of God are engaged with us in battle against the Red Dragon and his legions. Ephesians 6:12 says, "For we wrestle not against flesh and blood, but against principalities, against powers, against the rulers of the darkness of this world, against spiritual wickedness in high places."

Great ignorance is shown by the professed followers of Christ on the subject of fallen angels. Some even doubt that there is a personal devil. The Scriptures plainly show that there are myriads of these fallen spirits that throng the atmosphere surrounding the globe seeking a place of habitation. There are all kinds of demons making up the organized forces of darkness. There are some with greater strength than others, and of superior intelligence, and of course capable of occupying more responsible places in their Majesty's service. Demons are trained and fitted for the special work they have to do. Some of them are princes, and for this reason Paul says, "For we wrestle against principalities and powers." No doubt there are myriads of demons who are not allowed to leave the confines of perdition because of their incapabilities.

They would do great damage to the kingdom of darkness if they were let have their course. We have often heard it said, "The devil overshot his mark." We believe in a case of this kind that an inexperienced demon who was not equal to the occasion, brought defeat to his master's cause. Many of them are ambitious to become great leaders, as is clearly manifested by the way they work through human beings who try to obtain honors and distinction in this world. If Satan's ambition was to excel the Almighty God, of course many of those who co-operate with him are of a similar character.

There are other demons, however, who are not aspiring to become great, they are satisfied to enter human beings, through the lust of the flesh, and drag them down to the lowest depths where they live lives lower than the animals. When Satan tempted Christ in the wilderness he approached Him through the flesh. Knowing that He had been many days without food he tried to induce Him to turn stones into bread. But Jesus said, "It is written, Man shall not live by bread alone, but by every word that proceedeth out of the mouth of God." Then he tried to get him to commit the sin of presumption, which so many who are giving way to the flesh are doing. The sin of presumption is much more prevalent in this age than it has ever been in the history of the world, from the fact that the old red flesh dragon is filling the whole earth. Peter says, "But chiefly them that walk after the flesh in the lust of uncleanness, and despise government. Presumptuous are they, self-willed." He further states that such persons "have eyes full of adultery and cannot cease from sin." We see here that God's curse is pronounced upon those who are guilty of presumptuous sins. Presumption is the counterfeit of faith and is strongly rooted in the soil of fleshly lusts.

When Satan failed in the first and second attempts to overthrow the Son of God he took Him into a high mountain and showed Him all the kingdoms of the world, and said, "All these things will I give thee if thou wilt fall down and worship me." He did not send one of his arch-demons out to meet Jesus; the emergency was great and he went himself, but he lost all his ammunition and saw the utter futility of his efforts. The written Word was used in defense against him and furnished an armor that he could not pierce.

With an open Bible before us it is not difficult to understand the nature of demons. We can know their occupations and thoughts. They live in an unrestful state running to and fro seeking an entrance into the hearts of those they can bring under their control. There are proud demons, stingy demons, lying and thieving demons. In the panoplied armies of hell there are great demons of lust that are greater in strength and power than all other demons combined; they should be met with the sword of the Spirit and driven from their strongholds. Then will the kingdom of righteousness flourish in the earth and the witchcraft in which the "Tongues" movement is figuring so prominently get a blow that will bring the hidden things of darkness to light.

THE END

MODERN VAMPIRISM

A. Osbourne Eaves, 1904

MODERN VAMPIRISM

PREFACE

If an apology be needed for the appearance of this little book it is the increasing neurotic tendency of the age, when to be healthy is to be abnormal, and the dangers in which the wholesale dabbling with the unknown will enmesh the feet of the unwary. To the widely read there may be little new in the subject, but as this is primarily written for the general mass of people it may not be hackneyed, and will, it is hoped, be of service.

That the subject is one in which a keen interest is taken is shown by the fact of its being the most popular of the thirty odd lessons or essays written by the author, and its more complete form should make it more useful.

The writer gratefully acknowledges his indebtedness to several authorities on the subject, and these should be consulted by those whose interest may be sufficiently awakened in it.

A. OSBORNE EAVES Harrogate, May 1904.

PRELIMINARY CONSIDERATIONS

Want of space will prevent elaborate and detailed proofs being given of the statements made in the following pages. Most of the statements made have been verified by more than one of the investigators into the subjects dealt with, observers who have developed within themselves extensions of faculties

DEMONOLOGY

possessed by all, but latent as yet in most of us. Clairvoyance, telepathy, and the indestructibility of mind are accepted, as well as any other authenticated fact of nature. Those to whom these ideas are new, and who, naturally, require proof, may be referred to the latest works on psychology, Prof. James' *Religious Experiences*, the *Proceedings of the Society for Psychical Research*, Dr. Babbitts', *Principles of Light and Colour*, Mr. C.H. Hintons' *Scientific Romances*, and Myers' *Human Personality and its Survival after Death*. The last named work is very painstaking, embracing many years patient study, and comprising some 1,360 pages. The reader who after judicially weighing up the evidence placed before him is convinced that death ends all, is in a bad way. As Sir Oliver Lodge said a few years ago with regard to many of the phenomena giving evidence of there being more than five senses, those who denied them were simply ignorant. As there is atrophy of an organ after which it is absolutely useless, so there is atrophy of the mind. A man who has pursued a certain groove in thought is incapable of "changing his mind" however much he may desire to do so, just as intellectual giants like Darwin have lamented in their declining days that they had no taste for poetry, or lighter hobbies with which to occupy themselves. So it will be often found that person possessing the "seven great prejudices," or seventy might be nearer the mark, that Herbert Spencer referred to, and incapable of either entertaining ideas which run along channels foreign to their usual line of thought, or believing that whatever they are incapable of seeing or experiencing, every person must necessarily share similar limitations.

All life is consciousness; the two words, in fact, are synonymous. Whenever there is one there the other will be found, and it may be as truly said that wherever there is life there is form, however subtle or rarefied that form may be. Further, all life must have vehicles through which it can express itself. For example, a physical body is necessary to contact all that is physical. Therefore, immediately we seek to pass beyond the purely physical, say, the realm of emotions, a vehicle is necessary for its expression. So, too, when we think. We have changed our consciousness and with that change comes a change in vehicle. We are said to function in a zone, or area, appropriate to the type of consciousness used. That there is something apart from the physical we all know, as when we say "my head aches", "my feet are tired", "I am hungry", we admit that "I" possess something; that the body is not the "I". Yet that this something apart should require a vehicle has not dawned upon many people as yet; remember there can be no mind without matter, the highest consciousness of which we know anything consists of a filmy and extremely attenuated matter. As it is "matter" it occupies "space" and from these considerations it may be said that every vehicle of man has a corresponding place, sometimes termed the zone or plane.

Consciousness, also, is another name for vibrations; one cannot exist without the other. Metals, we are now told, with the air of something that has just been discovered, possess consciousness or life, This was taught thousands of years ago; every particle of matter is endowed with life. There is no such thing as "dead matter." Dead! A corpse is dead. There was never greater or more ceaseless activity going on within that body than the instant "life" leaves it. The work of disintegration, or putrefaction, in which the constituent elements are returned to their appropriate state, is a beautiful illustration of the laws of nature that motion is eternal, and that matter cannot be destroyed, but can only change.

An extension of consciousness, or abnormal consciousness, only means that there is a capacity to receive higher vibrations than is customary. The range of vibrations within which the consciousness of the average man moves is well defined, but by proper training it can be extended. For instance, it is well known that there are colors which the human eye is not sufficiently sensitive to detect in the spectrum. Muller says that the suns' rays extend below the red more than two octaves. Baron Reichenbach discovered some of these missing rays which he demonstrated by means of thousands of experiments with sixty persons, including physicians, professors, naturalists, etc, and which proved his odic light and color which was derided til the advent of the N-Rays, when it is admitted that rays are emitted from the body. Things move very rapidly now, and possibly before these lines have been in print the existence of half the phenomena discussed in the following pages will have been recognized, and the writer will have been flogging a dead horse. All we are waiting for are instruments still more delicate than those hitherto invented to register the subtler vibrations which surround man on every side, though he is ignorant of their existence.

The gaps in the spectrum, then, are not due to the absence of colors, but to the incapability of sense organs to cognate them. In the same way there are sounds which the human ear is deaf to; few people have a sufficiently keen ear to detect the cry of the bat; in fact not one of the five senses but what very imperfectly registers the phenomena of life, and it is due to these imperfections that other realms of nature are shut out to us as the infinitesimal creation was til the advent of the microscope. What the microscope has done in one direction hypnotism has done in another. Under hypnosis there is a strange extension of faculties in the field of sight, hearing, touch, smell, and taste, and the mental functions. Psychology has actually invented a terminology to cover the phenomena observed, and in the course of the next fifty years they may discover that the contentions of the old mesmerists were quite correct, though not expressed in such polished or terse language as they themselves employ. There is in ordinary hypnosis, however, a hiatus between the consciousness thus produced and the normal consciousness, which is seldom bridged over. What takes place during the period covered by the experiment? If the patient is left to "sleep" and is insensible to all physical pain, to the attempts to awaken him, except by his operator, where is the consciousness? He is unconscious, it will be said. There is no such thing as unconsciousness; except to one set of vibrations. Trance, somnambulism, catalepsy, even death, are but the changing of the consciousness, and it is with some of these other states of consciousness that we are concerned with the subject of vampirism.

MAN'S VEHICLES

It is not necessary to say much about the physical vehicle- the body, except that the type of life led and the purity or otherwise of the food taken have much to do with the building of subtler vehicles fitted to respond to the higher vibrations. As he builds a coarse foul physical body so he builds the next vehicle.

Interpenetrating the physical body is another usually known as the etheric double, because it is composed of ether, and is an exact duplicate of the grosser vehicle. As to how it can interpenetrate it we have only to remember that ether interpenetrates every particle of matter of which we have any knowledge, just as in a pint of water, there would be a pint of air, and as much of ether, so that really the water would occupy no more space for the presence of these additions. This etheric double is composed of four ethers- only one is known to modern science at the present- and is of a violet-gray in color, its fineness or the reverse depending on the type of physical body. Its purpose is to form a medium by which the life-force (called in the East, prana,) can pass along the nerves of the body, and by means of which impacts from without can be conveyed to the body. It is upon this that the physical body is molded. As the life which is poured forth from the sun (technically called Jiva) reaches the earths' atmosphere it is the work of this vehicle to transmute it into vitality for the use of the ordinary body. This transmutation or specializing is done by the spleen, the function of which has always been a mystery to physiologists. After being specialized, it courses over the body, bringing buoyancy, which in the case of very feeble or enervated constitutions, in clear sunlight frequently causes sneezing, and colds are "caught," the system being unable to stand the invigorating life rays. The vitality (prana) is a beautiful rose-tinted light, which after it has expended itself upon the body radiates outwards in every direction in bluish-white light or mist.

Anesthetics drive out the etheric double; so too do mesmeric passes. It cannot be contended that the circulation is retarded in the latter case, as it is not, but the prana of the operator takes the place of that of the subject. Cold also acts in a similar manner, and other forces, to which reference will be made in their place.

Within the etheric double, or rather interpenetrating it, lies another vehicle, composed of a matter of a luminous character, and therefore called by the ancients the "astral" body, though this is not after all a very happy term. It is affected by every passing thought or emotion, changing both in color and shape with inconceivable rapidity. On account of its great tenuity it is sometimes termed the fluidic body, or psychic effluvium. This matter has been gathered together by the man, unconsciously, so far as his ordinary brain consciousness is concerned, and is the expression of him on the plane on which he functions when using this vehicle.

Further it is the seat of desire, and the stronger the desires the more accentuated is this body, more especially if these desires are gross or impure, because the astral body pertains more to the animal part of man than the divine. As "man" is mortal, so is this vehicle, although its life is considerably longer than that of the body, in many cases existing for very lengthy periods, as long, in fact, as desire itself lasts. All feeling, suffering, enjoying connected with the senses are received by it, so that it is in constant use, but few people are aware of it; as has been said there is a want of unifying consciousness between these two consciousnesses, and it is at

DEMONOLOGY

night while the physical body is asleep that it leaves it. Many of the so-called "ghosts" are simply astral appearances of living or dead persons.

There are other vehicles of a higher character but it is not necessary to consider them for our purposes.

OTHER PLANES

The word plane is not a very satisfactory one, nor is zone much better, but one is perforce compelled to use either one or the other. One usually imagines that other realms of nature must necessarily exist outside the earth- in space. While there is no reason why this should not be the case since life invests every atom of the universe, yet it is difficult for some to conceive life interpenetrating life, and plane interpenetrating plane. Yet this must be so. Take the countless millions of lives of which our physical bodies are composed. Each little microbe has its separate consciousness, as the chemical atoms have when they display their likes and dislikes for their brother elements; it plays its little role and dies, although we are quite unaware of it. Its "plane" is the body, but we are scarcely cognizant of it. Again, in dreams, many of the senses are as realistic as though the actions depicted in them were actually taking place, and the illusions of time and space are admirably illustrated in this state.

Now in a very similar manner the astral plane exists. While we are functioning there in the astral body, which is the appropriate vehicle for it, as a ship is an appropriate vehicle when we wish to traverse water, a balloon for air, and a train or motor car for earth, it is very real to us, but we are dead to the real surroundings, such as the bed and room. So in like manner while the consciousness functions in the physical body, the man is dead to the astral which surrounds him on every side. Every night when he retires to slumber, his astral body slips out, and if not too lethargic and concerned with its own thoughts, it makes a tour of the plane, and passes through similar experiences that

DEMONOLOGY

it passes through during the day in the waking consciousness, though it cannot bridge over the two states. Where a man is able to extend his sense of sight or that of hearing he comes into conscious touch with the plane; the man attunes the rate of his vibrations to those of the plane- done unwittingly in most cases- and that is sufficient to put him in touch with it. A fair analogy is offered in the case of two strings of a musical instrument being tuned to the same pitch, or note, and if one is touched the other will take up the sound independently. Very similar, also, is the *modus operandi* of the Marconi apparatus, where each instrument must be tuned, so to say, to the same pitch.

There are seven subdivisions of this, the second division of nature, and six higher ones are formed into two classes, while the lowest stands alone, life on the sixth, as the author of *The Astral Plane* points out, being very similar to our own here, minus the physical body. The scenery is the same, but the phenomena on the plane are much more startling than on earth.

We are not concerned with the higher regions of this plane, and need not therefore pause to describe them, but a few words may be said regarding the lowest level. Our physical plane is said to be the background of it, and it may be likened to a dense black fog, rendering progress through it slow, uncertain, and unpleasant, and giving the traveler in it a tired, heavy, languorous feeling. Life here is like life in the foulest slums we can boast of.

THE INHABITANTS

Of the entities who inhabit these regions there are many, and among the human and living (i.e. living human beings) in addition to the lowest among mankind, are the black magician and his pupils- members of the Dugpa, Obesh, and Voodoo schools among others.

Among the "dead" is the ordinary person, but he does

not stay here long, the atmosphere not being conducive to tranquility or happiness. Generally speaking, the lowest class of man preponderates, the length of time they remain depending on many circumstances, and varying in duration. The averagely "good" man would not stay many months, probably not weeks, but others might remain there centuries, one factor in the question of duration depending upon the type of mind and the life previously led. The purer and more noble the life lived here, the shorter the period spent on the astral plane, because it is not mans' final home but only a temporary resting place, where he outwears the lower desires he carried with him at death. The existence of many persons, much engrossed with their own thoughts, is spent in a semi-conscious dreamy state. The majority of men, however, rarely recognize their innate divinity; the life of many is lower than that of the brutes, and the result is that they fall below the level of that inferior creation, recalling to mind Pascals' words; "Man, the shame and glory of the universe." Man lives ignorant of his birthright, pandering to the animal propensities in his nature, which he should have outgrown long ago, and he himself forges the fetters which bind him to earth.

One of the greatest mistakes in connection with the subject of death is that there is a wonderful transformation in the nature. Nothing, we are assured, can be further from the truth. The only difference between a man who has just "died" and a living one is that the former has shaken off a vehicle, as a man might take a coat off. As a great coat hampers movement to some extent so the physical body hampers freedom of movement, and there is a feeling of indescribable lightness which one sometimes experiences in dreams, by being so divested of this cumbrous weight. No conversion of a man who has led a low, ignoble, brutish life to a saint occurs; no, he retains his nature exactly as it was a few moments before death. Nature never jumps, it is said, and a quick change in regard to character is a pure myth. As it has taken years to form the character, so it takes many years to reform it. To take a homely, and perhaps rather crude analogy, the law of its being compels a cork to float on the surface, and a stone to rest at the bottom; cream invariably comes to the top, and mud just as inevitably sinks to the bottom, or with the chemical elements, some will come together whatever difficulties be placed in their way; others will as persistently refuse to coalesce.

And cut-and-dried theological systems would have us believe that at the casting off of the physical body a man goes to one of two places!

A man in the flush of youth may lead a life of excess, but as the vital powers decrease with advancing age, and he has become satiated with pleasure, he may lose his hold upon them, and in the course of time outwear them altogether; but should such a man be "cut off" in the heyday of his passions he will carry with him to the next state these unquenchable desires, but with no means of gratifying them, for he has lost the instrument which required the gratification- the physical body, and with it the organs which would enable them to receive the pleasure.

Suppose, for instance, a man were a confirmed drunkard, death would not deprive him of the unnatural thirst he had created; he would feel it in all its intensity, but would be unable to satisfy the craving in the slightest, except in a manner which will be described later.

Again, in the case of those removed by accident or suicide, in which no preparation of any kind has been made, and where all the life forces are in full play, if the life has been a degraded one then they will be alive to the horrors of this plane. They will be cut adrift, as it were with all their passionate nature strong upon them, and must remain on that plane until the time their death in an ordinary manner would have taken place. Thus a man killed at 25 who would otherwise have reached the age of 75, would spend half a century upon this plane. In case of the suicides, seeing they have not accomplished their end, namely, to put an end to existence, the return for earth-life grows upon them with terrible zest.

It is here that one of the dangers of vampirism occurs. If the experience they seek cannot be obtained without a physical body only two courses are open for them. One is to do so vicariously. To do this they must feed on the emanations arising from blood and alcohol; public houses and slaughter houses are thronged with these unhappy creatures which hang about and feed thus. From this standpoint the habit of offering blood sacrifices to propitiate entities, as found recorded in some of the worlds scriptures, becomes luminous, and the history of magic teems with such examples. Not content, however, with thus prolonging their existence on the lower levels of the astral plane the entities lure on those human beings whose tastes are depraved, causing them to go to all kinds of excesses, enticing them on in sensuality and vice of every kind. Each time a man yields to temptation the supremacy over him which these creatures hold becomes stronger; they gain possession of his will, til at length they control him altogether. How many men, who have hitherto lived a blameless life, have on the spur of the moment committed some heinous crime, and the public have marveled how they came to it? The explanation offered after the commission of the crime has often been to the effect that they could not tell what possessed them to do it but they felt a sudden impulse sweep over them and they obeyed it. Here, without a doubt, is the genesis of the conception of a tempter, and one feels more inclined to pity than to blame in many cases.

What is known as "obsession" is often brought about by the same means. As like attracts like, so a debased nature attracts to it either human or non-human entities of a similar nature, and these plunge the unfortunate man into vice and crime. Many will remember the historical case of the year 1864, where a whole community became possessed of the Devil; the demoniacs of Morzine, the sorceries of Vallyres, and those of the Presybeter de Cideville, and since then numerous isolated

DEMONOLOGY

cases have been reported from time to time. Exorcism was resorted to by the church, and in some instances this was successful but not invariably.

NON-HUMAN ENTITIES

Thanks to materialism most people have come to the conclusion that no life can exist which is not visible to the eye, and the existence of the microbe and whirling atom is very problematic to them. Yet Huxley said "Without stepping beyond the analogy of that which is known it is easy to people the cosmos with entities, in an ascending scale, until we reach something practically indistinguishable from omnipotence, omnipresence, and omniscience." Sir Wm. Crookes, the great physicist, in the Fortnightly, wrote; "It is not improbable that other sentient beings have organs of sense which do not respond to one or any of the rays to which our eyes are sensitive, but are able to appreciate other vibrations to which we are blind. Such beings would practically be living in a different world to our own. Imagine, for instance, what idea we should form of surrounding objects were we endowed with eyes not sensitive to the vibrations concerned in electric and magnetic phenomena. Glass and crystal would be among the most opaque of bodies. Metals would be more or less transparent, and a telegraph wire through the air would look like a long, narrow hole drilled through an impervious solid body. A dynamo in active work would resemble a conflagration while a permanent magnet would realize the dream of medieval mystics, and become an everlasting lamp with no expenditure of energy or consumption of fuel." Radium was not invented when these words were penned (1892) otherwise Sir William would have written with more assurance than he did.

This question of other entities and the impossibility of seeing them through the want of another "sense" is one the importance of which cannot be over-estimated by students who would fain recognize the plausibility of a hypothesis which settles so many problems, and the writer is therefore tempted to devote a little more space to it than he otherwise would.

Humanity is said to manifest in a three dimensional space, that is to say they exist surrounded by "space," which permits movement in but three directions. There is a limitation which all thinkers have recognized, and which Mr. Hinton, to whose work on the subject the reader has already been referred, if he is capable of keeping up sustained and sequential thought, for it must be confessed the book will be rather "stiff" to the untrained student, has cleared up, as far as it is possible in words to do so. We have length, breadth, and height, then, and can only move an object by a combination of three movements. It is impossible to think, in ordinary consciousness, of any other direction. Mr. CW Leadbeater very aptly shows the limitations of dimensions by contrasting those of a creature which possessed but two dimensions with ourselves who perceive three. "Think of some such microbe" he says, "suppose him to be living upon the surface of a sheet of paper. To him that sheet of paper might well seem to be the whole world, and we suppose him strictly limited to its surface. Not only could he never leave the surface either by rising above it or burying himself in it, but he could never have any conception of the meaning of our words up and down. Although he lived upon a surface, he would not know that it was a surface; to him the superficies of the thickness of an atom would be the world in which he lived. Imagine that this creature could reason; could he arrive at any way at the conception of the third dimension of up and down, which was absolutely invisible to him, and entirely outside of any experience which he has ever yet imagined? In order to arrive at this let us see what his limitations would be, and how any three dimensional object which came in his way would appear to him.

Notice, first, that considerations of size do not enter into the question. Our sheet of paper might just as well be imagined as many miles in length and in that case our microbe might be larger. So long as he is an entity only one atom thick and does not know of that thickness, his atom may be of any size that we choose. Notice that a line drawn on the paper would be for him an insurmountable obstacle. If we drew a line completely across the paper that line would divide his world into two separate parts and he could know of no way to pass from one part to another, for his world, being only the thickness of an atom, would be completely shut off by the line drawn on the paper from another world of the same nature which might be lying close to and beside his own, divided from it only by the thickness of the line. He would be entirely unconscious of what took place on the other side of that line even though it be all but touching him."

The writer goes on to show that if we could lift some object from that other world and drop it down into his, that object would be an apparition; if a square were drawn round him it would be absolutely closed to him on all sides and it would appear impossible that any creature could enter that square without coming through the sides: No box or safe that he could construct would ever be closed to us, with our three-dimensional sense. The question is considered at greater length and from the mathematical standpoint, but we are prevented from following it in all its detail, a perusal of this book for this alone would well repay perusal.

In this way it is possible to conceive of another dimension, which is peopled by entities differing in their constitution from ourselves and through the fineness of their organisms being invisible to the more solid inhabitants. On the astral plane, there are many other types of human beings than those discussed, and which the digression led us away from for the moment. Of these perhaps the most terrible are the vampire and werewolf.

The incubi and succubi of medievalists, and going still further back, the entities under different names, differ very little

DEMONOLOGY

from the vampire, about which so much was heard in 1730 in Hungary and Serbia. One reason why these countries are singled out is because their inhabitants have a strain of fourth-race blood in them and the true vampire belongs to this race. We ourselves are of the fifth great root-race, and have outgrown these beings of previous evolution. The Encyclopedia Britannica remarks on the subject of vampires; "The persons who turn vampires generally are wizards, witches, suicides, and persons who have come to a violent end, or who have been cursed by their parents or the church." It will be seen that there is much in this definition with which we can agree. Luckily for humanity these terrible creatures are very rare, and should become increasingly so as time goes on, for although they have the power to perpetuate their bodies for many centuries their victims are likely to become far fewer as they learn how to protect themselves against them.

The nature of these beings may be gathered from the following account, which is given in *Isis Unveiled*: About the beginning of the present century, there occurred in Russia, one of the most frightful cases of vampirism on record. The governor of the province Tch___ was a man of about sixty years, of a malicious, tyrannical, cruel, and jealous disposition. Clothed with despotic authority, he exercised it without stint, as his brutal instincts prompted. He fell in love with the daughter of a subordinate official. Although the girl was betrothed to a young man whom she loved, the tyrant forced her father to consent to his having her marry him; and the poor victim despite her despair became his wife. His jealous disposition exhibited itself. He beat her, confined her to her room for weeks together, and prevented her seeing anyone except in his presence. He finally fell sick and died. Finding his end approaching he made her swear never to marry again; and with fearful oaths threatened that, in case she did, he would return from his grave and kill her. He was buried in the cemetery across the river, and the young widow experienced no further annoyance, until, nature getting the better of her fears, she listened to the importunity of her former lover and they were again betrothed.

On the night of the customary betrothal-feast when all had returned, the old mansion was aroused by shrieks proceeding from her room. The doors were burst open and the unhappy woman was found lying on her bed in a swoon. At the same time a carriage was heard rumbling out of the courtyard. Her body was found to be black and blue in places as from the effect of pinches, and from a slight puncture on her neck drops of blood were oozing. Upon recovering she stated that her deceased husband had suddenly entered her room, appearing exactly as in life, with the exception of a dreadful pallor, that he had upbraided her for her inconstancy, and then beaten and pinched her most cruelly. Her story was disbeliever; but the next morning the guard stationed at the other end of the bridge which spans the river reported that just before midnight, a black coach and six had driven furiously past them toward the town, without answering their challenge.

The new governor, who disbelieved the story of the apparition, took nevertheless the precaution of doubling the guards across the bridge. The same thing happened, however, night after night; the soldiers declaring that the toll bar at their station near the bridge would rise of itself, and the spectral equipage sweep by them despite their efforts to stop it. At the same time every night the coach would rumble into the courtyard of the house; the watchers, including the widows' family, and the servants, would be thrown into a heavy sleep, and every morning the young victim would be found bruised, bleeding, and swooning as before. The town was thrown into consternation. The physicians had no explanations to offer; priests came to pass the night in prayer, but as midnight approached all would be seized with the terrible lethargy. Finally, the archbishop of the province came and performed the ceremony of exorcism in person but the following morning the governors' widow was found worse than ever. She was now

DEMONOLOGY

brought to deaths' door.

The governor was now driven to take the severest measures to stop the ever-increasing panic in the town. He stationed fifty cossacks along the bridge with orders to stop the specter carriage at all hazards. Promptly, at the usual hour, it was heard and seen approaching from the direction of the cemetery, the officer of the guard, and a priest bearing a crucifix, planted themselves in front of the toll bar, and together shouted "In the name of God and the Czar, who goes there?" Out of the coach window was thrust a well-remembered head, and a familiar voice responded; "The privy councilor of state and governor C.__!" At the same moment the officer, the priest, and the soldiers were flung aside as by an electric shock, and the ghostly equipage passed by them before they could recover breath.

The archbishop then resolved as a last expedient to resort to the time-honored plan of exhuming the body and pinning it to the earth with an oaken stake driven through its heart. This was done with great religious ceremony in the presence of the whole populace. The story is that the body was found gorged with blood, and with red cheeks and lips. At the instant that the first blow was struck upon the stake, a groan issued from the corpse and a jet of blood spurted high in the air. The archbishop pronounced the usual exorcism, the body was re-interred, and from that time no more was heard of the vampire.

How far the facts of this case may have been exaggerated by tradition we cannot say. But we had it years ago from an eyewitness, and at the present day there are families in Russia whose elder members will recall the dreadful tale."

The recital of this narrative will serve several purposes. In the first place it is unique in possessing more of the phenomena connected with vampirism than is usually found in a single instance, and this would lead a student of these subjects to accept it as being credible. A prerequisite in vampires of the type we are considering is cruelty and a strong individuality, and the fact of this man having been a governor of a province would support the latter assumption. Then there was the intensity of his jealousy, which dies hard, and that intensity was sufficient to keep the thoughts of the governor one-pointed. The binding oath was the seal to a compact of a terrible character, namely the returning after death to kill his wife. Naturally, seeing the renewal of an acquaintance which he has stepped in between, and knowing no doubt his wifes' preference for her old lover, the degree of hatred can well be imagined, which would be fanned into a flame when the young couple became betrothed. As has been stated, under ordinary circumstances, a man passing out of this life stays but a short time on the next plane, and he has no particular desire to come back, but the natural inclinations were different in the case we are dealing with. While very many persons leaving this plane are unable to communicate with those whom they have left behind, and which forms such an unanswerable argument to the skeptic, who calls for proof that the dead are near us and conscious, a strong nature will find means- generally by accident- for on that plane he is surrounded by laws as here, though these laws are of course strange at first. It is a matter of experiment. A case was reported in the daily press in April 1904, where a telegraphist could, by taking hold of the hands of two friends and making an effort of will, cause a coin to rise from the table several inches. Bulwer Lytton was credited with the power of compelling a letter to come to him across the room by his volition. A popular weekly also gave an experiment lately how a ping pong ball could be made to advance or recede by an effort of the will. Now these feats will before a few years have passed away be quite childish, but to most people such phenomena are surrounded by mystery and the occult. Yet it is but an application of the laws of mind, known to a few here and there and discovered by accident, as many of our most important inventions have been. So it is in other realms of nature. The majority of people who find themselves on the astral plane are at first quite helpless, and marvel to see others passing through solid (apparently) rock, living fire, raging water, or walk off precipices. It has been mentioned that the body changes its shape rapidly, and its color on this plane. So do many of the entities existing there, while a man who has studied the dynamics of thought can create by his thought, just as a Hindu fakir does, something which has no palpable existence, except in the mind of its creator for the time being. Yet it will have the semblance of reality.

The governor had by some means learned the laws by which it is possible to preserve his "dead" body after his death, that is, by vampirism, by the drawing of blood from some human being and thus fed his body in the grave which he may either leave, as in cases of materializations, or the blood may be brought to it. "As above so below" runs the Hermetic axiom, and instances in the animal kingdom of vampirism point to their possibility on higher planes.

Another instance, which is better known than the one just quoted, "The Bride of Corinth," sheds further light on the question. Six months after her death she appeared to a man who was staying in her fathers' house and even partook of some refreshments with him. Her return is soon discovered by a nurse who informs the girls' mother who, eventually, with a pardonable incredulity, goes into the room. Everything is in darkness however, the visitor evidently having retired for the night. In the morning she has an interview with the visitor, and learns that the daughter has been there, a ring belonging to the girl, who had left it in exchange for some trinket from the man, being recognized. This had been buried with her, and it is surmised that the body must have been exhumed, but as the girl promised to visit the house the next night nothing is said of their suspicions, The girl re-appears, and the parents being apprised of the fact by a servant whom they have set to watch, they see her and recognize her. Instead of being overjoyed the girl upbraids her parents for coming, saying that she has been permitted to spend three days with their visitor, but that now she must go to her appointed place, on saying which she falls down dead. In this case the body was quite visible, otherwise it would have been taken as a hallucination. The vault was opened but no body was found there, but the ring given to the girl by the young man was found lying upon the bier, The body was again buried outside the city with special ceremonies, it being believed that it was a case of vampirism.

If one reads the daily papers, instances where coffins have been accidentally opened have disclosed bodies which have all the appearance of life in them. It has been accounted for by supposing that it has been a case of premature burial, to prevent which, I believe, there is a society. There is no doubt cases of catalepsy are more frequent than is suspected; it has even been suggested that electric bells should be placed in the coffin which should act with the slightest movement, but it might easily be in some cases that the body had been artificially kept in a state of freshness with the hope that it could be used again. Without the full knowledge of the process of materialization and dematerialization, however, this artifice would avail little.

A variant in the type of vampire is seen in the following article, written by Dr. Franz Hartmann, the author of *Magic Black and White* and other well known works on occultism, who has devoted some twenty years to the study of these subjects. It is headed "A Modern Case of Vampirism."

In the night of December 31st, 1888, Mr. and Mrs. Rose (the names in this story are pseudonyms, but the facts are true) went to bed as poor people and on the morning of January 1st, 1889, they woke up finding themselves rich. An uncle to whom they owed their poverty because he kept them from coming into the legal possession of their rightful property, had died during the night. There are some occurrences of an occult character, connected with this event, which will be interesting to those who wish to find practical proofs and demonstrations in their investigations of the "night side of nature."

Mr. Rose is a young, but very clever, professional man in this city who, being at the beginning of his career, has therefore only an exceedingly limited number of clients. His young wife is one of the most amiable ladies whom it has been my good fortune to meet; a spiritually minded woman and more of a poetess than an economist. She had been brought up under the most affluent circumstances, her father being very rich, and she was the only and therefore the pet child in her luxurious home. It would be too complicated a task to tell how it happened that the property which she inherited fell first into the hands of her uncle, a spiteful and avaricious man. Sufficient to say that this man, whom we will call Helleborus, had by his intrigues and lawsuits managed to keep Mrs. Roses' property in his hands, giving her and her husband no support whatever. More than once they were forced to borrow money from their friends in order to keep themselves from starvation.

As "Uncle Helleborus" was in the last stage of consumption, their only hope was that his death would soon put an end to his lawsuits and bring them into possession of what rightfully belonged to them.

Uncle Helleborus however did not seem inclined to die. Year after year he kept on coughing and expectorating, but with all this he outlived many who predicted his death. After making to Mr. and Mrs. Rose a proposal of a settlement, which would have left him in possession of nearly all the property and given to them only a pittance, he went to Meran, last summer, to avoid the cold climate of Vienna.

Under the embarrassing circumstances they were much inclined to accept the settlement but they concluded to first consult about it a friend, an eminent lawyer, and this gentleman,

DEMONOLOGY

(whom we will call Mr. Tulip, as everybody in Vienna knows his real name), advised them to the contrary. This enraged Helleborus against Tulip, and starting into a blind rage he swore that if he found an opportunity of killing Tulip he would surely do so.

Mr. Tulip was an extraordinarily strong, well built and healthy man; but at the beginning of December last, soon after Mr. Helleborus' departure for Metan, he suddenly failed in health. The doctors could not locate his disease, and he grew rapidly thinner and weaker, complaining of nothing but extreme lassitude, and feeling like a person who was daily bled, Finally, on the 20th of December last, all Vienna was surprised to hear that Mr. Tulip had died. Post-mortem examination showing all the organs in a perfectly normal condition, the doctors found nothing better to register but death from *marasmus* (emaciation) as the cause of this extraordinary event. Strange to say, during the last days of disease (if it can be so-called) when his mind became flighty, he often imagined that a stranger was troubling him, and the description which he gave of that invisible personage fitted Mr. Helleborus with perfect accuracy.

During Mr. Tulips; sickness, news came from Meran that Mr. Helleborus was rapidly gaining strength and recovering from his illness in a most miraculous manner; but there were some people who expressed grave doubts as to whether this seeming recovery would be lasting. On the day of Mr. Tulips' funeral, Mr.___, a prominent member of the T.S. Now in Austria, remarked to Mrs. Rose; "You will see that now that Mr. Tulip is dead, his vampire will die too."

On January 1st 1889, Mr. Rose dreamed that he saw uncle Helleborus looking perfectly healthy. He expressed his surprise about it when a voice, as if coming from a long distance, said; "Uncle Helleborus is dead." The voice sounded a second time, and this once far more powerfully, repeating the same sentence; and this time Mr. Rose awoke with the sound of that voice still ringing in his ears, and communicated to his wife the happy news that "Uncle Helleborus was dead." Two hours afterward a telegram came from Meran announcing the demise of Uncle Helleborus which had occurred that very night, and calling upon Mr. Rose to attend the funeral. It was found that Mr. Helleborus had begun to grow rapidly worse from the day when Mr. Tulip died.

The only rational explanation of such cases, I have found in Paracelsus." -Franz Hartmann, M.D.

THE VAMPIRES' FATE

There can be no doubt that the strong wish to injure "Mr. Tulip" was sufficient to form a tie between the uncle and himself, which permitted the absorption of vitality from the one to the other, in a manner to be explained later.

It is only possible for a man to become a vampire by leading a really wicked and utterly selfish life. The most deeply-dyed villain has nearly always some one redeeming point and this would be sufficient to prevent so awful a fate befalling him as inclusion in this class of entity. There is in addition to the bodies described above a principle in which the soul inheres, and if an exceptionally evil life has been led then it becomes entangled as it were with the animal part of nature, and the soul becomes "lost." From such a class is the ancient vampire drawn. After death, instead of spending some years on the lower levels of the astral plane, he is drawn into his own place- Avitchi, the eighth sphere, whereon are consigned those who pass through the "second death." "That death" says the author of *Isis Unveiled*, "is the gradual dissolution of the astral form into its primal elements... the 'soul' as a half animal principle becomes paralyzed, and grows unconscious of its subjective half- the Lord, and in proportion of the sensuous development of the brain and nerves, sooner or later, it finally loses sight of its divine mission on earth. Like the Vourdalak, or vampire, of the

DEMONOLOGY

Serbian tale, the brain feeds and lives and grows in strength at the expense of its spiritual parent." Again: "Our present cycle is pre-eminently one of such soul deaths. We elbow soulless men and women at every step in life. Neither can we wonder, in the present state of things, at the gigantic failure of Hegels' and Schellings' last efforts at metaphysical construction of some system. When facts, palpable and tangible facts of phenomenal spiritualism happen daily and hourly, and yet are denied by the majority of 'civilized' nations, little chance is there for the acceptance of purely abstract metaphysics by the ever growing crowd of materialists. And when death arrives there is no more a soul to liberate... for it has fled years before."

Knowing what to expect the vampire endeavors by the aid of laws at present known but to a few to escape the justly merited fate that threatens, by preserving his physical body from decay. It can be kept in a cataleptic condition by the transfusion of human blood, which it accomplishes by fastening on those who are not strong enough to defend themselves against it.

Perhaps the most sensational fiction with regard to the Vampire after Sheridan le Fanu's "Carmilla" is to be found in "Dracula" but it is very morbid reading. Evidently the author has been working the subject up, judging from the story, and by means of a vivid imagination an exciting narrative has been produced. The book is quoted here because so much information in reference to the vampire is given which want of space forbids enlarging upon here. Robert Louis Stephenson's romance of the *Strange Case of Dr. Jeckyll and Mr. Hyde* illustrates other phases and may interest the reader.

SIR CONAN DOYLE

The dangers arising from the class of entity we have been considering are naturally limited, but there are other dangers to which a very large number of people are exposed. Truth, as is generally the case, supplies us with examples which fiction cannot easily equal, but are not always easily accessible; whereas fiction is, and often, unwittingly, it may be, places the less known facts of life in a clearer light. Thus we have in Sir Conan Doyle's little story "The Parasite" an object lesson on the subject of vampirism. It will be remembered how the vampire is introduced in the person of Miss Penelosa, who is described as being a small frail creature, "with a pale peaky face, an insignificant presence and retiring manner." Her eyes are remarkable however. The beginning of the power exercised over Professor Gilroys' fiancee, where the latter is placed in a mesmeric sleep, and then extended to the skeptical professor himself, who finds himself becoming thinner and darker under the eyes, and aware of a nervous irritability which he had not observed before, is all very significant. The further detailing of how this woman with the crutch obsesses the professor, projecting herself into his body and taking possession of it is related. "She has a parasite soul" he says; "yes, she is a parasite, a monster parasite. She creeps into my form as the hermit crab creeps into the whelks' shell." Realizing at last the womans' intentions on him, and the fact of his will becoming weaker, he seeks to withdraw himself out of her toils, locking himself in his bedroom and throwing the key into the garden beneath. He succeeds for the time being but learns on the occasion of his success that Miss Penelosa had been ill and that she had said that her powers forsook her at such times. One night, fearing to excite the gardeners' suspicions, pushes the key under the door instead of resorting to the old ruse of throwing it out of the window, and composes himself to read one of Dumas' novels;- "Suddenly, I was gripped- gripped and dragged from the cough. It is only thus that I can describe the overpowering nature of the force which pounced upon me. I clawed at the coverlet, I clung to the woodwork, I believe that I screamed out in my frenzy. It was all useless- hopeless. I must go. There was no way out of it. It was only at the outset that I resisted. The force soon became too overmastering for that. I thank goodness that there were no watchers to interfere with me. I could not have answered for myself if there had been. And besides the determination to get out, there came to me also the keenest coolest judgment in choosing my means. I lit a candle and endeavored, kneeling in front of the door, to pull the key through with the feather-end of a quill pen. It was just too short and pushed it farther away. Then with quiet persistence I got a paper knife out of one of my drawers and with that I managed to draw the key back. I opened the door, stepped into my study, took a photograph of myself from the bureau, wrote something across it, and placed it in the inside pocket of my coat, then started off for Wilsons."

He then finds himself in her presence and her hands in his and making professions that he loathes while he utters. He frees himself by a mighty effort and, in scathing language, empties the vials of his wrath on her head, and rushes away, the spell broken. The victory seemed to be of brief duration. Miss Penelosa recovers sufficiently to visit him and warns if he persists in scorning her love he may know what to expect. He laughs at her threats but almost immediately experiences her influence upon him. The unburdening of his troubles to his college professor does not relieve him of the demoniacal possession and the prescription of chloral and bromide is consigned to the gutter. The continuance of the vampires' wiles where she seeks to destroy his popularity as a lecturer by confusing his thoughts upon his subject, ending with the university authorities taking his lectureship from him, his lectures having become the laughing stock of the university, drive him to extremities.

"And the most dreadful part is my loneliness. Here I sit in a commonplace English bow-window looking out upon a commonplace English street, with its garish buses and lounging policemen, and behind me there hands a shadow which is out of all keeping with the age and place. In the home of knowledge I am weighed down and tortured by a power of which science knows nothing. No magistrate would listen to me, no paper would discuss my case. No doctor would believe my symptoms. My own most intimate friends would only look upon it as a sign of brain derangement. I am out of all touch with my kind."

Silently and with devilish subtlety, the woman winds her coils about him more closely, causing him to rob a bank, half kill a friend, and almost disfigure the features of the girl he loves. How far the machinations of the woman might have been carried is impossible but her death puts an unexpected end to them.

SOME MODERN CASES

Turning from fiction to fact, Mr. D. Younger gives one of several instances which have come under his notice of cases allied very closely to vampirism, in his book. A man came to him for help, having been recommended to him. He had been troubled for a long time with voices sounding in his ears and threatening him with bodily harm. The voices had pursued him even to Mr. Youngers' house in Bayswater, and the victim could then hear them talking. Mr. Younger, whom the writer remembers as a tall, well-made vigorous man, made a number of passes round the patient, and after a time the voices ceased, and have not returned since, as far as the writer is aware. The writer received a letter a few months ago from a French lady in London who had been staying in Harrogate last summer.

"When I went to Harrogate, I was better, and the distressing feeling of fright I had had constantly day and night vanished for a time, but it has now assumed its sway. It begins at night when I am out of doors; it is as if I was pursued. It always comes from behind like a large wave, over my right shoulder, and when I am in my room writing, it seems as though I had someone behind me. The sensation is oppressing, and I feel a weight over my shoulder blades, and when people pass near me, if they do not touch me, they hurt me. It has become so uncanny that I should like to know what it is and what is to be done."

DEMONOLOGY

The writer himself some years ago had a similar experience. It would be between four and five o'clock one morning when he was awakened by a voice which distinctly came from within, saying "you will have to come," at the same time there was an indescribable feeling as though part of himself was being forcibly torn from the body. Being interested in the phenomenon and wondering what it might be, the writer composed himself a moment after, emphatically declaring he would not go, to see if the sensation would be repeated. It was, and very unpleasantly this time, though wide awake, and it was deemed best to throw the influence off. There was a brief struggle, during which the voice again demanded that the personality should yield, then the sensation passed.

A friend of the writers' has had a somewhat similar feeling, where during the night, if lying upon the stomach he has felt himself gripped on the shoulders behind, with pressure on the small of the back, while the shoulders would be pulled backwards. He has been awakened by the sensation and the struggle has lasted a few seconds after being awake, so that it is no nightmare. This occurred twice, and on two other occasions he distinctly felt a solid body, like a dead body beside him in bed. Florence Marryat in *There is No Death* relates a very gruesome story along a similar line, and people who are subject to these experiences should never sleep alone. Many cases of epilepsy are no doubt instances of entities using the physical body of the victim.

A MODERN DEMONIAC

A case is quoted by Mr. WT Stead in *Borderland*, which came within his own personal knowledge. One day in January 1896, a young man, an officer in the British Army, came to his office, and said that some time back he had taken up automatic writing. This, for the benefit of those to whom the phrase may be new, is sitting with the mind passive, pen in hand, and permitting the hand to be used by ones' own inner

DEMONOLOGY

consciousness, or other entities. Many books have been so produced, the phenomenon being a very common one. Being charmed with the novelty of the thing the young man had neglected nearly every duty, allowing himself to be used eight to ten hours at a stretch at a time. Gradually the intelligence or entity gained such possession of his faculties that, as he said, "I no longer felt I belonged to myself. It dominates me by its will, and I do not know what the end will be." Mr. Stead expostulated with him, saying he should exert himself, but the young man said it was no use, as his will was under the influence. "He says", continued the young man, "that he will do me all the evil he can while I live, and after that, I am to be damned. But will you speak with him?" Being informed that the entity would take possession at any time, Mt. Stead continues; "I paused for a moment but I thought that as the evil spirit was in the habit of seizing without his will and to his own detriment, it would be permissible to allow him to enter in by an act of his own volition when he was with one who might possibly be the means of helping him in his deliverance; so I said 'yes, if he will talk he may come.' My visitor walked across the room and sat down without saying a word in a large easy chair. In a moment he became convulsed, his eyes closed, he fell backwards with his head on the couch, his chest heaved, rising and falling, while his body writhed as if convulsed. Not a word was said. I stood watching him silently, nor did he speak or make a sound beyond a low moan when the convulsions became more violent. After waiting for two or three minutes standing over him, I said at last, 'well!' Then there was another writhing movement of the prostrate form before me, and a very curious voice, quite different from that of my visitor, said to me..." but the dialogue is too lengthy to be reproduced here. It is sufficient to say that the entity claimed to be the grandfather of a girl whom the young man had ruined, and since then (some four months before) the grandfather had never left the young man, and told his interrogator that the officer dare not shave himself for fear her should cut his throat, which he (the old man) would see he did some day. While the conversation was going on the young man struck himself, and the face twinged with pain, which delighted the entity apparently.

"I can do anything with him now. Anything. He is mine altogether. I can make him go where I like, talk to him when I like; night and day torment hi. Keep it up. Oh! Yes, keep it up. And in four months cut his throat." the last sentence being accompanied by drawing his hand across his neck.

As to how he got ahold of this unfortunate man may be told in the entities' own words: "I was an officer in the army in my time and I think I ruined more women than any man I know. Then I came over here and for fifty years what have I had to do but go along seeing girls, pretty girls, falling in love with them and not being able to speak to them.

Tormented with the desire, but unable to gratify it, he watched until the young man took up a ouija board, and got answers from somebody, then thinks he will try handwriting. Takes a pen. I see him. I am passing. I see what he is doing. Remember about my grand daughter. I wait. I think I can get at him. Some day he thinks he will try automatic writing. Takes a pen in his old fist- ugh! I took his hand and wrote. Called myself 'Lucy' I did. Lucy, nice girl, always said her prayers, beautiful spirit; come to lead him into the paths of virtue. Ho! Did I not fool him... I have tortured him for four months. I will torture him for another four, then I will cut his throat- yes, I will!"

Mr. Stead brought this conversation to a termination by telling the obsessing entity that it would do nothing of the kind and that it would have to clear out, as it had been there quite long enough.

"He did not speak again. A few convulsive movements followed, a long sigh, and then the visitor slowly rose to his feet, rubbing his eyes."

DEMONOLOGY

Taxed with the story related to Mr. Stead the young man admitted its truthfulness, and was despondent as to being able to throw the evil influence off, though Mr. Stead pointed out that he, the young man, still had some will left as he would not have come to him had it been otherwise. Mr. Stead advised him to try and find the young lady who could help him, but the young man said that if he did he would kill him that night. I will conclude the article with the closing paragraph:

"I saw my unknown visitor once again. His control was more blasphemous and more defiant than before. The convulsions were worse, and the contortions more violent. It was a ghastly sight to see him writhing on the floor, tossed about until he was stiff and sore. It may have been incipient insanity. It certainly was not fooling. When the control passed the victim was calm and sane. If it be madness it was madness resulting from excessive experimenting with spiritualism. But I wish any materialistic doctor would take the man in hand. He would, I am sure, be less scornful in his comments upon that exploded superstition 'Demoniacal possession'."

In the following issue, Mr. Stead states that he received letters from the gentleman whose case has just been described, and that he had evidently not been relieved from the obsession.

A correspondent in Vancouvers' Island complains of voices and hands are laid on him, and the unfortunate object of these attentions dare not mention it to anyone on account of the risk of being considered insane.

Many people, among whom are fellows of the Royal Society and doctors, and others, are of opinion that many of the cases of insanity in our asylums are really cases of obsession, but with one exception, that there have been no experiments along this line to determine the point. It was certainly recognized by the early church, just as today it is by the Roman Catholic Church, and in the East the idea has always been common.

DEMON LOVERS

Right throughout the ages the theory of demon lovers has been a popular one, and like most superstitions, when investigated there is a sub-stratum of truth at the bottom. Although our position today enables us by the labors of many unwearied researches into the less known of natures' laws to understand much which was inexplicable, yet the facts of certain phenomena are not wholly explained by the hypotheses advanced. In fact, but a very minute corner of the veil has been lifted, and here as in every other department of nature the so-called simplicity is an utter misnomer. Hence cases occur where phenomena of a psychic character do not come under any of the well-defined categories into which they usually fall another explanation must be sought.

One of these is that of the demon lover. There are people who hold daily communication with what they believe to be their "twin souls" whom they call their "spirit brides" or "spirit lovers." The latter live upon the magnetism of those whom they are attracted to, and Dr. Hartmann contends that these vampires are exceedingly numerous as he had ample opportunity to observe during his experience. As he says, it is impossible to laugh the people out of their belief, as they "feel" the presence of these beings. Conversation takes place between them, questions asked and answered, and in some cases these entities have "materialized" so as to be seen by anyone. In olden times if a male was attached to a woman it was called an "incubus"; if a female attracted to a man its name was a "succubus." Apart from medieval writers, as another writer remarks: "The immense mass of evidence collected from many countries, by different scientific observers, and the medical men and others, cannot be set aside. Doubtless, if only one or two cases exist, we should explain them by the one word- 'hysteria'; but the accumulated mass of facts from so many different temperaments cannot be dealt with in this manner. We must accept the facts though we may differ as to their cause."

Among the narratives related by Dr. Hartmann are the following.

THREE STORIES

"A young lady at G___ had an admirer who asked her in marriage, but as he was a drunkard she refused and married another. Thereupon the lover shot himself, and soon after that event a vampire, assuming his form, visited her frequently at night, especially when her husband was absent. She could not see him but felt his presence in a way that could leave no room for doubt. The medical faculty did not know what to make out of the case, they called it hysterics and tried in vain every remedy in the pharmacopoeia, until she had at last the spirit exorcised by a man of strong faith. In this case there is an elemental making use of, and being aided by, the elementary of the suicide." (Elementals and Elementaries are species of entities found in nature.)

"A miller at D___ had a healthy servant boy, who soon after entering his service began to fail. He had a ravenous appetite, but nevertheless grew daily more feeble and emaciated. Being interrogated, he at last confessed that a thing which he could not see, but which he could plainly feel, came to him every night and settled upon his stomach drawing all the life out of him, so that he became paralyzed for the time being, and neither could move nor cry out. Thereupon the miller agreed to share his bed with the boy, and proposed to him that he should give him a certain sign when the vampire arrived. This was done, and when the sign was given the miller grasped an invisible but very tangible substance that rested upon the boys' stomach, and though it struggled to escape, he grasped it firmly and threw it in the fire. After that the boy recovered, and there was an end of these visits. Those who like myself have on

DEMONOLOGY

innumerable occasions removed 'astral tumors' and thereby cured the physical tumors, will find the above neither 'incredible' nor 'unexplainable.' Moreover the above accounts do not refer to events of the past but to persons still living in this country.

"A woman in this vicinity has an incubus, or as she calls it a 'dual' with whom she lives on the most intimate terms as a wife and husband. She converses with him and he makes her do the most irrational things. He has many whims, and she, being a woman of means, gratifies them. If her dual wants to go and see Italy, 'through her eyes', she has to go to Italy and let him enjoy the sights. She does not care for balls and theaters; but her dual wants to attend them, and so she has to go. She gives lessons to her dual and 'educates' him in the things of the world and commits no end of follies. At the same time her dual draws all the strength from her, and she has to vampirize everyone she comes in contact with to make up for the loss."

HYPNOTISM AND ITS DANGERS

Before closing this aspect, attention may be directed to hypnotism. There is grave reason to believe that we shall hear more cases like the above, and that there may even be a recurrence of the true vampire through the bare-faced exploitation of hypnotism which has been so marked a feature during the last few years. There have been persons who have unblushingly counseled the gaining of the control of other peoples' minds, so as to bend them to the experimenters' purpose. It cannot be too clearly stated that the human will is sacred, that any interference with it by any other person must lead to awful results, which cannot be contemplated. A law has been set in motion which will exact to the uttermost farthing the effects caused by the imposing of one will upon another. Law obtains in every part of the universe, however high up one may go- Emerson called it compensation- by which any wrong inflicted on a human being must react upon the doer. In modern

DEMONOLOGY

civilization the greater part of the time is spent in supplying each others' wants, and in the multifarious and complex transactions between man and man each is a voluntary party if an agreement is come to. This, of course, does not prevent the introduction of deception and sharp practices, but it certainly limits it; one is able to checkmate those who do not appear to be playing the game, but in hypnotism a secret and silent factor, more potent than any finesse done openly, is smuggled in and one man is made the tool of another. The law of the land recognizes "undue influence" in regard to the making of wills, etc, but it is here powerless to step in and shield the weak. A man is simply compelled against his will, or better understanding, to fall in with the wishes of another, being blind to the wrong he is doing himself, or how cruelly he is subverting his own interests and jeopardizing those of those most dear to him. No wonder the unscrupulous charlatan, pandering to the lowest side of human nature recognized in hypnotism a means of playing on the weakness of a large number of people and reaping considerable financial benefit from it. Hypnotism can only be legitimately used in disease and the eradication of bad habits, but even then some guarantee as to the character of the operator is required, for the magnetism of the operator is blended with that of the subject. In many a dabbler in this subject we have the nucleus of a vampire, and not only should the reader steer clear of the art but also refuse to be experimented upon by others, unless it is a case of disease, and only then when satisfied as to the bona fides and in the presence of a third friend. A hypnotist should be like Caesars' wife, but morals are often immaterial in the eyes of those professing to teach the art.

ELEMENTALS

In the Indian pantheon there are no fewer than 32,000,000 of various kinds of entities, and among these are the elementals. We are only concerned with one or two classes here, however- one we have already referred to- and these are known

DEMONOLOGY

as Rakshakras and Bhutas, and the brothers of the shadow, the latter being both living and dead. The latter class are cunning, full of vindictiveness, ever seeking to retaliate upon humanity, these ghouls live on the emanations of others or blood. They have, as it were, cheated nature, by their knowledge of the forbidden art, and most of the magic feats performed by dabblers are accomplished through their aid, helped by the elementaries. They rove the planes of nature and pounce down on people who lay themselves open to them.

THE VAMPIRE OF HEALTH

Sensitive people have often complained of a feeling of ennui, of being run down after being in the company of certain persons. Laurence Oliphant, in his Scientific Religion, remarks the fact, pointing out that one "cause of death is the drainage of vital atoms by human vampire organisms; for many persons are so constituted that they have, unconsciously to themselves, an extraordinary faculty for sucking the life principle from others, who are constitutionally incapable of retaining their vitality. Thus it is well known that old people can derive physical life from fresh young organisms by sleeping beside them, and the experience is common among invalids whose organisms have been rendered sensitive by illness, that the presence of certain people is exhaustive and of others life-giving... This constant change of vitality is a necessary condition of our existence as we are at present constituted, but as the laws by which it is governed are absolutely unknown to the medical profession, which does not treat patients except on their surfaces, an appalling account of wholesale slaughter now goes on unchecked. This might be greatly diminished if doctors would open themselves to divine illumination, and not relegate to the church that part of the human organism which, if they knew a little more about it, they would perceive comes directly within the sphere of their operations."

There is no doubt that vitality can be absorbed as above

DEMONOLOGY

quoted, robust people being drained by the modern vampire, and the information has been known for thousands of years. Doctors are puzzled and such cases make one more addition to the already long list of nervous diseases. What has happened in reality is, the life force or magnetism has been drawn out of him or her and has been absorbed like a sponge by the modern vampire. In the novel *As in a Glass Darkly* the author well describes such an instance. Breeders tell us that young animals should not be herded with old ones; doctors forbid young children being put to sleep with old people. We all remember David when old and feeble having his forces recruited by having a young person brought in close contact with him, and in the case of the late Empress of Russia, the sister of the Emperor of Germany, who was seriously advised by her physician to keep a young and robust girl in her bed at night. Readers of Dr. Kerners' *Seeress of Provost* will remember how Mde. E. Hause repeatedly stated that she supported life merely on the atmosphere of the people surrounding her.

THE AURA

In addition to the vehicles which have been mentioned as forming part of a human being there is a fine substance called the aura. Modern science will "discover" it in a few years, but of course, it will not be known by this name, it will be a new "ray" christened by the name of its "inventor." Perhaps as has been hinted, the N-Rays of M. Blondlot approach it most closely.

Painters in all ages have depicted a circle of light surrounding the heads of saints, called the "glory," nimbus, or aureole, indifferently in olden times. But more was then known about this subject, so that it is no mere freak of the imagination. The only fault of the painter was that he restricted this phenomenon to the head. As a matter of fact it surrounds the whole body to the extent of about eighteen inches. This was the odic fluid of Reichenbach. It is of a highly refined order of physical matter, seen by many people, just as some people see colors beyond what appears as a blank to others looking at the colors thrown on a sheet of paper by a prism. It is very complex, there being several grades of etheric matter in it. One of these grades is known as the health aura, and it is with this that we are chiefly concerned. It is the vehicle of the vital force on this plane, transmuting the life-energy poured out by the sun into health and strength. It has been referred to earlier in these pages as the prana, specialized from the Jiva. It is absorbed by the spleen, and thence runs over the whole body much in the same way that blood circulates through the veins, raying out from the center in every direction. As it uses the nerves as a medium, unless these are healthy, there is no free flow of this nerve-ether, or prana. In addition to this raying out, a healthy man flings off, much in the same way perspiration is thrown off, large quantities of his aura, so that wherever he goes he literally sprays health about him. It escapes from every pore, and can be directed to flow along certain channels. This radiation is a shield against disease; it may be compared to a rapidly revolving wheel, which if struck by some small body will fling it off at a tangent as soon as it comes into contact with it. It diminishes in quantity and suffers in quality from worry, injury to the body, ill health, grief, melancholy, hatred, anger, and any of the disintegrating forces which enter into daily life of those which are inherent in them and which surround them on every side.

    A man in bad health is like a sponge, and as soon as he comes in contact with a healthy person he draws the aura to him. If this drain goes on for long the healthy person is injured very much. All sensitive persons give off this aura very readily; it passes off without their consciousness, but it is only when brought into contact with people of a certain type that this happens, or when they attend *seances*. Only the very strong should attend these, unless they possess pure and strong individualities, as these can resist the onslaughts made by entities that materialize. All the phenomena of the seance room are produced by means of the magnetism of the sitters and the

DEMONOLOGY

"medium," as is well known to those who have studied the subject merely superficially.

THE REMEDY

Carrying the mind back to what has been said with regard to vibrations, all sensitive persons, or those who have hitherto been robust and suddenly find themselves losing strength without any adequate reason should set apart at least ten minutes a day to the cultivation of rendering the vitality impregnable to the attacks of the vampire, whether of the blood or of the vitality.

Here it may be as well to point out that there are two classes of persons particularly liable to take on the conditions of those with whom they are brought in contact, or to be drawn upon by outside influences. These are those born between 21st June and 21st July. Children born between these dates should not be placed with elderly people to sleep. The other class are those born between 21st February and 21st March. It has been found that persons born at these times are very mediumistic, and in one case the reason is that the influence of the moon is very marked. More than one writer has remarked upon the moons' vampirizing this earth, and retaining its vitality- dead as it may appear- through the emanations from the earth.

That vitality is transferable was proved by the old mesmerists, and the masseur of today emphasizes it. Many elderly people are massaged daily for no particular complaint but when they get run down or their bodily powers are declining, they find being rubbed by a healthy man or woman restores their energy and vim. One well known English member of parliament who, though advanced in years, gets through enough work to kill several men, has a medical rubber in constant attendance on him, and he admitted to him one day that had he not his assistance he could not keep the strain up. Masseurs know that strength goes from them and that it is not merely from the labor of rubbing. Retain your vitality, then. In *The Art of Fascination* some useful hints are given. To these may be added a few points. In the first place lead as pure a life as possible, avoiding alcohol, which retains evil magnetism, and attracts to yourself entities in and out of the body, there being a similar rate of vibration existing between you and them, and this places them in sympathy, as it were, with you, and able to affect you. In the same way a certain relationship exists between you and those who use corpses as food, living and dead human beings, and vampires and elementals, shells, and other species of entities that roam the lower levels of the next plane. In addition to this there is a vast mass- it takes the form of clouds and sometimes horrible shapes- of hatred resulting from the collective thoughts or sensations of all the slaughtered animals, tame and wild, and the blood, like alcohol, is a magnetic tie, as has been already seen. Purity of food, then, is essential.

Next is purity of thought. Sensuality, anger, malice, are differing rates of vibration, and these vibrations are taken up by others in the vicinity. The entertaining of a thought of evil towards another human being is fed and increased in consequence, so that the next time you repeat the thought it is with increased power. If indulged in much you create a center of evil, and this may be seized upon by some passing entity, which either attaches itself to you and feeds vicariously on your magnetism, and that of others ending in possession, or without being pounced upon by an astral inhabitant it will become a kind of alter ego, another stratum of consciousness, acquire a semi-consciousness of its own, and become to a large extent independent of you. This is the key to much of the phenomena of multiplex personality, and also accounts for the remark so frequently heard when a friend sees another whom he has not met for years; "How he has changed!" Every man is his own devil or god, just as he is responsible for whatever circumstances he is surrounded by, or his destiny in general. By thinking pure thoughts only, sympathetic, helpful thoughts, the matter of which your subtle vehicles is gradually built on vibrations corresponding with these qualities, and the lower thoughts perish for want of food. Further, just as evil thought is fed like a river is fed by a tributary, so in the same way high thinking and kindly thoughts attract those of a like nature.

Sympathy is of two kinds, however, and nearly always the wrong is indulged in. By feeling keenly and sympathizing with one in pain or suffering from a disease there is a tendency to reproduce the same symptoms in yourself, to say nothing of being unconsciously drained by the invalid. It is quite possible to sympathize with a friend without at the same time taking on his weakness. Let your sympathy be strong, that is to say, look at things from the most optimistic standpoint, which is the only true one. Don't humor him, and strengthen him in his negative aspect. We all know those people who are wet blankets wherever they go, whether it be the sick chamber or the busy mart. We also know those who like a ray of sunshine entering a dark cellar lights everything up. This is the aspect to take when visiting sick friends. Refuse to see the disease, talk only of the bright, the helpful, and not only are you cheering him up and practically creating life force, but you render yourself less likely to be drawn upon.

With regard to protecting yourself generally, when rising imagine that a shell is forming at the extremity of the aura. Picture a white mist, ovoid, becoming denser every moment. Just as in winter the breath is clearly visible with each exhalation, so as you breathe outward see in the mind the breath taking form. Use the will in addition and this will have the desired effect. Repeat about mid day, or whenever entering a crowd, or a low quarter of a city. At night again form this protective shell just before going to sleep, and you are not likely to be troubled with vampires.

Where there is a suspicion of the existence of an entity of the ghoul type the free use of garlic in a room is recommended, or placing small saucers of nitric acid on the

DEMONOLOGY

tables (out of the way of children and animals) for a short time daily, but not in the bedroom unless the window is left open each night, will be found to counteract any vampire influence. The use of incense in places of worship is not "superstition," or to have a theatrical effect, but to keep undesirable entities away just as the origin of church bells was to free the sacred edifice of their presence. The gargoyles seen on cathedrals etc, are the "demons" escaping. There is more in sound than the world dreams of, and there is a deep law underlying the breaking of a wine-glass when whistled into, or the walls of Jericho falling down after the blowing of an instrument, but this scarcely comes within our province here.

Just as certain smells are obnoxious to human beings- some even fatal, as is the case of inhaling chemical gases- so the burning of certain herbs, or food even, has definite effects on invisible beings; cases of tribal deities loving a "sweet savor" and the offering up of animals as sacrifice will occur to the reader, while to the student of medieval literature the rites connected with witchcraft will be better understood.

The Hindus sit on Kusa grass mats when meditating, as this fiber is said to resist bad elementals and evil influences. The use of fleniculis, burnt, is also recommended for the same purpose. The burning of dried garlic will also be found efficacious but is anything but pleasant.

In walking in the street you can prevent yourself being "tapped" by closing the hands, as the fingers conduct the magnetism freely, and many people lose much in this way, which is tapped up from the fingers by astral entities. The body may be "locked" to prevent any leakage in railway compartments, trams, etc, by clasping the hands and placing the left foot over the right, and thus form a complete circuit with ones' limbs. Just as electricity discharges itself from angles and points, so in the human body.

DEMONOLOGY

It is to be hoped that cremation will grow in favor as time goes on as it will put an end to the grave vampire. So long as the body remains, there is a strong desire on the part of man whose thoughts have been of the earth, earthy, and if he gain the occult knowledge as to keeping his corpse fresh he will not hesitate to use it. Sometimes when a body is destroyed another body will be obsessed for the purpose, or in the case of a human monster, a human being will not be depraved enough and the body of some ravenous animal will be selected, such as the wolf, whence comes the werewolf, which is urged madly on in its career of destruction, the entity partaking, vicariously, of the blood of its victims.

In folklore, fairy tale, and religion, there has been sound reason in virtue being triumphant over evil, because goodness is an actual shield, shedding an influence around it, which the malign forces cannot approach, still less penetrate. A good conscience is an invincible coat of armor, and it can be created atom by atom, by right thought and right living.

If man could but realize that he alone is the creator of so-called evil, that the earths' moral atmosphere formed by him in his ignorance permeates nearly all of us, whether we will or not, until we are soaked in pessimism, that obeying a general law like forces attract like forces, that again in obedience to law repeated additions of unkind, uncharitable, fierce, bitter and evil thoughts keep the strata of misery, greed, and crime ever active- if man realized this surely he would begin to build better. Until he does, however, he will continue to suffer and contribute to the worlds' stock of woe.

THE END

DEMONOLOGY

ON THE OPERATION OF DEMONS

Psellus (Or Psellos), 1682

MICHAEL PSELLUS' DIALOGUE BETWEEN TIMOTHY AND THRACIAN ON THE OPERATION OF DEMONS

TIMOTHY: Is it long, Thracian, since you visited Byzantium?

THRACIAN: Yes, it is long, Timothy; two years perhaps, or more: I have been abroad.

TIMOTHY: But where, and why, and engaged in what business, were you away so long?

THRACIAN: The questions you put would take too long to answer just now; I must devise Alcinius' narrative if I am obliged to particularize every thing I was present at, and every thing I endured, while constrained to associate with impious characters, those Euchitae, or, as many call them, Enthusiasts, have you not heard of them at all?

TIMOTHY: Why, I understand that there are among us individuals as godless as they are absurd, and that in the midst of the sacred they jeer but as to their dogmas, their customs, their laws, their proceedings, their discourses, I have not yet been able to learn any thing about them; wherefore I beg of you to tell me most explicitly whatever you know, if you are disposed to oblige an intimate acquaintance, I will even add, a friend.

THRACIAN: Even have it so, friend Timothy, though it be enough to give one a headache if he but attempt to describe the outlandish doctrines and doings of demonology; and though

DEMONOLOGY

you cannot possibly derive any advantage from such description- for, if it be true what Simonides says, that the statement of facts is their delineation, and that therefore the statement of unprofitable facts must be profitable, and the statement of unprofitable facts quite the opposite- what possible benefit could you derive from my delineating their seductive statements?

TIMOTHY: Nay, but I shall be greatly benefited, Thracian; surely it is not unserviceable for physicians to be acquainted with drugs of a deadly nature, that so none may be endangered by their use: besides, some of the particulars, at all events, will not be unprofitable. We have our choice, therefore, either to carry off from your disquisition what is profitable, or to be on our guard of it if it have anything pernicious.

THRACIAN: Agreed, my friend; you shall hear (as the poet says) truths certainly, but most unpleasant ones, but if my narrative advert to certain unseemly proceedings, I require of you, in common justice, not to be angry with me who relate them, but with those who do them. This execrable doctrine had its rise with Manes the Maniac, from him their multitudinous origins have flowed down as from a fetid fountain; for, according to the accursed Manes, there were two origins of all things: he, with senseless impiety, opposed a god, the author of evil, to God, the creator of every good- a ruler of the wickedness of the terrestrial, to the bounteous ruler of the celestial. But the demoniacal Euchitae have adopted yet a third origin; according to them, two sons, with their father, make the senior and the junior origin; to the father they have assigned the supra-mundane region solely, to the younger son the atmospheric region, and to the elder the government of things in the world- a theory which differs in nothing from the Greek mythology, according to which the universe is portioned out into three parts. These rotten-minded men, having laid this rotten foundation, thus far are unanimous in their sentiments; but from this point are divided in their judgments into three parties: some yield worship to both sons, maintaining, that though they are at variance, yet that both are equally deserving of being worshiped, because they are spring from one parent, and will yet be reconciled. But others serve the younger son as being the governor of the superior region, which extends immediately over the earth; and yet they do not absolutely disdain the elder son, but are on their guard of him, as of one who has it in his power to do them injury; while the third party, who are further sunk in impiety, withdraw altogether from the worship of the celestial son, and enshrine in their hearts the earthly alone, even Satan, dignifying him with the most august names, as, the first begotten, estranged from the father, the creator of plants and animals, and the rest of the compound beings.

Preferring to make suit to him who is the destroyer and murderer, gracious God! how many insults do they offer to the celestial, whom they pronounce envious, an unnatural persecutor of his brother, (who administers judiciously the government of the world) and aver, that it is his being puffed up with envy occasions earthquakes and hail and famine, on which account they imprecate on him, as well other anathemas, as in particular that horrible one!

TIMOTHY: By what train of reasoning have they brought themselves to believe and pronounce Satan a son of God, when not merely the prophetic writings, but the Oracles of divine truth everywhere speak but of one son, and he that reclined on our Lord's bosom (as is recorded in the Holy Gospel), exclaims, concerning the divine logos, "the glory as of the *Only-begotten* of the Father," whence has such a tremendous error assailed them?

THRACIAN: Whence, Timothy, but from the Prince of Lies, who deceives the understandings of his witless votaries by such vainglorious fiction, vaunting that he will place his throne above the clouds, and averring that he will be equal to the

DEMONOLOGY

highest; for this very reason he has been consigned to outer darkness: and when he appears to them, he announces himself the first-begotten son of God and creator of all terrestrial things, who disposes of everything in the world, and by this means, following up the peculiar foible of each, cheats the fools, who ought to have considered him an empty braggart and the arch-prince of falsehood, and overwhelmed with ridicule his pompous pretensions, instead of believing everything he says, and suffering themselves to be led about like oxen by the nose.

However, it will soon be in their power to convict him of being a liar, for if they insist on his making good his honored promises, he will turn out no better than the ass in lion's skin which, when it attempted to roar like a lion, its braying betrayed. At present, however, they resemble the blind, and the deaf, and the insane, since they cannot perceive, from the consanguinity of universal nature, that there is but one creator, nor hear that very consanguinity declaring the self-same truth, nor discover, by reasoning, that if there were two opposite creators, there would not be that one arrangement and oneness which binds all things together. As the prophet says, "the ox and the ass know their master and their master's crib," but these bid their master farewell, and have elected to the place of God the most abject of all creatures. "Scorched though they be with the fire," (as the Proverb says) they yet follow and precipitate themselves into that fire which has long been provided for him and his co-apostates.

TIMOTHY: But what profit do they derive from abjuring the divine religion received from their fathers, and rushing on certain destruction?

THRACIAN: As to profit, I do not know that they derive any, but I rather think not; for though the daemons promise them gold, and possessions, and notoriety, yet you know they cannot give them to any: they do, however, present to the initiated phantasms and flashing appearances, which these

DEMONOLOGY

men-detesters of God call visions of God. Such as wish to be spectators of them, gracious heavens! how many shameful things, how many unutterable and detestable must they witness! For everything which we consider sanctioned by law, and a doctrine to be preached, and a duty to be practiced, they madly disregard, nay, they even disregard the laws of nature; to commit their debaucheries to writing would only befit the impure pen of Archilochus, nay, I do think that were he present he would be loath to commemorate orgies so detestable and vile, as were never witnessed in Greece, no, nor in any barbarous land; for where or when did anyone ever hear that man, that august and sacred animal, ate excretions, whether moist or dry- a monstrosity which, I believe, not even wild beasts in a rabid state are capable of committing, and yet this is but the preliminary proceeding with these execrable wretches.

TIMOTHY: What for, Thracian?

THRACIAN: Oh, this is one of their secrets- they know best who do it: however, on my frequently questioning on this point, all I could learn was, that the daemons became friendly and affable on their partaking of the excretions. In this particular I was satisfied they spoke truth, though incapable of speaking it in other matters; since nothing can be so eminently gratifying to hostile spirits as to see man (who is an object of envy), man who has been honored with the divine image, fallen to such a state of degradation: this is putting the finishing stroke on their folly. Nor is this confined to the Antistites of the dogma (to whom they tack the appellation, apostles), but extends to the Euchitae and the Gnostics. But as to their mystical sacrifice, God preserve me! Who could describe it? I blush to repeat the shameful things I witnessed, and yet I am bound to repeat them, for you, Timothy, have already prevailed on me; I will therefore skim over them lightly, omitting the more shameful proceedings, lest I should seem to be acting a tragedy:

Vesperi enim luminibus accensis, quo tempore

DEMONOLOGY

salutarem domini celebramus passionem, in domum præscriptam deductis, quas sacrilegi sacris suis initiaverunt, puellis necum puellis libidinose volutantur in quamcumque tandem, seu sororem, seu propriam filiam, seu matrem quilibet inciderit. Siquidem et hac in re dæmonibus rem gratam facere arbitrantur, si leges divinas transgressi fuerint, in quibas cautum est, ne nuptiæ cum sanguine cognato contrahantur.

Having perfected this rite, they are dismissed; on the expiry of nine months, when the unnatural progeny of an unnatural seed is about being born, they meet again at the same place, and on the third day after parturition, tearing the wretched infants from their mothers, and scarifying their tender flesh with knives, they catch in basins the dripping blood, and casting the infants, still breathing, on the pile, consume them; afterwards, mingling their ashes with the blood in the basins, they make a sort of horrible compound, with which, secretly defiling their food, liquid and solid, like those who mix poison with mead, not only they themselves partake of these viands, but others also who are not privy to their secret proceedings.

TIMOTHY: What end do they propose to themselves by such revolting pollution?

THRACIAN: They are persuaded that by this means the divine symbols inscribed in our souls are thrust out and expunged, for so long as they continue there the daemon tribe are afraid and keep aloof, as one might from the royal signet attached to a cabinet; in order, therefore, to enable the daemons to reside in their souls they, without any apprehension, chase away the divine symbols, by their insults to heaven- and a profitable exchange they have made of it. But not satisfied with perpetrating this wickedness themselves, they lay a snare for others; the polluted viands tempting the pious also, who, without being aware of it, partake of the strange food, they like so many Tantali serving up their children for the entertainment.

DEMONOLOGY

TIMOTHY: Good heavens, Thracian! this is what my grandfather by the father's side predicted; for once being distressed, because some subverted as well the other privileges of the good as their acquisition of a liberal education, I asked him, will there ever be a restoration? He being then an old man, and very sagacious in farseeing coming events, gently stroking my head and fetching a heavy sigh, replied;

"My son, my child, do you imagine that they will ever again restore literature, or anything excellent? The time is at hand when men will live worse than wild beasts, for now the Antichrist is at hand, even at the doors, and evil precursors in the shape of monstrous doctrines and unlawful practices, no better than the orgies of Bacchus, must usher in his advent. And whatever things have been represented by the Greeks in their tragedies, as Saturn and Thyestes and Tantalus devouring their offspring, Oedipus debauching his mother, and Cinyras his daughters, all these fearful enormities will break in upon our state; but see my son, and be on your guard, for know, know for certain, that not only individuals from the illiterate and unpolished class, but many also of the learned, will be drawn away into the same practices."

These things, if I am to judge from the result, he spake prophetically; but I, when I recall to mind his words, which are as fresh in my memory now as when he uttered them, am surprised at what you tell me.

THRACIAN: And well you may be surprised; for, many as are the absurd nations described by historians in the far North, and the parts about Libya and Syria, yet I venture to say no one has ever heard of such impiety being practiced by them, no, nor by the Celts, nor by any other nation near Britain, though destitute of laws and in a savage state.

TIMOTHY: It is afflicting to think, Thracian, that such horrible practices should take up their abode in our quarter of the world. But a perplexity of long standing respecting daemons distresses me; among other things, I should like to know whether they are manifestly seen by the demoniacal wretches.

THRACIAN: Not a doubt of it, my friend, for this they all strive, might and main; their assemblage and sacrifice, and rites, and every horrible practice of theirs, are held for this purpose, to bring about a manifestation.

TIMOTHY: How then can they, being incorporeal, be seen with the visual organs?

THRACIAN: But, my good friend, they are not incorporeal; the daemon tribe have a body, and are conversant with corporeal beings, which one may learn even from the holy fathers of our religion, if one only addict himself heartily to magical practices. We hear many too relating how the daemons appeared to them in a bodily form; and the divine Basilius, who beheld invisible things (or at least not clear to ordinary eyes) maintains it, that not merely the daemons, but even the pure angels have bodies, being a sort of thin, aerial, and pure spirit; and in proof of this he adduces the testimony of David, most celebrated of the prophets, saying, "He maketh his angels spirits, and his messengers a flame of fire." And it must needs be even so, for when the ministering spirits are dispatched to their respective employments (as the divine Paul says) they must needs have some body, in order to their moving, becoming stationary and apparent; for these effects could not be accomplished otherwise than through the medium of a body.

TIMOTHY: How comes it then, that in most passages of scripture they are spoken of as incorporeal.

THRACIAN: It is the practice both with Christian and profane authors, even the most ancient, to speak of the grosser description of bodies as corporeal; but those which are very thin, eluding both the sight and touch, not only we Christians, but even many profane authors think fit to call incorporeal.

TIMOTHY: But tell me, the body which angels have by natural constitution, is it the same with that which daemons have?

THRACIAN: What folly! there must be a vast difference, for the angelic, emitting a sort of extraneous rays, is oppressive and intolerable to the visual organs: but as to the daemonic, whether it was once of this sort I cannot say, but so it would seem; (for Esaias disparagingly calls Lucifer "him that had fallen") now, however it is an obscure and darksome sort of thing, saddened in aspect, divested of its kindred light; but the angelic nature is immaterial, and therefore is capable of penetrating and passing through all solids, being more impalpable than the sun's rays, which, passing through transparent bodies, the opaque objects on this earth reflect, so as to render its stroke endurable, for there is something material in it; but nothing can interpose opposition to an angel, because they present opposition to nothing, not being homogeneous with any thing; on the other hand, the bodies of daemons, though constituted indistinct by their tenuity; are yet in some measure material and palpable.

TIMOTHY: I am becoming quite a sage, Thracian, (as the proverb says), by these novel accessions of knowledge; for to me, indeed, this is a novel fact, that some daemons are corporeal and palpable.

THRACIAN: There is no novelty in our being ignorant of many things, so long as we are men, Timothy, as the saying is; it is well, however, if, as ages advance, our good sense increases. Be assured of this, that in making these statements, I am not uttering lying rhapsodies, like the Cretans: and Phoenicians, but am persuaded of their truth from the savior's words, which affirm, that the daemons shall be punished with fire, a punishment they would be incapable of if incorporeal. Since a being that is destitute of a body cannot suffer in the body, therefore they must needs undergo punishment by means of bodies, constituted capable of suffering. Much, however, I have suppressed which I heard from some who adventured themselves to intuition; for my own part, I have never seen a being of that nature- heaven grant that I may never behold the fearful looks of daemons! But I conversed with a monk in Mesopotamia, who really was an initiated inspector of daemonic phantasms: these magical practices he afterwards abandoned as worthless and deceptive, and having made his recantation, attached himself to the true doctrine, which we profess, and assiduously applying himself, underwent a course of instruction at my hands; he accordingly told me many and extraordinary things about daemons; and once, on my asking, if daemons were capable of animal passion, "Not a doubt of it," said he. *Quemadmodum et sperma nonnulli eorum emittunt et vermes quosdam spermate procreant. Et incredible est, inquam excrementi quicquam dæmonibus inesse, vasave spermatica et vitalia vasa quidem eis, inquit me, hujusmodi nulla insunt, superflui autem seu excrementi nescio quid emittunt hoc mihi asserenti credito.*

But, said I, if they derive nourishment, they must derive it as we do? Marcus, the monk, replied; "some derive it by inhalation, as for instance a spirit resident in lungs and nerves, and some from moisture, but not as we do, with the mouth, but as sponges and ruddy fishes do, by drawing nourishment from the extraneous moisture lying around them, and they afterwards void a spermatic substance, but they do not all resemble each other in this particular, but only such descriptions of daemons as are allied to matter, such as the Lucifugus, and Aqueous, and Subterranean." And are there many descriptions of daemons, Marcus, I asked again?

"There are many, said he, and of every possible variety of figure and conformation, so that the air is full of them, both that above and that around us, the earth and the sea are full of them, and the lowest subterranean depths."

DEMONOLOGY

Then, said I, if it would not be troublesome, would you particularize each?

"It would be troublesome," said he, "to recall to mind matters I have dislodged from thence, yet I cannot refuse, when you command," and so saying he counted off many species of daemons, adding their names, their forms, and their haunts.

TIMOTHY: What's to hinder you then Thracian, enumerating them to us?

THRACIAN: I was not very solicitous, my good sir, to retain either the substance or arrangement of that conversation, nor can I now recollect it. What possible benefit could I derive from an over-solicitude to retain their names, their, haunts, and in what particular they resemble, and in what differ from each other? therefore, I have allowed such insipid matter to escape my memory, yet, I retain a little out of a great deal, and whatever you are curious about, if you inquire of me you shall know it.

TIMOTHY: This in particular I wish to know, how many orders of daemons are there?

THRACIAN: He said, there were in all six species of daemons, I know not whether subdividing the entire genus by their habit!, or by the degree of their attachment to bodies- be that as it may, he laid that the six orders were corporeal and mundane, because in that number all corporeal circumstances are comprised, and agreeably to it the mundane system was constituted; afterwards he observed, that this first number was represented by the scalene triangle, for that beings of the divine and celestial order were represented by the equilateral triangle, as being consistent with itself, and with difficulty inclined to evil, whilst human beings were represented by the isosceles triangle, as being in some measure liable to error in their choice, yet capable of reformation on repentance. On the other hand, that the daemonic tribe were represented by the scalene triangle, as being at variance with itself, and not at all approaching to excellence.

Whether he were really of this opinion or not, this is certain, he counted off six species of daemons, and first he mentioned Leliurium, speaking in his barbarous vernacular tongue, a name which signifies igneous. This order of daemons haunts the air above us, for the entire genus has been expelled from the regions adjacent to the moon, as a profane thing with us would be expelled from a temple.

But the second occupies the air contiguous to us, and is called by the proper name aerial; the third is the Earthly, the fourth the Aqueous and marine, the fifth the Subterranean, and the last the Lucifugus, which can scarcely be considered sentient beings. All these species of daemons are haters of God, and enemies of man, and they say, that the Aqueous and Subterranean are worse than the merely bad, but that the Lucifugus are eminently malicious and mischievous, for these, said he, not merely impair mens' intellects, by fantasies and illusions, but destroy them with the same alacrity as we would the most savage wild beast. The Aqueous suffocate in the water all that approach them; the Subterranean and Lucifugus, if they can only insinuate themselves into the lungs of those they meet, seize and choke them, rendering them epileptic and insane; the aerial and Earthly, with art and cunning stealthily approach and deceive mens minds, impelling them to unlawful and unnatural lusts. But how, said I, or what doing, do they accomplish this? is it by lording it over us, and leading us about wherever they please, as if we were so many slaves? Not by lording it over us, says Marcus, but by leading us into reminiscences, for when we are in an imaginative spirit, approaching by virtue of their spiritual nature, they whisper descriptions of sensual delights and pleasures, not that they actually emit distinct sounds, but they insinuate a sort of murmur, that serves with them the place of words.

DEMONOLOGY

But it is impossible, said I, they could utter words without sound? It is not impossible, said he, as you will perceive, if you only reflect, that when one is speaking to another at a distance, he must speak in a high key, but if he be near, he need barely murmur, and whisper into the ear of his auditor, and if one could approach the very essence of the soul, there would be no occasion for any sound whatever, but any word we pleased would reach its destination by a noiseless path; a faculty which they say is possessed by disembodied spirits, for they bold communication with each other in a noiseless manner, in the same way the daemons hold communication with us, without our perceiving it, so that it is impossible to discover from what quarter an attack may be made upon us.

You need have no doubt on this point, if you only consider what happens in the atmosphere; when the sun shines, he combines colors and forms, and transmits them to objects capable of receiving them, (as we may observe in mirrors); thus also the daemons, assuming appearances and colors, and whatever forms they please, transport them into our animal spirit, and occasion us in consequence a vast deal of trouble, suggesting designs, reviving the recollection of pleasures, obtruding representations of sensual delights, both waking and sleeping; sometimes, too, rousing the baser passions by titillation, they excite to insane and unnatural amours, and especially when they find warm perspiration cooperating; for in this way, donning Pluto's helmet, with craft and the most refined subtlety, they create a commotion in mens minds. The other description of daemons have not a particle of wit, and are incapable of cunning, yet are they dangerous and very terrible, injuring after the manner of the Charonean spirit, for (as they report) the Charonean spirit destroys every thing that comes in its way, whether boast man, or bird; in the same way these daemons terrifically destroy everyone they fall in with, injuring them in body and mind. and subverting their natural habits; sometimes they destroy not merely men, but even irrational animals, in the fire, in the water, or by casting them over

DEMONOLOGY

precipices.

TIMOTHY: But what can be their object in entering irrational animals? for this happened to the swine, at Gargasa (as the sacred writings attest). I am not surprised if, being hostile to men, they injure them; but what is the sense of their entering irrational animals?

THRACIAN: Marcus said that it was not from any motive of hatred, nor from any hostile intention, that they pounced upon some beasts, but from a vehement desire for animal heat; for, as they inhabit the most profound depths, which are cold to the last degree, and destitute of moisture, they are excessively cold; being contracted and pained in consequence, they naturally long for a moist and vivifying heat to revel in, and spring into irrational animals, and plunge into baths and pits; on the other hand, the heat that proceeds from fire they avoid, because consuming and scorching, but gladly attach themselves to the moisture of animals, as being congenial to their nature, but especially to that of man, as being most congenial of all; and when infused into them they occasion no small uproar, the pores in which the animal spirit resides being clogged. and the spirit confined and displaced by the bulk of their bodies, which is the cause of their agitating mens persons, and injuring their faculties, and obstructing their motions.

When a subterranean daemon assails one, he agitates and distorts the person possessed, and speaks through him, using the tongue of the sufferer as if it were his own member; but if a lucifugus daemon clandestinely possess a person, it occasions a relaxation of his whole system, stops his utterance, and almost leaves the sufferer dead; for this last species is more allied to earth than the others, and is therefore excessively cold and dry, and anyone it can secretly possess, it blunts and obscures all the sufferer's natural power; but, because it is irrational and totally devoid of intellect, being governed by irrational whim, it has no more dread of reproof than the most intractable wild beast, for which reason it is designated with great propriety dumb and deaf; nor can a sufferer be dispossessed but by divine power, procurable by prayer and fasting.

"But, Marcus," said I, "physicians would persuade us to be of another way of thinking, for they assert that such affections are not produced by daemons, but are occasioned by an excess or deficiency of humors, or by a disordered state of the animal spirits, and accordingly they endeavor to cure them by medicine or dietetic regimen, but not by incantation or purification." Marcus replied, "It is not at all surprising if physicians make such an assertion, for they understand nothing but what is perceived by the senses, their whole attention being devoted to the body.

Lethargy, syncope, cases of hypochondria, delirium, which they can remove by vomits, or evacuations, or unguents, it is quite correct to say that there are the effects of disordered humors; but enthusiasm, and mildness, and possessions, with which when one is seized he is incapable of making any use of his judgment, his tongue, his imagination, his senses, it is quite another thing moves and excites them, and speaks what the person seized is unconscious of uttering, though occasionally be prophesies something." With what propriety can these effects be called the disordered movements of matter?

TIMOTHY: How now, Thracian! do you yourself assent to what Marcus says?

THRACIAN: Most undoubtedly, Timothy; for how could I do otherwise, when I recollect what the holy Gospels relate concerning persons possessed with daemons, and what befell the man of Corinth at Paul's command, and how many wonderful things are related of them by the fathers; and moreover saw with my own eyes, and heard with my own ears, their doings at Elason; for a man in that place was in the habit of delivering oracles after the manner of the priests of Phoebus, and, among other things, predicted not a few concerning myself. Having collected the multitude of the initiated around him, he said;

"I apprise the present company of the fact that an individual will be sent against us, by whom the mysteries of our worship will be persecuted, and the mysteries of our service abolished; myself and many others shall be apprehended by that person; but, though he be very anxious to carry me off a prisoner to Byzantium, he shall not do it- not though he make many and vigorous efforts to accomplish it."

Such predictions he uttered, though I had never gone as far from the city as to the neighboring villages. He described, too, my aspect, deportment, and occupation, and many who used to pass to and fro told me the facts. At length, when I did apprehend him, I asked him how he came to be gifted with the prophetic art? He, though he did not wish to divulge the secret, yet, laboring under a laconic necessity, confessed the truth, for he said that he had come to the knowledge of demoniacal practices through a certain vagabond African, who, bringing him by night to a mountain, causing him to partake of a certain herb, spitting into his mouth, and anointing his eyes with a certain unguent, enabled him to see a host of daemons, from among which he perceived a sort of raven fly towards him, and down his throat into his stomach. From that time up to the present moment he could predict, but only respecting such things, and at such times, as the daemon who possessed him wished; but on passion week and the resurrection day, so much venerated by Christians, not though be himself should greatly desire it, is the daemon who possessed him disposed to suggest anything. These things he told me, and, when one of my followers struck him on the cheek, "you," said he, "for this one blow shall receive many; and "you," said he, turning to me, "shall, suffer great calamities in your person, for the daemons are fearfully incensed against you for subverting their service,

DEMONOLOGY

and will involve you in harassing dangers, such as you cannot by any possibility escape, unless some power superior to that of daemons extricate you." These things the polluted wretch predicted, as if uttering oracles from the Delphic Tripod; for they all happened, and I have been almost undone by the numerous dangers which beset me; from which my savior alone wonderfully rescued me; but who that has seen the oracle in which daemons play upon wind instruments, will say that madness in all its forms are but the vitiated movements of matter?

TIMOTHY: I am not at all surprised, Thracian, that physicians are of this way of thinking, for how many cannot at all understand this sort of thing? For my part, I was first of their opinion, until I saw what was absolutely portentous and monstrous in its character, which, as it is quite apropos to the present topic, I shall relate. An old man like me, and who has, besides, assumed the monastic habit, is incapable of telling a falsehood. I had an elder brother married to a woman, who was on the whole of a good disposition, but exceedingly perverse; she was, too, afflicted with a variety of diseases. She, in her confinement, was very ill, and raved extravagantly, and, tearing her bed gown, muttered a sort of barbarous tongue, in a low murmuring tone; nor could the bystanders comprehend what she said, but were in a state of perplexity, not knowing what to do in so desperate a case.

Some women, however (for the sex is very quick in discovering expedients, and particularly clever in meeting exigencies), fetched a very old bald headed man, with his skin wrinkled and sunburned to a very dark hue, who, standing with his sword drawn beside the bed, affected to be angry with the invalid, and upbraided her much in his own tongue; (I mention that, because he was an Armenian).

The woman replied to him in the same tongue; first she was very bold, and, leaning on the bed, rated him with great spirit; but when the foreigner was more liberal with his exorcisms, and, as if in a passion, threatened to strike her, upon this the poor creature crouched and shook all over, and, speaking in a timid tone, fell fast asleep. We were amazed, not because she was transported with frenzy, for that with her was an ordinary occurrence, but because she spoke in the Armenian tongue, though she had never up to that hour so much as seen an Armenian, and understood nothing but her connubial and domestic duties. On her recovery I asked what she had undergone, and if she could recall to mind anything that had occurred; she said she saw a sort of darksome specter, resembling a woman, with the hair disheveled, springing upon her; that in her terror she had fallen on the bed, and from that time had no recollection of what has occurred. She spoke thus on her recovery.

Ever since that event a sort of bond of ambiguity keeps me perplexed, as to how the daemon which harassed this woman could seem feminine, for we may well question whether the distinction of sex prevails among the daemons as among the creatures of earth; and, in the next place, how could it employ the Armenian tongue? for we can hardly conceive that some daemons speak in the Greek, some in the Chaldee, and others in the Persian or Syriac; and also why it should crouch at the. charmer's threats, and fear a naked sword; for how can a daemon, which can neither be struck nor slain, suffer from a sword? These doubts perplex me exceedingly; upon these points I require persuasion, which I think you the most competent person to afford, as you are thoroughly acquainted with the sentiments of the ancients, and have acquired a great deal of historical knowledge.

THRACIAN: I should wish, Timothy, to render reasons for the matters in question, but I am afraid we may seem a pair of triflers, you in searching for what no one has yet discovered, I in attempting to explain what I ought rather to pass over in silence, and especially as I know that things of this kind are made matters of misrepresentation by many; but since, according to Antigonus, one ought to oblige his friend, not merely in what is very easily performed, but sometimes also where there is something of difficulty, I will even attempt to loose this bond of ambiguity, reconsidering the matter which gave occasion to Marcus' discourses. He said that no species of daemon was naturally either male or female, but that their animal passions were the same with those of the creatures with which they were united; for that the simple daemonic bodies, which are very ductile and flexible, are accommodating to the nature of every form; for as one may observe the clouds exhibiting the appearance one while of men, at another of bears, at another of serpents, or some other animal, thus also it is with the bodies of daemons; but when the clouds are disturbed by external blasts, diversified appearances are presented; thus also it is with the daemons, whose persons are transformed according to their pleasure into whatever appearance they please, and are one moment contracted into a less bulk, the next stretched out into a greater length. The same thing we see exemplified in lubricious animals in the bowels of the earth, owing to the softness and pliability of their nature, which are not merely altered in respect of size, but also in respect of appearance; and that in a variety of ways; the body of daemons likewise is accommodating in both particulars: not only is it peculiarly yielding, and takes the impression of objects, but, because it is aerial, it is susceptible of all kinds of hues, as is the atmosphere; such is the body of daemons, owing to the imaginative energy inherent in it, and which extends to it the appearance of colors; for, as when we are panic struck, we first are pale, and afterwards blush, according as the mind is variously affected, owing to the soul extending such affections to the body, we may well suppose it is just the same way with the daemons, for they from within can send out to their bodies the semblance of colors; for which reason each, when metamorphosed into that appearance which is agreeable, extending over the surface of his body the appearance of color, sometimes appears as a man, sometimes is metamorphosed as a woman, and, changing those forms, it retains neither constantly, for its appearance is not substantial, but resembles what occurs in the atmosphere, or water, in which you no sooner infuse a color, or delineate a form, than straight away it dissolves and is dispelled.

We may perceive that the daemons are liable to similar affections, for in them color, and figure, and all appearance whatever is evanescent. In these things Marcus, as I conjecture, said what was probable; and from this time forward let not the question harass you, whether the distinction of sex exists in daemons on account of the genital member appearing in them, for these, whether male or female, are not constant nor habitual; therefore consider that the daemon which so much harassed the woman in confinement seemed like a woman, not because it was really and habitually feminine; but because, it presented the appearance of a woman.

TIMOTHY: But how comes it Thracian, that it does not assume now one form, and now another, like the other daemons, but is always seen in this form, for I have heard from many, that daemons of the female form only are seen by women in confinement?

THRACIAN: For this too, Marcus assigned a not improbable reason, he said that all daemons have not the same power and inclination that in this particular there is a great diversity among them, for some are irrational, as among mortal compound animals, now as among them, man, being endowed with intellectual and rational powers is gifted with a more discursive imagination, one which extends to almost all sensible objects, both in heaven, and around, and on this earth. Horses, oxen, and animals of that sort, with a more confined sort of imagination, which extends but to some things, which exercise the imaginative faculty, their companions at pasture, their stall, or their owners; and gnats, with flies and worms, have this faculty exceedingly restricted, not knowing any of them the hole they leave, where they proceed, or whither they ought to go, but exercising the imagination for the single purpose of aliment, in the same manner also the species of daemons are greatly diversified; for among them, some as the Imperial and aerial are possessed of a very discursive imagination, one that extends to every imaginable object; very different from them are the subterranean and Lucifugi.

They do not assume a variety of forms, for they are incapable of numerous spectral appearances, not being possessed of pliability and versatility of person; the Aqueous and Terrestrial, occupying an intermediate position with respect to those already described, are incapable of changing their forms, but in whatever forms they delight, in these they constantly continue. But you should not be at all perplexed, if the daemon that harassed the woman in confinement appeared feminine, for being a lascivious daemon, and delighting in impure moisture, changing its form, it naturally assumed that which is best adapted for a life of pleasure, but with respect to the daemon speaking in the Armenian tongue; that was a point Marcus did not clear up, it will be manifest, however, from the following considerations:

It is impossible to ascertain the peculiar tongue of each particular daemon, whether such a daemon speak in the Hebrew, or Greek, or Syriac, or other barbarous tongue; indeed, what absolute need have they of a voice, who usually hold intercourse without one? But as in the case of the angels of the nations, different angels being appointed over different nations, different angels must associate with each other, they use each the tongue of their respective nations; we may reasonably conclude, that it is the same way with the daemons, for which reason some of them with the Greeks delivered oracles in Heroics, but others with the Chaldees were evoked in Chaldee, whilst among the Egyptians they were induced to approach by means of Egyptian incantations, in the same manner too, the daemons among the Armenians, if they happen to go elsewhere,

DEMONOLOGY

prefer to use their tongue as if it were the vulgar tongue.

TIMOTHY: Be it so Thracian; but what suffering are they capable of, that they fear threats and a sword? what are they to be supposed capable of suffering from such, that they crouch with fear, and keep aloof?

THRACIAN: You are not the only person, Timothy, who has been perplexed on these points; before I heard your doubts on them I expressed mine to Marcus, and he to remove them observed, the various species of daemons are bold, and cowardly in the extreme, but especially such as are allied to matter. The aerial indeed possessing the largest share of intelligence, if one rebuke them, can distinguish the person rebuking, and no one harassed by them can be liberated, unless such a holy character as addicts himself to the worship of God, and relying on the divine power, calls to his aid the terrible name of the divine Logos.

Those that are allied to matter, unquestionably fearing a dismissal to abysses and subterranean places, and the angels who are usually dispatched against them, when one threatens them with these, and their being conveyed away to such places, and calls over them, the designation of the angels appointed to this office, are afraid, and thrown into great perturbation; so that from being deranged, they cannot discern who it is that threatens.

TIMOTHY: But what advantage, did he say, resulted from the service of the aerial daemons?

THRACIAN: He did not say, my good friend, that any good resulted from those proceedings; indeed the things themselves proclaim in a barefaced manner that they are made up of vanity, imposture, and a groundless imagination, however fiery meteors, such as are usually called falling stars, descend from them on their worshipers, which the madmen have the

DEMONOLOGY

hardihood to call visions of God, though they have no truth, nor certainty, nor stability about them, (for what of a luminous character, could belong to the darkened daemons,) and though they are but ridiculous tricks of theirs, such things as; are effected by optical illusions, or by means called miraculous? But really by imposing on the spectators; these things I wretched man discovered long since, and was meditating to abandon this religion, yet up to the present moment, I was kept fascinated, and my perdition had been inevitable, had not you extricated me by the path of truth, shining forth like a Pharos, placed to dispel the darkness of the sea, Marcus having spoke thus shed a flood of tears, and I consoling, him said, you can choose a fitter time for weeping, now it is seasonable to magnify your salvation, and return thanks to God, by whom both your body and soul are emancipated from perdition.

TIMOTHY: Tell me this, for I long to know it, whether the bodies of daemons are of such a nature, as to be capable of being struck?

THRACIAN: Marcus said, that they could be struck, so as to be pained by a powerful blow afflicted on the person. But how, said I, can that be, as they are spirit, and not solid nor compound, for the faculty of sensation belongs to compound bodies? I am amazed, said he, you should be ignorant of the fact, that it is not the bone or nerve of any is endowed with the faculty of sensation, but the spirit inherent in them, therefore, whether the nerve be pained or refreshed, or suffer any other affection, the pain proceeds from the emission of spirit into spirit, for a compound body is not capable of being pained by virtue of itself, but by virtue of its union with spirit, for when dissected or dead, it is incapable of suffering, because deprived of the spirit; also a daemon being altogether spirit, and of a sensitive constitution in every part of it, sees and hears, and is capable of the sense of touch, without the intervention of organs of sense, it is pained after the manner of solid bodies, with this difference, however, that whereas when they are divided, they are with difficulty, or never made whole, this when divided, straightway unites, like the particles of air or water, when some solid body displaces them; but though the spirit unites swifter than speech, yet is it pained in the very moment of separation; this is the reason why it fears and dreads the points of iron instruments- and exorcists, well aware of their aversion, when they do not wish the daemons to approach a specific place, set darts and swords erect, and provide certain other things, either diverting them from that spot by their antipathies, or alluring them to another by their attachments. In these particulars, Marcus' explanation respecting the daemons, in my judgment, seemed probable.

TIMOTHY: But did he tell you this Thracian? did he tell you whether the daemons were gifted with foreknowledge?

THRACIAN: Yes, but not a causal or intelligent, nor experimental foreknowledge, but merely conjectural, for which reason it most generally fails, so that they scarcely ever utter a particle of truth.

TIMOTHY: Can't you describe to me, the nature of that foreknowledge, which is inherent in them?

THRACIAN: I would describe it, if time permitted me, but now 'tis time to return home, for as you see, the air around is hazy, and charged with rain, and if we sit here in the open air, we will be wet through and through.

TIMOTHY: Friend, consider what you do, leaving your discourse unfinished.

THRACIAN: Don't be uneasy, my best friend, for please God, the first opportunity you and I meet again, I will make good whatever is wanting, and, that in the Syracusan style.

THE END

THE DEVIL: HIS ORIGIN, GREATNESS, AND DECADENCE

Albert Reville, 1870

THE DEVIL

TRANSLATOR'S PREFATORY NOTES

Although the appearance of this essay in the Revue des Deux Mondes must have brought it under the notice of a large number of educated Englishmen, there remain not a few to whom a translation may be serviceable. Of these, there are some who regard belief in the personality of the devil as an essential of true religion; there are others who have already, come to the conclusion that such belief makes faith in our Heavenly Father's perfect wisdom, and man's free will, impossible, and that this form of superstition not only plies the weak with unworthy motives of conduct, but is a far slighter check upon the misbehavior of depraved persons than is commonly assumed by theologians; and there are, doubtless, some who, not having experienced in themselves, nor observed in others, its injurious effects, regard the matter with indifference.

To those who thoughtfully reject the dark belief, this interesting essay requires no comment; but among such as hold it upon "Scriptural grounds," there may be some who are not too prejudiced to bear with the translator while, in no carping spirit, he ventures to ask, through the following questions, whether Scripture authorizes as distinctly as it is generally supposed to do, a doctrine which reason condemns as based upon no evidence, and as a fruitful source of mischief.

Do Moses and the older Prophets appear to have so much as heard of the devil? Is not the Old Testament Satan a common noun, meaning an adversary, a hindering influence? (1 Chron. XXI, 1; Psalm CIX, 6). Is not, for instance, the Hebrew word translated adversary in the narrative of Balaam (applied there to the "Angel of the Lord"), the word which is translated elsewhere Satan? (Numbers XXII, 22).

(NOTE: As the account of the Fall (Genesis III.) is regarded by many as containing a mention of the Devil, we may be allowed to remark (apart from any question as to whether the episode is mythical, allegorical, or a simple record of facts) that, however general may be the notion, which Milton's grand imaginings have done much towards establishing, that the serpent was an incarnation of the Evil One, there is nothing in the narrative to support it. "The serpent was more subtle than any beast of the field." What is there here to show that the woman was surprised by any extraordinary display of subtlety on the part of the serpent, or that the animal was the mere instrument of an arch-fiend? Indeed, the curse pronounced upon the serpent race is inconsistent with such a supposition. S. Paul, in referring to the temptation of Eve (2 Cor. XI, 3), says nothing of the Devil's part in it; the serpent is not even a Satan, but simply the serpent.)

Did not the Jews derive many of their notions of devils and hells, so firmly held by the Pharisees of Christ's time, from their long intercourse with, the Persians?

Have not our translators of the New Testament, perplexed by the ambiguity of the Greek idiom, sometimes erred by their arbitrary suppression of the Greek article?

(Christ, for instance, is made to say, "Satan cometh," "Satan hath bound," "I beheld Satan," etc, instead of *the* Satan.)

Is it not open to question whether, where Christ's words seem to confirm the notion of a personal Satan, he is doing more than accommodate his language to the popular mode of expressing the power of evil? When Christ declares that one of his disciples is a devil, and when he addresses another as Satan, does he not use the word in its sense of adversary; and have these expressions any value in supporting the assertion that he taught the personality of the devil?

Has not the arbitrary treatment by our New Testament translators of the Greek word *diabolos*, which signifies an accuser, a slanderer, done much towards personifying the devil?

(Ex. gr., S. Paul (1 Tim. III, 11) says that the wives of deacons must not be "devils;" that (2 Tim. III, 2-3), in the last time men shall be "devils;" aged women (Titus II, 3) are to be exhorted not to be "devils," etc. Here we have, in our version, "slanderers," and "false accusers;" but where the word appears to the translators to point to the orthodox devil, the specific term is arbitrarily used.)

The inquiry whether the "possessed of devils" were sufferers from physical infirmities which were popularly attributed to the agency of evil spirits, deserves consideration, but is distinct from the question of the diabolarchy.

Does the Temptation of Christ establish the personality of the devil, seeing that this episode in the life of our Lord has by many orthodox expositors of ancient and modern times been regarded as parabolic? In the oft-quoted passage in which the "adversary, the devil," of the converts to whom S. Peter wrote, is described as "a roaring lion" (1 Peter V, 8), does not careful perusal of the context (IV, 14-19, etc.) make it clear that the sharp exercise of the Roman rule, and no hellish Tempter, is referred to?

The value of carefully comparing Scripture with. Scripture cannot be over-rated; but Reference Bibles not infrequently induce such comparison as misleads the student. The passage just quoted supplies a case in point. In the book of

DEMONOLOGY

Job, where Satan answers the question, "Whence comest thou?" by the words, "From going to and fro in the earth, and from walking up and down in it," reference will be found to the above passage in S. Peter's epistle; and, if only the personality of the devil is first admitted, the two accounts of his roaming habits will blend very readily.

"He roves," Cruden writes, "full of rage, like a roaring lion, seeking to tempt, to betray, to destroy us, and involve us in guilt and wickedness." But does the Satan of the book of Job, a poem, be it remembered, of Gentile, not of Jewish origin, bear any likeness to the Devil of the orthodox? Satan, in company with other "sons," or angels, of God, appears in the presence of the Lord, and, both in questioning the integrity of Job, and in chastening him with those trials that result in his increased happiness, acts, not as the Arch Rebel, but as the diligent servant of God. Again, in the Epistle of Jude, 19, occurs the passage, "Yet Michael the archangel when contending with the devil he disputed about the body of Moses, durst not bring against him a railing accusation, but said, The Lord rebuke thee." We are referred from Jude to Zachariah III, 2. Here Satan stands, it is true, with, a capital S; but a glance shows that here, as in so many other instances, "an adversary" is the correct translation.

In 1 Cor. V, 5; and in 1 Tim. I, 20, is it possible to understand by "Satan" the diabolarch? No inquiries have been suggested as to the "dragon," "Satan," "devil" of the Apocalypse, because it is well known that the most opposite views have been taken by divines as to the whole drift of the book of Revelation, while there is hardly a passage in it that has not been used to support contradictory theories; and because the canonicity of the book regarded in the second century as a forgery of Cerinthus, omitted in the list of books of the New Testament by the Council of Laodicea, and passed over in silence by Cyril of Jerusalem, Chrysostom, Theodore of Mopsuestia, and Theodoret is also well known to be a vexed question with biblical scholars.

And if in the above, and in other places, it is not conceded that we should understand by Satan and Devil, the adverse power of Rome, the obstacle opposed to the spread of the Gospel by individuals within or outside the Church, physical hindrance (2 Cor. XII, 7, and 1 Thes, II, 18), or that "law of sin" which Paul found within him, we may still be suffered to ask: Is there any passage in the Epistles where the dangerous endeavors of the Tempter of our race are exposed?

How is it that where the nature of temptation is set forth, as notably in the following passage, this special business of the devil is altogether ignored? "Let no man say when he is tempted, I am tempted of God, for God cannot be tempted with evil, neither tempteth he any man. But every man is tempted, when he is drawn away of his own lust and enticed. Then when lust hath conceived, it bringeth forth sin, and sin when it is finished bringeth forth death." James I. 13-15.

This passage goes far to confirm the opinion of many that the serpent of the "Fall" symbolizes carnal pleasure.

Are we at all warranted in supposing an implied intervention of the devil when Christ speaks as follows? And if "false-witness" is not the "father of lies," what is?

"OUT OF THE HEART PROCEED EVIL THOUGHTS, MURDERS, ADULTERIES, FORNICATIONS, THEFTS, FALSE WITNESS, BLASPHEMIES." Matt. XV. 19.

-H. A.

DEMONOLOGY

AUTHOR'S PREFACE

This little book will be found to contain the substance and general plan of the two lectures I gave at Strasbourg towards the close of last autumn, and the almost literal reproduction of the article published by me in the Revue des Deux Mondes of the 1st January, 1870.

The occasional alterations that may be remarked are, perhaps, explained by the difference that naturally suggests itself between a discourse, delivered in a Protestant Church, and an article subjected to the conditions of publication imposed by such a periodical as the above, and, again, between this and a pamphlet placed before the public upon the writer's sole authority.

These alterations, moreover, affect the-form only of the essay, and a few details; its basis, and the development of the ideas, remain unchanged. I would take advantage of this opportunity of thanking my Strasbourg hearers for the kind interest of which they have given me so many proofs, and of which the publication of this essay is at once a result and a new mark.

-A. R.
Rotterdam, January, 1870.

DEMONOLOGY

HISTORY OF THE DEVIL

HIS ORIGIN, GREATNESS, AND DECADENCE

Among fallen majesties whom Time, still more than sudden revolutions, has compelled to descend slowly from the thrones they occupied, there are few whose prestige has been as imposing and as prolonged as that of the king of hell, SATAN. In speaking of him, we may safely use the expression, fallen majesty; for those among our contemporaries who still profess belief in his existence and power, live absolutely as if they held no such belief, we shall presently see how those lived who did seriously believe in the devil, and when faith and life are no longer in harmony, we have a right to say that faith is dead. I am speaking of course, of our educated contemporaries; the rest can no longer be taken into consideration in the history of the human mind. To give a general view of the belief in a devil, with an account of its transformations and evolutions, will, we think, be interesting. It affords well-nigh a biography. An opportunity of doing this is afforded by a remarkable work for which we are indebted to a theological professor of Vienna. Notwithstanding its occasional diffuseness, Professor Roskoff's book is an encyclopedia of all that concerns the subject; and the author will not grudge us the aid we shall derive from his treasury of erudition. May the University of Vienna, invigorated by the events which have changed the face of Austria, pay the arrears she owes to European . scholarship by producing such books as this!

I

The origin of the belief in the devil carries us back to very early times; and, as is the case with all more or less dualistic faiths, faiths, that is, based upon the radical opposition of two supreme principles, we must seek it in the human mind, developing itself in the bosom of a Nature whose aspect is now

DEMONOLOGY

favorable, now hostile. There is a certain relative dualism, an antagonism of the ego and the non-ego which reveals itself from man's birth. His first breath is painful to him, for it makes him weep. To learn to eat, to walk, to speak, is a struggle to him; and, later, the work upon which his preservation depends will reproduce this perpetual struggle under other forms. When the religious sentiment awakens within him, and, at the onset, searches its object and its food in the visible creation, he finds himself face to face with phenomena which he personifies, which are, on the one hand, lovable and loved, as the aurora, and the life-sustaining vegetation, with the rain that refreshes and fertilizes it; and, on the other hand, frightful and terrible, as storm, thunder, and darkness. Hence come good gods and evil gods. As a general rule, and in virtue of that naive egotism which alike characterizes the childhood of individuals and of peoples, the dreaded gods are more adored than the loving deities who always do good of their own accord and unasked. This way, at least, the remarks converge of all the voyagers who have closely observed those peoples of both hemispheres who retain their savage state. We need not add that their divinities have, properly speaking, no moral character. They do good or harm according to their nature; and that is all.

Herein they do but resemble their worshipers. Man, indeed, always projects his own ideal upon the divinity he adores; and, if we consider the matter carefully, it is still thus that he arrives at the possession of all he can understand of divine truth. He has always a feeling that his god is perfect; and this is the main point; but the features of that perfection are always more or less those of his ideal. Two young swine-herds in a remote province of Austria, were once asked, "What would you do if you were Napoleon?" "I," said the younger, "would always use up the whole butter pot on my bread." "And I," said the other, who no doubt thought this answer lacked poetry, "I would watch the pigs on horseback." In like manner, a Bushman, when invited by a missionary who had instilled into him some notions of morality to give a few proofs that he could

DEMONOLOGY

distinguish between right and wrong, said, "It is wrong for another man to come and take away my wives; it is right for me to go and take his." The gods of savages are, necessarily, savage gods. They have, for the most part, frightful forms; just as their worshipers think it proper to make themselves look hideous when they go to battle, or even when they adorn themselves. The odd, the grotesque, is to them the beautiful; whatever is uncommon is mysterious; and the unknown is terrible. The poet must pardon us if we assert that the religion of peoples of this category is simply the adoration of genii or demons of bad repute. When, passing from savage peoples who live solely by hunting and fishing, we come to pastoral and, especially, to agricultural races, this adoration of evil deities is no longer so exclusive. Still, even among these the worship of the terrible gods predominates.

Take by way of illustration the simple prayer of the Madagascans, who acknowledge, among many other, two creating divinities, Zanihor, the author of good things, Nyang, of evil things: "Zamhor! To thee we offer no prayers. The good god needs no asking. But we must pray to Nyang. Nyang must be appeased. Nyang, bad and strong spirit, let not the thunder roar over our heads Tell the sea to keep within its bounds! Spare, Oh Nyang, the ripening fruit, and dry not up the blossoming rice! Let not our women bring forth children on the accursed days. Thou reignest, and this thou knowest, over the wicked; and great is their number, Nyang. Torment not, then, any longer, the good folk."

It would be easy to multiply the facts which show that the large place fear has in their piety compared with veneration or love, is a characteristic feature of the religion of primitive peoples. Hence come the enormous quantity of mischievous beings of a lower rank, recognized by all inferior religions, and which we meet with in the popular superstitions which adhere so pertinaciously to religions of a more exalted spiritual level.

DEMONOLOGY

In the grand mythologies, as those of India, of Egypt, or Greece, the apparent duality of nature is reflected in the distinction between the gods of order and production, and those of destruction and disorder. The feeling that in the long run order gains the upper hand in the contest between the opposing forces of nature, inspires myths; thus, Indra overcomes the storm-cloud; Horus avenges his father Osiris, wickedly slain by Typhon; and Jupiter vanquishes the Titans. Brahminism, when developed, shows us Siva, the god of destruction, concentrating and arranging the elements which disturb the universe.

Siva is still the most adored of the Hindu gods. In Semitic polytheism, dualism becomes sexual; or else the sun, always the chief object of adoration, the supreme god, is conceived under two forms, one smiling, the other terrible, Baal or Moloch.

This two-fold character of the adored divinities is no less remarkable when we study the most poetical and serene of polytheisms, that of Greece. Like all the others, it has its root in the worship of the visible world; but more than elsewhere, unless we except Egypt, the Greek gods join to their physical nature a corresponding moral physiognomy. They conquered the agents of confusion who, under the name of Titans, Giants, Typhons, threatened to disturb established order. They are, then, the invincible preservers of the established order of things; but as, after all, this regular order is far from being always in conformity with man's physical and moral good, it follows that the Greek gods have, all of them, in varying proportions, their pleasing and their somber aspect. Phoebus Apollo, for instance, is a god of light, a civilizer, the inspirer of art, the purifier of the earth and of the soul; and yet, he sends also plague, he is pitiless in his vengeance, and it is not very prudent to form close friendships with him. The same may be said of his sister Diana, or, rather, of the moon, who appears now with the charming features of a fair and chaste virgin, now with the sinister physiognomy of Hecate, of Brimo, or of Empusia. The azure horizons of the sea are at first beautiful blue birds then, sea-maidens, of surpassing beauty to the waist, who bewitch navigators by their sweet love-songs: but woe to those who allow themselves to be seduced! This physiognomy, in which good and evil are mingled, is common feature of the Hellenic pantheon, and reproduces itself unfailingly, from the supreme pair, Jupiter and Here (Juno), to the wedded occupants of the lower world, Aedoneus or Pluto, and his wife Proserpina, the strangler.

Like reflections are suggested by the Latin mythology and, where original, this is even more dualistic than the polytheism of Greece. It has its Orcus, its Stryges, its Lares and Lemures. The Slavonic mythology has its white and its black god. The divinities of our Celtic forefathers were by no means attractive, and the Germano-Scandinavian gods possessed valuable qualities allied with faults which made all intercourse with them very awkward, to say the least. Wherever in our own day belief in brownies, white-ladies, fairies, goblins, sprites, and the like has survived, we find the same admixture of good and evil qualities. These fragments of the great divine host of olden times are at once graceful, attractive, and generous, when they are in the mood; but also capricious, spiteful, and dangerous. We must keep this distinctly before us in entering upon an inquiry into the origin of our devil; for we shall find that he is of the composite order, and that many of his essential features connect him with the somber elements of all the religions which preceded Christianity.

But there is among those religions one which, from this special point of view, deserves that we ponder awhile over its fundamental doctrines, namely, that of the Zend Avesta, or, in more common parlance, the Persian religion. For here it is that we see the divine hierarchy, and creeds under the sway of a systematic dualism which extends over the whole world, including moral evil. The gods of light and the gods of darkness divide time and space between them. We do not speak here of

DEMONOLOGY

Zarvan-Akarana, the Endless Time who gave birth to Ahura Mazda, or Ormuz, the good god, and to his brother Angramainju, or Ahriman, the god of evil; for this is a philosophical notion of much later date than that original and characteristic point of view of the Zend religion which simply recognizes two equally eternal powers which are constantly struggling together, and which meet in combat on the surface of the earth as well as in the hearts of men. Wherever Ormuz plants good, Ahriman sows evil.

The history of the moral fall of the earliest men, due to the treachery of Ahriman, under the form of a serpent, presents the most surprising analogies with the parallel account given in Genesis. Hence the assertion that the tale is merely borrowed from the Persian. I think this opinion is ill-founded, for in the Iranian myth the evil genius is disguised, while in the Hebrew account it is a genuine serpent that speaks and acts, and who involves his race in the punishment he entails upon himself. We must, then, concede to the latter history the advantage of greater antiquity, if not as to its actual form, at least with regard to its original idea. The substituting a god in disguise for an animal that reasons and speaks, points to a reflection unknown in the ages that gave to myths their earliest form. Such reflection, in later times, led the Jews to see their Satan under the features of the serpent of Genesis, although the canonical text by no means countenances such a supposition.

I prefer, therefore, to regard the two myths, Hebrew and Iranian, as two unequally ancient variations of one and the same primitive theme, traceable, possibly, to the times when Iranians and Semitics still lived together under the shade of Ararat.

However this may be, one thing remains clear, that in the most seriously moral polytheism of the old world we meet with a religious conception which approaches very nearly to that which Semitic monotheism has handed down to us under the name of the devil or Satan. Ahriman, like Satan, has his

DEMONOLOGY

legions of bad angels, whose only thought is to torment and ruin mortals. It is not solely physical ills, storms, darkness, floods, diseases and death, that are attributed to them, but bad desires and sinful deeds. The good man is, therefore, a soldier of Ormuz, fighting under his command against the powers of evil; while the wicked man is a servant and, at last, an instrument of Ahriman. The Zend doctrine taught that at last Ahriman would be overcome, and would even be a convert to good. This trait distinguishes him advantageously from his Jewish-Christian brother. But here again we may ask in how far this fair hope formed part of the primitive religion. Certain it is that there is a very close likeness between the Jewish Satan and the Persian Ahriman; and in this there is nothing strange, if we bear in mind that the Persians are the sole polytheistic people with whom the Jews, emancipated by them from the Chaldean bondage, maintained a long and friendly intercourse.

There were some among Christian theologians, Origen, for instance, for he believed in the final conversion of Satan. Still, we must dissent from the wide-spread opinion which sees in Satan a transplanting of the Persian Ahriman into the religious soil of Semiticism. It is true that the Jewish, as well as the Christian, devil owes much to Ahriman. From the moment when the Jewish Satan makes his acquaintance, he imitates him, adopts his methods, his conduct and his tactics, and forms his infernal court upon the same pattern; in a word, he transforms himself into his likeness. But ere this, obscure and ill-defined as was his life, Satan existed.

Let us endeavor to sum up his history as traced in the Old Testament. The Israelites, and this is now clearly demonstrated, in common with other Semitic peoples, long believed in the plurality of gods; and the dualism which is at the bottom of all polytheisms has, as a necessary consequence, re-appeared among them under the forms peculiar to the ethnic group to which they belong. In proportion as the worship of Jehovah became more and more exclusive, this dualism changed its forms. The fervent worshiper of Jehovah, while he still believed in the real existence of the neighboring deities, such as Baal and Moloch, could not but regard these immoral, cruel, and hostile gods with much the same eye as was turned upon the demons of a later age. We may go so far as to suspect some debris of a primitive dualism, or of an antagonism between two once rival gods, in that enigmatic being, the despair of exegetists, who, under the name of Azazel, haunts the desert, and to whom, on the day of atonement, the high priest sends a goat on whose head he has laid the sins of the people. But we must add, that in historic times the meaning of this ceremony seems to have been lost to those who performed it; and that, in truth, nothing can be more in opposition to anything like dualism than the Jehovistic point of view in all its strictness. With the exception of the books of Job, Zechariah, and Chronicles, all three of which are among the least ancient of the sacred collection, not a word is said about Satan in the Old Testament, not even and this we repeat because in spite of the evidence of the text, the mistake we point out is so common not even in Genesis. Jehovah, when once adored as the one true god, has not, could not have, a rival. Nothing happens, nothing is done on earth, which is not subject to his will; and more than one Hebrew author attributes to him directly, without the least reservation, the suggestion of errors and faults that are afterwards referred to Satan. Jehovah hardens those whom he will harden; Jehovah destroys those whom he chooses to destroy; and no one has a right to question his justice. But, as he was believed to be supremely just, it was admitted that in hardening the heart of the wicked, he did so that they might dig their own graves; while in distributing according to his will good and evil, he did so in such sort as to reward the righteous and punish wrong-doers. It was impossible to adhere constantly to this notion, so convenient in theory, but so often belied by experience; but it was long held, and a proof of this will be seen in the kind of religious ideas out of which we shall see Satan come forth.

DEMONOLOGY

Hebrew monotheism did not exclude belief in heavenly spirits, in sons of God (ben Elohim), in angels whose office it was to surround the throne of the Eternal, like a holy guard. They awaited his orders, performed his will, and were in some sort the agents of divine government. Upon them devolved the direct application of the punishments and mercies of God.

Consequently, there were among them some whose offices inspired fear rather than confidence. We find, for instance, an angelic messenger punishing Saul for his misdeeds, by troubling with dark fancies which David's harp alone can dissipate. It is an angel of the Eternal who appears with a naked sword in his hand to Balaam, as if ready to pierce through, or who destroys in one night a whole Assyrian army. In course of time an angel was distinguished among the rest whose special function in the heavenly court was that of accuser of men, and whom we might regard as the personification of a guilty conscience.

Sovereign justice doubtless decided alone, and in the fullness of its power; but not until after some adverse debate. Now, he whose profession it was to prosecute men at the divine tribunal was an angel whose name Satan simply means adversary, in both the legal and proper sense of the word. Such is clearly the Satan of the Book of Job; he is a member of the heavenly court, and is one of the sons of God, although it is his special concern to accuse men. He has become so suspicious through his constant practice as public prosecutor, that he believes in no human being's goodness, not even in that of Job the just; and supposes the purest manifestations of piety to result from interested motives. We see the character of this angel begin to tarnish; and the history of Job shows that when his purpose is to exhaust the resignation of a just man, he spares nothing to effect it. It is again as the accuser of Israel that Satan appears in the vision of Zechariah (III, 1). This special character of his, together with the settled belief that angels took part in human affairs, caused Satan, unaided by any help from

DEMONOLOGY

Ahriman, to be feared by the Israelites as the worst enemy of mankind; and a tendency arose, under both public and private misfortunes, to suspect his evil agency. It resulted from this that those fatal inspirations which earlier Jehovism attributed immediately to Jehovah himself, came to be regarded as proceeding from Satan. In the history of David we have a curious instance of this evolution of religious belief. David one day was possessed by the unlucky, and to the theocratic republicanism of the prophets of his time impious idea of numbering his people. In the second boot of Samuel (XXIV, 1) we are told that "the anger of the Lord was kindled against Israel, and he moved David" to give the necessary orders for this census; while, on the other hand, where the self-same history is related in the first book of Chronicles (XXI, 1), we have these words: "And Satan stood up against Israel and provoked David to number Israel." Nothing could show better than these parallel passages the change that had come about during the interval between the composition of these two books. From this time forward the monotheist will attribute to the Adversary the evil thoughts and the calamities which in former times would have been traced directly to God. We may even presume that this solution of certain problems that had begun to trouble him carried with it some religious comfort; for in proportion as our conception of God becomes more elevated, it becomes harder to rest content with the childish theories that satisfied less thoughtful ages.

In the part of adversary of mankind, of mar-plot, we find the true origin of the Jewish and Christian devil. We must not, therefore, identify him too readily with the more or less wicked divinities of polytheistic religions. That he has affinities with them which grow closes and closer, we admit fully; but the certificate of his birth is clearly written; and if even the Jews had never come into contact with the Persians, Jewish tradition would still have given us a fully-equipped Satan. Satan, then, is neither the son nor even the brother of Ahriman; but a time came when the resemblance was so great, that it was easy to confuse them. We may say, in short, that while Ahriman is physical evil that has become moral evil also, Satan is moral evil becoming physical evil. This is the secret of his increasing sway.

Indeed, in the so-called apocryphal books of the Old Testament, distinguishable from the canonical books of the same volume by the Alexandrine and Persian elements which they contain, Satan is seen growing in importance and influence. The Seventy, in translating his name by diabolos, from whence comes our word devil, retain the exact definition of his early character of accuser. But he comes to be something very different from that.

He is an agent provocateur of the highest order; a very exalted personage, who, jealous to rise to a still loftier eminence among angels of the highest rank, was banished from heaven with the other spirits who were his accomplices in ambition. To hatred of men he now adds hatred of God and it is here that the imitation of Ahriman begins. Like the Persian demon, he is at the head of an army of evil beings who execute his orders. Many of these we know by name. Among others is Asmodeus, the demon of pleasure, who plays an important part in the book of Tobit, and whose Persian origin has been rendered unquestionable by the learned researches of M. Michel Breal. In consequence of his growing importance and his absolute separation from the faithful angels, Satan has a distinct kingdom, and a residence in the subterranean hell. Like the Persian Ahriman, he sought to spoil the work of creation, and waged war on men, whose innocent happiness was insupportable to him. And then it is agreed that he it was who, like Adam, beguiled the first woman under the guise of the serpent. It was he who introduced, death with all its horrors; and hence his most formidable antagonists are those who through their great holiness are able to warn their fellows against his insidious attacks.

DEMONOLOGY

A multitude of diseases, those especially which through their singularity and the absence of external symptoms defied natural explanations, as madness, epilepsy, St. Vitus's dance, dumbness, certain forms of blindness, etc, were attributed to his agents. Millions of fiends, obedient to his commands, were supposed to stream constantly from the depths of hell, and like the night demons of the old faith preferred, for their, haunts deserts and wildernesses. But there they grew weary, they were thirsty, they wandered about and found no rest; and their great resource was to take up their abode in a human body, that they might absorb its substance and refresh themselves with its blood. Sometimes many of them would occupy the same frame. Hence the demoniacs and the possessed of whom we read so often in the gospel narrative. Still, the Jewish mythology did not press to the utmost this likeness to Ahriman. Satan never wages war directly upon God. Certain formulas, in which the name of the Most Holy is the chief, sufficed to exorcise, to drive away, him and his angels. His power was strictly limited to the circle which it had pleased the divine wisdom to trace; so that the dualism remained very incomplete. But, for the Jewish Satan, no conversion was considered possible. As Prince of incurable evil, and knowing that the divine decrees doomed him to a final and irremediable defeat, it was held that he would persist in wickedness, and serve as executioner to supreme justice by tormenting for ever those whom he had drawn into his dreadful toils.

Such was the feeling on this head among the Jewish people when the gospel was first preached. The development of the Messianic ideas did much towards enriching the popular faith. If, as they believed, the devil dared not encounter God himself, nor even the highest of his angels, still he did not fear to resist openly his servants on the earth. Now the Messiah was to be the servant of God par excellence. He was to appear in order to establish the kingdom of God among the human race, which was almost wholly in the power of the devil and his angels; so that Satan would defend his dominions to the utmost

DEMONOLOGY

against the Messiah, whose work might be summed up as consisting in a close and victorious struggle with the "prince of this world." This point of view we must never allow to escape us in our study of the gospels. Satan and the Messiah personified, on either hand, the power of evil and the power of good, fighting over every contested point a battle in which no quarter was given. Never, therefore, could Jesus have passed for the Messiah in the eyes of his countrymen, if had not been accounted stronger than the evil spirits, whenever those possessed were brought to him.

Modern theology, which has well-nigh repudiated the Devil, has dwelt much upon the question whether Jesus himself shared the belief of his contemporaries in regard to satanism. To treat this question adequately, it would be necessary to enter upon inquiries which are foreign to the history of the devil. We will simply remark that there is no authority for thinking that Jesus, out of consideration for popular beliefs, would have feigned a faith which he did not hold; to which we would add, that the principles of his religion were not in themselves favorable to this kind of faith. The idea that God is the Father of all, is not easily reconciled with the existence of a devil.

Nowhere does Jesus make belief in the devil one of the conditions of admission into the Kingdom of God; and were the devil a mere idea, a bare symbol, these considerations would remain literally the same. Purity of heart, thirst for justice, love for God and man, these are all of them essentials which are entirely independent of the question whether Satan exists or not. So that, whenever Jesus speaks in a general, abstract sense, without regard to the circumstances of time and place, he removes the person of Satan from his field of instruction. He declares, for instance, that our evil thoughts come from our heart; while, according to the satanic theory, they ought to be referred to the devil. Still, he evidently availed himself of the popular belief on this head, as a form or image to which he attributed no positive reality. It furnished him with matter for

DEMONOLOGY

parable. He addressed as Satan, one of his disciples who sought to withdraw him from approaching sufferings, and who, through very affection, became a momentary tempter. A like observation suggests itself in studying the theology of St. Paul at least, in his authentic epistles. St. Paul evidently believes in the devil; and yet with him moral evil is connected with the earthly nature of man, and not with the external and personal action of the fiend.

In a word, the teaching of Jesus and Paul does not anywhere combat the belief in the devil; but it can do without, and tends to do without it. In our own day we see abundance of good Christians who do not at all concern themselves about the king of hell; but this belief was one of those germs (of which the Gospel contains many) which required another intellectual atmosphere for their development. What precedes has explained to us why there is so much more about the devil in the New than in the Old Testament.

The belief in the devil and the expectation of the Messiah had a parallel growth. Be it remarked, however, that if the New Testament often speaks of Satan and his angels, of spirits "of the air," and of the devil, "*quoerens quam devoret*," its descriptions of them are almost colorless. A kind of spiritual reserve still veils all conceptions of this order. The devils are invisible; no palpable body is attributed to them; and a multitude of superstitions which will grow out of the idea that they can be seen and handled, are as yet unknown.

Nevertheless, from this point of our history we may consider the origin of Satan as closed. We see him here as the link that connects polytheistic dualism with just that degree of relative dualism which Jewish monotheism could support. We are now to see him develop himself under new forms; but he has already attained a shape which we can no longer ignore. He stands before us the old *Satanas*, the bugbear of our forefathers, in whom is centered all that is unholy and frightful and lying in a word, he is the ideal of evil.

II

The earliest ages of Christianity, far from developing that side of the Gospel which tended to banish the devil to the regions of symbolism and personal uselessness, served to extend his dominion, by multiplying his interventions in human affairs. He served as a scape-goat upon which the first Christians could expend their horror of heathen institutions. For some time Christians did not draw a very distinct line between the Roman Empire and the empire of Satan. This essentially Jewish point of view did not last long; but the favorite theme of most apologists was to attribute whatever polytheism presented, whether fair or foul, good or bad, to the devil's cunning and pride. Wherever the beautiful and the good were found united, this, in their eyes, was neither more nor less than so much truth artfully mixed by the enemy of mankind with fearful error, in order to retain a better grasp upon man, who could not be held under the sway of sheer falsehood.

The Alexandrian school alone was more reasonable; but it had little hold upon the mass of the faithful. And now the idea spread that Satan was at bottom but a ridiculous, though for long a powerful, rival of the one adorable God. Led by a thirst for honor and dominion, he had aped, as well as he could, the divine perfections, but had only succeeded in producing a hateful caricature. But, such as it was, the caricature had blinded the nations. This subject suggested to Tertullian one of those characteristic sayings in which his satirical temper delighted: "Satan," said he, "is God's ape;" and the saying lived. The Greco-Roman gods became to Christians, as well as to Jews, demons who had usurped divine rank. The licentiousness of pagan customs, too often consecrated by traditional religious ceremonies, furnished a sort of popular justification to this view, which was heightened by the moral superiority which the early Church had, generally, a fair right to contrast with the corruptions that surrounded her. Satan, therefore, became, more than ever, the "prince of this world."

But let us not forget one very important circumstance, namely, that other currents external to the Christian Church contributed to spread abroad the belief in evil spirits. Polytheism in its decline obeyed its true nature; it became more and more dual. Its latest forms, those for instance which were marked by what they derived from Platonism and Pythagorism, were all saturated with dualism, and thus opened a large field to the imagination for the creation of every kind of evil genius. At that epoch, asceticism, which consists in slowly killing the body under the pretext of developing the soul, was not peculiar to the most exalted members of the Christian Church, but was found wherever a religious morality was practiced. The ecstasies which were physiologically generated by fasting, gave all the appearance of reality to the imaginary beings they evoked. Apollonius of Tyana drove away as many foul spirits as a Christian saint. As Professor Roskoff very justly observes, the doctrine of angels and devils presented to both Jewish polytheism and Christian monotheism a sort of neutral territory on which, to a certain point, they could meet.

The religious movements known under the name of gnostic sects, which represent, in various proportions, a mixture of heathen, Jewish, and Christian views, have as a common feature the belief in fallen angels who are the tyrants of men and the rivals of God. The great success of Manicheism, that confluence of Persian dualism and Christianity, is due to the leaning of public opinion towards whatever portrayed a systematic struggle between the genius of evil and the genius of good. The Talmud and the Kabbala were subjected to the same influence. We must not regard Christianity as alone responsible for the prominent place Satan took in the concerns of this world; it was a universal tendency of the epoch, and we should be more correct in regarding Christianity as affected thereby in common with all other contemporaneous forms of religion.

DEMONOLOGY

The Jewish Messiah became to Christians the Savior of guilty humanity. This is why we see the radical antagonism between Satan and the Messiah reflected in the primitive doctrine of redemption. From the close of the second century, this doctrine is summed up in a grand drama in which Christ and the devil are the principal actors. The multitude were contented to believe that Christ, descending into hell, had, in virtue of his right as the stronger of the two, taken from Satan the souls he had carried captive. But this rude idea underwent a refinement. Irenaeus taught that man, after the fall, having become Satan's rightful property, it would have been unjust on the part of God to deprive him by violence of his own; and that Christ, as a perfect man, and therefore independent of the devil, offered himself a ransom for the human family, which bargain the devil accepted.

Soon, however, it became clear that the devil had made a very foolish reckoning, as Christ did not remain, after all, in his power. Origen, whose ecclesiastical teachings must not always be taken as literally exact representations of his real opinions, became the organ of views which freely admitted that both Christ and Satan had played their parts very cleverly, seeing that the devil believed he should keep in his power a prey which was worth more to him than the whole human race, while Christ knew very well that he should not remain in Satan's hands. This view, which made Jesus the deceiver at the cost of Satan, scandalous as it appears to us, was, nevertheless, a success, and long predominated in the Church. Ecclesiastical poetry, popular preaching, and even pontifical assertion, extended it in all directions, dramatized it, consecrated it. One can readily understand that this way of regarding redemption did not go towards diminishing the devil's sway over men's minds. Nothing did more to increase fear of the enemy than vague descriptions of the immensity of his power, and of the risk run by exposure to his attacks; especially as, by a singular contradiction from which the ancient theology never succeeded in extricating itself, of the devil, although declared vanquished, overthrown, and rendered powerless by his victor Christ, did not the less maintain his infernal sway over a large majority of mankind.

The saints alone could count themselves safe from his ambushes; and, according to the legends which now began to spread, great was the prudence and energy they required to escape him. Everything turned upon this constant state of watchfulness. Baptism dwindled into an exorcism. To become a Christian, was to renounce the devil with his pomps and works. Expulsion from the fold of the Church, whether for immoral behavior, or for heterodoxy, was the being "delivered over to Satan." It was thus that during this period the doctrine of the fall of the evil angels was developed. We now find it taught that devils were referred to in that mythic passage of Genesis where the "sons of God saw the daughters of men that they were fair, and took them wives of all that they chose," licentiousness being considered as the original sin and never-ending concern of evil spirits; and again, as this hypothesis did not explain the anterior presence of a wicked angel in the earthly paradise, the fall of the rebel fiends was dated from the moment of the Creation.

Augustine thought that in consequence of this fall, their bodies, which were formerly subtle and invisible, became dense. And here we have the beginning of a belief in the visible apparitions of the devil Then came another notion, that devils, in order to gratify their lust, took advantage of the night to surprise young persons while asleep; and hence the succubus and incubus which played such a prominent part in the middle ages. Saint Victor, according to the legend, was overcome by a demon who had artfully assumed the form of a young seductress who had lost her way at night tune in the woods. The councils, from the fourth century, enjoined bishops to keep a close watch over those in their dioceses who practiced magic arts, the inventions of the devil; and wicked women are spoken of who are supposed to run the fields by night in the train of Diana and other heathen goddesses.

But as yet these imaginary sabbaths are regarded as but dreams suggested by Satan to those whose vicious inclinations gave him a hold over them. Ere long, however, all became real and material.

There was not a saint to whom the devil did not at least appear once under a human form. Saint Martin even met him so disguised as to represent Christ. For the most part, however, in his quality of angel of darkness, he appeared as a man, and quite black, under which color he was wont to escape from the heathen temples and idols that had been thrown down by the zeal of converts to the new religion. And then came the idea that one could make an agreement with the devil, by which the soul might be exchanged for the object of one's greatest desire. This notion dates from the legend of Theophilus, a sixth century saint. He, in a moment of wounded pride, made himself over formally to Satan; but, being devoured by remorse, he got the Virgin Mary to recover the fatal document from the evil one.

This legendary episode, written with the express object of extending the worship of Mary, necessarily had important results. The devil, moreover, saw his prestige increase still further, when the conversion of the invaders of the Empire, and the missions sent into countries that had never formed part of the Roman dominions, introduced into the bosom of the Church a mass of grossly ignorant people, who were still impregnated with polytheism. The Church and State, which had been united since Constantine's time, and were still more closely cemented under Charlemagne, did what they could to refine the coarse minds of those whose teachers they had become; but, to do this effectually, the temporal and spiritual powers had need to be themselves less under the sway of the very superstitions they desired to repel. If some among the more clever of the Popes succeeded in combining with their political plans a certain amount of toleration for customs and errors that seemed ineradicable, the great majority of bishops and missionaries firm believed that by insisting upon the extirpation of polytheism they were fighting against the devil and his host. They inoculated their converts with the same belief; and thereby considerably prolonged the existence of the heathen divinities. The good old rural spirits died hard. The sacred legends contain many of them, and comparative mythology recognizes not a few ancient Celtic and Teutonic gods among the patron saints of our ancestors.

Saint Nicolas, Saint Victor, Saint Denis with the "head carrying" saints in general, Saint Ursula (Horsela), Saint Venetia, and many others of less fame, enter into this category. For a long time, and without its being looked upon as a renunciation of the catholic faith, it was usual in England, France, and Germany, to offer presents, now out of gratitude, now through fear, to the spirits of the fields and forests, women especially adhering to such old customs. But as the Church still regarded as demons and devils all superhuman beings who were not saints or angels, seeing that the character of the old gods had nothing angelical in it, an interchange, or, rather a transformation, was effected. The good side of these deities served, under new names, to enrich the kingdom of the saints, the kingdom of the demons had what was left. Belief in the devil, which in the earlier ages had something elevated in it, became simply gross and stupid. At the beginning of the middle ages certain animals, as cats, toads, rats, mice, black dogs, wolves, were regarded as specially selected by the devil and his servants for symbols, auxiliaries, and even as temporary disguises. In our own times even, we generally find these animals were consecrated or sacrificed to the divinities whom demons have replaced.

Traditions of human sacrifices offered up in honor of the ancient gods, account doubtless for the notion that Satan and his slaves have a relish for human flesh. The were-wolf who eats children has been by turns a god, a devil, and a sorcerer who went to the sabbath under the guise of a wolf that he might not be recognized. We all know that there is no witch without her cat. Vermin, that sore which then as now was but too common a scourge among populations devoid of all sense of cleanliness, was also to be laid at the door of the devil and his servants. A time came when the idea that the devil had a distinct bodily shape became settled; and this form was that of the ancient fauns and satyrs, with horns, protruding legs, hairy skin, tail, cloven foot or horse's hoof. It would be easy to accumulate here semi-burlesque, semi-tragic details. But we prefer marking the salient points of the development of belief. We have reached a period at which we must look at it under a new light.

Among the Jews of the times immediately preceding the Christian era, Satan had become the adversary of the Messiah; with the early Christians he was the direct antagonist of the Savior of mankind: but to the middle ages Christ was up in heaven, far away; and the immediate, living organism, in which his kingdom on earth was to be realized was the Church, between which and the devil the war was thenceforward to be waged. The faith of the peasant consists simply in believing what the Church believes. Ask him what the Church believes, and he will answer boldly, "What I believe." And if in the times of which we are speaking the question had been put, "What does the devil do?" the answer would have been "What the Church does not do;" while to the question, "And what is it that the Church does not do?" the response would have amounted to this, "What the devil does."

The sabbaths which the ancient councils, when referred to thereupon, treated as appertaining to imaginary regions, had now been something very real. The Germanic idea of fealty, the idea that fidelity to the suze-rain was the first of virtues, just as treason on the part of the vassal was the greatest of crimes, was introduced into the Church, and contributed not a little to give to aught approaching infidelity to Christ the color of the blackest depravity. The wizard was as faithful to his master the devil as

DEMONOLOGY

was the good Christian to his heavenly liege; and just as vassals came yearly to render homage to their lord, so did the feudal servants of Satan hasten to pay him like honor, either on some accustomed day or at a special convocation. The weird chase through the air of wizards and witches, as they hastened to the nightly rendezvous, was no other than a transformation of the Celtic and German myth of the Wild-Huntsman. But the master who awaited them was a sort of god; and in the grand assemblies of the devilish horde he was honored by the celebration of a burlesque of the mass; the spirit of evil being worshiped by reversing the ceremonies which serve to glorify the author of good. The very name of sabbath came from the confusion of devil-worship and mere noncatholic rites; the Church having placed on the same footing Jews, excommunicate persons, heretics, and necromancers. To this confusion there was one circumstance which contributed greatly. Into most of the sects that had revolted against the Church (and above all the one which holds so exalted and so sad a place in French history, that of the Albigenses) the old gnostic and Manichaean leaven had thoroughly instilled itself.

Dualism was the principle of their theology. This accounts for the idea that at their religious meetings, which rivaled the mass, they simply said the mass service backwards, a mode of worship which was in high favor with Satan. If, bearing this in mind, we remember how easily in medieval times the State allowed itself to be persuaded that its main business was to exterminate heretics, we shall cease to wonder at the severity of the penal laws directed against supposed sorcerers.

The absorbing nature of the belief in the devil during the middle ages is the point we wish to make clear. Those who have still this faith can hardly imagine to what a degree it then controlled men's whole lives. It was the one fixed idea with every one, particularly from the thirteenth to the fifteenth century, the period at which we may consider this superstition to have reached its climax. A fixed idea tends, among those whom it possesses, to center everything in itself. When, at the present day, we observe closely those of our contemporaries who devote themselves to spiritualism, it is surprising to see how fertile their imagination becomes when they are busy in interpreting in favor of their hobby the most trifling and unimportant circumstances.

The unlatching of a half-closed door, an insect describing arabesques in its flight, the fall of a badly-balanced article, the creaking of furniture at night-time, any one of these petty accidents suffices to give wing to their fancy. If we generalize such a mental state, by substituting faith in the incessant interventions of the devil for the harmless illusions of our spiritualists, we shall get a fair notion of what took place in the middle ages. Among the numberless records from which we might quote, we will take the Revelations of the Abbot Richalmus, who lived in Franconia some seven hundred years ago, and who belonged to the Cistercian order.

These Revelations, though now forgotten, had formerly a wide-spread fame. Abbot Richalmus boasted the possession of a special power of discerning and detecting the machinations of Satan's satellites, who moreover, according to the abbot, were especially given to playing their impish tricks upon churchmen and good Christians. And right diabolically did they worry the poor man! From his distraction during mass to the nausea that too often troubles his digestion, from the discords of the choir-men to the fits of coughing that interrupt his sermons, all is of fiendish agency.

"For instance," says he to his attendant, "when I sit down to holy studies, the devils make me feel heavy with sleep. Then I stretch my hands beyond my cuffs to give them a chill. Forthwith the spirits prick me under my clothes like so many fleas, which causes me to put my hands there; and so they get warm again, and my reading grows careless." They love, he tells us, to make people ugly. To one they give a red nose, to another cracked lips. If a man likes to close his mouth decently, then they make his lower lip droop. "Come," he says to his acolyte, "just look at my lip; for twenty years has an imp clung to it, just to make it hang down." And so on, in the same strain. When asked whether there are many devils who thus wage war with man, the abbot Eichalmus replies that each one of us is as closely surrounded by them as a man when plunged in the sea is by the waves.

Fortunately, the sign of the cross was generally enough to disconcert them; but not always, for they understand well the human heart, and know how to take advantage of its weak side. One day, when some monks were gathering together stones under the abbot's orders, for the purpose of building a wall, he heard a young devil who was hidden under them call out very distinctly, "What a troublesome task!" This he did that he might dispose the monks to grumble at the labors imposed upon them.

To the sign of the cross, he tells us, it is often useful to add the aid of holy water and salt. Evil spirits cannot bear salt.

"When I am at dinner, and the devil has taken away my appetite, as soon as I have tasted a little salt it comes back to me; and if, shortly afterwards, I lose it again, I take some more salt, and am once more an hungered." Here we have the old idea that salt was preservative, vivifying, agreeable to gods and men; and, consequently, opposed to whatever is ungodly. In the hundred and thirty chapters which make up his Revelations, the abbot scarcely does anything but subject to his one fixed idea the most trivial events of domestic and, particularly, of convent life. But the popularity this book, which was published after his death, enjoyed, proved that he had simply abounded in the notions of his contemporaries. Innumerable parallels may be found in the literature of the age. The Golden Legend of Jacobus de Voragine, one of the most popular books of the middle ages, would suffice as an illustration.

DEMONOLOGY

This incessant turning of the thoughts devil-ward, had two equally logical consequences, though they were of a very opposite character. It had its comic and its serious aspect.

Through seeing Satan everywhere, a familiarity with him was engendered, and by a kind of unconscious mental protestation against the imaginary monsters created by traditional teaching, people got so bold as to manage his horned majesty very easily. The legends pictured him always as so miserably outdone by the sagacity of saints and holy priests, that his reputation for cleverness gradually waned. It was thought by no means impossible to turn his stupidity to account. Had he not, for instance, been such a simpleton as to get architects out of hobbles by supplying them with splendid plans for the cathedrals of Aix-la-Chapelle and Cologne? It is true that at Aix he had bargained for the soul of the first person who entered the church, and at Cologne for that of the architect himself; but then he was outwitted, after all. At Aix, a wolf was goaded into the newly-finished church; at Cologne, the architect, having got possession of the promised plan, instead of giving Satan a proper deed by which his soul was made over, suddenly draws from under his gown a bone of one of the eleven thousand virgins, which he thrusts into the evil one's face, who makes off with a thousand oaths. It is well known how prominent was the part assigned him in the medieval religious plays.

The popular imagination still pictured the redemption as a divine stratagem by which the enemy of mankind was fairly duped; and thus it was easy to conceive a host of other cases in which Satan was caught in his own net.

What laughter his scrapes excited among the good folk! There are ample reasons for believing that he became the personage who was the most to their taste, if he did not gain the largest share of their sympathy. The rest of the dramatic persons had their parts traced out for them by tradition; in his case there was always room for a little extemporaneous acting. For a long time he represented the comic element of the sacred drama. His character, half mountebank, half grim, was conveniently flexible.

In France, where there has always been an inclination to subject the theater to precise rules, there were popular pieces called devilries, vulgar and often obscene masquerades, in which at least four devils were expected to display their gambols, and, from which it would seem we get the expression, *faire le diable a guatre*. In Germany, too, the devil was an amusing character on the stage. There is an old Saxon "mystery" of the Passion, in which Satan repeats as a mocking echo the last words of Judas while he hangs himself; then, when according to the sacred tradition the bowels of the traitor gush out, he puts them into a basket, and sings an appropriate ditty as he carries them off.

But all this did not prevent the devil's generally causing terrible fear. To go to the play was, in the middle ages, much the same as going to church. When there, there was nothing to hinder one's making a butt of the hated being whose malice was powerless to harm the actors in the sacred performances. But listening to mysteries could not be made the main business of life; and the realities of every day soon restored his prestige. The number of persons who were suspected of having dealings with Satan was enormous; so great, that when the success of an enemy or of a bold plot seemed otherwise inexplicable, it was at once set down to Satanic agency. Enguerrand de Marigny, the Templars, poor Joan of Arc, and many other illustrious victims of political hatred, were convicted of witchcraft. Among the Popes themselves, some, as John XXII., Gregory VII., and Clement V., encountered the same suspicion.

At this epoch the notion arose that agreements made with the devil must be signed with the blood of those in league with him, that it might be clearly understood that their persons

DEMONOLOGY

and lives were his; while the old Italian superstition was resuscitated by which one's enemy was destroyed by mutilating or piercing little waxen figures, made in his image, and placed under a spell.

Councils were summoned expressly to check the supposed spread of witchcraft. Pope John XXII., himself accused of necromancy, declared, in a bull promulgated in 1317, what bitter grief was caused him by those compacts made with the devil by his physicians and courtiers, by which other men were led to take part in the like impious doings. From the thirteenth century, the crime of sorcery was placed on a level with the greatest offenses; and popular ignorance was but too ready to furnish fuel to the zeal of the inquisitors. At Toulouse a noble lady, fifty-six years of age, Angela de Labarete by name, was the first who was burned as a sorceress, in which special quality she formed part of the great auto-da-fe which took place in that city in 1275. At Carcassonne, from 1320 to 1350, more than four hundred executions for witchcraft are on record.

Up to the end of the fourteenth century, however, these horrible displays were localized, but in 1484 a decree of Pope Innocent VIII. extended trial for witchcraft over the whole of Christendom. Then began in Europe that hideous witch-hunt which marks the climax of the belief in the devil, which concentrated and condensed it during more than three centuries; and which at last, succumbing to the moral force of modern times, was to carry away with it the dark belief from which it

III

In the fifteenth century a momentary lull of orthodox fanaticism rendered the inquisitor's task somewhat difficult in the treatment of heresy proper. On the banks of the Rhine as well as in France, people seem to have begun to weary of the insatiable ghoul that threatened everybody, while it healed none of the ills of the Church to which it had been applied as a sovereign remedy.

Faith in the Church itself as a perfect and infallible institution was tottering, and the inquisitors carried to the Holy See their murmurs at the increasing obstacles placed in their way by local powers and parish clergy. Still, even those whose faith in the Church was shaken, and who inclined towards religious toleration, did not propose to leave a free course to the devices of the devil and his agents. It was at this time that the famous bull Summis desiderantes appeared, by which Innocent VIII added to the power of the officers of the Inquisition that of prosecuting those guilty of witchcraft, and of applying to them the rules which hitherto had only been aimed at *depravatio haeretica*. Long is the list of machinations enumerated in the pontifical bull, from; tempests and the destruction of crops to the spells cast upon men and women to prevent the increase of the human family. Armed with this bull, which thundered the severest pains and penalties against the refractory, and which was confirmed by other decrees of the same sense and origin, the inquisitors Henry Institoris and Jacob Sprenger wielded that Witch-Hammer, Malleus Maleficarum, which was long throughout Europe the standard code of action against those suspected of sorcery.

It received the sanction of the Pope, and the approval of the Emperor Maximilian and of the theological faculty of Cologne. The perusal of this heavy and wearisome treatise can hardly fail to provoke a shudder; a careful study of the false put in the stead of the true, of the repeated sophisms with which the book abounds, of the pedantic folly with which its authors heap together whatever can give a shadow of likelihood to their nightmares, together with the cold-blooded cruelty which dictates their prosecutions and summonses, this could not but disgust the modern student, were it not his duty to bring to the bar of history one of the most lamentable aberrations that have warped the conscience of humanity.

DEMONOLOGY

Everything is explained in this conjuring-book. We learn why the devil enables his servants to change themselves *reali transformatione et essentialiter* into wolves and other dangerous animals; why it is heresy to disbelieve in the power of magic; how the incubi and succubi work their ends; why the number of witches is greater than ever; why David in olden time drove away the spirit that troubled Saul by showing him a harp in the form of the cross, etc. We are told, again, that the reason why there are more witches than wizards lies in the fact that women are more ready than men to be beguiled by the devil's promises; and this, because the fluidity of their temperament makes them more easily acted upon by his inspiration; (in a word, because being weaker than men they readily seek supernatural aid in order to satisfy their vengeance or their sensuality.)

All manner of recipes are recommended to persons who have the good sense to guard themselves against the charms that may be practiced upon them. The sign of the cross, holy water, the judicious use of salt, and of the name of the Holy Trinity, are among the principal exorcisms.

The sound of bells is accounted a very energetic preservative; and therefore it is well to ring them during storms, as the evil spirits, who cannot support the sacred sound, are thereby driven away, and checked in their work of perturbation. This superstitious custom, which has lasted to our own day, denotes clearly the confusion of demons ecclesiastic with the old divinities of storm and tempest.

But what is above all worthy of attention, is the mode of criminal action developed in this book, and which became law everywhere. It is exactly based upon the prosecutions instituted by the Inquisition against heretics. As witchcraft was the outcome of a league with the devil it presupposed the abjuration of the baptismal vow, and was, consequently, a kind of apostasy, a heresy of the gravest order. Denunciations without proof were

DEMONOLOGY

admitted. Even public hearsay sufficed to bring the charge under the judge's scrutiny. The depositions of all comers were received, no matter how infamous, no matter whether or not they were the enemies of the accused parties. The trial was to be as summary as possible, and useless formalities cut short. The witch was to be cross-questioned until something peculiar was detected in her life that served to strengthen the suspicions which hung over her. The judge was not obliged to name her accusers. She was allowed a defender, who knew no more of the matter than she did, and who had to limit what he said to the defense of the person accused, but not of her criminal acts, as this would turn suspicion upon himself. Confession was to be obtained by torture, together with all the circumstances connected with the offense.

In order to obtain full and prompt confession, her life might be promised her; but and this is expressed in so many words such promise was not binding. Torture was to be repeated every three days, and the judge was to use all needful caution lest its effects should be neutralized by charms hidden about the person of the accused. He was even to abstain from looking her in the face, seeing that witches had been known to be gifted by the devil with an influence which made judges who thus gazed on them unable to pronounce their condemnation. When at last she had been well and rightly convicted, she was to be delivered over to the secular arm, to be put to death without further parley. This rapid glance is enough to show that the unhappy creatures who fell into the clutches of this terrible tribunal, might well leave all hope at their prison door.

There is nothing more shocking than an attentive examination of witch trials. Women were always, as we have seen it learnedly explained, in the majority. Hatred, jealously, vengeance, and, more than all, suspicions caused by wretchedness and ignorance, found in these trials a vent of which they did not fail to avail themselves. Not infrequently, poor creatures were the victims of their own imagination, stimulated by an hysterical temperament, or by the fear of hell fire. Those who in our own day have had an opportunity of examining cases of religious mania know how readily women believe themselves fallen from grace and given over to the power of the evil one. All such sad cases, which are now treated with the greatest tenderness in institutions devoted to their care, were then looked upon as "possessions" of the devil, or as witches, and, horrible to think of, not a few of them believed it themselves!

Many related that they had been to the sabbath, and had given themselves up to the most shameful excesses. Greatly must such confessions have aggravated the danger of those who denied with the firmness of innocence that they had committed the abominations of which they were accused. Torture was at hand to tear from them what they refused to say, and thus the belief took deep root in the minds of the judges, even when they were comparatively humane and just, that over and above crimes committed by natural means, there was a long list of offenses the supernatural origin of which made them doubly heinous. And how was it possible to deal too sharply with such offenses?

In the single year 1485, and in the district of Worms alone, eighty-five witches were delivered to the flames. At Geneva, at Basil, at Hamburg, at Batisbon, at Vienna, and in a multitude of other towns, there were executions of the same kind. At Hamburg, among other victims, a physician was burnt alive because he saved the life of a woman who had been given up by the midwife. In Italy, during the year 1523, there were burnt in the diocese of Como alone more than two hundred witches. This was after the new bull hurled at witchcraft by Pope Adrian VI. In Spain it was still worse; there, in 1527, two little girls of from nine to eleven years of age denounced a host of witches, whom they pretended to detect by a mark in their left eye. In England and Scotland, political influence was brought to bear upon sorcery; Mary Stuart was animated by a

DEMONOLOGY

lively zeal against witches. In France, the Parliament of Paris happily removed business of this kind from the ecclesiastical tribunals; and under Louis XI., Charles VIII, and Louis XII. there were but few condemnations for the practice of magic; but from the time of Francis I., and especially from Henry II, the scourge re-appeared. Jean Bodin, a man of sterling worth in other respects, but stark mad upon the question of witchcraft, communicated his mania to all classes of the nation. His contemporary and disciple, Boguet, showed how that France swarmed with witches and wizards. "They increase and multiply on the land," said he, "even as do the caterpillars in our gardens. Would that they were all got together in a heap, so that a single fire might burn them all at once."

In Savoy, Flanders, the Jura Mountains, Lorraine, Beam, Provence, and in almost all parts of France, the frightful hecatombs were seen ablaze. In the seventeenth century the witch-fever somewhat abated, though it burst out here and there, centralizing itself chiefly in the convents of hysterical nuns. The terrible histories of the priests Gaufridy and Urban Grandier are well known. In Germany, and particularly in its southern parts, witch burning was still more frequent. In one small principality at least 242 persons were burnt between 1646 and 1651; and, *horribile dictu*, in the official records of these executions we find that among those who suffered were children of from one to six years of age! In 1657 the witch-judge, Nicholas Eemy, boasted of having burnt 900 persons in fifteen years. It would even seem that it is to the proceedings against sorcery that Germany owes the introduction of torture as an ordinary mode of getting at the truth. Mr Roskoff reproduces a catalog of the executions of witches and wizards in the episcopal town of Wurzburg in Bavaria, up to the year 1629. He enumerates thirty-one executions in all, not counting some regarded by the compilers of the catalog as not important enough to mention. The number of victims at each execution varies from two to seven. Many are distinguished by such surnames as The Big Hunchback, The Sweetheart, The Bridge-keeper. The Old Porkwoman, etc.

Among them appear people of all sorts and conditions, actors, workmen, jugglers, town and village maidens, rich burghers, nobles, students, magistrates even, and a fair number of priests. Many are simply entered as "a foreigner." Here and there is added to the name of the condemned person, his age and a short notice. Among the victims, for instance, of the twentieth execution figure "Little Barbara, the prettiest girl in Wurzburg;" "a student who could speak all manner of languages, who was an excellent musician *vocaliter et instrumentaliter*;" "the master of the hospice a very learned man" We find, too, in this gloomy account, the cruel record of children burnt for witchcraft; here, a little girl of about nine or ten years of age, with her baby sister, younger than herself (their mother was burnt a little while afterwards); here, boys of ten or eleven; again, a young girl of fifteen; two children from the poor-house; the little boy of a councilor... The pen falls from one's hand in recapitulating such monstrosities. Cannot those who would endow catholicity with the dogma of papal infallibility hearken, before giving their vote, to the cries that rise before God, and which history re-echoes, of those poor innocent ones whom pontifical bulls threw into the flames?

The seventeenth century saw the rapid diminution of trials and tortures. In one of his good moments, Louis XIV. mitigated greatly the severity of this special legislation. For this he had to undergo the remonstrances of the parliament of Rouen, which believed society would be ruined if those who dealt in sorcery were merely condemned to perpetual confinement. The truth is, that belief in witchcraft was so wide-spread that, from time to time, even throughout the seventeenth century, there were isolated executions. One of the latest and most notorious was that of Renata Saenger, superior of the convent of Unterzell, near Wurzburg (1748). At Landshut, in Bavaria, in 1756, a young girl of thirteen years was convicted of impure intercourse with the devil, and put to death. Seville, in

DEMONOLOGY

1781, and Glaris, in 1783, saw the last two known victims to this fatal superstition.

IV

A weapon has sometimes been framed against Christianity out of these brutal deeds. It has been affirmed that they are traceable to a belief with which Christianity alone had inoculated nations who would have otherwise ignored it. This point of view is superficial, and historically inaccurate. The fault really lies at the door of dualism, which is far older than the Christianity it has outlived. Pagan antiquity had its necromancers, its magicians, its old ghoul-like lamias, and venefacoe, who were no less feared than our witches. We have shown that dualism is inherent in all forms of nature-worship; that these "natural" religions, when at their full development, result, as in Persia, in India, and even in the latest evolutions of Greco-Roman paganism, in an eminently dualistic conception of the forces or divinities which direct the course of events: that the Jewish Satan owes, not his personal origin, but his growth and total depravity, to his contact with the Persian Ahriman; and that the Satan of the Christians inherited in his turn, and his angels with him, the worst side of the character of the vanquished divinities, together with the most frightful of their symbolisms. Indeed, the devil of the middle ages is at once heathen, Jewish, and Christian. He is Jewish and Christian, because moral evil is his proper domain; for the physical evils of which he is the author arise solely out of his eager desire to corrupt men's souls, which, for their part, only give themselves up to him for criminal purposes; and he is so inasmuch as his power, great as it may be, cannot transcend the boundaries it has pleased divine authority to mark out. He is heathen in all that he retains of the old polytheistic belief. The medieval faith in demons may be regarded as paganism taking its "revenge," or as the non-absorbed residuum of polytheism, perpetuating itself under new forms.

DEMONOLOGY

It was not solely the authority of the Church that prolonged the reign of Satan and his angels; it was mainly the intellectual condition which is betrayed, up to an epoch approaching our own, by all works of any scientific pretension during the whole period anterior to Bacon and Descartes. Anything like real knowledge of nature did not exist; that her laws were inviolable, had yet to be declared. Alchemy, astrology, and the medical practice of the time, all turned upon magic; they, no less than the theology of the age, were based upon belief in occult influences, in talismans, in the power of words, and in impossible transmutations. Even after the Renaissance, what a mystic and superstitious medley is presented in the physiological doctrines of Cardan and Paracelsus and Van Helmont! The general state of men's minds, determined, I acknowledge, to a great extent by the Church, but by the Church while herself undergoing the influence of preponderating ideas has been the real cause of that long series of follies and abominations which constitutes the history of the devil in the middle ages and in modern times. The proof of this may be seen in the fact that, at a time and in countries where the Church was still very powerful and by no means lenient, the belief in the devil gradually faded out of real life, suffered repeated attacks, and at last fell into ridicule without such a grave change in the ideas of enlightened Europe being signalized by any remarkable persecution. The imagination of the ages of ignorance sometimes takes a prophetic flight. The old writer tells us how that at the hour of night appointed by the king of hell for the sabbath of his faithful followers, demons, witches, and wizards assemble from all parts of the rendezvous. The place of meeting is generally a waste heath, a forest glade, or a naked mountain-top.

They come from every quarter of the horizon, breathless, disheveled, frenzied. Scarcely have they alighted, ere they turn towards Satan to pay him their dismal homage. He contemplates with pride the great army of the accursed. They are his, body and soul. The wind moans as it passes over the hellish gang. The moon scarcely dares to peer through the dark fringes of the heavy clouds. Bats, owls, ospreys hover in its pale rays. Soon the sacrilegious ceremony ends, and the orgies begin; nameless dances, contortions, yells, the blasphemies of the damned, a deafening rout! Woe to the benighted wanderer who becomes the unwilling witness of these hideous revelries! But suddenly a low but clear sound is heard. It is the crow of a cock in the neighboring village. A ray of light silvers the horizon. With it, everything vanishes; every vestige of the whirling throng is gone. The very grass shows no trace of the footsteps of the gang. What has happened? The old writers learnedly explain the transformation. Neither Satan nor his followers, they tell us, can hear the daylight.

It is light, then, that drives away devils, wizards, and witches. Little did those who said this know how truly they spoke. It is, in very truth, the light of a purer religion and of a more genuine science that has dispelled the night-mare of the middle ages.

The two great causes which worked a deep change in the general state of the intellect, and thereby brought about the irretrievable decadence of belief in the devil, were the indirect influence of the Reformation, and the progress of science. It may seem surprising that we mention the Reformation here. The sixteenth century reformers in no sense opposed faith in the devil. Luther held to it closely; and so did most of his friends. It was owing to a certain coolness of intellect, to a distrust of whatever gave too free play to the imagination, that Calvin was always very cautious in speaking of a subject which turned the best heads; but lie did not the less share the common notions of Satan and his power; and he asserted them more than once. It was an indirect, but not on that account a less cogent, influence to which we refer. What, among the nations who embraced the Reformation, struck the first blow, and a very telling one, at his infernal majesty, was, that all fear of him was taken away by virtue of the newly proclaimed principles. The idea of the absolute authority of God, which was so all-absorbing among the Protestants of the seventeenth century, that idea which they pushed to the paradox of predestination, quickly led them to regard Satan as a mere instrument of the divine will, and his doings as simply the means it pleased God to use in accomplishing his hidden designs. The Christian's faith enabled him to despise the rebel angel, who was powerless to harm the elect. We know what sort of reception he had when he paid Luther a visit at Wartburg. The simplification of the ritual, and the discredit of the supernatural power that had been attributed to the clergy, tended greatly to free the minds of the simple from the weary incubus. Exorcisms, whether at baptism, or in supposed cases of demoniacal possession, were done away with; those performances, that so terrified the imagination, in which the priest, flourishing his holy water brush, attacked the devil with dashes of water, repaid by the evil one in frightful blasphemies, were at an end. People ceased to believe in incubi and succubi. If, here and there, a person was thought to be possessed, prayer and moral exhortations were the only remedies employed; and ere long it became a very rare thing to hear demoniacs spoken of among Protestant peoples. The idea that the Bible miracles were the only true ones, illogical as it was, led people to live on from day to day without fearing or expecting any more to occur.

The devil's miracles were the first to lose their credit when the decline of belief in the supernatural began. Thus Satan lapses into just what he was in the first century, or even to something less, a tempting, invisible, impalpable spirit, whose suggestions must be resisted, and from whom regeneration alone delivers us, and that surely. Even his old part in the drama of the redemption is no longer conceded to him. All now is transacted immediately between the faithful and his God.

For it is now God and no longer Satan, who is held to take the ransom offered by Jesus for the deliverance of sinners, in a word, without as yet thinking of denying Satan's existence and power, the Reformation, while still making great use of his name in popular teaching and preaching, by slow degrees dismisses him to an abstract, ideal sphere, without any clear connection with everyday life. Had he been looked upon simply as a convenient personification of the power of moral evil in the world, Protestant piety would have been but little affected. French Catholicism in its palmiest period, the seventeenth century, while influenced much more than is generally supposed by the Reformation, presents a very similar character. With what moderation do its most illustrious representative men, Bossuet, Fenelon, and even such preachers as Bourdaloue, treat this part of Catholic doctrine. Good taste takes with them the place of rationalism; and who, after reading their works, wonders that a Louis Quatorze, scant as was his tenderness in dealing with religious questions, could show himself skeptical in the matter of witchcraft, and less superstitious than the Parliament of Rouen?

Even in ages of the darkest ignorance, there were disbelievers in witches and wizards. The Lombard law, by a remarkable exception, forbade the prosecution of masks, as sorcerers were called in Italy. A king of Hungary of the eleventh century forbade mention to be made of them, for the simple reason that they did not exist. Agobard, Archbishop of Lyons, classed belief in sabbaths among the absurdities bequeathed by paganism to the ignorant. The *Malleus Maleficarum* certainly had in view opponents who denied not only witchcraft, but also the intervention of the devil in human concerns, seeing that it insisted upon both in labored scholastic arguments. At the time when trials for leagues with the devil were in full vogue, there was a brave Jesuit named Spee, whose humane feelings got the better of the spirit of his order. While engaged in the charge of souls in Franconia, it was his duty to accompany to the stake, during a few years, more than two hundred persons convicted of witchcraft. One day the Archbishop of Mayence, Philip of Schoenborn, asked him why he, a young man of scarcely thirty, had gray hair already. "Through grief," he replied, "for the

DEMONOLOGY

many wizards I have had to prepare for death, no one of whom was guilty." It was he who wrote a *Cautio Criminalis*, printed under his name in 1631, and which, without denying witchcraft, or even the lawfulness of the penalties directed against it, entreats inquisitors and magistrates to increase their precautions against condemning so many innocents to capital punishment. Before Spee's time, a Protestant physician attached to the person of Duke William of Cleves had written in the same strain a book of considerable learning for the age, the fruit of distant voyages and numerous observations, in which, while he admitted the reality of magic, he denied witchcraft properly so called, and sharply charged the clergy with keeping alive popular superstitions, and making good folk believe that the troubles they could not help them through were the work of sorcerers who had sold themselves to the devil. It required no little courage to speak out thus in those days. To take the part of wizards was to expose one's-self to the charge of witchcraft; and in these sad annals examples are not rare of judges and priests who, victims of their humanity or their justice, were sentenced and burned with, those whom they had sought to save. The French physician Gabriel Naude undertook the same treatment of the question in his *Apology for Men accused of Magic* (1669). But the causes the slow influence of which we have described had not yet so far transformed men's minds that they were able to emancipate themselves from the devil. A total demolition of the edifice was necessary on the one hand, and, on the other, a religious justification of this destruction. Here, as elsewhere, progress could only go on effectively upon the condition that religious sanction was blended with purely rational arguments. This law of human progress verifies itself in all times and with regard to all questions. If it is resisted, public opinion divides itself into two camps, which mutually hold one another in check; frowning at each other, without advancing a step. What had come through the Church, must pass away through the Church. The honor of striking a decisive blow at the superstition we are examining is due to the Dutch pastor Balthazar Bekker, who appeared in the lists, not only in the name of good sense

DEMONOLOGY

and humanity, but as a theologian, and published his famous work, entitled, The Enchanted World (1691-1693). Four thousand copies exhausted in two months, the rapid translation of this thick book into all the languages of Europe, and the hot controversies it excited, all of which it has survived, suffice to show what a mark the work made upon the age.

It is quite true that the demonstrations of the Dutch theologian would not have like value in our eyes. Not yet venturing, for instance, to emancipate himself from the Scriptures, which he regarded as of infallible authority, he twists and turns the text in such a manner as to pare away the doctrine of a personal devil who busies himself with the actions and thoughts of men. He succeeds, however, in drawing attention to many details, not hitherto noticed, which go to prove that the Scriptural teaching about the devil is neither definite, nor harmonious, nor in conformity with the opinions of the middle ages. He subjects to a pitiless criticism all the threadbare arguments that, on the ground of experience, had been used to uphold popular prejudice. His discussion of the trial of Urbain Grandier and the Ursulines of Loudun, which was still within every one's memory, must have greatly struck his readers. A fact like this, that could be analyzed with the documents in one's hands, threw a clear light upon a heap of other more obscure cases of an older date, which had been constantly appealed to by the partisans of the devil.

For the first time, too, universal history was laid under contribution to show that belief in devils established an incontestable relationship between the polytheistic and Christian faiths. The whole spirit of the book is summed up in the aphorisms with which it ends: "There is no witchcraft where there is no faith in it; do not believe in it, and it will cease to be. Get rid of all these silly old-wives' fables, and exercise yourselves in godliness." Here was true prophecy; but it was not given to the author to see it fulfilled. To making light of Satan he added the offense, a very grave one in the eyes of Dutch orthodoxy, of being a zealous Cartesian. He was deprived of his living by a synod, and died soon afterwards. But the career of his book could not be checked; and it made its way well. From the date of its appearance, the cause of the devil may be considered as rejected by the tribunal of scientific theology. The progress of the human mind, and the knowledge of nature and modern philosophy, did the rest.

The spirit of science, as constituted since the time of Bacon and Descartes, no longer tolerates the hurried conclusions that so easily gained the assent of the ages in which imagination bore rule, and in which men's readiness to pronounce judgment upon obscure questions was proportioned to their ignorance. Experimental philosophy, the only true method, gives as much solidity to the theses it verifies, as it inspires distrust of whatever avoids the scope of examination. Beyond all doubt there are essential truths which we cannot subject to the test of experience; but these, to say the least, compensate us for that drawback by their close affinity with our nature, our life, and our conscience.

If, for instance, it could be said that belief in the devil commended itself to us on account of its great moral usefulness, in that it improves those who share it, and elevates a man's character by making him. more pure and brave and unselfish, then there would be good motives for trying to save it from the formidable attacks of modern reason. But the reverse is the case. Belief in the devil necessarily tends to blunt the sense of individual culpability. If I do wrong, not because I am bad, but because another, whose power is stronger than my own will, has driven me into wrong-doing, then my fault is certainly lessened, if not annulled. We have passed under review the wretched superstitions, the dangerous follies, and terrible crimes, which this belief so long inspired. But the disproof of witchcraft carries with it, some may urge, no disproof of the existence of a personal evil genius, against whom men must defend themselves, as against a foe who goes about perpetually seeking to lead them on to sin. But let such reflect whether witchcraft can be so easily severed from the principle of which it is the offspring.

Once admit the devil, and wizards follow as a matter of course. If there is really a being of superhuman strength, who seeks, as it is said, to work our moral ruin, for his private satisfaction, is it not evident that, in order the better to accomplish his end, he will try to catch weak souls, by putting in their way the means of procuring what they desire? It is quite consistent that belief in the devil should have found its definite outcome in belief in sorcerers, and that this latter, having succumbed before experience, should have carried in its ruin the belief in the devil himself. If there is, in good sooth, a devil, then there are wizards; and since there are no such things as wizards, it is clear there is no devil. This is what the condensed good sense of the three last centuries authorizes us to conclude; and this conclusion still awaits refutation.

The eighteenth century made the mistake of supposing that traditional beliefs could be destroyed by turning them into ridicule. When a belief that has for awhile been derided has deep roots in the human conscience, it easily survives the sarcasms of which it has been the object; and the time comes when those sarcasms no longer move laughter, for they chafe the innermost feelings of religious persons, and the good taste of the sensitive. But in the devil's case the laughter of the eighteenth century has remained victorious. The truth is, the devil is ridiculous. That being who is presented to us as so cunning, so malicious, so cleverly selfish, who strives unceasingly to carry on the troublesome business of corrupting men's souls, turns out to be very foolish. When, brought down from the heights where poetry and mystery have sometimes succeeded in placing him, he is subjected to close inspection and confronted with plain truth, Satan becomes a mere absurdity; and ever since this has been clearly seen it has become impossible to honor him by acknowledging his real existence.

We could have lengthened our retrospective study of the works which, during the eighteenth century, and even in our own times, have continued a controversy that will henceforward be aimless. Ever since a true knowledge of the constitution of the universe has dissipated the allusions which formed an indispensable frame to the picture of the Satan of olden time a fixed dome above, an earth in the midst, and a hell under the earth ever since we have been compelled to see God's presence live and move in all things, there is no more room left in the world for the devil. Nothing could be more wearisome and puerile than the endeavors of certain reactionary theologians, in Germany and elsewhere, to restore a shadow of reality to the old phantom, while at the same time escaping the gross superstitions to which, even these retrograde divines can no longer commit themselves. In vain is an attempt made to preserve for him something like an honorable position in some few dogmatic treatises, and in pietistic hymns. This, when not met by sheer indifference, does but annoy those of the clergy and laity who are pervaded by a healthy tone.

By them Satan is still tolerated as an expression, a type, a symbol which the language of religion has sanctioned; and this is all. But to allow him any place in civil or domestic codes, to admit him into actual life, this is now quite out of the question; *non possumus*. But is there absolutely no good to be got out of this error of such long standing, which occupies so much space in the history of religions, and dates from their very sources? Must we admit that, in this particular, the human mind has for all these centuries been feeding upon what is absolutely false? This cannot be so. There must surely be something in human nature which has pleaded in its favor, and has maintained from generation to generation a faith which is contradicted by experience. I will not assert, with some who have thought upon the matter, that the explanation lies in the ease with which this doctrine of the devil solved the problem of the origin of evil; for the truth is, that it solved nothing. It carried into heaven the problem that seemed insoluble on earth. But what did this avail?

The main stay of faith in the devil, or the one constituent of that faith, is the power of evil in and around us. I wonder at the singular tranquility with which almost all our French philosophers face this question, or rather forget it, while they dilate in eloquent phrases upon free-will. Let us look at the facts as they really stand. The truth is, that the best among us is a long way behind the ideal that he sets before him; he is too weak to realize this ideal; and, if he is sincere, he acknowledges his shortcomings. The truth is, that our weak morality is too often at the mercy of those urgings within us of the "Old Adam," that animal, carnal man, we carry within us, which has so often given the lie to the proud satisfaction we bestow upon ourselves so complacently.

Another truth is this, that we are at every moment carried into evil by the social influences that surround us, and against the mischievous and impulsive current of which few have energy enough victoriously to hold their own. We must not fall into the extreme of those theologians who have taught the total depravity of the human race, and with it a method of regeneration; as if even a miracle could regenerate a totally corrupted nature.

Observation proves that we are selfish, but capable of loving; that we are naturally sensual, but not less naturally attracted by the splendor of the true and the good; that we are very imperfect, but still perfectible. The first condition of progress is to feel wherein we fail. This is why the "Kingdom of heaven" is promised to the "poor in spirit," to those, that is, who are conscious of their poverty. If we would so rive as to satisfy our conscience, we must learn to repel victoriously those attacks with which selfish sensuality, flesh and blood, and worldly fascinations assail us. This is the devilish power from which we must set ourselves free. There is a sense in which we may say we are all of us more or less "possessed." The mistake lies in personifying this power of evil. When theists say there is a personal God, they do not ignore the faultiness of the notion of personality as derived from our own human nature; but as it is impossible for us to conceive any other mode of existence save personality and impersonality, and as God must possess all perfection, they declare, lacking a better term, that he is personal because he is perfect, and because impersonal perfection is a contradiction. Evil, on the other hand, which is the diametrical opposite of the perfect, is necessarily impersonal. Against its baneful seductions, against its ever direful sorcery, must we wrestle, so that our true human personality, our moral personality, may triumphantly disengage itself from the soil allotted for our growth. Upon this condition depends its attaining to the regions of pure and steadfast morality, where naught that has the likeness of Satan can hinder our ascent Good-ward. This alone remains of the doctrine of the devil. But this alone concerns our moral health; and this must never he forgotten.

THE END

DEMONOLOGY

THE PIASA: THE DEVIL AMONG THE INDIANS

P.A. Armstrong, 1887

CHAPTER I

From the evening and the morning of the sixth day, from the beginning when God created the heaven and the earth, and darkness was upon the face of the deep, and the spirit of God moved upon the face of the waters, and God said: Let there be light in the firmament of the heavens to divide the day from the night, and give light upon the earth, and made two great lights, the greater to rule the day and the lesser to rule the night, and plucked from his jeweled crown a handful of diamonds and scattered them broadcast athwart the sky for brilliants to his canopy, and stars in his firmament, down through the countless ages to the present, all nations, tongues, kindreds and peoples, in whatsoever condition, time, clime or place, civilized, pagan, Mohammedan,barbarian or savage,have adopted and utilized signs, motions, gestures, types, emblems, symbols, pictures, drawings, etchings or paintings as their primary and most natural as well as direct and forcible methods and vehicles of communicating, recording and perpetuating thought and history. Even that great book of books and history of histories the Holy Bible teems with examples of this character from the first chapter of Genesis to the last chapter of Revelations.

Our syllabaries or alphabets are but a series and system of types, symbols and emblems which, by the aid of machinery and printers' ink, bristle with thought and are the vehicles of recording history.

Sign or gesture language is the primary method of direct communication, from the beginning to the present, while object language is, and ever has been, the indirect mode of not only

DEMONOLOGY

communicating but preserving history. The former is of more universal use than the latter, for it always has and always will exist and be utilized by the entire human family, civilized or savage, and extends to every animal existence, flesh, fish and fowl. While gesture language is direct, it is but transient, because not recorded so as to be preserved. On the other hand object language is direct in its communication and most graphically and indelibly recorded.

The entire series of object language may well be embraced in the term now in general use pictograph or a writing by pictures, which conveys upon sight and instantaneously records by graphic means the thought, act or deed intended by the artist, without words, syllables or letters, and maybe delineated upon any hard substance wood, stone, metal, bone, slate, dried hide, etc.

When delineated upon rock or stone these pictographs have been aptly named petroglyphs by the learned German archaeologist, Dr. Andree, of Stuttgart, which means rock delineations, or pictures.

By signs or gestures the infant first attempts and finally succeeds in attracting attention and indicating its wants, and no other means of communication is known between persons entirely ignorant of each other's language and deaf mutes. The secondary method is by sounds or oral language, which is of the greatest importance and universal use. Object language, or pictographs, is the tertiary method, and though not so generally used, its communication being of a more permanent and enduring form, its lessons are of greater importance in history than sign or oral language. There can be no doubt of the fact that pictographs were the precursors and parents of our syllabaries or alphabets, and the indirect expressions of ideas formed in oral speech, hence their importance to the ethnologist depends upon the light they may shed upon the evolution of human culture. If by their aid we may learn the wisdom of the

DEMONOLOGY

ages in which no written history was kept except these crude pictures, then indeed will they have served a noble purpose.

The importance of pictographs to the human race cannot be over-estimated in their production of the smaller and systematized letters and types which have been the direct means of preserving and perpetuating history, science and knowledge, through the alphabet which seems to have been known and brought into use some 3,400 years ago or about 1,500 years before the Christian era. Whether letters and the alphabet were invented by the Egyptians, Ninevehans, Phoenicians or Chinese is a disputed question, for they all claim the honor. Rollin says letters were taken from Syria to Greece by Cadmus about the year 1455 B. C.

The first discovery of pictographs and petroglyphs in the United States dates back only about three hundred years, but they are more plentiful in this than any other country; and the American Indians have shown a versatility as well as much talent in their execution, as well as design. Indeed they have in many instances combined the art of etching, or engraving, and that of painting with fine effect, and seem to have had some practical aim or object in view in the production of each delineation. To be enabled to correctly interpret and fairly understand the purport and meaning of Indian pictographs, and more especially their petroglyphs, which are of greater interest and importance to the ethnologist and archaeologist, we must become familiar with their traditions, mythologies, customs, habits, dress, religious beliefs and modes of worship. Their petroglyphs as a rule being much larger than their pictographs, and incised or cut into the face of the rock and the incisions or tracings filled with paint, they are much better preserved as well as larger than their pictographs.

Add to this the fact that the Indian is naturally averse to manual labor, and the cutting or engraving of the hard rock with such instruments as he could improvise was slow and tedious

DEMONOLOGY

work, none but the most important objects and events were delineated upon the rocks, hence their petroglyphs are vastly more important as records than their pictographs. Again, there is another difference between these two kinds of delineations, namely, all their pictographs we can or have found are of comparatively modern date, while their petroglyphs as a rule are ancient. This may be accounted for, in part at least, by the fact that their pictographs were simply painted and usually on perishable material, while their petroglyphs were etched, cut or incised and then painted, and the painting renewed from time to time, kept them well preserved.

A very general system of pictographs is now in use by the Indians of the plains, by means of which they keep a record of the leading events of each year which thereby becomes an annual calendar, which they call winter counts.

Not infrequently do they keep this kind of chronology for a century upon a single buffalo hide. That of Lone Dog, a Dakota Indian, embraces over seventy years and covers only about half the surface of one buffalo robe. These pictographs commenced with the year 1800, near the center of the robe, and subsequent years up to 1872 are arranged in elliptical circles around it. The first year is represented by three sets of parallel black lines of ten each, showing that thirty Dakotas were killed by the Crow Indians that year. The next year is represented by the naked bust of an Indian, literally covered with red blotches, showing that small-pox killed many Indians that year, etc. Many of these pictographs are apt illustrations of the ideologies intended to be conveyed. The meteoric shower of November 13, 1833, is represented by a picture of the moon and a host of falling stars, leaving a large streak trailing after each. Indian pictographs may be numbered by hundreds of thousands in the United States while their petroglyphs are comparatively few, less than one to a thousand, yet they have been found all over the country from Maine to California, on rocks, boulders, ledges, canyons, caves and grottoes. Sandstone surface especially is prolific with these delineations, and are of three classes.

    1st. Simply paintings upon the rocks, usually in three colors, red, green and black.

    2nd. Etched or cut upon the rock.

    3rd. First incised, or etched, and then painted, the lines of paint following the incised lines. The first above described kind is far more numerous than either of the others.

    The Indians not only understand the art of compounding and mixing paints that withstand the elements, but are adepts in that art. Though they know nothing of the use of linseed oil and turpentine in the preparation of paint they have a substitute which is more lasting. By boiling the tails of the beaver together with the feet of the elk, deer, moose or antelope, they obtain a glutinous, oily substance with which they mix their earth-pigments and oxides of iron, copper and zinc, burnt bone, etc., whereby they are able to produce colors of the most enduring kind. Though the Indian never understood the art of blending colors so as to produce varieties of shade, he well understood primary colors and used them to advantage in producing all the prismatic shades. Their paint brushes were constructed of small pieces of soft wood, chewed or pounded at the end into fibers, but more recently they used tufts of antelope hair tied around small sticks. Their implements for drawing, etching, cutting, carving, scratching, pecking or engraving petroglyphs were few and decidedly pristine and simple.

    They consisted of small pieces of sharp-pointed rocks obsidian, flint and quartz predominating. But after coming in contact with white people the Indians soon discovered the great superiority of well-tempered steel over the very best qualities of obsidian or quartz in the manufacture of engravers for stone etchings, and have very generally adopted a short thick-bladed knife for that purpose. For tracing pens they used a piece of dry buffalo rib or hard wood, dipped in a thin, colored glue which was spread along the line intended to delineate the object of the petroglyph. The tracings served as lines for incising, scratching and pecking, as well as for final painting. Like every other nation and people of earth the red man attaches great significance to colors.

To them black is an emblem of sorrow, anguish and death; red of defiance, anger and war; yellow of treachery, jealousy and inconstancy; green of hope, joy and victory; blue of truth, love and constancy. By arranging the cardinal colors side by side in various forms they had a species of sign alphabet by means whereof they communicated as well as perpetuated a large amount of information and history. Nearly every rock cavern, as well as smooth-faced perpendicular ledge of any considerable altitude throughout the entire western hemisphere, when discovered by the white man, were converted into maps, charts and histories by the aborigines, whereon were recorded in that most graphic language, petroglyphs, the great events of the preceding ages, and could we but correctly read and fully interpret this silent language, the early history of the Occident, like that of the orient, would teem with deeds of heroism and daring. The rocks at Oakley Springs, Arizona, and the valley of the Kanawha, West Virginia, alone would furnish an encyclopedia of stirring events of the most intense interest.

The valley of the Mississippi, though producing but comparatively few petroglyphs, exhibited some of the grandest and by far the most mysterious ever found in this or any other country in the world, known as the Piasa, and described by Father Marquette, the celebrated Jesuit priest, who was of noble descent and born in Picardy, France, and came as a missionary to Canada in the year 1665, where he soon learned to speak the language of some half dozen Indian tribes, from whom he heard of the existence of a great river in the west which they called Mesche-cebe, or the great river. Some of them called it Natme-sipon, or the river of fishes; others called it Chusa-gua,

DEMONOLOGY

Sassagonly, and Mala-bianchi, and subsequently the French called it La Palisade Escandido, Colbert, or St. Louis. M. Talon was the French intendant of Canada at the time, but had been ordered to Paris in the fall of 1672. From Marquette and others he had heard stories about this great unknown river of the west and determined to investigate the matter.

Before leaving Canada he selected M. Joliet a successful merchant of Quebec, who had much experience among the Indians, to conduct the expedition. Joliet selected Marquette as his chief assistant and adviser to accompany him in this hazardous enterprise, and on the 13th of May, 1673, with only about a half dozen men they embarked in their canoes and struck out on their long, lonesome and dangerous voyage of discovery.

They did not reach the Mississippi until the 17th of June. Marquette says (See his discoveries of the Mississippi, published in Paris in 1681):

"We met from time to time numberless fish which struck so violently against our canoes that at first we took them to be large trees which threatened to upset us. As we were descending the river we saw high rocks with hideous monsters painted on them and upon which the bravest Indian dare not look. They are as large as a calf, with head and horns like a goat, their eyes are red, beard like a tiger's and a face like a man's. Their tails are so long that they pass over their bodies and between their legs under their bodies, ending like a fishes tail. They are painted red, green and black, and so well drawn that I could not believe they were drawn by the Indians, and for what purpose they were drawn seems to me a mystery."

Again he says:

"Passing the mouth of the Illinois we soon fell into the shadow of a tall promontory, and with great astonishment

DEMONOLOGY

beheld the representation of two monsters painted on its lofty limestone front. Each of these frightful figures had the face of a man, the horns of a deer, the beard of a tiger, and the tail of a fish, so long that it passed around the body, over the head and between the legs. It was an object of Indian worship, and greatly impressed me with the necessity of substituting for this monstrous idolatry the true God."

Father Hennepin, another early explorer of the wilds of the west, published a small volume in 1698 entitled, "A new discovery of a vast Country in America," which he dedicated to William III, King of Great Britain, says, pages 168 to 170:

"This made our voyage the more easy, for our men landed several times to kill some Fowl and other Game with which the Banks of the Mischasipi are plentifully stocked; however, before we came to the River Illinois we discovered Messorites who came down along the River, but as they had no Pyrogues with them we crossed to the other side, and to avoid any surprise during the night we made no fire and thereby the Savages could not discover whereabouts we were, for doubtless they would have murdered us, thinking we were their enemies.

I had quite forgot to relate that the Illinois had told us that towards the Cape which I have called in my map St. Anthony, near the nation of the Messorites, there were some Tritons and other Sea Monsters painted which the boldest Men durst not look upon, there being some enchantment in their face. I thought this was a story, but when we came near the place they had mentioned we saw instead of these Monsters a Horse and some other Beasts painted upon the Rock with Red Colors by the Savages. The Illinois had told us likewise that the rock on which these dreadful Monsters stood was so steep that no man could climb up to it, but had we not been afraid of the Savages more than of the Monsters we had certainly got up to them. There is a common tradition among the people that a great number of Miamis were drowned in that place, being pursued by the Savages of Matsegamie, and since that time the Savages going by the Rock use to smoke and offer Tobacco to these Beasts to appease, as they say, the Manitou, that is, in the Language of the Algonquins and Accadians, an Evil Spirit, which the Iroquois call Otkon, but the Name is the one thing they know of him.

While I was at Quebec I understood M. Jolliet had been upon the Mischasipi and obliged to return without going down the River because of the Monsters I have spoken of who had frighted him, as also because he was afraid to be taken by the Spaniards, and having an opportunity to know the truth of that Story from M. Jolliet himself, with whom I had often traveled upon the River St. Lawrence. I asked him whether he had been as far as the Arkansas. That Gentleman answered me that the Outtaouats had often spoke to him of these Monsters, but that he had never gone further than the Hurons and Outtaouats, with whom he had remained to exchange our companies' Commodities with their Furs. He added that the Savages had told him that it was not safe to go down the River because of the Spaniards, But notwithstanding this Report I have found nowhere upon the River any mark as crosses and the like that could persuade me that the Spaniards had been there and the Savages inhabiting the Mischasipi would not have expressed such admiration as they did when they saw us if they had seen Europeans before. I'll examine the question more in my second volume."

In his second volume Hennepin says he had seen Father Marquette, from whom he got the following description:

"Along the Rocks I have mentioned we have found one very high and steep and saw two Monsters painted upon it which are so hideous that we were frighted at the first sight, and the boldest Savage dare not for their Eyes look upon them. They are drawn as big as a Calf, with two horns like a Wild Goat. Their Eyes are Red, their Beard is like that of a Tiger, and their

DEMONOLOGY

Body is covered with Scales. Their Tail is so long that it goes over their Heads and then turns between their Fore-Legs under the Belly, ending like a Fish-Tail. There are but three Colors, namely, Red, Green and Black, but those Monsters are so well drawn that I cannot believe that the Savages did it, and the Rock whereon they are painted is so steep that it is a wonder to me how it was possible to draw those Figures. But to know to what purpose they were made is a great Mystery. Whatever it be our best Painters would hardly do better."

Two immensely large petroglyphs of a monster or more properly speaking, monsters, for they do not appear to have been alike, though substantially so, as will be seen by reference to the engravings herewith given were found, first incised or cut upon a layer of bluish gray sandstone overlying a bed of limestone on the north bank of the Mississippi, immediately where the Illinois State prison was built at Alton, Illinois, which were quite distinct when that locality was first settled by the white people, and traces of their outlines remained until the rock whereon they were delineated was quarried by the convicts of the penitentiary as late as about the year 1856. From the mouth of the Illinois river at Grafton to Alton, Illinois, a distance of twenty miles, the Mississippi river runs from west to east, and its north bank or Illinois side is a high bluff, the highest point being the eastern end. This bluff is but a continuous perpendicular strata of limestone, ranging from forty to fifty feet high, with a layer of bluish gray fine grit sandstone, about twenty feet deep, lying on the top or over the limestone, and upon this sandstone, at an elevation of some eighty feet above the base of this ledge of rocks and the river's surface, these monsters were incised and afterwards painted. They were of about equal size and measured thirty feet in length by twelve feet in height. From their hideous shape and size they were a mortal terror to all the Indian nations of the then northwest.

Each nation had one or more traditions connected therewith, some calling them The Piasa, others called them The

DEMONOLOGY

Piusa. In painting these monsters but three colors were used red, emblematic of war and vengeance; black, symbolic of death and despair; and green, expressive of hope and triumph over death in the land of dreams, beneath, beyond the evening star, where they located their happy hunting grounds.

In estimating the size of these petroglyphs, Father Marquette did not take into consideration their great elevation nor the distance from his canoe to the rock wall where they were delineated. Why he did not mention the fact of their having the wings of a bat, but of the shape of an eagle's, is not easily explained, yet as a matter of fact they were both supplied with those appendages beyond a doubt, as there are several persons still living who bear testimony to the fact from having seen them. They also had four legs, each supplied with eagle-shaped talons. The combination and blending together of the master species of the earth, sea and air, as shown in these petroglyphs so as to present the leading and most terrific characteristics of the various species thus graphically arranged, is an absolute wonder and seems to show a vastly superior knowledge of animal, fowl, reptile and fish nature than has been accorded to the Indian.

Indeed, they seem to have been made by some person familiar with the Holy Scriptures, for we read from them as follows:

"And the first beast was like a lion and the second like a calf, arid the third beast had a face as a man, and the fourth beast was like a flying eagle. As for the likeness of their faces they four had the face of a man and the face of a lion on the right side, and the face of an ox on the left side; they four also had the head of an eagle.

And their wings were stretched upwards, and when they went I heard the noise of their wings like the noise of great waters. The first was like a lion, and had eagle's wings. And another beast, like a leopard, appeared, which had upon its back four wings of a fowl. And a fourth beast appeared, dreadful and terrible, and exceedingly strong, and it had great iron teeth. And behold, a great red dragon, having seven heads and ten horns, and his tail drew the third part of the stars. And he had two horns like a lamb, and he spake like a dragon.

And to the woman were given two wings of an eagle, that she might fly into the wilderness. Behold, there came up from the sea an eagle. And she spread her wings over all the earth, and all the winds of the air blew on her and were gathered together. And I beheld as it were a roaring lion chased out of the woods, and I saw he sent a man's voice unto the eagle.

And therefore appear no more, thou eagle nor thy horrible wings, nor thy wicked feathers, nor thy malicious heads, nor thy hurtful claws, nor all thy vain body."

These quotations from the Holy Scriptures might be extended to a great length, all tending to show that the ancient Israelites believed in the existence of a veritable corporeal and visible Devil, to whom they attributed the power of all evil, and symbolized under various forms, shapes and names. To Mother Eve he assumed the shape of the serpent, with the voice of a man, and by false representations and blandishments induced her to dupe and deceive her husband. While more generally described in the Bible as the leviathan or dragon, he is frequently mentioned as the "old serpent," "enemy," "evil spirit," "unclean spirit," "evil one," "wicked one," "liar," "lying spirit," "father of lies," "crooked serpent," "piercing serpent," "prince of the power of the air," "great red dragon," "abaddon," "beast," "apollyon," "adversary," "accuser of his brethren," "serpent," "spirit that works in the children of disobedience," "Belial," "Beelzebub," "god of this world,' "power of darkness," "ruler of the darkness of this world," "prince of the devils," "tempter," "murderer," "devil," "Satan," etc.

DEMONOLOGY

All of these names and terms were used as being synonymous and convertible, representing a fixed, firm and abiding faith in the existence of one or more all-bad being, essence or principle, which is the active and implacable enemy of the human race. Though indefinite and divergent in opinion as to whether there were but one or a legion of these evil spirits, agencies or devils, as well as to whether they had a real definite corporeal or merely a spiritual existence, it is a significant fact that all nations, kindreds and tongues in every clime, time and place, whether Christian, Mohammedan or savage, are united in one great prevailing faith and belief in the existence of certain agencies or spirits which are ever busy in making mischief among, and causing sorrow, pain, grief and suffering to the people of earth, to which they apply as many different names, shapes and attributes as the stars in heaven. Nor do they confine the persecutions of these evil spirits to their earthly existence, but connect them with vivid imagination to that other and fondly hoped-for better life beyond the grave, whither they fear these tormentors will follow them.

In very many leading characteristics, customs and beliefs the North American Indians very closely resemble those of the ancient Israelites, when they first came in contact with the Europeans. Like them they believed in the existence of one great and all-powerful being or spirit which should be and was the object of adoration. Of the God-head or Christ they had no tradition, and consequently no belief; hence the subtleties and nice distinctions of the trinity, Father, Son and Holy Ghost of the Christian they did not comprehend and would not believe.

Red Jacket said: "If the Great Spirit so loved the pale-faces that he sent his only son to them, and they killed him, then the white people did very wrong, and should be punished for this evil deed. If he had sent his son to the red men he would have been well fed and kindly treated."

Though the Indians, like Christianized white men,

DEMONOLOGY

believe in the existence of a multiplicity of good spirits, one alone is chief, whom they know as the Manitou or Sowana, corresponding with our God or Jehovah, and the universality of this belief in the existence of an all-powerful Supreme Ruler of the universe among all nations and peoples of earth constitutes the strongest argument and most irrefutable proof of the existence and active agency of an indulgent, loving Father or God, whose hearty earnings are constantly leading and drawing his children home.

> "Where buds and flowers of blooming spring
> In brightest robes abound,
> And sweetest odors constant bring
> In never ceasing round;
> Where birds of richest plumage shine,
> Of fairy form and fair,
> And softest melodies combine
> To charm the vocal air."

The celebrated Sauk chief, Black Hawk, who, all things considered, was probably the ablest Indian that ever lived, and certainly one of the purest and noblest of his race, said:

"The Great Spirit has the care of all beings created. Some believe in two spirits, one good, the other bad, and make feasts for the bad spirit, to keep him quiet, thinking that if they can make peace with him the good spirit will not hurt them. If the Great and Good Spirit wishes us to believe and do as the whites, he could easily change our opinions, so that we could see, think and act as they do. We are nothing as compared to His power, and we feel and know it. We have men among us like the whites, who pretend to know the right path, but will not consent to show it without pay. I have no faith in their path, but believe every man must make his own path."

Red Jacket said:

DEMONOLOGY

"If the Great Spirit desires us to believe in the white man's religion why has He not given us a book like the one he gave them, that we might read and understand His will? He knows what is best for His red children, and we do but follow His will."

But Black Hawk, with all his piety and sound judgment, believed in manifold good and bad spirits, as illustrated by his idea as to how corn, beans and tobacco were first discovered by his race, which was that "a beautiful woman was seen to descend from the clouds and alight upon the earth by two of our ancestors who had killed a deer and were sitting by the fire roasting a part of it to eat. They were astonished at seeing her, and concluded she was hungry and had smelt the meat. They immediately went to her, taking with them a piece of the roasted venison. They presented it to her. She ate it, telling them to return to the spot where she was sitting at the end of one year and they would find a reward for their kindness and generosity. She then ascended to the clouds and disappeared. The men returned to their village and explained to the tribe what they had seen, done and heard, but were laughed at by their people. When the period had arrived for them to visit this consecrated ground where they were to find a reward for their attention to the beautiful woman of the clouds, they went with a large party, and found where her right hand had rested on the ground corn growing, where the left hand had rested, beans, and immediately where she had been seated, tobacco."

In speaking of the island of Rock Island the old chieftain said:

"It was our garden, like the white people have near their big villages, which supplied us with strawberries, blackberries, gooseberries, plums, apples and nuts. A good spirit had charge of it, which lived in a cave in the rock immediately under the place where the fort now stands (old Fort Armstrong, torn down in 1845). This guardian spirit has often been seen by our people.

DEMONOLOGY

It was white, with large wings like a swan's, but ten times larger. We were particular not to make much noise in that part of the island which it inhabited for fear of disturbing it, but the noise at the fort has since driven it away, and no doubt a bad spirit has taken its place."

He does not claim to have ever seen this good white spirit, with wings ten times larger than those of a swan, which would make it fully as large as the Piasa, but says that many of his people had seen it. Thus it is apparent that the Indians believed in the corporeal existence of winged spirits, both good and bad, and to their minds all that was good and desirable was attributed to good spirits, while all that was terrible and disastrous was charged to the account of bad spirits. By referring to the two engravings given as the Piasa, or Piusa, it will be observed that the artist who originated and executed them has embodied all the more dreadful characteristics contained in the foregoing Biblical descriptions of the devil. Here do we behold the wings and talons of the eagle, united to the body of the dragon or alligator, with the face of a man, the horns of the black-tailed deer or elk, the nostrils of the hippopotamus, the teeth and beard of the tiger, the ears of the fox, and the tail of the serpent, or fish, with the scales of the salamander, so nicely arranged and fitted together as to preserve the distinctive characteristics of each and produce a picture of all that is the most horrible, alike in animal, fowl, fish and reptile nature in a single graphic view. That king of birds, the eagle, has ever been considered by all nations and peoples the emblem and symbol of speed, strength, ferocity and quick perception. The deer and elk, the fleetest of the animal creation, and the tiger the most pugnacious and ferocious.

The fox is the symbol of cunning, and possesses the sharpest sense of hearing. The hippopotamus is indigenous alike to land and sea, with the strength and courage of the lion, united to the ferocity of the tiger, and a hide which may be termed bullet-proof. The dragon as above shown is the prototype and

DEMONOLOGY

representative of Satan, and the serpent is his twin brother, while man is the image of his Maker, and by divine command received "dominion over the fish of the sea, and over the fowl of the air, and over every living thing that moveth upon the earth." Whether conceived and executed by the Indian, Mound Builder or white man, these petroglyphs were fearfully grand in conception and stupendously large in dimension. Some writers in describing them have said their scales rivaled the rainbow in their gaudy coloring, but we are inclined to the opinion they were in error in that respect. The Mississippi was the great highway of travel to the Indians, which forced them against their will to pass these pictured monsters. Knowing this fact the Indian voyagers as a rule prepared for an attack upon these petroglyphs as they passed, while some offered sacrifices and burnt offerings to appease their supposed anger toward the worshipers, others offered prayer and supplications to them for mercy and forgiveness, or set up a doleful howl, accompanied with objurgations and lamentations, but the great mass of the braves and warriors sent poisoned arrow heads and bullets at them, so that between the hail and storms of a long, long period of time, together with the indentations made by arrow heads and bullets the whole face of the rock where these petroglyphs were delineated was pitted as if from a severe attack of small-pox, which fact led to the belief that the scales were variegated in color. Yet it is possible they were painted of different colors. If such was the case these petroglyphs must have presented a most beautifully horrid sight, rendering them far above any other specimen of aboriginal art found in the United States.

While it is more than probable they were the conception and production of the Indians, they may have been made by white men and of recent date anterior to their discovery by Father Marquette, who first saw them about the first of August, 1673. Marquette was the first white man to describe the majestic Upper Mississippi, and has therefore been accredited with its discovery, yet we are satisfied that it had been not only seen but traversed by other white men nearly forty years before

DEMONOLOGY

his discovery. This fact is clearly established by the Jesuit records. The Franciscan friar, LeCaron, reached the rivers of Lake Huron in 1616. The Duke de Richelieu obtained a charter, known as the grant of New France, from Louis XIII, in 1627, which embraced the whole basin of the St. Lawrence and of such streams as flow directly into the sea, also to the country now known as Florida, and entered upon his possession in 1632, and in 1634 Peres, Brebeuf and Daniel, who were soon followed by Lallemaid, penetrated the heart of the Huron wilderness and established two missions and built the first house of the society of Jesus, and named it St. Ignatius. M. Nicollet, a French trader, located on the Ottawa river in 1618, and in 1620 on the border of Lake Huron.

Pere Lejeuni writes that Nicollet discovered the Wisconsin river in 1639. He says:

"M. Nicollet, who has penetrated farthest into those most distant regions, has assured me that if he had pushed on three days longer on a great river which issues from the second lake of the Hurons (Lake Michigan) he would have found the sea. Now I strongly suspect this sea is on the north of Mexico, and that thereby we could have an entrance in Japan and China."

Parkman says: """As early as 1639 Nicollet ascended the Green Bay of Michigan and crossed the waters of the Mississippi."

While it is improbable that Nicollet saw the Mississippi on his first visit to Wisconsin in 1634, where he met in one general assembly "four thousand warriors who feasted on six score of beavers before whom he appeared in a robe of state adorned with figures of flowers and birds, approaching with a pistol in each hand he fired both at once, and the astonished natives hence styled him 'Thunder Panther,'" it is more than probable he both found and traversed it in 1639. Father Jean

DEMONOLOGY

Dequerre went from Sault St. Marie to the Illinois river in 1652 and established a flourishing mission, probably near Starved Rock, possibly at Peoria, Ill. He visited many Indian tribes down that river, and fell a martyr to his faith in the midst of his Christian labors. In 1654 a couple of French fur traders or voyagers joined a band of Ottawa Indians on an extended hunting expedition to the western wilds, of five hundred leagues, which extended through two years, when they returned accompanied by fifty canoes and two hundred and fifty men. That they not only traversed the "Father of Waters," but followed it from the mouth of the Wisconsin to the mouth of the Mississippi, or even to the gulf, is very probable, but they wrote no history of their trip, as they were upon a hunting, not an exploring voyage.

Father Jean Charles Drocoux went from Quebec to the Illinois river and returned in 1657. Pere Renne Mesnard left Quebec on a mission to the far west in 1660, and traversed Lake Superior and thence to Green Bay, reaching Keweena, where he wandered into the forest the next year and was either killed or starved to death. Father Claude Allouez started on a mission to the far west in 1665, and reached the falls of St. Mary in September, and from thence went to the great village of the Chippewas at Chegoimegon, where a grand inter-tribal council was held at which the Pottawattamies from Lake Michigan, the Sauks and Foxes from the west, the Hurons from north of Lake Superior, the Sioux from the head waters of the Mississippi, as well as the Illinois, assembled. From these Indians he received a most bewitching description of a noble river flowing south, on which they dwelt, and whose adjacent prairies they assured him were replete with immense herds of buffalo and deer. Their representations created a strong desire in him to explore this Indian paradise. He returned to Quebec in 1667. In 1668 Claude Dablon and Pere Marquette established the mission of St. Marie, which is the oldest European settlement in Michigan. M. Talon, the Canadian intendant, sent Nicholas Perrot on a mission in 1669 to arrange a general conference with all the

DEMONOLOGY

Indian nations of that locality to assemble at St. Mary. He visited Green Bay, from whence he was escorted by the Pottawattamies to Chicago.

In 1669 Allouez visited Green Bay and thence up Fox River of Wisconsin to the principal villages of the Mascoutins, and in the fall of 1670 Dablon joined him when they returned to Green Bay to establish the Mission of St. Xavier. A great congress of the Indian nations was held at St. Mary in May, 1671, where the cross was raised, and by its side a column was planted and marked with the lilies of the Bourbons. The cross was borne by Allouez and Dablon through the lands of the Mascoutins, Kickapoos, Miamis, Sauks and Foxes in Wisconsin and Illinois, so when Father Marquette and Sieur Joliet explored the Fox and the Wisconsin rivers, reaching a Mascoutin village on the bank of the Wisconsin about the 5th of June, 1673, they found the cross erected by Allouez and Dablon in May, 1671, and reaching the Mississippi on the 17th of June, 1673, they descended that great waterway to the mouth of the Missouri.

Passing an Indian village about a hundred miles below the mouth of the Wisconsin, they were hospitably received by a band of the Illinois Indians, who welcomed them in the figurative language of the Indian: "Frenchmen, how bright the sun shines when you come to visit us; all our village awaits you, and you shall enter our wigwams in peace." After entering and smoking the calumet they were invited to visit the great chief of the Illinois, and were told by him that the "presence of his guests added flavor to his tobacco, made the river more calm, the sky more serene and the earth more beautiful." Thus it is shown that Nicollet had found and partially, at least, explored the Mississippi thirty-four years before Marquette, and the French fur traders with their escort of Ottawas had almost to a certainty explored that mighty river some nineteen years before Marquette and Joliet, so that it is barely possible that either these traders or Nicollet may have engraved these monsters upon the rocks for a purpose, but what that purpose may have been can only be surmised at this late day. Knowing the superstitious nature of the Indians these French traders, or voyageurs as they were then called, may have made their homes in one of the caverns in the cliffs and cut and delineated those petroglyphs upon the sandstone rock with the points of their knives for the purpose of frightening the Indians away from their cavern rendezvous, and thereby protecting their lives and property, but it is very improbable that these French voyagers painted them, for they could hardly have had the means of doing so, and if they did the storms of some nineteen years between the time they must have done the work and the time when Marquette saw them would have thoroughly obliterated the paint. Another reason why they did not make those petroglyphs is that they would have frightened their allies the Ottawas who accompanied them added to the fact that white men were seldom known to make petroglyphs, while such works are common to the Indian races, convinces us that they were the entire work of the Indians.

While not disputing the statement of Prof. Russell, hereinafter given, relative to the innumerable human bones he found in one of these caves, nor attacking his suppositious theory of their being the work of the Piasa, we suggest that this cave may have been used as a burial place by the Mound Builders or Indians, where their dead were deposited from generation to generation, it being dry and protected from rains, storms and dampness, the bones were long in crumbling to decay. It is a great loss to science and ethnology that the intrusive changes of the swiftly flowing waters of the Mississippi, together with the rains and storms of two centuries have entirely obliterated these caves and carried away their deposits, so that no vestige of them now remains. Nor, indeed, have we any photographs or other pictures of these monsters known to be accurate. They were delineated on the river side of the rock and destroyed before any efforts were made to even take "counterfeit presentments of them." Hence we only have representations taken from a couple of paintings made from descriptions given by those who were familiar with them. The engravings we herewith give were taken from photographs of these paintings.

The one with the elk's horns and serpent's tail was painted by T. F. Ladd, of Whitehall, Ill., the other by an artist sent thither from Washington, D. C. for that purpose. Whether the petroglyphs were made just alike, and the difference between them occurred from painting, or whether they were dissimilar, as shown in the engravings, we cannot say, but presume our engravings are accurate representations of each, and that they were dissimilar as they were delineated on the rock. These petroglyphs were badly marred and defaced before any white man settled in that locality, and though nearly alike in conception and execution they are somewhat dissimilar in the shape of their horns and tail, and the manner of its carriage.

The one with the tail passing over the back between the wings, thence over the head and back between the legs, with the fish terminal, comes more closely to Marquette's description than the other, yet in their main features and combination they approximate very closely; and while there were several traditions among the Indians of the then northwest relative to them none but that of the Miamis mention but one monster. Some of the traditions say the Piasa was fond of bathing in the Mississippi and a very rapid swimmer, and when disporting in the tide raised such a commotion in the water as to force great waves over the banks, inundating the adjacent country. Others, that when mad (and it always was mad at the sight of an Indian) it thrashed the ground with its tail until the whole earth shook and trembled.

There were several other petroglyphs upon the same strata between Alton and Grafton, but insignificant in size as compared with these. One represented two birds in attitude of fighting over an apple or ring which was carved on the rock between them. Another of a bird and a small animal contending for a similar prize. Another was a small Grecian cross. But we will not attempt to theorize upon these smaller petroglyphs, but refer the reader to the work of the Honorable William McAdams, the ethnologist and archaeologist of Alton, Illinois, who either now has or soon will publish a work on the pictographs of the Mississippi Valley, and is of the opinion that these monster petroglyphs, together with the numerous lesser ones of that locality, were a chronological history of the great events which transpired away back in the dim misty past, to some far more intelligent people than the Indian, and is inclined to the belief that they were made by that mysterious but very intelligent pre-historic race of this country, whom we call the Mound Builders, who are only known by the relics of their wonderful works, and what appears from these works to have been their great advancement in a knowledge of the arts and sciences, more especially engineering and fort-building.

They also had not only a knowledge of the utility of metal but were experts in the manufacture of copper instruments and hardening them so as to cut granite. They also well understood the art of making pottery and bricks, and must have been as numerous along the banks of the Mississippi as the inhabitants on the banks of the Tiber. While these people might have made these petroglyphs we are clearly of the opinion that they did not, and are the more confirmed in this belief by the fact that they have never heretofore been accredited with keeping any such records, while it is a well settled fact that the Indians not only made petroglyphic records before the advent of the Europeans to this continent but have kept it up ever since.

Besides this it is absolutely certain that these petroglyphs were of a more recent date than the age of the Mound Builders, because the elements would have entirely effaced them if not renewed from time to time, which could hardly have been done, since the Mound Builders became extinct thousands of years ago, unless we assume that the Indian is either the descendant of, or the immediate successor to, the possession of this vast continent, neither of which is tenable nor reasonable. The difference in the anatomical formation of these two races forbids this assumption. While the fact that the Indians had no tradition or other evidence of their having overcome and subdued the occupants of this vast country, nor that there were any former people here, establishes beyond doubt that the Indians were in no way connected with the Mound Builders or had any knowledge of their existence, but they utilized their tumuli or mounds for their burial grounds, whereby the name "Indian Mounds" obtains, and even at this late period, when science and research are illuminating the dark caverns and hidden nooks of nature's laboratory, there are very many intelligent people who believe these mounds were the production of the Indians. But whether these monster petroglyphs were the conception and work of the red or white man the naked fact still exists that they embodied in a strikingly graphic view so many elements of horror, dread and fright to the Indians of that locality that even the boldest and bravest of them dare not gaze upon the great red eyes and horrid shape of these cold, inanimate pictures, away up on the smooth stone wall, nearly a hundred feet above the river.

Such was their dread of them that in passing up and down the Mississippi which was their only highway at this point they steered their canoes so as to hug the opposite shore, while few, indeed, dared even look in the direction of the rock whereon these dreaded monsters were delineated, with elevated wings, as if about to swoop down and destroy every living creature upon the broad face of the river. Their position upon the rock was in a straight horizontal line, close together, with their heads facing the east. When discovered by Marquette they seemed to have been recently painted in red, black and green, and were certainly horrid enough in their aspect to frighten the learned and trusting Jesuit, who says, "they frighted me" If they were objects of fright to him how much more so must they have been to the superstitious sons of the forest, who believed in the existence of a multiplicity of real, corporeal, bad spirits, henos,

DEMONOLOGY

or devils, chief of which was represented by the Piasa their devil of devils.

CHAPTER II

The North American Indians, like the pale faces, have their historians, orators and statesmen, with this difference in their production and growth; theirs are carefully selected and educated to the special profession and make it their life-study and calling, while ours spring up like magic with a kind of spontaneity not unlike Jonah's gourd or mushrooms the growth of a single night. Though the Indian has no books and is ignorant of the alphabet and penmanship he has two modes of preserving and recording history tradition and pictographs or petroglyphs.

The art of preserving history in detail among the Indians is by tradition, hence its accuracy largely depends upon the tenacity of the memory of their historians, and the accuracy with which their traditions are handed down from father to son, from generation to generation. Their great events and periods are graphically shown and preserved in pictographs and petroglyphs as before shown. But they have no other means of preserving their history in narrative form and detailed order than tradition.

Though visionary and unreal, still their traditions have much foundation of fact, and are full of interest to the student and thinker. The Illini tradition of the Piasa is from the pen of the late Prof. John Russell, of Jersey county, Illinois, a scholar, writer and poet of considerable repute. Indeed, his beautiful epic entitled, "The Worm of the Still," gave him a world-wide fame as a poet. He came from the Empire State away back in the "thirties" and located in Jersey county, where he engaged in teaching school and writing for the public press. Having come in almost daily contact with the Indians of that locality, which is near Alton, where the pictures of these monsters were

DEMONOLOGY

delineated, he heard several Indian traditions pertaining to the Piasa, and was especially interested in that of the Illini or Illinois confederacy, and to fully understand the locality he visited it in company with a competent guide in March, 1848, and explored the cave near where these monsters were delineated on the rock, and wrote up the results of his exploration and had it published in "The Evangelical Magazine and Gospel Advocate," printed and published at Utica, in the State of New York, in the July number, 1848, and republished in the February number of "Manford's Magazine," of Chicago, 1887, which is as follows:

"The Piasa; an Indian Tradition of Illinois:

No part of the United States, not even the highlands of the Hudson, can vie in wild and romantic scenery with the bluffs of Illinois. On one side of the river, often at the water's edge, a perpendicular wall of rock rises to the height of some hundred feet. Generally on the opposite shore is a level bottom or prairie of several miles in width, extending to a similar bluff that runs parallel with the river. One of these ranges commences at Alton and extends, with a few intervals, for many miles along the left bank of the Illinois. In descending the river to Alton the traveler will observe between that town and the mouth of the Illinois a narrow ravine, through which a small stream discharges its waters into the Mississippi. The stream is the Piasa. Its name is Indian, and signifies in the Illini, 'the bird that devours men.' Near the mouth of that stream, on the smooth and perpendicular face of the bluff, at an elevation which no human art can reach, is cut the figure of an enormous bird, with its wings extended. The bird which this figure represents was called by these Indians the Piasa, and from this is derived the name of the stream. The tradition of the Piasa is still current among all the tribes of the Upper Mississippi, and those who have inhabited the valley of the Illinois, and is briefly this:

'Many thousand moons before the arrival of the pale-

DEMONOLOGY

faces, when the great Magalonyx and Mastodon, whose bones are now dug up, were still living in the land of the green prairies, there existed a bird of such dimensions that he could easily carry off in his talons a full grown deer. Having obtained a taste of human flesh from that time he would prey upon nothing else. He was artful as he was powerful, and would dart suddenly and unexpectedly upon an Indian, bear him off into one of the caves of the bluff and devour him. Hundreds of warriors attempted for years to destroy him, but without success. Whole villages were nearly depopulated, and consternation spread through all the tribes of the Illini. At length Ouatogo, a chief whose fame extended even beyond the great lakes, separating himself from the rest of his tribe, fasted in solitude for the space of the whole moon and prayed to the Great Spirit, the Master of Life, that he would protect his children from the Piasa. On the last night of his fast the Great Spirit appeared to Ouatogo in a dream, and directed him to select twenty of his warriors, each armed with a bow and poisoned arrow, and conceal them in a designated spot.

Near the place of their concealment another warrior was to stand in open view as a victim for the Piasa, which they must shoot the instant that he pounced upon his prey. When the chief awoke the next morning he thanked the Great Spirit, and returning to his tribe told them the dream. The warriors were quickly selected and placed in ambush as directed. Ouatogo offered himself as the victim.

He was willing to die for his tribe. Placing himself in open view of the bluff he soon saw the Piasa perched on the cliff, eyeing his prey. Ouatogo drew up his manly form to its utmost height, planting his feet firmly upon the earth he began to chant the death song of an Indian warrior. A moment after the Piasa arose into the air and swift as the thunderbolt darted down upon the chief. Scarcely had he reached his victim when every bow was sprung and every arrow sent to the feather into his body. The Piasa uttered a wild, fearful scream, that resounded far over the opposite side of the river, and expired. Ouatogo was safe. Not an arrow, not even the talons of the bird had touched him. The Master of Life, in admiration of the generous deed of Ouatogo, had held over him an invisible shield. In memory of this event the image of the Piasa was engraved on the face of the bluff.'

Such is the Indian tradition. Of course I do not vouch for its truth. This, however, is certain, the figure of a large bird cut in the solid rock is still there, and at a height that is perfectly inaccessible. How and for what purpose it was made I leave for others to determine. Even at this day an Indian never passes that spot in his canoe without firing his gun at the figure of the bird. The marks of the balls are almost innumerable. Near the close of March of the present year I was induced to visit the bluffs below the mouth of the Illinois and above the Piasa. My curiosity was principally directed to the examination of a cave connected with the above tradition, as one of those to which the bird had carried his victims. Preceded by an intelligent guide, who carried a spade, I set out on my excursion. The cave was extremely difficult of access, and at one point of our progress I stood at an elevation of one hundred and fifty feet on the face of the perpendicular bluff, with barely room to sustain one foot. The unbroken wall towered above me, while below was the river. After a long and perilous clambering we reached the cave, which was about fifty feet above the surface of the river. By the aid of a long pole, placed on a projecting rock and the upper end touching the mouth of the cave, we succeeded in entering it. The Mississippi was rolling in silent grandeur beneath us; high over our heads a single cedar hung its branches over the cliff, on the blasted top of which was seated a bald eagle. No other sound or sign of life was near us. A Sabbath stillness rested on the scene.

Not a cloud was visible in the the heavens, not a breath of air was stirring. The broad Mississippi lay before us calm and smooth as a lake. The landscape presented the same wild aspect as it did before it had met the eyes of the white man. The roof of the cavern was vaulted, the top of which was hardly less than twenty feet high. The shape of the cave was irregular, but so far as I could judge the bottom would average twenty by thirty feet. The floor of the cave throughout its whole extent was one mass of human bones. Skulls and other bones were mingled together in the utmost confusion. To what depth they extended I am unable to decide, but we dug to the depth of three or four feet in every quarter of the cavern and still we found only bones. The remains of thousands must have been deposited there. How and by whom and for what purpose it is impossible to conjecture."

Such is the tradition of the dread Piasa, as given by Prof. Russell, as common among the great confederation known as the Illini. His statement that the place where this monster was delineated was so high that no human art could reach it shows that he had but little knowledge of the use of blocks and pulleys as a means of reaching elevated places. To the painter of the present day eighty feet elevations have no terror and offer but little inconvenience. We think he made a mistake in saying the wings of this monster were represented as being extended.

He probably intended to use the words "elevated, as in the act of starting to fly," which would be more strictly in accordance with the position of the wings, as shown by the engravings, or, in the language of the evangelist, "their wings were stretched upward." It will be observed that each wing has five hook shaped pendants, representing dagger-shaped horns, which may have been intended to represent the ten horns of the great red dragon described in Revelations. While Pere Marquette called them monsters, Prof. Russell called it (for he only mentioned one) a bird; and indeed, it, or they, may have been called bird, beast, saurian or reptile with equal propriety, since all are combined in the representation, with a little of the man thrown in to make this wonderful combination of aerial, mundane and saurian what is it?

From the fact that the Mississippi is liable to wash out

new channels and change its course, the strong probability is that at the time these petroglyphs were made its channel was considerably south of its present one and that there was a large depth of earth lying at the base of the present perpendicular stone wall which extended up to the bed of the sandstone on which they were cut, so that the artist for he who conceived and executed them was an artist of marked ability stood upon the ground to do his work, and that since then the swift waters of the "Father of Waters" have cut out its present channel, sweeping the earth into the gulf, leaving these monster petroglyphs some eighty feet above the river's surface.

Assuming this to be true their elevation is no wonder. When and by what tribe, nation or confederation of Indians the particular locality about Alton, Ill., was first settled, like the origin of the Indian race, is an unsolved and in all human probability ever will remain an unsolvable mystery, unless we adopt the theory advanced by some ethnologists and beg the question by saying, they are indigenous to the Western Hemisphere, or, like Topsy, were "never born but grown." Others advance the hypothesis of their being the offspring of that wonderful people of whom we see so much and know so little the Mound Builders. The advocates of this theory urge as a reason for their belief their divergence from all European nations in their physical structure and color.

Prominent among points of difference is the fact that in the pile or hair of the European the coloring matter is distributed by means of a central canal, while in the Indian it is incorporated in the fibrous structure; but the most clearly defined difference is in the shape of the hair under the microscope. That of the Indian being round; the white man, oval; the negro, flat. If these stolid, lazy, ignorant, hunting and fishing people are the descendants of the once powerful, intelligent, industrious, pastoral Mound Builders, then, indeed, may we exclaim, in the language of Mark Antony, "O, my countrymen, what a fall was there!" Others claim that they are a

DEMONOLOGY

derivative race, and sprang from some of the ancient Asiatics, while others assert, with considerable reason to back them, that they are the offspring of the lost tribes of Israel, described by Esdras, "these are the ten tribes which were carried away prisoners out of their own land in the time of Osea, the king, whom Salamanaser, the king of Assyria, led away captive into another land. But they took this counsel among themselves, that they would leave the multitude of the heathen and go forth into a farther country, where never mankind dwelt.

And they entered into Euphrates by the narrow passage of the river. For the Most High then Showed signs for them and held still the flood till they were passed over. For through that country there was a great way to go, namely, of a year and a half, and the same region is called Asareth."

By assuming that away back in the early days when "the waters were being divided and gathered together in one place, and the dry land appeared" the western limits of America were united to Asia on the west and Europe on the east, we can readily see how the Indians as well as animals from the present Eastern Hemisphere crossed over to this. Though, like the ancient Scythians, the Indians scalped their victims and tortured their prisoners; and like the Tartars, in the shape of their canoes and manner of marching in single file, the great similarity of their religious customs and habits to those of the ancient Jews in many of their leading characteristics, among which were their offering sacrifices and burnt-offerings to appease and please their deities, and celebrating the passover in their harvest or crane dance, are, indeed, very strong arguments in favor of their Hebrew origin and descent. Yet no generally accepted theory or hypothesis has been accepted by the ethnologists upon this question, so we are left in the dark to grope our way to the light as best we can. We have given much time and study to the mythologies, customs, habits and religious practices of the Indians, which has confirmed our belief in their Jewish origin, and that they probably came to this continent away back of the

DEMONOLOGY

Christian era, and are possibly the descendants of the lost tribes of Israel, described by Esdras in the Apocrypha, as before indicated.

When the white people first discovered the Upper Mississippi nearly all of its banks and adjacent country were in the full and undisputed possession of a powerful Indian confederacy, known as the Illini. This confederacy was originally composed of possibly fifty Indian nations, united under one set of sachems or chiefs, and originally came from the shores of the Gulf of Mexico and banks of the various streams entering it.

Having lived there for centuries they from time to time ascended the Mississippi, each time going a little farther up they finally took complete possession of that great river with its adjacent lands. The powerful and warlike Miamis, according to their tradition, were once a member of that great confederacy, and had their principal village at or near where the city of Alton, Illinois, now stands. Their tradition was related to us nearly sixty years ago by a chief, and is substantially as follows:

THE MIAMI TRADITION OF THE PIASA

Several thousand winters before the pale-faces came to this country there existed the most powerful Indian confederacy ever known. Their principal country was upon the bank of the broad water, into which the Mestchecepe (now spelled Mississippi), or great river, flows. Here they lived and were prosperous and happy for many thousand winters. Their warriors became as numerous as the trees in the forest, and were as brave as the bear, strong as the buffalo, swift as the elk and cunning as the fox. Their long residence and great multitude in that country resulted in killing off the buffalo, elk, moose and deer, until game became so scarce that their hunters were forced to keep constantly extending their hunting grounds farther north, and the Mestchecepe being their principal highway they

DEMONOLOGY

ascended that great river in their canoes, but frequently came in contact and conflict with other tribes, always overcoming and conquering them; for it was the pride and glory of the warriors of this confederacy that they were Illini, which signified in their language, "we are men, not dogs or cowards."

As their hunting parties advanced up the Mestchecepe their families followed, until they reached the great lakes in the north. When they reached the country about the mouth of the Missouri, or muddy river, and thence up to the mouth of the Illinois, and up that stream to its source they found the entire surrounding country full of game of every kind known to them, in inexhaustible quantities.

Its woods abounded in fruits, flowers, nuts and wild honey of the richest flavor and sweetest taste; while its creeks, rivers and lakes teemed with fish and eel so thick as to impede their navigation, even by canoe. In short, it was a perfect Indian paradise. "Where corn, tobacco, squash and bean, luxuriant to the view, In one unbroken round was seen, The gift of Manitou."

Immense herds of buffalo, moose, elk and deer listlessly roamed over the broad savannas, daintily nipping earth's luxuriant beard the grass too fat and happy to even heed the approach of the Indian hunter.

> "In such a paradise the game
> Of every species, every name,
> Was quickly found on every hand,
> To rich reward the hunter band."

Here the lordly Indian could, with but little effort on his part, daily feast upon:

> Roast bear and bison, elk and moose.
> Roast deer and turkey, brant and goose,

DEMONOLOGY

> Baked woodchuck, antelope and coon,
> Baked squirrel, rabbit, duck and loon,
> Broiled pheasant, chicken, lark and quail,
> Broiled woodcock, plover, snipe and rail,
> Fried lobster, turtle, fish and crabs,
> Fried eels and clams, fried eggs and squabs,
> Boiled maize, potatoes, rice and squash,
> Boiled pumpkins, beans and succotash,
> Parched acorns, artichokes and corn,
> Parched roots and nuts of various form,
> Wild apples, cherries, grapes and plum,
> Wild berries and wild honey-comb.

Powerful in numbers, they soon became lax in discipline, because they were so much dreaded by surrounding nations that they were never attacked. Naturally lazy, their easy lives led to indolent habits and reckless living, united to a long period of peaceful relations between them and their surrounding nations drove the cultivation of the art of war into "innoxious desuetude." Their great numerical strength and slothful habits resulted with them as with every other great nation in being the rock upon which their confederacy was broken and shattered to atoms, never again to be united, for it is a fact that the cohesive attraction which holds an Indian nation together is weakened as the nation increases in size. The larger the number the greater the prize in reaching its chief command, which offers temptations to the unscrupulous and ambitious leaders of each powerful gentes or phratry to intrigue and plot for its command, which sooner or later results in a complete rupture, generally ending in a bitter, if not exterminating, internal war.

The Illini became insolent, oppressive and greedy to such a degree as to forget the greatest of all Indian virtues hospitality to strangers when the Great Spirit determined to punish them as He did the inhabitants of Sodom and Gomorrah, because they had become thoroughly wicked and transgressed His law. First afflicting them with the most dreaded plague to the Indians smallpox which carried away thousands upon thousands, and scarcely had this plague subsided ere He sent evil spirits among them to encourage and inaugurate jealousies, intrigues, plots and revolts, not only among the confederacy, but among the different tribes composing it. Assassinations, murders and revolutions followed until the once almost omnipotent Illini were severed and torn to segments by internal wars.

Nor did their afflictions end with the collapse of the confederacy, but the most implacable wars sprang up between the broken segments of the Illini, which not infrequently terminated in the utter annihilation of some of its tribes. The Miamis and Mestchegamies (generally spelled Michigamies) were among the most powerful tribes or nations of the Illini, and their territories joined each other, while their principal villages were only some twenty miles apart, both on the north bank of the Meschecepe, one near the mouth of the Illinois, the other near where Alton now stands. A bitter and relentless war had been carried on between these two nations, which had been friends and allies for generations before. Murders and robberies were of such daily occurrence that hunting and fishing parties were compelled to go in large bodies, ever ready to repel attacks. Each nation had a lookout or signal station, where sentinels were always on duty to signal everything which might indicate approaching danger.

That of the Mestchegamies was upon the upper, the Miamis the lower, point of the rock promontory, extending almost continuously between their villages. Overlying the rocks there was sufficient soil to support the growth of large oak trees, on the limbs of which platforms of poles were made for their sentinels. Each sentry-tree commanded a view of the surface of the Mestchecepe between the two villages and over the bluff on the south; but owing to several deep ravines leading from the north, cutting their path through the promontory to reach the river, an army might pass along some of these canyons or ravines without being seen from either of their lookouts. There were two caves entering the rock near the lower end of the promontory, some fifty feet above the river's current, in which two huge monsters, with the body and claws of an alligator, wings of an eagle, but ten times larger; horns of an elk or deer, ears of a fox, face of a man, mouth, teeth and beard of a tiger, and tail of a serpent or fish, made their homes, but spent the greater part of their time resting and dozing upon some high part of the rocks, or flying over the country. One of these was fond of bathing, and a good swimmer; while the other seemed to be delighted with its ability to beat the earth with its monstrous bony tail.

Though of horrid shape and mien they had never molested the Indians other than by their loud noises. The voice of one resembled the roaring of a buffalo bull, the other the shrill scream of the panther. They had lived there so long without doing violence to the Miamis that they considered them good spirits, and were very careful about disturbing or scaring them away, notwithstanding the Indians knew these monsters as devil birds, and that they were of sufficient strength to pick up and carry off a young buffalo, and in fact lived and battened on deer, elk and young buffalo, upon which they swooped down and clutched with their powerful claws or talons and bore off to their cavern homes in the cliff to devour at their leisure.

Thus matters stood until one bright September morn, when the Mestchegamies left their village in force to steal a march upon and stealthily attack their mortal foes; and on that same morning the Miamis attempted to play the same game upon the Mestchegamies. The latter got the earlier start and reached the upper end of the lower Piasa canyon as the Miamis reached its lower end. Each were intending a surprise and slaughter of their enemies by passing through this canyon, the Miamis up, the Mestchegamies down it. Both sides were in force and fully armed for war. Soon they came face to face in the narrow canyon, where escape from a desperate battle was impossible except by abject flight. But no such thought was entertained by either side. With the war-whoop of their respective nations the dread battle shock was inaugurated.

Every brave and warrior resolved to conquer or die in the narrow defile. Quarter was neither given nor expected. In the midst of this fierce and bloody encounter, and at a moment when the ranks of the Mestchegamies were wavering as if about to yield or fly, two dread monsters, like the war horse of the Scriptures "snift the battle from afar" and came flying up the canyon, uttering bellowings and shrieks, while the flapping of their wings upon the air roared out like so many thunderclaps.

Passing close over the heads of the combatants each selected and picked up in his huge talons a Miami chieftain and bore him off above the now terrified and utterly demoralized Miamis, who believed the Great Spirit had sent these dread monsters, or bad spirits, to aid and assist their enemies. And as each bore away in its cruel claws a struggling, squirming, howling, groaning, screaming chieftain, the horrified Miamis, distinctly heard them calling, pleading and imploring for assistance, which they could not give; the bravest heart ceased to beat and the strongest limbs were paralyzed with terror. They were incapable of either thought or act until aroused to a sense of their position by the fierce war-whoop of the Mestchegamies, who were now sure of victory, since the Great Spirit had sent these monsters to fight their battles for them. All order was gone from the Miamis, and their leaders being carried away by the monsters, a panic set in and ran riot through the ranks, and thousands were slaughtered by the fierce Mestchegamies or forced into the Mississippi by the terrible onslaught and drowned. Instead of a battle it was a massacre, a holocaust, which only ceased with the close of day, since the Indians never fight in the darkness of the night. Though by no means annihilated the Miamis were so badly crippled as a nation that they fled towards the Wabash and crossed that stream ere they felt safe. Here they remained during generation after generation,

DEMONOLOGY

"Gathering their brows like gathering storm
Nursing their wrath to keep it warm,"

Never forgetting nor forgiving the Mestchegamies or the monsters, but like Hamilcar, the Carthagenian, who caused his son, Hannibal, to swear eternal enmity to Rome, each father related it to his son from generation to generation, and swore them to avenge the terrible massacre of their ancestors in the canyon on the Mestchecepe.

In the meanwhile the Mestchegamies had reunited with the Peorias, Cohokias, Tamaroas and Kaskaskias, forming another confederacy known as the Illinois. Though less formidable in numerical strength than their predecessors the Illini, the Illinois were a very powerful and warlike confederacy, and soon became the absolute owners and masters of a vast territory, bounded on the east by the Wabash, south and west by the Metschecepe, running north almost to Lake Michigan. They soon became a proud, haughty, domineering and extremely selfish confederacy, and guarded their rights of territory with rigorous exactitude. Every trespass upon their hunting grounds was promptly and severely punished. The closer they guarded their territory against trespass from the hunters of surrounding tribes the greater was their temptation; for the Indian like Mother Eve, has a strong desire for forbidden fruit, and feels bound to do that which he is forbidden to do if it breaks his neck.

Hence large hunting parties were formed and raids made into the territory of the Illinois, which exasperated them in turn, resulting in numerous murders and small battles, followed by a few cold-blooded massacres. In this way the passions of these naturally vengeful people were wrought up to a white heat, when nothing but revenge and slaughter was thought of. This was the long-wished and patiently waited for time for the Miamis to wipe out the score between them and the Mestchegamies, for:

DEMONOLOGY

"Time at last sets all things even,
And if we do but watch the hour,
There never yet was human power
Which could evade, if unforgiven,
The patient search and vigil long,
Of him who treasures up a wrong."

Generation after generation had come and gone to find the Miamis plotting, planning and scheming some means of paying off their deadly enemies the full amount of their sufferings and loss, not only in their own coin, but with compound interest. By persistent and untiring efforts they succeeded in organizing a powerful Indian confederacy, about the year 1760, known as the Peuotomies, which was composed of many, if not quite all the Indian nations of the then northwest who spoke the Algonquin language; among whom the Miamis, Pottawattamies, Ottawas, Chippewas, Sauks and Foxes were prominent actors in the long and sanguinary struggle which followed close upon the formation of the Peuotomies. Revenge has ever been the controlling passion of the Indian, impelling him to fight like a demon for its accomplishment. This was the strongest incentive to the Peuotomies in the war, to which was added a desire for the possession of the magnificent territory of the Illinois.

The great war chief, Sugar, of the Pottawattamies, was their commander-in-chief. His height, as shown by a measurement of his skeleton made by us in 1831, must have been six feet six inches; while his weight certainly approached three hundred pounds. (He was buried in a wooden pen on the south bank of the Illinois river, a few miles above Starved Rock.) Big Elk, the war chief the Mestchegamies, commanded the Illinois, who were not only fighting for revenge upon their enemies on account of numerous murders and robberies committed on them by the Peuotomies, but for everything dear to the Indian home, country, and the graves of their sires.

DEMONOLOGY

With such prizes to contend for, and such armies to contend, the war was not only terrific but long and implacable. Commencing near the Wabash above Vincennes in the early spring it lasted until the following winter. Step by step the Peuotomies drove the Illinois from point to point, fighting as they went, until they reached Blue Island, near Chicago, where a most terrific battle took place, lasting several days, which resulted in, not only the defeat of the Illinois, but in breaking up their army and scattering them in segments and ignominious flight. A considerable portion of them however, under Big Elk, fled down the Des Plaines river to the place where the city of Joliet now stands, where they were overtaken by the Peuotomies, flushed with their late signal victory. Here another sanguinary battle occurred, in which the Illinois fought with desperation, but were again defeated in a great slaughter. From here they again fled down the Illinois river, but were overtaken at the point where the city of Morris now stands, where another severe struggle ensued, resulting in a victory for the Peuotomies, but at the cost of the lives of many of their bravest and best soldiers, among whom was the great Chippewa chief Nucquette who was buried in one of the tumuli near where he fell, and a red cedar pole placed at the head of his grave to mark the spot. This pole still stands where it was put over a hundred and twenty five years ago, and is now in a good state of preservation, and is located on Wauponsee street, near the Court House, in Morris.

The loss of the Illinois in this battle was far greater than that of their enemies, and again they fled down the Illinois, endeavoring to descend that river to the Mississippi, but were overtaken by the victorious Peuotomies, who not only cut off their passage down that river but surrounded them on all sides, thus cutting off every avenue of escape. Standing on the south bank of the Illinois river, about eight miles below the city of Ottawa, is a singularly shaped St. Peter's sandstone rock, which rises up from the river's edge one hundred and forty-seven feet. Its surface embraces an area of about half an acre, and is overlaid with earth several feet deep, studded with a few small red cedar trees. It is circular in shape and its walls are nearly perpendicular, except a small space on the south side, where persons can climb up. But this passage way is so narrow that it was easily defended by those on its summit. In their sore need and desperate extremity, the remnant of the Illinois, who had fled in this direction with Big Elk, their chief, sought refuge upon this rock. But the besiegers at once surrounded the rock, holding their lines beyond the reach of the arrows of the besieged; and thus cut off all supplies of food. There were crevices worn in the face of this rock immediately above the water in the river, so deep and large as to permit an Indian to pass all along the river side of the rock, so when the famishing besieged lowered a vessel by means of a rawhide string for water an Indian in the crevice below seized the string and jerked the drawer head foremost from the rock into the river, a distance of nearly one hundred and fifty feet. To avoid this certain death the water-drawers ran their leather cords around the body of a tree or stump, unwinding it slowly, and thus lowered their water vessels down. But this proved abortive, for the Peuotomies, who were stationed along the crevices below, cut the cord with their scalping knives, and, being sheltered by the projecting rock above they could not be dislodged by the Illinois. Thus were the besieged completely cut off from food and water, without which they could live but a few days at best. The segment of the Illinois here penned up on this cold inhospitable rock were chiefly Mestchegamies, the mortal foes of the Miamis, while the latter were their most insatiable tormentors, and ever and anon kept shouting to them: "Now send forth your devil-birds for food and water; call forth your Piasas to keep you from the Pauguk (god of death), whose chattering teeth are tearing and rending your trembling cowardly bodies." To these cruel taunts the brave but now famishing Mestchegamies hurled back their defiance: "The Miamis are dogs and squaw-papooses, who fight only with their mouths and dare not meet men face to face in fair battle. If you will allow us to come down from this rock and meet us on the plain, weak and hungry as we are, we will send

DEMONOLOGY

you flying like so many howling coyotes, as our ancestors did in the canyon on the Mestchecepe long ago, and that, too, without assistance from devil-birds or Piasas." Nor were thirst and famine the only enemies the Illinois were forced to contend with; winter, stern, cold and stormy, had set in. The angry winds howled over and around this perpendicular rock like searching demons, from whose piercing shafts they had no shelter, nor were they half clad. This small high rock is but a dissevered part of the south bluff of the Illinois river, and its height is no greater than the next point of the rock bluff immediately east, and is separated from it by a deep gulch, about two hundred yards wide at the top. Upon this last named point the Chevalier La Salle erected a Fort, surrounded with ditches and embankments, in November, 1682, and called it Fort St. Louis, in honor of the then King of France.

Fort St. Louis was occupied and held by Tonti, the one armed Italian lieutenant under La Salle until 1702 or a period of twenty years; but no vestige, save the ditches and earthen breast works, remained at the siege of the Illinois on Starved Rock. Many of the Peuotomies, more especially the Miamis and Pottawattamies, were armed with rifles or muskets, and experts in their use; and by lying down behind the earthen embankments of the old fort they could pick off the Illinois on Starved Rock, which was within easy rifle range. Thus instead of a refuge and place of safety, Starved Rock proved to be a death trap and a snare to the Illinois. What between thirst, hunger, cold and the deadly bullets of their implacable enemies their tortures were worse than those described in Dante's Inferno.

Bearing all like heroes as they were, the physically feeble Illinois made a dash for life and liberty the first dark night after their entrapment by climbing down from the rock and rushing through the beleaguering lines. Eleven only of their entire number succeeded in making good their escape. All the rest who were able to leave the rock that cold, stormy night,

DEMONOLOGY

crossed the dark and silent trail from which there is no return.

Thus perished this remnant of the Illinois who sought safety on this rock, which from thence forward has been known by no other name than Starved Rock.

Though badly defeated in this long and bloody war the Illinois were by no means crushed out of existence, but the Mestchegamies were virtually annihilated, never again to be known among the red men save by tradition. Thus at last were the Miamis terribly avenged upon their bitterest enemies after waiting and watching for an opportunity generation after generation. As the result of this long war the Illinois were confined to the territory in southern Illinois, and the Miamis regained their ancient village and territory surrounding Alton, Illinois. But upon their return, after an absence of a thousand moons, they found the image of the devil-bird or Piasa upon the rock near where these monsters had been the cause of their great loss of life and country, which fact had been kept green in their minds by tradition, and could they have reached the place of their delineation upon the perpendicular wall they doubtless would have effaced them so that no mark or even scratch should indicate where they were. But as the place was some eighty feet high they were compelled to wreak their spite and hate upon these cold images by shooting at and cursing them. If these traditions are true, then, indeed, the temporary assistance of the Piasato the Mestchegamiesin their desperate battle with the Miamis, in the canyon near Alton, Illinois, instead of a blessing proved to be a terrible curse to them, soon after, by the great sacrifice of their people to feed the ever hungry monsters which seemed to have a special taste for Indian flesh, and would touch no other.

The time when the Piasa existed in this country, according to the Illini tradition, was "many thousand moons before the arrival of the palefaces," while that of the Miamis says, "several thousand winters before the pale-faces came."

DEMONOLOGY

Though indefinite as to the exact time or period both indicate a very long period of time many centuries and may be construed to go away back to the mesozoic or middle-life geological period, known as the age of reptiles, when the monster saurians existed in great numbers and varieties, among which were the ichthyosaur, with the general shape of the dolphin, snout of the porpoise, head of the lizard, jaws and teeth of the crocodile, vertebra of the fish, sternal arch of the water-mole, paddles of the whale, trunk and tail of a quadruped. It had a short, thick neck, large head, enormous mouth, with as high as 160 inches long, round, sharp teeth. It had for its playmate and companion another monster called the plesiosaur, with the head of a lizard, feet of a crocodile, neck of a swan, trunk and tail of a quadruped, ribs of the chameleon and paddles of the whale. His body was shorter and much larger than that of his companion, while in general size they were nearly equal. And there were other monsters in those days, among the most notable of which were the pterodactyl, or wing-fingered monstrosity, which in every point of the horrible surpassed the ichthyosaur and plesiosaur. It was an aerial beast, bird or reptile, with wings shaped like those of the bat. Its bones were hollow like those of the bird, but it had no feathers, and though its bill resembled that of the bittern, it was full of long, sharp teeth like those of the shark. Instead of two legs and feet it had four of each. The fore legs seemed to have come out at the butt of its wings and rested upon them. In shape they resembled human arms, with talons like the eagle in shape but much longer.

It probably could walk on its hind legs with folded wings. Its legs, like its arms, were supplied with long and powerful talons. Its spread of wings was from fifteen to twenty five feet. The fossil remains of some twenty-five species of this monster have been found, and it is sometimes called the pterosaur or flying lizard. There were other monster lizards in those days, some of which were, nearly or quite one hundred feet long, known as dinosaurs (terrible-lizards), megalosaurs, hylaeosaurs, iguanadons, etc. The megalosaur, as shown by the skeleton restored and now in the Crystal Palace at Sydenham, England, is really a most hideous monster, with immense body, legs and tail, all covered with armor scales.

Another great monster of the frog species, called the labyrinthodon, then lived. Its general shape was that of a frog, but it had the teeth of an alligator, while its head was protected by a natural helmet and its body with scales. But the most singular monster of the age yet discovered and its shape and component parts analyzed is the ramphorhyncus, which seems to be a connective link between birds, beasts and reptiles. Its body and neck resemble that of the Piasa, while its tail is identical with it, except it is pictured as dragging behind instead of being carried around the body or over its back and head . The shape of the head is drawn to resemble that of a duck, with the long bill of a snipe or bittern, but is full of sharp, round teeth, like those of the crocodile. It had four legs, with eagle's talons, and a pair of bat-like wings. When on the ground it traveled on all fours, dragging its long tail trailing behind, and when flying it must have wrapped it around its body, under its wings or around its huge neck. Its entire length from head to tip of tail was probably thirty feet or more. In many respects the Piasa is a faithful copy of the ramphorhyncus. The form, shape and description of the Piasa, according to the Indian traditions were painted from actual sight of the living subject; that of the ramphorhyncus is from collecting its badly decomposed bones, and from their form, shape and size constructing an ideal monster.

We are strongly of the opinion that they were but one and the same species, and that the Indians' representation upon the rock is by far the truer one of this extinct monster. While there are several close resemblances between the pterodactyl and the Piasa, as shown in the petroglyphs,the similarity between them and the ramphorhyncus is more strikingly clear. Thus may the traditions of these Indians be true, and their petroglyphic history of the Piasa may enable the scientist to

DEMONOLOGY

reconstruct his ramphorhyncus into the shape and form of the Indians' Piasa.

If these petroglyphs were the work of the Indian, and of this we have but little doubt, they show that he had a knowledge, real or traditional, of the existence of these monsters of the geological reptile age. And it is true that many of the finest specimens of these extinct monsters, as well as those of the post tertiary period, have been found in the United States. The badlands of Arizona and the cretaceous rocks of the State of Kansas are specially prolific in the production of skeletons of the extinct saurians, while the bones of the mastodon and other monsters of the tertiary period are scattered all over this country. Our conclusions may be summed up in a few words, as follows:

First. The Indians appeared upon this continent before the extinction of the huge reptiles and saurians of the mesozoic age.

Second. That among the still existing saurians or reptiles when the Indians appeared was one huge monster that could walk, run, fly and swim, known to the Indians as the Piasa whose bones have been found and reconstructed into the saurian, or reptile, known to science as the ramphorhyncus. The best specimens of the anatomy of the ramphorhyncus ever found was lately discovered by Prof. Marsh in Kansas.

Third. That this saurian or reptile was of immense size, great strength and voracious appetite with decidedly cannibal propensities, and feasted upon Indian flesh.

Fourth. That these petroglyphs were made by the Indians many centuries after the extinction of these monsters as a means of preserving and refreshing their tradition; or, in other words, their tradition was a very old one while these petroglyphs were comparatively of recent date and made by persons who never saw the Piasa, but made them to correspond with the descriptions given in their tradition.

And lastly the manifest similarity and close analogy between the noble, patriotic and heroic conduct of this great Indian chief, Ouatogo, in offering himself as the victim of the dread Piasa to save his nation from utter destruction and annihilation upon the banks of the majestic Mississippi to that of the Chief of all Chieftains, Immanuel, in offering up his young life upon the cross on Mount Calvary, as a sacrifice and propitiation for the sins of the world, is such as to attract our special wonder, while the simple but beautiful faith of these sons of the forest in the loving kindness and ever watchful care of an all-over-ruling power, as expressed in the few words:

"The Great Spirit held an invisible shield over Ouatogo which protected him from the talons of the monster and the arrows of his men," challenges our admiration. Thus in the character of Ouatogo do we see a type and symbol of "the Lamb of God that taketh away the sin of the world."

THE END

A TRYAL OF WITCHES

John Russel Smith, 1839

TRYAL OF WITCHES AT THE ASSIZES

TO THE READER

This Tryal of Witches hath lain a long time in a private Gentleman's hands in the Country, it being given to him by the Person that took it in the Court for his own satisfaction, but it came lately to my hands, and having perused it, I found it a very remarkable thing, and fit to be Publish'd; especially in these times, wherein things of this nature are so much controverted, and that by persons of much Learning on both sides. I thought that so exact a relation of this Tryal would probably give more satisfaction to a great many persons, by reason that it is pure Matter of Fact, and that evidently Demonstrated; than the Arguments and Reasons of other very Learned Men, that probably may not be so Intelligible to all Readers; especially, this being held before a Judge, whom for his Integrity, Learning, and Law, hardly any Age, either before or since could parallel; who not only took a great deal of pains, and spent much time in this Tryal himself; but had the Assistance and Opinion of several other very Eminent and Learned Persons; So that this being the most perfect Narrative of any thing of this Nature hitherto Extant, made me unwilling to deprive the World of the Benefit of it; which is the sole Motive that induced me to Publish it.

FAREWELL:
London, 1682.

DEMONOLOGY

A TRYAL OF WITCHES

At the Assizes and General Gaol delivery, held at Bury St. Edmonds for the County of Suffolk, the Tenth day of March, in the Sixteenth Year of the Reign of our Sovereign Lord King Charles II. before Matthew Hale, Knight, Lord Chief Baron of His Majesties Court of Exchequer; Rose Cullender and Amy Duny, Widows, both of Leystoff, in the County aforesaid, were severally indicted for Bewitching Elizabeth and Ann Durent, Jane Booking, Susan Chandler, William Durent, Elizabeth and Deborah Pacy:

And the said Cullender and Duny, being arraigned upon the said Indictments, pleaded Not Guilty: And afterwards, upon a long Evidence, were found GUILTY, and thereupon had Judgment to DYE for the same.

The Evidence whereupon these Persons were convicted of Witchcraft, stands upon divers particular Circumstances.

I: THREE of the Parties above-named, viz. Ann Durent, Susan Chandler, and Elizabeth Pacy, were brought to Bury to the Assizes and were in a reasonable good condition: But that Morning they came into the Hall to give Instructions for the drawing of their Bills of Indictments, the Three Persons fell into strange and violent fits, screeching out in a most sad manner, so that they could not in any wise give any Instructions in the Court who were the Cause of their Distemper. And although they did after some certain space recover out of their fits, yet they were every one of them struck Dumb, so that none of them could speak neither at that time, nor during the Assizes until the Conviction of the supposed Witches.

As concerning William Durent, being an Infant, his Mother Dorothy Durent sworn and examined deposed in open Court, That about the Tenth of March, Nono Caroli Secundi, she having a special occasion to go from home, and having none in her House to take care of her said Child (it then sucking) desired Amy Duny her Neighbour, to look to her Child during her absence, for which she promised her to give her a Penny; but the said Dorothy Durent desired the said Amy not to Suckle her Child, and laid a great charge upon her not to do it. Upon which it was asked by the Court, why she did give that direction, she being an old Woman and not capable of giving Suck? It was answered by the said Dorothy Durent, that she very well knew that she did not give Suck, but that for some years before, she had gone under the reputation of a Witch, which was one cause made her give her the caution: Another was, That it was customary with old Women, that if they did look after a sucking Child, and nothing would please it but the Breast, they did use to please the Child to give it the Breast, and it did please the Child, but it sucked nothing but Wind, which did the Child hurt. Nevertheless after the departure of this Deponent, the said Amy did Suckle the Child: And after the return of the said Dorothy, the said Amy did acquaint her, that she had given Suck to the Child contrary to her command. Whereupon, the Deponent was very angry with the said Amy for the same; at which the said Amy was much discontented, and used many high Expressions and Threatening Speeches towards her; telling her, That she had as good to have done otherwise than to have found fault with her, and so departed out of her House: And that very Night her Son fell into strange fits of swounding, and was held in such terrible manner, that she was much affrighted therewith, and so continued for divers weeks. And the said Examinant farther said, that she being exceedingly troubled at her Childs Distemper, did go to a certain Person named Doctor Jacob, who lived at Yarmouth, who had the reputation in the Country, to help children that were Bewitch'd; who advis'd her to hang up the Childs Blanket in the Chimney-corner all day, and at night when she put the Child to Bed, to put it into the said blanket, and if she found anything in it, she should not be afraid, but to throw it into the Fire. And this Deponent did according to his direction; and at night when she took down the Blanket with an intent to put her Child therein, there fell out of the same a great Toad, which ran up and down the hearth, and she having a young youth only with her in the House, desired him to catch the Toad, and throw it into the Fire, which the youth did accordingly, and held it there with the Tongs; and as soon as it was in the Fire it made a great and horrible Noise, and after a space there was a flashing in the Fire like Gun-powder, making a noise like the discharge of a Pistol, and thereupon the Toad was no more seen nor heard. It was asked by the Court, if that after the noise and flashing, there was not the Substance of the Toad to be seen to consume in the fire? And it was answered by the said Dorothy Durent, that after the flashing and noise, there was no more seen than if there had been none there. The next day there came a young Woman a Kinswoman of the said Amy, and a neighbour of this Deponent, and told this Deponent, that her Aunt (meaning the said Amy) was in a most lamentable condition having her face all scorched with fire, and that she was sitting alone in her House, in her smock without any fire. And thereupon this Deponent went into the House of the said Amy Duny to see her, and found her in the same condition as was related to her; for her Face, her Leggs, and Thighs, which this Deponent saw, seemed very much scorched and burnt with Fire, at which this Deponent seemed much to wonder. And asked the said Amy how she came into that sad condition? and the said Amy replied, she might thank her for it, for that she this Deponent was the cause thereof, but that she should live to see some of her Children dead, and she upon Crutches. And this Deponent farther saith, that after the burning of the said Toad, her Child recover'd, and was well again, and was living at the time of the Assizes. And this Deponent farther saith, That about the 6th. of March, 11° *Car.* 2. her Daughter Elizabeth Durent, being about the Age of Ten Years, was taken in like manner as her first Child was, and in her fits complained much of Amy Duny, and said, That she did appear to her, and Afflict her in such manner as the former. And she this Deponent going to the Apothecaries for some thing for her said Child, when she did return to her own House, she found the said Amy Duny there, and asked her what she did do there? and her answer was, That she came to see her Child, and to give it some water. But she this Deponent was very angry with her, and thrust her forth of her doors, and when she was out of doors, she said, You need not be so angry, for your Child will not live long: and this was on a Saturday, and the Child dyed on the Monday following. The cause of whose Death this Deponent verily believeth was occasion'd by the Witchcraft of the said Amy Duny; for that the said Amy hath been long reputed to be a Witch, and a person of very evil behaviour, whose Kindred and Relations have been many of them accused for Witchcraft, and some of them have been Condemned.

The said Deponent further saith, that not long after the death of her Daughter Elizabeth Durent, she this Deponent was taken with a Lameness in both her Leggs, from the knees downward, that she was fain to go upon Crutches, and that she had no other use of them but only to bear a little upon them till she did remove her Crutches, and so continued till the time of the Assizes, that the Witch came to be Tryed, and was there upon her Crutches; the Court asked her, That at the time she was taken with this Lameness, if it were with her according to the Custom of Women? Her Answer was, that it was so, and that she never had any stoppages of those things, but when she was with Child.

This is the Substance of her Evidence to this Indictment. There was one thing very remarkable, that after she had gone upon Crutches for upwards of Three Years, and went upon them at the time of the Assizes in the Court when she gave her Evidence, and upon the Juries bringing in their Verdict, by which the said Amy Duny was found Guilty, to the great admiration of all Persons, the said Dorothy Durent was restored to the use of her Limbs, and went home without making use of her Crutches.

II: As concerning Elizabeth and Deborah Pacy, the first

DEMONOLOGY

of the Age of Eleven Years, the other of the age of Nine Years or thereabouts; as to the Elder, she was brought into the Court at the time of the Instructions given to draw up the Indictments, and afterwards at the time of Tryal of the said Prisoners, but could not speak one Word all the time, and for the most part she remained as one wholly senseless as one in a deep Sleep, and could move no part of her body, and all the Motion of Life that appeared in her was, that as she lay upon Cushions in the Court upon her back, her stomach and belly by the drawing of her breath, would arise to a great height; and after the said Elizabeth had lain a long time on the Table in the Court, she came a little to her self and sate up, but could neither see nor speak, but was sensible of what was said to her, and after a while she laid her Head on the Bar of the Court with a Cushion under it, and her hand and her Apron upon that, and there she lay a good space of time, and by the direction of the Judge, Amy Duny was privately brought to Elizabeth Pacy, and she touched her hand; whereupon the Child without so much as seeing her, for her Eyes were closed all the while, suddenly leaped up, and catched Amy Duny by the hand, and afterwards by the face; and with her Nails scratched her till Blood came, and would by no means leave her till she was taken from her, and afterwards the Child would still be pressing towards her, and making signs of Anger conceived against her.

Deborah the younger Daughter was held in such extream manner, that her Parents wholly despaired of her life, and therefore could not bring her to the Assizes. The Evidence which was given concerning these Two Children was to this Effect:

SAMUEL PACY a Merchant of Leystoff aforesaid, (a man who carried himself with much soberness during the Tryal, from whom proceeded no words either of Passion or Malice, though his Children were so greatly Afflicted,) Sworn and Examined, Deposeth, That his younger Daughter Deborah, upon Thursday the Tenth of October last, was suddenly taken with a

DEMONOLOGY

Lameness in her Leggs, so that she could not stand, neither had she any strength in her Limbs to support her, and so she continued until the Seventeenth day of the same Month, which day being fair and Sunshiny, the Child desired to be carryed on the East part of the House, to be set upon the Bank which looketh upon the Sea; and whil'st she was sitting there, Amy Duny came to this Deponents House to buy some Herrings, but being denyed she went away discontented, and presently returned again, and was denyed, and likwise the third time and was denyed as at first; and at her last going away, she went away grumbling; but what she said was not perfectly understood. But at the very same instant of time, the said Child was taken with most violent fits, feeling most extream pain in her Stomach, like the pricking of Pins, and Shreeking out in a most dreadful manner, like unto a Whelp, and not like unto a sensible Creature. And in this extremity the Child continued to the great grief of the Parents until the Thirtieth of the same Month. During this time this Deponent sent for one Dr. Feavor, a Doctor of Physick, to take his advice concerning his Childs Distemper; the Doctor being come, he saw the Child in those fits, but could not conjecture (as he then told this Deponent, and afterwards affirmed in open Court, at this Tryal) what might be the cause of the Childs Affliction. And this Deponent farther saith, That by reason of the circumstances aforesaid, and in regard Amy Duny is a Woman of an ill Fame, and commonly reported to be a Witch and a Sorceress, and for that the said Child in her fits would cry out of Amy Duny as the cause of her Malady, and that she did affright her with Apparitions of her Person (as the Child in the intervals of her fits related) he this Deponent did suspect the said Amy Duny for a Witch, and charged her with the injury and wrong to his Child, and caused her to be set in the Stocks on the Twenty-eighth of the same October; and during the time of her continuance there, one Alice Letteridge and Jane Buxton demanding of her (as they also affirmed in Court upon their Oathes) what should be the reason of Mr. Pacy's Childs Distemper? telling her, That she was suspected to be the cause thereof; she replyed, Mr. Pacy keeps a great stir about his Child, but let him stay until he hath done as much by his Children, as I have done by mine. And being further examined, what she had done to her Children? She answered, That she had been fain to open her Child's Mouth with a Tap to give it Victuals.

And the said Deponent further deposeth, That within two days after speaking of the said words being the Thirtieth of October, the eldest Daughter Elizabeth, fell into extream fits, insomuch, that they could not open her Mouth to give her breath, to preserve her Life without the help of a Tap which they were enforced to use; and the younger Child was in the like manner Afflicted, so that they used the same also for her Relief. And further the said Children being grievously afflicted would severally complain in their extremity, and also in the intervals, That Amy Duny (together with one other Woman whose person and Cloathes they described) did thus Afflict them, their Apparitions appearing before them, to their great terrour and affrightment: And sometimes they would cry out, saying, There stands Amy Duny, and there Rose Cullender; the other Person troubling them.

Their fits were various, sometimes they would be lame on one side of their Bodies, sometimes on the other; sometimes a soreness over their whole Bodies, so as they could endure none to touch them; at other times they would be restored to the perfect use of their Limbs, and deprived of their Hearing; at other times of their Sight, at other times of their Speech sometimes by the space of one day, sometimes for two; and once they were wholly deprived of their Speech for Eight days together, and then restored to their Speech again. At other times they would fall into Swoundings, and upon the recovery to their Speech they would Cough extreamly, and bring up much phlegme, and with the same crooked Pins, and one time a Two-penny Nail with a very broad head, which Pins (amounting to Forty or more) together with the Two-penny Nail were produced in Court, with the affirmation of the said Deponent, that he was present when the said Nail was Vomited up, and also most of the Pins. Commonly at the end of every fit they would cast up a Pin, and sometimes they would have four or five fits in one day.

In this manner the said Children continued with this Deponent for the space of two Months, during which time in their Intervals this Deponent would cause them to Read some Chapters in the New Testament. Whereupon this Deponent several times observed, that they would read till they came to the Name of Lord, or Jesus, or Christ; and then before they could pronounce either of the said Words they would suddenly fall into their fits. But when they came to the Name of Satan, or Devil, they would clap their Fingers upon the Book, crying out, This bites, but makes me speak right well. At such time as they be recovered out of their fits (occasion'd as this Deponent conceives upon their naming of Lord, or Jesus, or Christ,) this Deponent hath demanded of them, what is the cause they cannot pronounce those words, They reply and say, That Amy Duny saith, I must not use that name. And farther, the said Children after their fits were past, would tell, how that Amy Duny, and Rose Cullender would appear before them, holding their Fists at them, threatning, That if they related either what they saw or heard, that they would Torment them Ten times more than ever they did before. In their fits they would cry out, There stands Amy Duny, or Rose Cullender; and sometimes in one place and sometimes in another, running with great violence to the place where they fancied them to stand, striking at them as if they present; they would appear to them sometimes spinning, and sometimes reeling, or in other postures, deriding or threatning them. And this Deponent farther saith, That his Children being thus Tormented by all the space aforesaid, and finding no hopes of amendment, he sent them to his Sisters House, one Margaret Arnold, who lived at Yarmouth, to make tryal, whether the change of the Air might do them any good. And how, and in what manner they were afterwards held, he this Deponent refers himself to the Testimony of his said Sister. Margaret Arnold, Sworn and Examined, saith, That the said Elizabeth and

DEMONOLOGY

Deborah Pacy came to her House about the Thirtieth of November last, her Brother acquainted her, that he thought they were Bewitch'd, for that they vomited Pins; and farther Informed her of the several passages which occurred at his own House. This Deponent said, that she gave no credit to that which was related to her, conceiving possibly the Children might use some deceit in putting Pins in their mouths themselves.

Wherefore this Deponent unpinned all their Cloathes, and left not so much as one Pin upon them, but sewed all the Cloathes they wore, instead of pinning of them. But this Deponent saith, that notwithstanding all this care and circumspection of hers, the Children afterwards raised at several times at least Thirty Pins in her presence, and had most fierce and violent Fitts upon them. The Children would in their Fitts cry out against Rose Cullender and Amy Duny, affirming that they saw them; and they threatned to Torment them Ten times more, if they complained of them. At some times the Children (only) would see things run up and down the House in the appearance of Mice; and one of them suddainly snapt one with the Tongs, and threw it into the fire, and it screeched out like a Rat. At another time, the younger Child being out of her Fitts went out of Doors to take a little fresh Air, and presently a little thing like a Bee flew upon her Face, and would have gone into her Mouth, whereupon the Child ran in all haste to the door to get into the House again, screeching out in a most terrible manner; whereupon, this Deponent made haste to come to her, but before she could get to her, the Child fell into her swooning Fitt, and at last with much pain straining herself, she vomitted up a Two-penny Nail with a broad Head; and after that the Child had raised up the Nail she came to her understanding; and being demanded by this Deponent, how she came by this Nail? she Answered, That the Bee brought this Nail and forced it into her Mouth.

And at other times, the Elder Child declared unto this Deponent, that during the time of her Fitts, she saw Flies come unto her, and bring with them in their Mouthes crooked Pins; and after the Child had thus declared the same, she fell again into violent Fits, and afterwards raised several Pins. At another time, the said Elder Child declared unto this Deponent, and sitting by the Fire suddainly started up and said, she saw a Mouse, and she crept under the Table looking after it, and at length, she put something in her Apron, saying, she had caught it; and immediately she ran to the Fire and threw it in, and there did appear upon it to this Deponent, like the flashing of Gunpowder, though she confessed she saw nothing in the Childs Hand.

At another time the said Child being speechless, but otherwise, of perfect understanding, ran round about the House holding her Apron, crying hush, hush, as if there had been Poultrey in the House; but this Deponent could perceive nothing: but at last she saw the Child stoop as if she had catch't at something, and put it into her Apron, and afterwards made as if she had thrown it into the Fire: but this Deponent could not discover any thing; but the Child afterwards being restored to her speech, she this Deponent demanded of her what she saw at the time she used such a posture? Who answered, That she saw a Duck.

At another time, the Younger daughter being recovered out of her Fitts, declared, That Amy Duny had been with her, and that she tempted her to Drown her self, and to cut her Throat, or otherwise to Destroy herself. At another time, in their Fitts they both of them cryed out upon Rose Cullender and Amy Duny, complaining against them; Why do you not come your selves, but send your Imps to Torment us?

These several passages as most remarkable, the said Deponent did particularly set down as they daily happen'd, and for the reasons aforesaid, she doth verily believe in her conscience, that the Children were bewitched, and by the said Amy Duny, and Rose Cullender; though at first she could hardly

DEMONOLOGY

be induced to believe it.

As concerning Ann Durent, one other of the Parties, supposed to be bewitched, present in Court. Edmund Durent her Father Sworn and Examined; said, That he also lived in the said Town of Leystoff, and that the said Rose Cullender, about the latter end of November last, came into this Deponents House to buy some Herrings of his Wife, but being denyed by her, the said Rose returned in a discontented manner; and upon the first of December after, his Daughter Ann Durent was very sorely Afflicted in her Stomach, and felt great pain, like the pricking of Pins, and then fell into swooning fitts, and after the recovery from her Fitts, she declared, That she had seen the Apparition of the said Rose, who threatned to Torment her. In this manner she continued from the first of December, until this present time of Tryal; having likewise vomited up divers Pins (produced here in Court.) This Maid was present in Court, but could not speak to declare her knowledge, but fell into most violent fits when she was brought before Rose Cullender. Ann Baldwin Sworn and Examined, Deposeth the same thing as touching the Bewitching of the said Ann Durent.

As concerning Jane Booking who was so weak, she could not be brought to the Assizes:

Diana Booking Sworn and Examined, Deposed, That she lived in the same Town of Leystoff, and that her said Daughter having been formerly Afflicted with swooning fitts, recovered well of them, and so continued for a certain time; and upon the First of February last, she was taken also with great pain in her Stomach, like pricking with Pins; and afterwards fell into swooning fitts and so continued till the Deponents coming to the Assizes, having during the same time taken little or no food, but daily vomiting crooked Pins; and upon Sunday last raised Seven Pins. And whilst her fits were upon her she would spread forth her Arms with her hands open, and use postures as if she catched at something, and would instantly close her hands again; which being immediatly forced open, they found several Pins diversly crooked, but could neither see nor perceive how or in what manner they were conveyed thither. At another time, the same Jane being in another of her fitts, talked as if she were discoursing with some persons in the Room, (though she would give no answer nor seem to take notice of any person then present) and would in like manner cast abroad her Arms, saying, I will not have it, I will not have it; and at last she said, Then I will have it, and so waving her Arm with her hand open, she would presently close the same, which instantly forced open, they found in it a Lath-Nail. In her Fitts she would frequently complain of Rose Cullender and Amy Duny, saying, That now she saw Rose Cullender standing at the Beds feet, and another time at the Beds head, and so in other places. At last she was stricken Dumb and could not speak one Word, though her fitts were not upon her, and so she continued for some days, and at last her speech came to her again, and she desired her Mother to get her some Meat; and being demanded the reason why she could not speak in so long time? She answered, That Amy Duny would not suffer her to speak. This Lath-Nail, and divers of the Pins were produced in Court.

As concerning Susan Chandler, one other of the Parties supposed to be Bewitched and present in Court. Mary Chandler Mother of the said Susan, Sworn and Examined, Deposed and said, That about the beginning of February last past, the said Rose Cullender and Amy Duny were Charged by Mr. Samuel Pacy for Bewitching of his Daughters. And a Warrant being granted at the request of the said Mr. Pacy, by Sir Edmund Bacon, Baronet, one of the Justices of the Peace for the County of Suffolk, to bring them before him, and they being brought before him were Examined, and Confessed nothing. He gave order that they should be searched; whereupon this Deponent with five others were appointed to do the same; and coming to the House of Rose Cullender, they did acquaint her with what they were come about, and asked whether she was contented that they should search her? She did not oppose it, whereupon they began at her Head, and so stript her naked, and in the lower part of her Belly they found a thing like a Teat of an Inch long, they questioned her about it, and she said, That she had got a strain by carrying of water which caused that Excrescence. But upon narrower search, they found in her Privy Parts three more Excrescences or Teats, but smaller than the former: This Deponent farther saith, That in the long Teat at the end thereof there was a little hole, and it appeared unto them as if it had been lately sucked, and upon the straining of it there issued out white milkie Matter.

And this Deponent farther saith, That her said Daughter (being of the Age of Eighteen Years) was then in Service in the said Town of Leystoff, and rising up early the next Morning to Wash, this Rose Cullender appeared to her, and took her by the hand, whereat she was much affrighted, and went forthwith to her Mother, (being in the same town) and acquainted her with what she had seen; but being extreamly terrified, she fell extream sick, much grieved at her Stomach; and that Night after being in Bed with another young Woman, she suddenly shrieked out, and fell into such extream fits as if she were distracted, crying against Rose Cullender; saying, she would come to bed to her. She continued in this manner beating and wearing her self, insomuch, that this Deponent was glad to get help to attend her. In her Intervals she would declare, That some time she saw Rose Cullender, at another time with a great Dog with he: She also vomited up divers crooked Pins; and sometimes she was stricken with blindness, and at another time she was Dumb, and so she appeared to be in Court when the Tryal of the Prisoners was ; for she was not able to speak her knowledge; but being brought into the Court at the Tryal, she suddenly fell into her fits, and being carryed out of the Court again, within the space of half an hour she came to her self and recovered her speech, and thereupon was immediatly brought into the Court, and asked by the Court, whether she was in condition to take an Oath, and to give Evidence, she said she could. But when she was Sworn, and asked what she could say against either of the

DEMONOLOGY

Prisoners? before she could make any answer, she fell into her fits, shrieking out in a miserable manner, crying Burn her, burn her, which were all the Words she could speak.

Robert Chandler, father of the said Susan, gave in the same Evidence, that his Wife Mary Chandler had given; only as to the searching of Rose Cullender as aforesaid. This was the sum and Substance of the Evidence which was given against the Prisoners concerning the Bewitching of the Children before mentioned. At the hearing this Evidence there were divers known persons, as Mr. Serjeant Keeling, Mr. Serjeant Earl, and Mr. Serjeant Bernard, present. Mr. Serjeant Keeling seemed much unsatisfied with it, and thought it not sufficient to Convict the Prisoners: for admitting that the Children were in Truth Bewitched, yet said he, it can never be applyed to the Prisoners, upon the Imagination only of the Parties Afflicted; For if that might be allowed, no person whatsoever can be in safety, for perhaps they might fancy another person, who might altogether be innocent in such matters.

There was also Dr. Brown of Norwich, a Person of great knowledge; who after this Evidence given, and upon view of the three persons in Court, was desired to give his Opinion, what he did conceive of them; and he was clearly of Opinion, that the persons were Bewitched; and said, That in Denmark there had been lately a great Discovery of Witches, who used the very same way of Afflicting Persons, by conveying Pins into them, and crooked as these Pins were, with Needles and Nails. And his Opinion was, That the Devil in such cases did work upon the Bodies of Men and Women, upon a Natural Foundation, (that is) to stir up and excite such humours superabounding in their Bodies to a great excess, whereby he did in an extraordinary manner Afflict them with such Distempers as their Bodies were most subject to, as particularly appeared in these Children; for he conceived, that these swooning Fits were Natural, and nothing else but that they call the Mother, but only heightned to a great excess by the subtilty of the Devil, co-operating with the

DEMONOLOGY

Malice of these which we term Witches, at whose Instance he doth these Villanies.

Besides the particulars above-mention'd touching the said persons Bewitched, there were many other things Objected against them for a further proof and manifestation that the said Children were Bewitched. As First, during the time of the Tryal, there were some experiments made with the Persons Afflicted, by bringing the Persons to touch them; and it was observed, that when they were in the midst of their Fitts, to all Mens apprehension wholly deprived of all sense and understanding, closing their Fists in such manner, as that the strongest Man in the Court could not force them open; yet by the least touch of one of these supposed Witches, Rose Cullender by Name, they would suddenly shriek out opening their hands, which accident would not happen by the touch of any other person.

And least they might privately see when they were touched, by the said Rose Cullender, they were blinded with their own Aprons, and the touching took the same Effect as before. There was an ingenious person that objected, there might be a great fallacy in this experiment, and there ought not to be any stress put upon this to Convict the Parties, for the Children might counterfeit this their Distemper, and perceiving what was done to them, they might in such manner suddenly alter the motion and gesture of their Bodies, on purpose to induce persons to believe that they were not natural, but wrought strangely by the touch of the Prisoners. Wherefore to avoid this scruple it was privately desired by the Judge, that the Lord Cornwallis, Sir Edmund Bacon, and Mr. Serjeant Keeling, and some other Gentlemen there in Court, would attend one of the Distempered persons in the farther part of the Hall, whilst she was in her fits, and then to send for one of the Witches, to try what would then happen, which they did accordingly; and Amy Duny was conveyed from the Bar and brought to the Maid: they put an Apron before her Eyes, and then one other person touched her hand, which produced the same effect as the touch of the Witch did in the Court. Whereupon the Gentlemen returned, openly protesting, that they did believe the whole transaction of this business was a meer imposture.

This put the Court and all persons into a stand. But at length Mr. Pacy did declare, That possibly the Maid might be deceived by a suspition that the Witch touched her when she did not. For he had observed divers times, that although they could not speak, but were deprived of the use of their Tongues and Limbs, that their understandings were perfect, for that they have related divers things which have been when they were in their fits, after they were recovered out of them. This saying of Mr. Pacy was found to be true afterwards, when his Daughter was fully recovered (as she afterwards was) as shall in due time be related- For she was asked, whither she did hear and understand any thing that was done and acted in the Court, during the time that she lay as one deprived of her understanding? and she said, she did; and by the Opinions of some, this experiment, (which others would have a Fallacy) was rather a confirmation that the Parties were really Bewitched, than otherwise; for say they, it is not possible that any should counterfeit such Distempers, being accompanied with such various Circumstances, much less Children; and for so long time, and yet undiscovered by their Parents and Relations: For no man can suppose that they should all Conspire together, (being out of several families, and, as they Affirm, no way related one to the other, and scarce of familiar acquaintance) to do an Act of this nature whereby no benefit or advantage could redound to any of the Parties, but a guilty Conscience for Perjuring themselves in taking the Lives of two poor simple Women away, and there appears no Malice in the Case. For the Prisoners themselves did scarce so much as Object it. Wherefore, say they, it is very evident that the Parties were Bewitched, and that when they apprehend or understand by any means, that the persons who have done them this wrong are near, or touch them; then their spirits being more than ordinarily moved with rage and anger at them being present, they do use more violent gestures of their Bodies, and extend forth their hands, as desirous to lay hold upon them; which at other times not having the same occasion, the instance there falls not out the same.

21y: One John Soam of Leystoff aforesaid, Yeoman, a sufficient Person, Deposeth, That not long since, in harvest time he had three Carts which brought home his Harvest, and as they were going into the Field to load, one of the Carts wrenched the Window of Rose Cullenders House, whereupon she came out in a great rage and threatned this Deponent for doing that wrong, and so they passed along into the Fields and loaded all the Three Carts, the other two Carts returned safe home, and back again, twice loaded that day afterwards; but as to this Cart which touched Rose Cullenders House, after it was loaded, it was overturned twice or thrice that day; and after that they had loaded it again the second or third time, as they brought it through the Gate which leadeth out of the Field into the Town, the Cart stuck so fast in the Gateshead, that they could not possibly get it through, but were inforced to cut down the Post of the Gate to make the Cart pass through, although they could not perceive that the Cart did of either side touch the Gate-posts. And this Deponent further saith, That after they had got it through the Gate-way, they did with much difficulty get it home into the Yard; but for all that they could do, they could not get the Cart near unto the place where they should unload the Corn, but were fain to unload it at a great distance from the place, and when they began to unload they found much difficulty therein, it being so hard a labour that they were tired that first came; and when others came to assist them, their Noses burst forth a bleeding: so they were fain to desist and leave it until the next Morning, and then they unloaded it without any difficulty at all. Robert Sherringham also Deposeth against Rose Cullender, that about Two Years since, passing along the Street with his Cart and Horses, the Axletree of his Cart touched her House, and broke down some part of it, at which, she was very much displeased, threatning him, that his Horses should suffer for it; and so it happen'd, for all those Horses, being Four in Number,

DEMONOLOGY

died within a short time after: since that time he hath had great Losses by the suddain dying of his other Cattle; so soon as his Sows pigged, the Pigs would leap and caper, and immediately fall down and dye. Also, not long after, he was taken with a Lameness in his Limbs that he could neither go nor stand for some days. After all this, he was very much vexed with great Number of Lice of an extraordinary bigness, and although he many times shifted himself, yet he was not any thing the better, but would swarm again with them; so that in the Conclusion he was forc'd to burn all his Clothes, being two suits of Apparel, and then was clean from them.

As concerning Amy Duny, one Richard Spencer Deposeth, That about the first of September last, he heard her say at his House, That the Devil would not let her rest until she were Revenged on one Cornelius Sandeswell's Wife. Ann Sandeswell, Wife unto the above-said Cornelius, Deposed, That about Seven or Eight Years since, she having bought a certain number of Geese, meeting with Amy Duny, she told her, If she did not fetch her Geese home they would all be Destroyed; which in a few days after came to pass. Afterwards the said Amy became Tenant to this Deponents Husband for a House, who told her, That if she looked not well to such a Chimney in her House, that the same would fall: Whereupon this Deponent replyed, That it was a new one; but not minding much her Words, at that time they parted. But in a short time the Chimney fell down according as the said Amy had said. Also this Deponent farther saith, That her Brother being a Fisherman, and using to go into the Northern Seas, she desired him to send her a Firkin of Fish, which he did accordingly; and she having notice that the said Firkin was brought into Leystoff-Road, she desired a Boatman to bring it ashore with the other Goods they were to bring; and she going down to meet the Boat-man to receive her Fish, desired the said Amy to go along with her to help her home with it; Amy Replyed, She would go when she had it. And thereupon this Deponent went to the Shoar without her, and demanded of the Boat-man the Firkin, they told her, That they

DEMONOLOGY

could not keep it in the Boat from falling into the Sea, and they thought it was gone to the Devil, for they never saw the like before. And being demanded by this Deponent, whether any other Goods in the Boat were likewise lost as well as hers? They answered, Not any. This was the substance of the whole Evidence given against the Prisoners at the Bar; who being demanded what they had to say for themselves? They replyed, Nothing material to any thing that was proved against them. Whereupon the Judge in giving his direction to the Jury, told them, That he would not repeat the Evidence unto them, least by so doing he should wrong the Evidence on the one side or on the other. Only this acquainted them, That they had Two things to inquire after. First, Whether or no these Children were Bewitched?

Secondly, Whether the Prisoners at the Bar were Guilty of it? That there were such Creatures as Witches he made no doubt at all; For First, the Scriptures had affirmed so much. Secondly, The wisdom of all Nations had provided Laws against such Persons, which is an Argument of their confidence of such a Crime. And such hath been the judgment of this Kingdom, as appears by that Act of Parliament which hath provided Punishments proportionable to the quality of the Offence. And desired them, strictly to observe their Evidence; and desired the great God of Heaven to direct their Hearts in this weighty thing they had in hand: For to Condemn the Innocent, and to let the Guilty go free, were both an Abomination to the Lord.

With this short Direction the Jury departed from the Bar, and within the space of half an hour returned, and brought them in both GUILTY upon the several Indictments, which were Thirteen in Number, whereupon they stood Indicted. This was upon Thursday in the Afternoon, March 13, 1664. The next Morning, the Three Children with their Parents came to the Lord Chief Baron Hale's Lodging, who all of them spake perfectly, and were as in good Health as ever they were; only Susan Chandler, by reason of her very much Affliction, did look

DEMONOLOGY

very thin and wan. And their friends were asked, At what time they were restored thus to their Speech and Health?

And Mr. Pacy did Affirm, That within less than half an hour after the Witches were Convicted, they were all of them Restored, and slept well that Night, feeling no pain; only Susan Chandler felt a pain like pricking of Pins in her Stomach. After, they were all of them brought down to the Court, but Ann Durent was so fearful to behold them, that she desired she might not see them. The other Two continued in the Court, and they Affirmed in the face of the Country, and before the Witches themselves, what before hath been Deposed by their Friends and Relations; the Prisoners not much contradicting them. In Conclusion, the Judge and all the Court were fully satisfied with the Verdict, and thereupon gave Judgment against the Witches that they should be Hanged. They were much urged to confess, but would not. That morning we departed for Cambridge, but no Reprieve was granted: And they were Executed on Monday, the Seventeenth of March following, but they Confessed nothing.

END OF THE TRIAL

APPENDIX

A Witch, according to old descriptions, was generally blessed with a "wrinkled face, a furred brow, a hairy lip, a gobber tooth, a squint eye, a squeaking voice, a scolding tongue, a ragged coat on her back, a scull-cap on her head, a spindle in her hand, and a dog or cat by her side;" and Lord Coke pithily describes a "Witch to be a person that hath conference with the devil, to consult with him or to do some act." In former times the most eminent men and philosophers (Sir Thomas Brown for instance) were not proof against the prevailing opinions. A modern writer observes, that one would imagine that the establishment of Protestanism would have conduced to the abolition of this lamentable and pernicious credulity. But the Reformation did not arrive with great rapidity at its full extent,

DEMONOLOGY

and the belief in Witchcraft long continued to "overspread the land." Indeed it has been proved by Hutchinson, in his Essay on Witchcraft, that the change of religion at first rather augmented than diminished the evil.

A degree of importance, hardly credible in these times, was attached to it; and in the sixteenth century the unbelievers were accounted "Sadducees, Atheists, and Infidels!" One of the most eminent divines of the day, a strenuous advocate in the belief of Witchcraft, characterizes them thus in the most forcible language! It is not surprising, therefore, that the supposed dabblers in the infernal art were hunted out and exposed to the most dreadful cruelty and oppression, not only from those who imagined they had suffered under their charms, but from the very laws of the realm also. The first trial of any note took place in 1593. Three persons, old Samuel and his wife and daughter Agnes, were condemned at Huntingdon, before Mr. Justice Fenner, for bewitching a Mr. Throgmorton's family, etc. A few years after, an advocate for this belief appeared from no less a quarter than the throne itself. King James I. in his *Demonologie*, completely superseded Reginald Scot's *Discoverie of Witchcraft*, a work which completely unmasked the whole machinery, and was a storehouse of facts on the subject. The infection, commenced at the throne, soon reached the Parliament, and (as it has been observed the greatest part of mankind have no other reason for their opinions than that they are in fashion) a statute was passed in the first year of King James, having for its object, as expressed in the preamble, "the more effectual punishment of those detestable slaves of the devil, witches, sorcerers, enchanters, and conjurers." The punishment was enacted to be the pillory for the first offense (even though its object were not effected) and death for the second. "Thus was the detestable doctrine established both by law and fashion, and it became not only unpolite but criminal to doubt it; and, as prodigies are always seen in proportion as they are expected, witches were every day discovered, and multiplied so fast in some places, that Bishop Hall mentions a village in

DEMONOLOGY

Lancashire where their number was greater than that of the houses." There was dreadful havoc in that county after this law had passed. Lancashire has always been remarkable for the number of its witches. Though the information we have to go upon cannot, of course, be considered as very accurate, yet it has been ascertained that between the commencement of the statute in question (1602) and the year 1701, in the space of one century, 3192 persons were executed for the crimes of Witchcraft and Sorcery! The act alluded to was rigorously enforced during this period, and the above calculation is probably under the mark, and does not include the numbers that were tried on suspicion, but acquitted for want of sufficient proof of the charges alleged against them.

WITCHCRAFT IN SUFFOLK: In 1644, one Matthew Hopkins, of Manningtree, in Essex, who styled himself Witch-finder General and had 20s. allowed him for every town he visited, was, with some others, commissioned by Parliament to perform a circuit for the discovery of witches, during this and the two following years. Thus authorized, they went from place to place, through many parts of Suffolk, Norfolk, and Huntingdonshire; but what appears still more astonishing, they caused 16 persons to be hanged at Yarmouth, 40 at Bury, and others in different parts of the county to the amount of 60 persons! Butler, in his *Hudibras*, alludes to this when he makes his hero say:

> "Has not this present Parliament
> A ledger to the devil sent,
> Fully empowered to treat about
> Finding revolted witches out?
> And has not he within one year
> Hang'd threescore of them in a shire?"

A Mr. Lowes, an innocent and aged clergyman, vicar of Brandeston, was among the victims sacrificed by this impostor and his associates. A cooper and his wife, and fifteen other women, were by the same influence all condemned and executed at one time at Bury! Besides the arts used by Hopkins to extort confession from suspected persons, he had recourse to swimming them; which was done by tying their thumbs and great toes together, previously to throwing them into the water : if they sunk it was a proof of their innocence, but if they floated they were guilty. This method he pursued till some gentlemen, indignant at his barbarity, tied his own thumbs and toes, as he had been accustomed to tie those of other persons, and when put into the water, he himself swam, as many others had done before him. By this expedient the country was cleared of him. Hudibras alludes to this when, speaking of Hopkins, he says:

> "Who after proved himself a witch,
> And made a rod for his own breech."

The following curious Letter is copied from a manuscript in the British Museum:

"From Mr. Manning, Dissenting Teacher, at Halstead, in Essex, to John Morley, Esq., Halstead.

Halstead, Aug. 2, 1732.

Sir- The narrative which I gave you in relation to witchcraft, and which you are pleased to lay your commands upon me to repeat, is as follows; There was one master Collett, a smith by trade, of Haveningham, in the County of Suffolk, who, as 'twas customary with him, assisting the maide to churne, and not being able (as the phrase is) to make the butter come, threw a hot iron into the churn, under the notion of witchcraft in the case, upon which a poore labourer, then employed in carrying of dung in the yard, cried out in a terrible manner, 'they have killed me, they have killed me;' still keeping his hand upon his back, intimating where the pain was, and died upon the spot.

DEMONOLOGY

Mr. Collett, with the rest of the servants then present, took off the poor man's clothes, and found to their great surprise, the mark of the iron that was heated and thrown into the churn, deeply impressed upon his back. This account I had from Mr. Collett's own mouth, who being a man of unblemished character, I verily believe to be matter of fact.

I am, Sir, your obliged humble servant, SAM. MANNING."

An old gentleman, who died at Polstead, in Suffolk, some years ago, lamented till his death a sight he had lost when a boy, only for the want of five pounds; a man having undertaken for that sum to make all the witches in the parish dance on the knoll together; and though he grew up a penurious man, and lived a bachelor till fifty, he never ceased to lament that such an opportunity of seeing these weird-sisters collected together, never occurred again. He used to say he had seen a witch swam on Polstead Ponds, and "she went over the water like a cork." He had, when a boy, stopped a wizard on his way to Stoke, by laying a line of single straws across the path; and, concealed in a hedge, he had watched an old woman (alias witch) feeding her imps in the form of three blackbirds.

Witch-finding at Newcastle: Mention occurs of a petition in the common council books of Newcastle, dated March 26th, 1649, and signed, no doubt, by the inhabitants, concerning witches, the purport of which appears, from what followed, to have occasioned all such persons as were suspected, to be apprehended and brought to trial. In consequence of this, the magistrates sent two of their sergeants into Scotland, to agree with a Scotchman, who pretended knowledge to find out witches by pricking them with pins, to come to Newcastle, where he should try such as should be brought to him, and have twenty shillings a-piece for all he should condemn as witches, and free passage thither and back. When the Sergeants brought the witch-finder on horseback to

DEMONOLOGY

town, the magistrates sent their bellman through the town, ringing his bell and crying, all people that would bring in any complaint against any woman for a witch, they should be sent for, and tried by the person appointed. Thirty women were brought into the Town Hall, and had pins thrust into their flesh, and most of them were found guilty.- It appears by an extract from the registry of the parochial chapelry of St. Andrews, in Scotland, that one man and fifteen women were executed at Newcastle for witchcraft; and there is a print of this horrid execution in Gardner's England's Grievance Discovered, 1655, reprinted at Newcastle, 1796.- When the witch-finder had done in Newcastle, and received his wages, he went into Northumberland, to try women there, and got £3. a-piece; but Henry Ogle, Esq., laid hold on him, and required bond of him, to
answer at the sessions. He escaped into Scotland, where he was made prisoner, indicted, arraigned, and condemned for such-like villainy exercised in Scotland, and confessed at the gallows that he had been the death of above 220 women in England and Scotland, for the gain of 20s. A-piece!- Sykes's Local Records.

WITCHCRAFT IN LANCASHIRE: In 1634, seventeen Pendleforest witches were condemned in Lancashire, by the infamous contrivances of a boy only eleven years of age, and his father. Among other charges equally wonderful and miraculous, this little villain deposed that a greyhound was transformed by their agency into "one Dickenson's wife," etc. These poor creatures, however, obtained a reprieve, and were sent to London, where they first viewed and examined by his majesty's physicians and surgeons, and then by "his majesty himself and the council."

The result was that the boy's contrivances were exposed and properly punished. In 1664, Alice Hudson, who was burnt at York, said she received money from the devil, ten shillings at a time!

DEMONOLOGY

ORIGIN OF WALTZING: The origin of that elegant accomplishment, waltzing, is derived from the orgies of the devils and witches during the ceremony of initiation, who on these occasions never failed to dance. Each had a broomstick in her hand, and held it up aloft. "Also that these night-walking, or rather night-dancing, devils brought out of Italy into France that dance which is called La Volta"- See Bodin in his *Lib. de Demonomania*, and Scot's *Discoverie*. This is certainly the origin of the modern waltz; and that it should take its derivation from so diabolical a source is much to be lamented. Some, however, have endeavoured to trace the waltz from certain feasts of Bacchus, called Orgia.

WITCHCRAFT IN ESSEX: About the year 1576, seventeen or eighteen persons were condemned for witchcraft at St. Osyth, in Essex. An account of them was written by Brian Darcy, with the names and colors of their spirits!- See Scot's Discovery.

In 1645, fifteen persons were condemned for witchcraft at Chelmsford, and hanged- some at Chelmsford and some at Manningtree. Another died in gaol. Another died as going to execution. They were condemned at a Sessions by the Earl of Warwick, and some Justices of the Peace.- Hutchinson's Essay.

About half a century ago, the inhabitants of the rural village of Great Totham, Essex, were witnesses of one of those strange ceremonies, the swimming of a person who was suspected to be a witch. From a person who was present and saw the whole of the proceedings, and upon whose veracity I can rely, I have collected the following particulars: At an old cottage, a part of which is still standing, situate on the western side of Totham Hill, to the right of the road leading to Beckingham, dwelt an old widow-woman of rather singular habits of the name of Scotcher. One morning in harvest time, she and her daughter, who, with her husband, lived with her, were found by one Master Fitch, a small farmer at Great

DEMONOLOGY

Totham, who happened to be accompanied that morning by the village blacksmith, a person of the name of Acers, in one of the fields of the former, gleaning- it being but just light, and a much earlier hour than the rest of the inhabitants were accustomed to go out into the fields to glean. On being told that they had no right to be there at that time of the morning, and ordered to leave the field, they were much offended, and Scotcher became very abusive. At length, finding that words would not prevail, Acers went and procured a hedge-stake, and, assisted by Fitch, drove them out of the field by force. Acers used his weapon only in terrorem; but after they had driven them out of the field, being much excited by their conduct, he seized hold of both the offenders, and knocked their heads together with great force, telling Scotcher that she was a Witch, and that he would have her swam. This threat was actually put into execution a few days after, in the presence of a great number of the villagers, at 'Totham Pond,' (now laid dry and cultivated,) situate by the side of the road leading from Maldon to Colchester.

The suspected witch, after having been stript of all her habiliments save her under garment, her feet and hands confined together, and a rope tied round her waist, to enable the officiating person to pull her out of the water again, if they found she was in danger of drowning, was put into a large tub, where she was received by Acers, who, all being arranged, immediately shoved the tub from the side, and continued floating it until they had got to the deepest part of the pond, when he threw her into the water, and she swam, Although she tried all she could, and even 'dived down into the water like a duck,' said my informant, 'she could no more sink than a piece of cork!' After she had been worried about in the water for some time, she was taken out and allowed to depart; those assembled being quite satisfied that she was one of those 'slaves of the Devil,' yclept a Witch!

According to Strype, Bishop Jewel, preaching before the Queen, in 1558, said: "It may please your grace to

DEMONOLOGY

understand that witches and sorcerers, within these few last years, are marvelously increased within your grace's realm. Your grace's subjects pine away, even unto the death, their colour fadeth, their flesh rotteth, their speech is benumbed, their senses are bereft. I pray God they never practice further than upon the subject."... "This," says Strype, "I make no doubt was the occasion of bringing in a bill, the next parliament, for making enchantments and witchcraft felony." One of the bishop's strong expressions is, "These eyes have seen most evident and manifest marks of their wickedness."

In Archbishop Cranmer's Articles of Visitation, 1549, is the following: "Item, You shall enquire, whether you know of any that use charms, sorcery, enchantments, witchcraft, soothsaying, or any like craft, invented by the Devil."

John Bell, minister of the gospel at Glaidsmuir, says: "Providently, two tests appeared to discover the crime; if the witch cries out 'Lord, have mercy upon me!' when apprehended; and the inability of shedding tears, because, as a witch could only shed three tears, and those with her left eye, her stock was quickly exhausted; and that was the more striking, as King James I. shrewdly observes, since other women in general are like the crocodile, ready to weep upon every slight occasion.

About the year 1679, a witch was condemned at Ely, but reprieved by King Charles II., and afterwards the fellow that pretended to have been bewitched, was hanged at Chelmsford, in Essex, and confessed that he had counterfeited his fits and vomitings.- Hutchinson's Essay.

In 1716, Mrs. Hicks, and her daughter aged nine, were hanged at Huntingdon for selling their souls to the Devil, and raising a storm, by pulling off their stockings and making a lather of soap! With this crowning atrocity, the catalogue of murders in England closes, the penal statutes against witchcraft being repealed in 1736, and the pretended exercise of such arts being punished in future by imprisonment and pillory. Barrington, in his observations on the statute 20 Henry VI., does not hesitate to estimate the numbers of those put to death in England on the charge of witchcraft at 30,000!

THE END

APPENDIX: EXCERPTS FROM OTHER WORKS

Please note that I have taken material only from works I have personally edited so that I can more easily note which page the reader can peruse if they wish to see the mentioned passage.

I: **Abaddon and Manahaim**, Joseph F. Berg, 1856

This particular little text offers us a snippet here which shows a reformed protestant view of the subject of Satan and Hell: Here we see Berg offer the view that demoniacs and the insane are *not* the same thing:

"Those who were possessed, differed from persons oppressed by forms of insanity in the accuracy with which they reasoned. Amid all the diversities of mania to which a commission of lunacy is awarded we find two great principles established in the phenomena of insanity. The unhappy subjects of mental disease, in the ordinary affairs of life, either reason correctly on false premises, or they reason incorrectly on right grounds, or they blend right and wrong in inextricable confusion. The daemoniacs, on the contrary, reasoned correctly- they assumed right premises and deduced right inferences. Their words were always adapted to the occasion, without any sort of incoherency." (p.38)

Berg then further elaborates (p. 39) and points out that the demon possessed are regarded as intelligent beings in the Bible- from the literalists' perspective that makes sense, as is noted further, that if diseases and demons are synonymous, one would have to claim (if one takes the Bible literally) that as diseases came out of the afflicted upon the command of Jesus, they had to be silenced and not suffered to speak; which of course diseases cannot do.

DEMONOLOGY

It is perhaps worth noting that Satan and Abaddon (or Apollyon) are not the same being within general demonology. I have seen a few people use them as though they were interchangeable (also technically the case with Gehenna and Sheol.) Here is another snippet from the same work:

"The Hebrews, and all the nations of the earth, before the coming of the Messiah, felt his power as Abaddon, the DESTROYER. But he has another name, APOLLYON, in the Greek tongue." (p. 87)

II: **All About Devils**, Moses Hull, 1890

This strictly rational and blatantly antireligious pamphlet gives us a quite academic explanation for the concept of lakes of fire as spoken of in the Bible and in other mythology:

"The exact location of Lake Avermis, and Surbonus and other mythological places, are like Sodom and Gomorrah, hard to determine. But they were somewhere in what was once the valley of the Nile. These lakes had neither outlet nor inlet. The water came in by the overflow of the Nile and passed out by evaporation.

Decaying vegetation in the region of these lakes gave the smell of brimstone, and the rolling of the waves in the light of the moon caused the lake to look like a huge lake of fire. Huge phosphoric insects flying over the lakes looked like balls of fire, or sparks from the lake. A slow fever, generated by the poisonous miasma arising from the lake, was supposed to be an infliction from the god Typhon, confined in the bottom of that lake; hence it is to this day called typhus or typhoid fever." (p. 23-4)

Moses Hull offers various views of Satan, Hell, demons, and other supernatural concepts in the work, referring to the

DEMONOLOGY

Devil as a reformer and the Christian god as generally evil.

III: **Ars Goetia**, First in English by Samuel Mathers, 1904

This particular interesting work is invaluable for those who wish to study demonology, and is one of the works compiled into what became the infamous Lemegeton. This particular book in that selfsame work is purely black magic and involves complex rituals designed to literally summon demons, of which the work lists 72 explicitly as being various princes and regents in the infernal regions.

A single demon ought to suffice for the purposes of this work as illustrative of the nature of demons spoken of within the text, which reign over varied amounts of inferior troops arranged in a hierarchical structure with lesser imps in turn commanded by dukes and archdukes.

It ought perhaps to be noted that the Ars Goetia and the larger Lemegeton to which it belongs are sometimes conflated with the Greater Key of Solomon.

From the Ars Goetia: (p. 48)

STOLAS

The thirty sixth spirit is Stolas, or Stolos. He is a great and powerful Prince, appearing in the shape of a mighty raven at first before the Master but after he taketh the image of a man. He teacheth the art of astronomy, and the virtues of herbs and precious stones. He governeth 26 Legions of spirits; and his Seal is this...

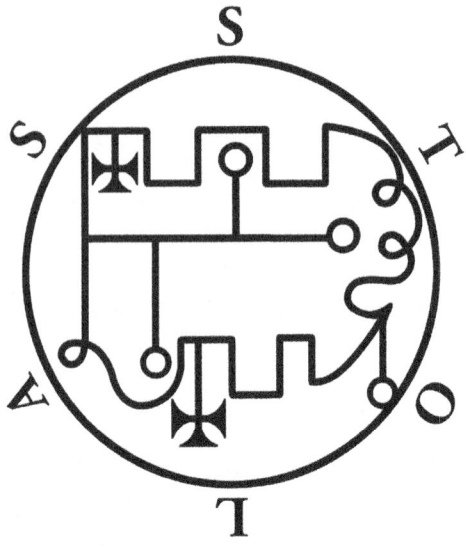

The seal of Stolas

IV: **Is the Devil A Myth?**, CF Wimberley, 1913

The following comes from the objectively Pentecostal background of its author, who relegates both liberal religion and rationalism to "quackery":

"No being, beside the Godhead, is more familiar with the secret hopes and impulses of the soul- than Satan. The long-haired quack on the street, bawling his 'junk,' is not half so anxious to defraud the crowd as Satan is to prescribe remedies that will not cure. His chief aspiration is to flood the land with bogus treatments which not only fail to cure, but they preempt the disease-infected spots so as to prevent the introduction of the genuine remedy. The quack doctor is, no doubt, pleased when an imaginary cure has been wrought by his wares; but Satan is filled with wrath if some of his formulas strike deeper than he anticipated, and a soul emerges from darkness unto light. This, however, does not often occur- he is too cunning to advertise to a hungry, sin-sick world that which will bring permanent relief." (p. 49.)

V: **The Religion of Babylonia and Assyria**, Theophilus Pinches, 1906

This work is rather dry and academic but contains a fairly large amount of demonological lore. I will quote a bit here verbatim as it shows the extremely categorical and varied nature of demons and evil spirits recognized by that system:

"The *uttuku*. This was a spirit which was supposed to do the will of Ann, the god of the heavens. There was the utukku of the plain, the mountains, the sea, and the grave

The *alu*. Regarded as the demon of the storm, and possibly, in its origin, the same as the divine bull sent by Istar to attack Gilgamesh, and killed by Enki-du. It spread itself over a man, overpowering him upon his bed, and attacking his breast.

The *edimmu*. This is generally, but wrongly, read *ekimmu,* and translated 'the seizer' from *ekemu*, 'to seize.' In reality, however, it was an ordinary spirit, and the word is used for the wraiths of the departed. The 'evil edimmu' was apparently regarded as attacking the middle part of a man.

The *gallu*. As this word is borrowed from the Sumerian *galla*, which has a dialectic form, *mulla*, it is not 'improbable that it may be connected with the word *mula*, meaning 'star,' and suggesting something which is visible by the light it gives possibly a will-o'-the-wisp, though others are inclined to regard the word as being connected with gala, 'great.' In any case, its meaning seems to have become very similar to 'evil spirit' or 'devil' in general, and is an epithet applied by the Assyrian king Assur-bani-apli to Te-umman, the Elamite king against whom he fought.

DEMONOLOGY

The *ilu limnu*, 'evil god' was probably originally one of the deities of Tiawath's brood, upon whom Merodach's redemption had had no effect.

The *rabisu* is regarded as a spirit which lay in wait to pounce upon his prey.

The *labartu*, in Sumerian *dimme*, was a female demon. There were seven evil spirits of this kind, who were apparently regarded as being daughters of Anu, the god of the heavens.

The *labasu*, in Sumerian *dimmea*, was apparently a spirit which overthrew, that being the meaning of the root from which the word comes.

The *ahhazu*, in Sumerian *dimme-kur,* was apparently so called as 'the seizer', that being the meaning indicated by the root.

The *lilu*, in Sumerian *lila*, is generally regarded as the 'night-monster' the word being referred to the Semitic root *lil* or *layl*, whence the Hebrew *layil*, Arabic *layl*, 'night'. Its origin, however, is Sumerian, from *lila,* regarded as meaning 'mist.' To the word *lilu* the ancient Babylonians formed a feminine, *lilithu*, which entered the Hebrew language under the form of Lilith, which was, according to the rabbins, a beautiful woman, who lay in wait for children by night. The *lilu* had a companion who is called his handmaid or servant

The *namtaru* was apparently the spirit of fate, and therefore of greater importance than those already mentioned. This being was regarded as the beloved son of Bel, and offspring of Eres-ki-gal or Persephone, and he had a spouse named *Hus-bi-saga*. Apparently he executed the instructions given him concerning the fate of men, and could also have power over certain of the gods.

BIBLIOGRAPHY

In this following bibliography I have attempted to include both academic/irreligious and strictly uncritical works, with a few inclusions from non-Western cultural sources. A casual stroll across the internet will allow the reader to find thousands upon thousands of works which reference demons and associated topics like the burning times, Judeochristian Satan, Hell, etc.

I have included no bibliographic entries for the works I have cited prior in this compilation because I felt it wrong to have so many entries inevitably under my own name. I did include, however, a few volumes which I edited. In the case of the Book of Tobit, Testament of Solomon, and Ophiolatreia, I listed the works under "Warwick, Tarl", since the authors were not known (King Solomon did not write the two former and while we "probably" know who wrote Ophiolatreia and the rest of the Phallism series, we cannot technically be sure. I entered "Private Printing" for the authorship in my own edition because of this.)

Alexander, W.M: *Demonic Possession in the New Testament*, 1902.

Ashton, John: *The Devil in Britain and America*, 1896.

Brown, Robert: *Demonology and Witchcraft*, 1889.

Calmet, Augustine: *The Phantom World,* 1850.

Canonicus: *Letters to the Rev. William E. Channing D.D. On the Existence and Agency of Fallen Spirits*, 1828.

Carus, Paul: *The History of the Devil and the Idea of Evil*, 1900.

DEMONOLOGY

Conway, Moncure: *Demonology and Devil Lore* (Two volumes), 1879.

Davies, T. Witton: *Magic, Divination, and Demonology Among the Hebrews and their Neighbours*, 1898.

Defoe, Daniel, *The Political History of the Devil*, 1840.

Dobbins, Frank S: *Gods and Devils of Mankind*, 1897.

Drake, Samuel: *The Witchcraft Delusion in New England* (Three Volumes), 1866

Elworthy, Frederick: *The Evil Eye; An Account of the Ancient and Widespread Superstition*, 1895.

Gilpin, Richard: *Daemonologia Sacra*, 1867.

Hall, Frederic T: *The Pedigree of the Devil,* 1883.

Harris, Dean: *Essays in Occultism, Spiritism, and Demonology,* 1919.

Jannaway, Frank G: *Satans Biography*, 1909.

Lavater, Ludwig, *Of Ghostes and Spirites Walking by Nyght*, 1572.

Mathers, Samuel: *The Greater Key of Solomon*, 2016.
(Please note that I edited this edition and it was re-illustrated by Eli Fousteris.)

Mathers, Samuel: *The Lesser Key of Solomon, Lemegeton*, 2018.
(Please note that I edited this edition, cleaning up the format considerably.)

DEMONOLOGY

Michelet, Jules: *The Sorceress, a Study in Middle Age Superstition*, 1905.

Oesterreich, T.K: *Possession, Demoniacal and Other*, 1930.

Peebles, J.M: *The Demonism of the Ages*, 1904.

Perley, M.V.B: *Salem Village Witchcraft*, 1911.

Rodker, John (Publisher) *Malleus Maleficarum*, 1928. (English translation with various inclusions by Montague Summers. Invaluable.)

Rudwin, Maximilian: *Devil Stories, an Anthology*, 1921.

Scot, Reginald: *The Discoverie of Witchcraft,* (1886 ed.)

Seymour, John D: *Irish Witchcraft and Demonology*, 1913.

Spalding, Thomas: *Elizabethan Demonology,* 1880

Steele, W.A: *Getting Along Without the Devil*, 1919.

Summers, Montague, *The History of Witchcraft and Demonology*, 1926.

Thacher, James: *An Essay on Demonology, Ghosts and Apparitions*, 1831.

Thimpson, R. Campbell: *The Devils and Evil Spirits of Babylonia*, 1904.

Tremearne, Major A.J.N: *The Ban of the Bori*, 1914.

Trithemius, Johannes, *Steganographia*, 1606. (Note:

Digitized by multiple sources in and from Latin.)

Warwick, Tarl (Editor) *Ophiolatreia, Serpent Worship*, 2016.

Warwick, Tarl (Editor) *The Book of Tobit*, 2017.

Warwick, Tarl (Editor) *The Testament of Solomon*, 2015.

Whatley, R: *A View of the Scripture Revelations Respecting Good and Evil Angels*, 1856.

Young, Joseph: *Demonology; or, the Scripture Doctrine of Devils*, 1861.

THE END

Made in the USA
Coppell, TX
28 June 2023